OCR

AS AND A LEVEL MUSIC

Study Guide

OCR
Oxford Cambridge and RSA

An OCR endorsed textbook

First published 2017 in Great Britain by
Rhinegold Education
14-15 Berners Street
London W1T 3LJ, UK
www.rhinegoldeducation.co.uk

You should always check the current requirements of your examination, since these may change.

Editor: Toby Knowles
Cover and book design: Fresh Lemon Australia

OCR AS and A LEVEL Music Study Guide
Order No. RHG280
ISBN: 978-1-78558-162-5

Exclusive Distributors:
Music Sales Ltd
Distribution Centre, Newmarket Road
Bury St Edmunds, Suffolk IP33 3YB, UK

Printed in the EU

OCR AS AND A LEVEL MUSIC

Study Guide

HUW ELLIS-WILLIAMS, MARIA JOHNSON & SUSAN ROBERTS
with performance chapter by Richard Bristow

RHINEGOLD EDUCATION

Contents

The authors

Huw Ellis-Williams

was brought up in Bangor and read Music at the University of Oxford. He was Head of Music and Head of Sixth Form at a comprehensive school in north Wales. He has examined for OCR and was a part of the team that wrote the OCR specifications for AS and A Level Music. A pianist, organist and occasional composer, Huw enjoys being involved with the local community as a conductor and accompanist.

Maria Johnson

read Music at the University of Cambridge and has a master's degree in Education from the Open University. She has taught music in both the state and private sectors to students aged between seven and eighteen years old, and now works at Clifton High School in Bristol. Maria has been an examiner and moderator since 2005 and examines at GCSE and AS Level. She also teaches the piano and plays the organ regularly for church services, but stays well away from the pedals!

Susan Roberts

has a master's degree in Composing, Analysis and Criticism from the University of Surrey. She has taught music in a wide range of schools, principally in the 11–18 age range as well as in Sixth Form Colleges. She currently works in freelance practice as a music therapist. Working as an A Level examiner and moderator both nationally and internationally for over 20 years, Sue's involvement with delivering INSET has included the development of well-received materials and Schemes of Work for A Level teachers. Sue is an enthusiastic advocate of 20th-century and contemporary music, and her interest in the way that musicians learn to compose has taken her on travels across three continents.

Welcome to the OCR Study Guide

This Study Guide covers both the AS Level and A Level in Music. The new AS and A Level specifications are available for teaching from September 2016.

AS Level and A Level are separate qualifications.

The A Level is designed as a two-year course. The assessment takes place at the end of the second year.

- This guide is intended for students who will complete their A Level studies in either 2018 or 2019.

The AS Level can be studied in one year or over two years. Your school or college will advise you of the options available to you. AS Level is intended to be 'co-teachable' with A Level. This means that some of the AS Level course is useful preparation for A Level.

- This guide is intended for students who will complete their AS Level studies in either 2017 or 2018.

Both AS and A Level examinations consist of three components:

- Performing – a video of your performance recital. This should be recorded in March, April or May of the exam year.
- Composing – an audio performance of your compositions, with a score, lead sheet or written description. This should be submitted before May 15 of the exam year.
- Listening and Appraising – a written examination in May or June. The examination will include: (i) questions on recordings of extracts from unfamiliar music, (ii) questions on prescribed music (including recorded extracts), and (iii) essay questions.

All three components are marked by OCR examiners.

The courses focus on the following six Areas of Study:

Area of Study 1	**Instrumental Music of Haydn, Mozart and Beethoven**
Area of Study 2	**Popular Song: Blues, Jazz, Swing and Big Band**
Area of Study 3	**Developments in Instrumental Jazz, 1910 to the present day**
Area of Study 4	**Religious Music of the Baroque Period**
Area of Study 5	**Programme Music, 1820–1910**
Area of Study 6	**Innovations in Music, 1900 to the present day**

Performing, Composing, and Listening and Appraising

OCR encourages you to connect the three activities of performing, composing and appraising music.

Everything that you do when you study music is connected. When you perform, you are listening and learning about composing. When you compose, your listening and performing skills are helping you. When you listen, your experience in performing and creating music is helping you make judgements that deepen your understanding of music.

The final assessment is divided into three separate components. In one year or two years of studying music you have the opportunity to integrate performing, composing and listening. In doing so, you will become a better musician!

For example, you could:

- Perform a piece by Haydn, discuss the cadences, then use similar cadences in a composition.
- Listen and compare a song sung by Ella Fitzgerald with a performance by another singer, then vary the phrasing and articulation in your own performance.
- Research ideas for a composition brief for Area of Study 3 by analysing compositions by a contemporary jazz musician.
- Form a quartet to sing or play the parts in a chorale by Bach. Write your own chorale setting to be tried out by the same group.
- Write a composition brief for your own instrument modelled on Mussorgsky's *Pictures At An Exhibition*.
- Choose one innovative composing technique since 1900 to study in detail. Perform a short extract to show your class how the technique works.

How many Areas of Study do I need to study?

Your teacher will give you guidance about what you need to study. A guide to the minimum required for the assessment is given below.

	A Level	AS Level
Performing	Free choice	Free choice
Composing	At least one	At least one
Listening and Appraising	AoS1 and AoS2 At least two others	AoS1 and AoS2 At least one other

In practice you may study a wider range of topics because of the options available to you in Performing and Composing. For example:

- Your Performing recital may include instrumental music by J. S. Bach or vocal music by Robert Schumann. This type of music falls outside the Areas of Study. However, they are perfectly valid choices for your performance.
- In Composing you are required to set your own brief for one of your pieces. You may choose to study the techniques of a style of music that is not included in the Areas of Study.

Assessment

The table provides a quick guide to the components of the assessment for A Level and AS Level.

You have a choice of route through A Level:

- Route A (Performing A and Composing A) has more marks for Composing.
- Route B (Performing B and Composing B) has more marks for Performing.

Of course, you have to complete more work in your preferred component. Since an A Level is a two-year course, you may be able to leave your final decision until the second year. Talk to your teacher about the best choice for you.

At AS Level there are equal marks available for Performing and Composing. There is no choice of route.

The Listening and Appraising examination counts for 40% of the marks at both A Level and AS Level.

A Level H543					
EITHER **A Level Components 1, 3 and 5**	Performing A 6–9 minutes **25%**	AND	Composing A 8 minutes **35%**	AND	Listening and Appraising Exam 2½ hours **40%**
OR **A Level Components 2, 4 and 5**	Performing B 10–15 minutes **35%**	AND	Composing B 4 minutes **25%**		
AS Level H143					
AS Level Components 1, 2 and 3	Performing 6–9 minutes **30%**	AND	Composing 4½ minutes **30%**	AND	Listening and Appraising Exam 2 hours **40%**

Studying Music at AS Level and A Level

Use your time well. Use the beginning of the course to develop your own knowledge, skills and experience.

Plan how to build your skills over a period of time. Reflect on what you can do at the beginning of the course. Make a list of what you would like to achieve in the short term, middle term and long term.

Develop and improve your skills as a musician. Learn to pick out a tune on a keyboard. Learn to play a keyboard with both hands, well enough to play chords. Learn to sing or pitch a note, sing or play from notation, play by ear and improvise. Any of these skills are really useful.

If your knowledge of notation is shaky, try to play something from a printed copy every day. You will soon improve and develop confidence in understanding how notated music works.

Keep a log or diary of your listening. Make a note of composers and performers – titles of pieces, first impressions, ideas for your own compositions, links with other music you are familiar with.

Keep your notes, worksheets, printed materials, etc. in folders. Organise your folders either by topic (Performing, Composing, Listening, Areas of Study) or in order of date (Term 1, Term 2, etc.). Review your notes from time to time. Build up a store of knowledge that you can rely on and use for your revision.

Plan a practice schedule. Get into good habits. Try to have a routine. Try not to leave performing or composing to the last minute.

Experience as much live music as you can. Look for opportunities to perform in ensembles at your school, in your area or at county or national level. Compose your music for others to perform or listen to. Listen to the work of other musicians. Go to live performances of music.

Explore sources of information. Read about music in books, magazines, newspapers and online. Discover reliable sources of information, including sources of scholarship. You may be lucky enough to have a good library locally, especially if your local college or university has a music department. You may be able to access a public subscription to the online Grove Dictionary of Music and Musicians (see **www.oxfordmusiconline.com**).

Music scores for older music are often available in online editions. Modern editions are usually available only in print.

Have an open mind. Be patient with unfamiliar music. Some music is immediately exciting, but some takes time to understand. Listen to the opinions of others. Be ready to change a first opinion. Be curious about new styles and techniques.

How to use this study guide

This study guide has been written by experienced teachers and musicians to help you prepare for AS Level and A Level. The separate sections on Performing, Composing and the Areas of Study for Listening and Appraising are designed to help you study for the assessments at the end of the course.

This is not a text book. It doesn't contain everything you need to know. It does not replace the performing, composing, and listening and appraising that you will do as part of your AS Level or A Level Music courses. You will want to take the advice of your teachers about what will work best for you.

There is plenty of useful advice in this book. This study guide can be used as a starting point for you to explore the content of the course. It can also be used as a revision tool at the end of the course.

In the end this makes up only part of the whole picture. You have to take the final decisions that will allow you to benefit most from your study of music at AS Level and A Level:

- You have to choose your pieces and decide how to perform them.
- You have to decide on your composition briefs and how to complete them.
- You have to explore the music for the listening examination.
- You have to write about your knowledge and judgements on the music in the Areas of Study.

We wish you every success in studying these courses and gaining the qualification through your hard work. Above all you should aim to become an all-round musician, with a deeper understanding of performing, composing, and listening and appraising.

Performing music

Why do we perform?

For many, performance is the principal reason for wanting to study music at an advanced level. Performance encompasses everything from a formal concert or gig at a prestigious venue with a sizeable audience to a more informal session with no audience; it can be as public or as private as we decide.

Performance strongly influences our sense of individual musical 'ownership' and many of us will have our favourite recordings of pieces that somehow appeal to us. The art of achieving an excellent performance is to understand how to communicate the notated composition so that it 'speaks' to the audience. Performance is more than simply playing the notes of a composition; it is about understanding what the composer of the music is trying to tell the audience, and enhancing this to make the music come alive. We must perform with subconscious passion and fully conscious intelligence.

Within this unit there are a number of different choices which you can make at both AS and A Level, outlined below:

Unit outline:

AS Level Music

For the AS Level Performance unit, you must submit:

- A minimum of 6 minutes of music consisting of two contrasting pieces from the following list:
  - Solo piece(s) on one or more than one instrument or voice
  - Ensemble performance
  - Accompanying another performer
  - Realisation using Music Technology

This is externally assessed via audio-visual recording and is marked out of a total of 75 marks. This unit in its entirety is worth 30% of the total AS Level. The maximum duration of performances is 9 minutes. Performances may include improvisation, where appropriate.

Assessment is based on:

- Knowledge and fluency
- Technical control
- Realisation of performance markings and/or conventions

A Level Music

At A Level, there are choices that you can make which allow you to choose whether your 60% coursework has greater weighting on composition or performance.

This means that each coursework paper can be worth either 25% or 35% depending on where your strengths as a musician lie, named as 'Performing A' and 'Performing B'.

Clearly, if choosing a 35% performance option, you must then choose the 25% composition option and vice versa.

Performing A – 25% total A Level

This unit is identical to the AS requirements, giving a recital of 6 to 9 minutes which might involve solo performance, ensemble performance, accompanying or realisation using music technology. Be sure to choose pieces that contrast in style and their use of the elements in order to best promote your musical technique. This option is marked out of 75 and is worth 25% of the total A Level marks.

If choosing this option you must select Composing A.

Performing B – 35% total A Level

This is a larger unit (105 total marks) with a higher weighting on performance, requiring you to perform a recital that lasts for a minimum of ten minutes, choosing from:

- Solo piece(s) on one or more than one instrument or voice
- Ensemble Performance
- Accompanying another performer
- Realisation using Music Technology

Furthermore, there is a requirement for your pieces to fit the following requirements:

Section A: Free Choice

- At least **two contrasting** pieces of your choice, allowing you to show off your expressive potential as a musician by achieving an accurate, controlled, expressive and fluent performance.

Section B: Focused Study

- At least **one further** piece, which has been chosen to develop and demonstrate an in-depth understanding of repertoire idiomatic to the instrument or voice.

This unit is marked out of 105 and is worth 35% of the total A Level marks. Performances should not exceed 15 minutes. If choosing this option you must select Composing B.

Live performances

Live performances refer to music that is produced by playing an instrument or singing, either performed unaccompanied or with an accompaniment on piano, guitar (or similar), backing track, or a small group of other live musicians, producing an ensemble.

Your part and chosen pieces should enable you to demonstrate your technical and expressive control of your chosen medium and should not be doubled by other parts, allowing the examiner to hear your performance fully.

Make sure that your recital meets the specification in terms of duration and that you understand how the mark scheme will be applied.

Assessment

As with many coursework units, this unit is assessed by different bands to enable the examiner to decide on a mark.

Where the band statement is convincingly met by the performance, then the top mark in that band should be awarded; where the performance adequately meets the statement, a middle-range mark should be awarded; where the performance just meets the band statement, the lowest mark should be awarded.

While the marks and total weightings change between the AS and A Level options, the criteria forming the marking bands are the same.

Within your performances there needs to be an awareness of the following aspects:

- **Knowledge and Fluency:** to what extent does your performance match the technical demands of the piece? Is it accurate to the notation/lead sheet? Does your performance show critical understanding?
- **Technical Control:** Are there any concerns with intonation, breathing, bowing or pedalling? Is the tempo appropriate? Have you met the technical demands of the music you are playing? If singing, is your diction suitable for the performance? Have the challenges of the piece been met in your performance? Do you manage to communicate your performance fully on the recording? Does the recording promote an emotional reaction in the listener? Is there a sense of occasion, with judicious use of silence and musical energy? Is the recording exciting to listen to?

Full requirements for this unit can be found on the OCR website, www.ocr.org.uk.

- **Realisation of performance Markings/Conventions:** To what extent are you following the given dynamics, articulation and expressive features of the music? Are there specific (perhaps unmarked) conventions to the music that you are/are not following, such as ornamentation in a Baroque piece? Are these appropriate to the character of the piece? Is there a clear understanding of the period and style of the piece? If using improvisation, is this appropriate to the chosen style?

The level of difficulty is also important to consider; pieces for the entire programme should be equivalent to Grade 6 for all major exam boards (ABRSM, Trinity, Rockschool and so on). No extra credit is given for pieces harder than this standard, though the top two bands for Technical Control are not accessible if the whole or part of the recital falls below this standard.

Recital Preparation

The key element to achieving success in this unit is to ensure that you prepare for your final performance thoroughly.

It is exceptionally useful to listen to other musicians perform your pieces on publicly available resources (such as Spotify, YouTube or radio), making notes on what they do to ensure they communicate fully with the audience. No two performances are the same, but this approach will enable you to research your pieces and gain a greater understanding of the potential of the piece.

Some points to help you plan your recital effectively:

- If your recital requires the use of either an accompanist or an ensemble of musicians, it is wise to ensure that they have sufficient time to learn the music and to rehearse it with you. Often the biggest challenge to learning new music is ensuring that your part fits with the music surrounding it.
- Take time to rehearse and perform your pieces in a variety of different contexts to gain confidence in your repertoire. Establish whether you perform best in front of an audience or without an audience.
- Note what level of difficulty your pieces are and time them to ensure you meet the recital timings as set out in the specification.
- It is useful to record your performances throughout the course as it gives you a chance to listen to them after the performance and assess them to the mark scheme, setting targets for improvement.
- If necessary, establish a tuning routine well in advance of your final performance. It is not advisable to wait for your accompanist to tell you if you are sharp or flat; you should have the musical confidence by the time your final recording is made to do this yourself.

Consider making a 'performance log' to record your thoughts on different performances of your pieces. Writing ideas down as you go will greatly help you when you are putting your final recital together.

Remember that your final recordings must be made between 1st March and 31st May in the year of examination.

Putting your recital together

Decide early on when planning your recital where **variety** will occur; this could be in musical style/period, technique or approach, or a combination of all of these. Avoid learning a programme of pieces which lacks variety – it is harder to award marks for such recitals and goes against the specification requirements.

The pieces chosen should offer variety in style and approach and allow for you to demonstrate a range of expression and techniques. Beware of long passages of music which are written only for the accompaniment; it is impossible for you to score marks when you are not playing. Backing tracks can be used and these are especially useful in Rockschool contexts. Remember that your submitted recital needs to be performed and recorded in one uninterrupted 'take', including any false starts, although you may record the whole recital more than once and submit the best one.

Sample AS Level Recital – Electric Guitar

This sample AS Level recital for electric guitar uses backing tracks to enable the performance to sound complete and is based around a Rockschool Guitar Grade 6 standard.

The use of backing track is useful in ensuring the candidate keeps in time and means that practice is made easier by not needing other musicians for rehearsal. As the programme is of Grade 6 standard, the whole mark range is accessible for Technical Control.

Artist	Title	Grade	Duration
Bennett	'Mohair Mountain'	Rockschool 6	2:55
Morgan	'Striped Shirt'	Rockschool 6	2:30
Muse	'Supermassive Black Hole'	Rockschool 6	2:50

This varied programme offers chances to show off many different skills including:

- Changes in time signature and tempo offer a chance for you to show technical control in 'Mohair Mountain', as does the improvisation in the solo, which features dynamic changes. The $\frac{7}{8}$ passages are particularly impressive when played fluently, evoking the rock style.
- A contrast of style is achieved in 'Striped Shirt' with a slower tempo, $\frac{6}{8}$ time signature and greater focus on lyrical musical lines, including semiquaver runs.
- The Muse track has many technical aspects to it including slides, bends and hammer-on/pull-off semiquavers. By ending with the most technically complex piece, a sense of energy is brought to the entire recital.

Sample A Level Recital – Soprano

This sample A Level recital uses Grade 8 pieces to form a chronological vocal recital. As the recital is above Grade 6, the full mark scheme is accessible. However, do take care here; there are no extra marks available for going beyond Grade 6 and the technical demands will be significantly increased, meaning that your overall mark might be lower if the pieces are too difficult for your current musicianship.

The pieces offer significant contrast in mood and the techniques required to effectively communicate the different texts.

Composer	Title	Grade	Duration
Durante	'Danza, danza, fanciulla'	ABRSM 8	1:40
Gluck	'O del mio dolce ardor' from *Paride ed Elena*	ABRSM 8	4:00
Debussy	'Nuit d'étoiles'	Trinity 8	3:00
Bernstein	'Something's Coming' from *West Side Story*	ABRSM 8	2:20

This programme offers many chances to show off different musical techniques:

- The Durante provides an arresting start to the recital: a fast tempo requiring attention to diction and an independent accompaniment allowing the voice to characterise the text and the performer to immediately communicate to the audience. The ascending scales offer excellent potential for scoring high marks if the intonation is precise and fully controlled.
- The Gluck offers a contrasting aria, with a slower tempo and greater chance to shape melodic character via short cadenza passages. Care should be taken here to ensure these are fully communicated to the accompanist to ensure a tight sense of ensemble.
- The Debussy is the emotional heart of the recital, with the chance to really shape the text and the unfolding storyline. The vocal line is entirely independent from the accompaniment, giving a chance to demonstrate excellent ensemble skills. The repeated passages offer a chance to change the vocal tone to reflect the different meanings of the text, especially on the line 'Je rêve aux amours défunts' ('I dream of bygone loves').
- The Bernstein offers a lighter conclusion to the recital, being more inspired by jazz and in a major key with a fast tempo. Anticipated rhythms, cross-rhythms and syncopation create significant musical excitement and end the recital with much energy.

All of these pieces in this recital offer plenty of material to meet the requirements for Section B – Focused Study, as all contain techniques that are highly idiomatic to the genre.

Both of these example recitals offer variety and meet the specification requirements in terms of duration of the complete performance.

Performance documentation

Remember that you need to provide a suitable stimulus to the examiner to assess your recital.

This could be in the form of:

- a **notated score**, which contains all the relevant information via notation to assess accuracy and the expressive intentions of the composer.
- a **lead sheet** which should contain pertinent information to allow the examiner to assess the extent to which your performance meets the composer's intentions.

Improvisation

Improvisation is permitted as a part of this unit. However, you must ensure that you provide information on what the improvisation is based on – for example a chord sequence, melodic fragment, a riff, a scale or a mode – to enable the examiner to assess the recording.

A piece that is entirely improvised is unadvisable to submit for this examination owing to the nature of the assessment.

Recording

There are many ways in which to ensure that your audio-visual recording is of an appropriate quality for this component.

It is important to consider the venue in which you are performing: its acoustic, as well as the time of day that you are performing. It is advisable to check the balance of the final mix to ensure that the performance is being captured in a way that truly reflects the performance you give. This is, after all, all the examiner has to go on to assess your performance.

Performing

When you step up to perform, breathe deeply, and if there is an audience present, smile and make eye contact.

There is much power in taking a few seconds before you start to perform in being silent to allow the audience to settle and encourage them to focus on what is about to happen. Similarly, after your piece has finished, consider waiting for a second or two before moving, allowing what you have just performed to settle and end without a sense of haste.

Summary for Live Performance

When planning your recital it is useful to remember the following points:

- Build variety into your recital pieces through changes in style, period, approach or technique, or a combination of these.
- Aim for pieces that are ambitious in standard but not beyond your technical control as a musician.
- Time your pieces to ensure they meet the specification requirements.
- Research your pieces to establish where the emotional peaks and troughs of the piece are, keeping a 'performing log' to track your work.
- Highlight areas that are more technically complex in your pieces and devote regular rehearsal time to meeting these challenges, remembering that slow practice is best to secure the music to muscle memory.

- Establish clear practice routines from the very start of the course, including tuning your instrument and communicating with your accompanist.
- Perform your pieces often.
- Record your performances, allowing for you to listen back to them and gain an understanding on which areas are successful and which require more work.
- Be active within the recording process - where the microphone is placed, the acoustic of the room, and the balance of the recording are all important factors. Consider how you are dressed and present yourself; this is what your examiner will see.

QUESTIONS ON LIVE PERFORMANCE

1. If you can get hold of the audio, look at the AS Level Electric Guitar recital (on page 14), listen to the tracks in order and consider if the recital works as a musical whole. Would you change any of the pieces? Would you change the order? Why?
2. Doing the same for the A Level Soprano recital, list areas where this recital might enable you to score highly on the assessment scheme. Which parts are more complex and might cause marks to be lost?
3. Now consider your own AS or A Level recital. Make a list of potential pieces for your recital, listing the positives and negatives of each piece, as well as the level of difficulty and the timings.
4. Discuss your ideas with your fellow students, other musicians and friends. This will not only enable you to improve your recital, but also to help your fellow A Level musicians in their work.

Music Technology Performances

These performances refer to music that is produced using music technology software: including sequencers (such as Cubase or Logic) and multi-track recording using microphones to capture live sound.

Please note that it is not acceptable to simply use a sequenced performance which has no live sound. While the initial skills demanded by this option might seem like a sharp contrast to the Live Performance option, the overall effect is similar; the desire to produce a musical performance that is satisfying to the audience's ear.

Assessment

The mark scheme for performances using production via music technology uses the same criteria as live performing.

- **Knowledge and Coherence:** similar to live performance, but ensuring that your track and final recording are completely fluent and accurate.
- **Technical Control:** this refers to the use of specific software functions, production techniques and balance to aid the overall sound quality of the performance.
- **Realisation of Performance Markings/Conventions:** similar to live performance, ensuring that the expressive qualities of the song are evidenced in your recording.

Preparation

Many of the points discussed for Live Performance ring true for this unit also. It is vital that you fully research your chosen pieces and listen to them to understand their individual characteristics, recording your thoughts as you progress by using a performance log.

The challenges in this unit come from your technical ability to use the technology available to you. Remember that performers who are completing a live performance may well have been having lessons on their instrument for many years, allowing for them to progress to a high standard. You need to be proficient on the software you are using to complete your performance, and this may include doing many small projects to familiarise yourself with the technology prior to starting work on your final recital.

Some points to help you plan your recital effectively:

- If your production requires the use of other musicians to perform pieces for you to capture, remember to be organised, giving them notice of when you would like to record the music. Be active within the process, ensuring that they are performing the music with technical and expressive control.
- Experiment with your recordings and use of a sequencer, producing different versions that use the software to its full potential. Remember that the mark scheme awards successful use of software under Technical Control.
- Ensure you have a thorough knowledge of the instruments you are using in your performance. How can you make an acoustic guitar sound strummed on a sequencer? How is the original effect being achieved, and how can you produce something similar?
- Give thought to pieces as you practise and develop your technological understanding. How many tracks are involved in each piece? Does the programme offer variety, high complexity of musical character and considerable expressive variety?
- Experiment with microphone placement, noticing how the recorded sound quality alters when the position of the microphone or the type of microphone changes.

Performance documentation

You need to provide the examiner with evidence to assess your performance against the mark scheme. Unlike the live performance option, this can be an annotation accompanied by a score which contains all the details of the processes, devices and techniques used, as well as any other information that you feel is relevant.

You should provide the examiner with as much information as possible to allow them to understand how your final recital has been produced.

Essential equipment

This performing option is reliant on having good quality music technology equipment available to enable you to be able to show the full range of skills required in the assessment scheme.

At a basic level, you should have access to and a working knowledge of:

- Sequencing software (e.g. Cubase or Logic) and VST instruments
- Notation software (e.g. Sibelius)
- A mixing desk
- Condenser microphones
- Dynamic microphones
- High-quality speakers and headphones.

QUESTIONS ON PRODUCTION

1. Research, define and create short musical examples to demonstrate the following processes:
   a. Panning
   b. Quantise
   c. Reverb
   d. EQ
2. Consider how you might use the production software to closely imitate the following features of live musical performance, producing short examples to demonstrate your points:
   a. Acoustic guitar - strumming
   b. Piano - pedalling
   c. Strings - changes in bowing
   d. Woodwind/Brass - breathing
3. Consider which microphones you might use and how you might place them for the following acoustic instruments:
   a. Electric guitar
   b. Vocals
   c. Drum kit

Being accurate and expressive

No matter which option or combination of options you elect to take for this component, there will come a point where you might be able to perform your piece accurately but it does not yet quite have the emotional control to be fully effective. Your teacher may well comment that the performance is accurate but lacks musical interest; how can we achieve both to obtain the highest marks?

When we are learning a piece of music we often focus on learning the notes in front of us, perhaps by interpreting a score or lead sheet, and there can be no doubt that this is a vital first stage in the learning process. However, this is only half of the story; while we might be playing the notes in the right order, we need to understand how to communicate the expressive demands of the piece beyond what the score is telling us.

When you research your pieces by listening to different recordings you will hopefully find many contrasting performances. Listen to as many varied performances as you can, commenting on how each performer interprets the specific features of the music. To what extent does each performance communicate a sensitive and mature understanding of style and period? How does your favourite recording achieve this?

Example Performance Activity

This activity can be done with any piece, providing you have two or more contrasting recordings. Completing this exercise for some or all of your chosen pieces would be a useful way to engage with the assessment criteria.

Search YouTube for student recitals of well-known pieces – for instance you could search for 'Rondo Alla Turca Student Recital' for a piano recital, or 'Meditation From Thais' for a violin recital. Find two contrasting performances of the same piece (on the same instrument) to listen to. The age of the performers isn't really relevant in this situation – what's important is that you can compare, contrast and assess two different performances of the same musical material.

As a class, listen to the performances, marking them to the assessment scheme in the specification (available on the OCR website) and adding a comment to justify the mark awarded. Be as honest and objective as possible! Consider specific moments where you are awarding or taking away marks, noting down why you feel this is appropriate. Hopefully the two recitals will exemplify the issues discussed above regarding communicating expressive control into your performances, as well as the obvious technical challenges.

Discuss your ideas with fellow musicians and friends. You may wish to use a table like this to order your thoughts:

		Performance 1	Performance 2
Knowledge and Coherence	25		
Technical Control	25		
Realisation of Performance Markings/Conventions	25		
Level of Difficulty?			
Other points for discussion			

During your discussion, consider:

- Did you award similar marks? Were there differences? Why might these have happened?
- Where in the piece did you award marks for expressive control? Where did you feel this control was not being met?
- How could the candidate improve communication via the recording?
- What advice would you give the candidate for each performance?

END OF COMPONENT QUESTIONS

1. Complete the assessment activity above for your chosen repertoire using recordings available online or via CD/radio. Consider how each performance would do when marked using the assessment criteria.
2. Compile these features into your own performances, taking care to ensure an overall sense of stylistic appreciation of each piece.
3. Finally, assess your own recordings in the same way against the assessment criteria, setting yourself suitable practice targets to gain credit for your work.

Composing

Composing is a creative craft with invention at its heart. It reflects something of the uniqueness of you, the composer. The process of composition will also help you to learn a number of disciplines and skills.

You will need to combine technical understanding with carefully considered, well-informed musical judgement in order to compose music.

This will mean acquiring a number of skills, possibly including:

- Developing an understanding of the possibilities of the human voice.
- Developing knowledge of how various instruments are played - their range, timbre, notation and other characteristics.
- Gaining skills in the use of technological hardware to generate or work with further possibilities in sound. It may require exploring the possibilities of software programmes that will allow you to manipulate, refine and experiment with music and sounds.

You will certainly need to develop an acutely critical listening ear. This is crucial for:

- The evaluation of your own work.
- Enabling you to be more alert to the creative processes involved in all the music you listen to or perform.

Making connections and links

You can learn about composition by intimately studying great musical works, both those from earlier points in music history and those by contemporary composers.

There is a link between composition and performing. Take notice of all that is happening in the music you play as a soloist, as well as the music you play alongside others in ensemble. Performing with a critical ear can generate ideas and provide starting points for your own composing.

Common approaches at AS and A Level

At the core of both AS and A Level qualifications is the requirement to compose two pieces of music:

- **Section 1** The exam board will issue six composing briefs relating to each of the Areas of Study. You will choose ONE task to complete.
- **Section 2** Learners will construct their own brief for a composition.

Additionally, for those who wish to specialise in composing at A Level:

- **Section 3** A set of three technical exercises.

The OCR brief for Section 1 will be made available to centres via the exam board website on September 1 of the academic year in which the course is to be completed.

A summary of the composing options

Composing option	%	Section 1	Section 2	Section 3	Total minimum duration
AS Level (02)	30%	OCR brief (35 marks)	Learner brief (40 marks)		4½ minutes
A Level Composing A **(03)**	35%	OCR brief (35 marks)	Learner brief (40 marks)	Technical Exercises (30 marks)	8 minutes
A Level Composing B **(04)**	25%	OCR brief (35 marks)	Learner brief (40 marks)		4 minutes

At AS Level, composing and performing each carry 30% of the total qualification marks.

At A Level there are two possibilities and they focus around whether you wish to allocate the higher weighting of marks to composition or to performance.

The combinations of composing and performing and their respective weightings are:

Composing A (03)	**35%**	**Performing A (01)**	**25%**
	OR		
Composing B (04)	**25%**	**Performing B (02)**	**35%**

You may have clear ideas about which specialism you wish to take from the start of your course but it is also possible to make your decision later on; discussions with your teachers can help you with this.

What will be included in your final submission?

Component element	Submission requirements
Section 1 **A Level/AS Level**	■ Audio recording of composition ■ Score, lead sheet or written account of composition
Section 2 **A Level/AS Level**	■ Audio recording of composition ■ Score, lead sheet or written account of composition ■ Learner set brief
Section 3 **A Level (03)**	■ Audio recording of composition exercises ■ Score, lead sheet or written account of exercises

What are examiners looking for?

The work submitted in the composition component will be completed during the course under the close supervision of your teacher and will be submitted to OCR for assessment.

Keeping the assessment criteria in mind as you progress in your composing work will help you to make sure that you are on target to meet the requirements of this component. Full details of the criteria used by examiners to assess your work are available on the OCR website.

A summary of how you will be assessed is provided here.

The three sections of the composition module

Section 1: Board Set Brief

You will be assessed on:

Response to brief and ideas (15 marks)

- The musical appropriateness of your response to the commission in the light of the specific genre, tradition or style of the brief.
- Aural familiarity.
- The quality of your ideas, structure, expressive communication.

Compositional techniques (10 marks)

- The techniques you use to assemble, connect and develop your ideas; melodic and harmonic understanding.
- Idiomatic understanding of the chosen medium; creative use of textures.

Communication (10 marks)

- Accurate, expressive, coherent, detailed communication of your composing intentions.

Section 2: Learner Set Brief

Assessment areas are the same as for Section 1, but you will also be assessed on:

Effectiveness of the learner set brief (5 marks)

- The quality of your brief as an effective starting point is credited here.

A Level - Composing A

Section 3: Technical Exercises

The specific requirements of the exercises are outlined later in this chapter.
The assessment of the exercises can be summarised as:

Language (10 marks)

- The use of pitch, rhythm and texture as appropriate to the chosen area.
- Idiomatic writing for voice/instruments.

Technique (10 marks)

- Specific techniques appropriate to the chosen area; structure.

Compositional coherence (10 marks)

- The way in which ideas, language, techniques and use of the chosen medium combine.

Notating, recording and writing about your composition

The specification allows choice in the way you communicate your musical ideas.

An audio recording is required for each section but you will decide what is the most appropriate written way to present your compositions, whether this is some form of music notation (including graphic notation) or a written account. The selective use of screenshots of relevant computer-related technical processes could make a useful contribution to writing about your composition. In order to get the top marks you should consider carefully how you will communicate the detail of your music - expressive elements such as dynamics, tempi, phrasing, mood, character, articulation, balance and technological factors may all be relevant.

You do not have to perform in your own compositions and you may realise them through music technology. Other musicians may perform your music. If they do so without notation, you must explain in your written description how you conveyed to the musicians what you wanted them to play. Extended improvisations by performers in a jazz or popular music context, for example, cannot be directly credited to the composer. Group compositions are not allowed. You should avoid any ambiguity in the presentation of your work.

Section 1
Board set brief

This section looks at how to compose a piece of music by responding to a brief set by OCR. The guidance given in the section applies to both AS and A Level qualifications.

Organising your time

If you are studying for an AS qualification, the choice of Board set briefs will be posted online from the start of your course.

At A Level, before the Board set brief becomes available in the second year of your course you will be able to absorb chosen aspects of the Areas of Study. Plan and prepare in your first year and work on the composition for which you design your own brief. If you are taking the Composing A option, you will be able to research, prepare and work on the technical exercises for Section 3.

Although there is a requirement for a minimum duration of AS and A Level compositions, submissions should not be lengthy unless this can be justified musically. Quality of musical content always wins over quantity.

Give yourself plenty of time. Play your compositions to family or friends to get a 'fresh ear' on your work. Be honest with yourself and ask others to be constructively critical about sections of your work that seem to be less successful than others. You may need to make some changes or transform and refine your ideas. Sometimes a section of music may legitimately take a calmer, more static role in the midst of highly energised music, for example, but if you sense the music is losing focus, take control and enjoy making improvements.

Have an attitude that every sound, every note, every rhythmic idea – everything in your music is important and worth your full attention.

How will your response be assessed?

The marking criteria, set out earlier, are quite clear about what will be expected of the content of your composition and are therefore required reading before you start your work.

The connections between your composition and the characteristics and features of the related Area of Study need to be clear. You may want to support this by the inclusion of a short explanatory commentary.

There is no expectation that you will compose entirely in **pastiche**; there is room to show your own creative and inventive understanding within the parameters of the task.

Establishing a way of working – outlining a methodology

The following steps might form the basis of your compositional approach to the Board set brief:

- EVALUATE the brief fully.
- CONNECT with the elements of the Area of Study; consider the possibility of further RESEARCH.
- COMPOSE by shaping, constructing, and assembling; allow time to reflect on the responses of teachers/family/others.
- RECORD with time to rehearse and make changes in the light of the performing experience; allow time to comprehensively edit a technology-assisted performance.
- DOCUMENT the creation of your work, using text, notation, audio, or whatever might be appropriate.

The following sample briefs will help you to think through this suggested pattern of working. You can adopt or modify it to suit your own style.

DOCUMENTATION

Evidence of your research and learning, together with a demonstration of a clear link with the Area of Study, should be clear from the composition. You may like to include a short commentary with your submission.

SAMPLE BRIEF

Area of Study 1
Instrumental music of Haydn, Mozart and Beethoven

This section offers a sample brief that takes Area of Study 1 as its focus. Remember that this is just a 'sample' brief – you will need to find your own way of working on your actual briefs, but hopefully this example will give you ideas on how to achieve that.

Task

Compose a minuet and trio movement to be performed in the gardens of the Schloss Esterházy as summer entertainment for visitors to the palace. Make use of instruments appropriate to the Classical period, writing for an ensemble of four to ten instrumental parts, without voices.

Evaluate the brief fully

This could be approached systematically via the following tasks:

- Define minuet and trio: how and in what context do Classical composers use this form?
- The venue: research this thoroughly and gain insights to the setting and occasion.
- Instruments: which appropriate instruments from this period could you use?

MINUET AND TRIO

A dance-like structure in $\frac{3}{4}$ time surviving from the Baroque period and present as part of larger Classical structures such as the symphony.

Connecting with the Area of Study – relevant repertoire

General features that you will come to appreciate, as characteristic of music of the Classical period, will include balanced phrases, clear melodies often using scale and arpeggio patterns, a relatively restrained mood, modulation to related keys, and a harmonic language that is typical of the period.

Forms such as sonata form became established in the Classical period, and you will study these in preparation for the Listening and Appraising paper.

Some examples of research that may add to your growing understanding of the characteristics of this Area of Study are outlined in the following exercises.

SCORES IN THE PUBLIC DOMAIN

Many of the scores referred to in the exercises can be downloaded free of charge from www.imslp.org.

Exercise 1

1. Listen to the minuet and trio of Sonata in A, Hob. XVI: 5. It is believed to be an early piano sonata written by Haydn.

2. Write the chord symbols to describe the harmonies above each crotchet beat, notating the modulation to the tonic minor key in the trio.
3. The external ternary structure of the minuet and trio is clear with a return to the minuet section after the trio. Show how the internal binary structure of each section functions using a diagram.

Exercise 2

1. Listen to the minuet and trio movement of Haydn's Symphony No. 55.

2. Notice how much the rhythm gives character to the melody. How are the features of four semiquavers (e.g. the appoggiatura in the first full bar), two semiquavers followed by a quaver rest, and staccato crotchets used in the remainder of the material in this movement?
3. In the trio there is a flowing cello melody in the lowest part of the texture which contrasts well with the predominantly 'melody-and-accompaniment' texture of the minuet. What other features in the trio provide contrast?

Exercise 3

1. Listen to the minuet and trio of Mozart's Symphony No. 33 in B♭ major, K. 319, focusing on the way the instruments are combined and used in their sections.
2. Complete the following table. Some of the information has been completed for you as a model. The bar numbers are approximate, with each phrase containing an **anacrusis** opening.

Minuet			Strings	Horns	Oboe and Bassoon
	a	b. 1–8	Vln 1 + 2 doubling for 4 bars; Vla/VC/CB accompaniment with some independent melodic and rhythmic interest.	Tonic and dominant punctuation coupled to the wind section.	Adding weight to the cadences.
A		b. 9–16			
	b	b. 17–24			
		b. 25–32			

Trio			Strings	Horns	Oboe and Bassoon
B	a	b. 33–40	Flowing melody Vln 1 Counterpoint arpeggio figure Vln 2 Vla/VC/CB 4 bars punctuating accompaniment followed by 4 bars flowing bass		Oboes in thirds partially doubling the second part of the violin phrase.
	b	b. 41–48			
A	Repeat of minuet				

For most of us, composing tends to start with sound rather than notation. Musical 'doodling' away from a computer screen, using your voice or an instrument, is a great place to start experimenting with ideas.

You might start working with a chord sequence. Another way of starting is to consider elements of your piece, such as whether to work in a major or minor key or whether to break your music down into eight-bar phrases - bearing in mind all you have learned about the characteristic basics of melody shaping in the Classical period.

Another way of working is to practise shaping ideas by continuing from a known starting point. This will help you with the structure and character of the music and then you can work on constructing complete ideas of your own.

Known starting points

Exercise 4

The starting point below is taken from the finale of Act 1 of Mozart's opera, *Don Giovanni*.

1. Continue the violin melody line above for a further four bars with a suitable modulation.
2. Compose a further eight bars of melody retaining some characteristics of the opening bars but taking the music in a new direction.
3. Work with the adapted opening of the trio section from Haydn's Symphony No. 67, noticing how Haydn uses the highest range of the violin for this solo upper part. Complete an appropriate harmony for the lower parts.

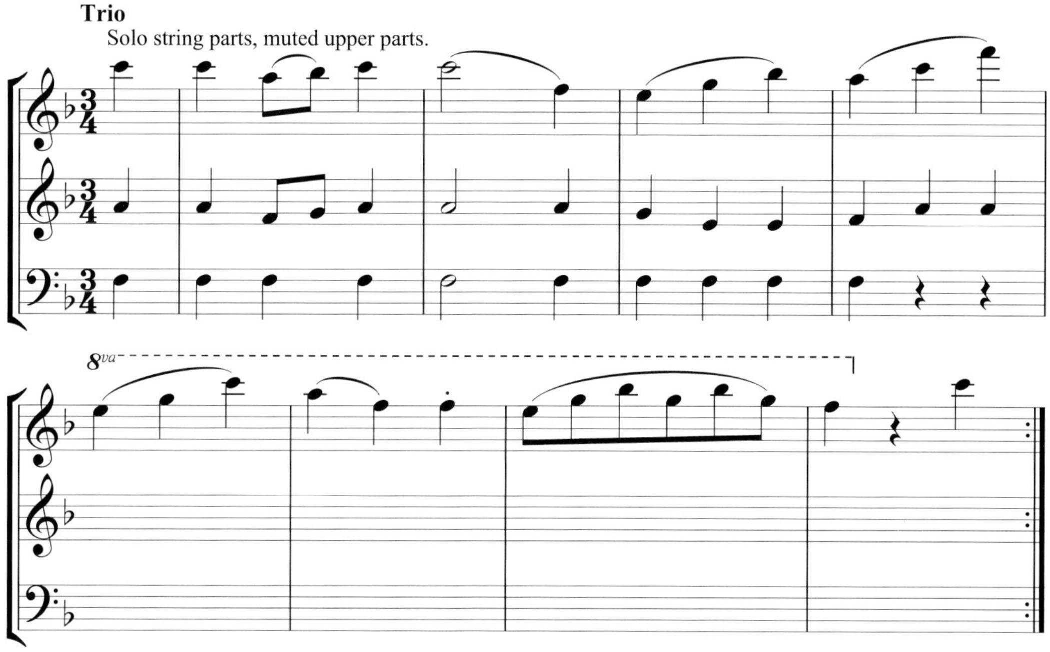

4. Compose and harmonise a further 16 bars to complete the trio and include a modulation to the dominant key at an appropriate place. The pedal is a unifying textural idea throughout the trio and contrasts with the texture of the minuet before it (not included here).
5. Using a shortened version of the structural plan of Mozart's minuet and trio from Symphony No. 33 in B♭ major K. 319, given earlier, choose your own small ensemble of appropriate instruments to compose a minuet and trio of your own invention. Remember that complete pastiche is not required.

Schloss Esterházy, Austria

Recording

You may have your chosen musicians available to rehearse and record a live performance of your final composition. You might use a synthesised/sampled simulation of any instruments you might have missing from your ensemble.

You may also use music technology to record your composition. Remember that aspects of performance - such as phrasing, articulation detail and expression - should be audible on your recording whatever means you choose to realise your work.

Area of Study 5
Programme music, 1820-1910

SAMPLE BRIEF

Task

Compose a short piece in the style of a concert overture, for a production of Shakespeare's *Macbeth*. It is to be performed in the grounds of Brodie Castle by a touring theatre company as part of a Scottish tourist initiative. You should write for at least four orchestral instruments typically used between 1820 and 1910, with or without the addition of a piano.

Evaluate the brief fully

A close evaluation of each aspect of the brief should be made. Some things you might consider include:

- Define 'concert overture' - what is the purpose and structural outline of this musical form?
- Shakespeare's *Macbeth* - familiarise yourself with a succinct synopsis of the play so that its characters, plot and other elements are known.
- Where is Brodie Castle and what is its significance? Will an outdoor performance have any bearing on your choice or number of instruments?
- Make a list of 'typical' instruments found during this period in the works you study. Think about the instruments that form the backbone of the orchestra and chamber ensembles, considering the size of the overall ensemble as well as the heightened and extended use of brass instruments, for example.

Connecting with the Area of Study - relevant repertoire

If you are studying AoS5 as part of your course, you will become familiar with the larger orchestras used to create music with a highly expressive, dramatic character.

Overtures from the period that take their inspiration from Shakespeare's texts include Mendelssohn's *A Midsummer Night's Dream* Op. 21 and Tchaikovsky's fantasy-overture, *Romeo And Juliet.*

A MIDSUMMER NIGHT'S DREAM SCORE

A free score of the overture can be found on the IMSLP (Petrucci Music Library) website.

A more detailed study of Mendelssohn's *A Midsummer Night's Dream* Op. 21 can be instructive in preparation for the *Macbeth* task. Mendelssohn's orchestra is of fairly modest dimensions but he does include the ophicleide - a deep bassoon-shaped brass instrument with a tone approximating that of a tuba - for its fine, deep tone.

This single movement is written in an adapted sonata form structure, which can be represented in the following way:

1-249	Exposition
250-393	Development
394-619	Recapitulation
620-end	Coda

In the Exposition, Mendelssohn presents us with a rich array of musical ideas that correspond to characters or essential ideas in the narrative.

Listen to the entire piece twice, marking the score on the second hearing with the main structural divisions. Identify the thematic material with the help of the information in the following exercise.

Exercise 5

The opening woodwind chords are transcribed here and signify the mysterious dreamworld of enchantment that Mendelssohn lays out before us:

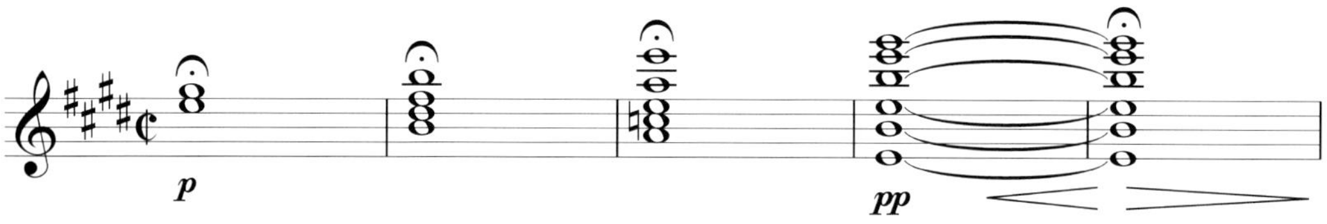

Note how many times this idea returns and where in the structure of the overall movement it is repeated.

Following these introductory chords, further musical ideas are presented.

The Fairies' music:

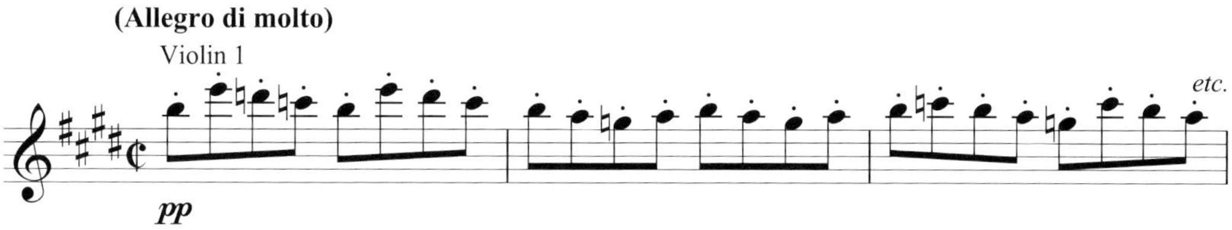

Notice the inventiveness of the orchestration of this idea as the violins play **divisi** in four independent parts very soon after the start of this music.

The bold, ceremonial music of Theseus and his court:

The music of the lovers grows in amongst these ideas and reaches its strongest statement in octaves at bar 158, with flutes doubling the violin part.

Note how the addition of performance detail in the score here - bowing and phrase marks with a soft dynamic - is an essential part of the invention of this expressive theme.

Exercise 6

1. Make a study sheet of your discoveries when exploring the Overture, including notation of the main thematic materials.
2. Write out the music that represents Bottom and the braying of a donkey (starting at bar 197). How does the articulation of this music contribute to the humorous character of the idea?
3. Write out the fanfare horn calls that represent the royal hunting party from bar 222.

In the Development section, the music of the fairies comes under the spotlight and is developed by transforming the staccato quaver motif using different keys.

Exercise 7

1. How does the music at the end of the Development section portray Lysander and Hermia as they sleep?
2. Trace the return of each of the Exposition themes in the Recapitulation.
3. What is the musical content of the Coda section?

Macbeth composition – getting started

A study of an appropriate work in preparation for the main task gives rise to a number of possibilities.

The characters, scenes and locations of *Macbeth* can be identified and considered for their musical potential. It would be wise to be selective and consider fewer themes than Mendelssohn does in his overture given the smaller scale of the piece you will be writing.

In addition to the characters and context of the play there is also a strong undertone of psychological dimensions at work. Is there a suggestion of a parallel here between the magical opening chords of the Mendelssohn overture and an idea that could represent the darker elements deep at work in Macbeth's psyche?

To adopt the formal structure of the Mendelssohn in your own work, with a development that explores a single thematic idea, would demonstrate a close understanding of the traditions and conventions of the overture as found in the programme music of this period.

Exercise 8

1. Compose a number of ideas that might represent the three witches.
2. What instruments might you use to construct contrasting themes for Macbeth and Banquo? Explore ideas using performance detail such as articulation and dynamic markings to give clarity to your thematic ideas.
3. How might Banquo's theme reappear in ghostly form?

Area of Study 6
Innovations in music, 1900 to the present day

SAMPLE BRIEF

Task

Compose a piece of music that portrays the meeting of different cultures or traditions. It is to be performed at the opening of the International Conference on Environment and Climate Change in Rome.

Make use of any appropriate musical techniques you have learned about from this area of study. You may compose using any medium, including acoustic and amplified instruments; you may also choose to work with music technology in an electro-acoustic environment.

Evaluate the brief fully

There are several parts to the brief.

- The international dimension of this brief is clear. It has musical potential. The purpose of the conference involves an international gathering of contributors and the environment and climate change are issues of international interest and concern. What sort of music might be appropriate for such a gathering?
- Music of different cultures or traditions – this rather ambiguous description is inclusive of the various traditions of world music as well as strands of music within art music and popular music. It includes, for example, various forms of jazz or music that combines different cultural elements.
- Electro-acoustic music is a term that covers a broad range of electronic music possibilities. It may include the collecting, generating, modification and organising of sounds. Important early pioneers in this field include Pierre Schaeffer and Edgar Varèse, who were known for using **found sounds**.
- The use of acoustic and amplified instruments and electronic sounds are permitted, alone or in combination in this brief. Voice is not excluded.

Connect with the Area of Study – relevant repertoire

Repertoire with an 'international' dimension

The following table is just one example of an appropriate set of pieces that has relevance to the brief.

Debussy: *Pagodes* (1903)	The composer suggests oriental scales and rhythms.
Bartók: *Romanian Dances* (1915) *15 Hungarian Peasant Songs* (1914–18) *Music For Strings, Percussion And Celesta* (1936)	The piano works are based on authentic melodies from Bartók's research and field studies. This orchestral work does not quote folk music directly but demonstrates an interpretation of folk music, fused together with the composer's own style.
Cage: *Amores* (1943)	Cage was influenced by Colin McPhee's interest in the Balinese gamelan.
Messiaen: *Oiseaux exotiques* (1956) *Turangalîla-Symphonie* (1946–48)	Use of Hindu and Ancient Greek rhythms. Influence of the gamelan is seen in the extensive use of metal percussion.
Volans: String Quartet No. 1 (1986)	Influences include Basotho concertino music and traditional Nyungwe music of Mozambique.

Innovation in structure

Exercise 9

1. Listen to a recording of Charles Ives' *Three Places In New England*, Movement II: Putnam's Camp. Identify some of the musical ideas supporting the narrative, including 'borrowed' melodies and rhythmical ideas. How might this layering of musical events be adapted for use in response to this Board set brief?
2. Listen to a recording of Steve Reich's *Different Trains*. Identify the various sounds, musical ideas and 'borrowed' materials in the first section: 'America – Before the War'. Reich talks of his piece as both a documentary and a musical reality. How might a 'musical documentary' approach be used in response to this set brief?
3. Compile a study log of your research findings for both these pieces.

Innovation in the use of sound sources

Some seminal works to investigate might include:

Voice	Musique concrète	Electronic music
Stockhausen: *Stimmung*	Pierre Schaeffer: *Étude aux tourniquets* – toy tops and percussion instruments	Stockhausen: *Gesang der Jünglinge*; *Kontakte*
Meredith Monk: *Do You Be*	Matthew Herbert: 'The Truncated Life Of A Modern Industrialised Chicken' from the album *Plat du Jour*. (2005)	Kraftwerk: *Autobahn*
Berio: *Sequenza III*		Tangerine Dream: *Phaedra*

A performance of Meredith Monk's *Songs Of Acension*

YOUTUBE AS A RESOURCE

YouTube is an excellent source of important historical footage, documenting key developments in music innovation during the 20th century.

Notation and reporting

If you choose to venture into electro-acoustic music it will be important to keep good records of the processes involved at each stage of your work.

Keep details of sound sources and the means by which any manipulations are made. This is especially important if your work cannot be notated conventionally. Graphic scores and diagrams can provide effective support in a written document.

Composing – getting started

As you work it may help you to construct a simple mind map of the most important elements of your research and listening experience in relation to this Area of Study.

Composing begins by making simple choices out of a range of options. A visual document such as a mind map can help you see the bigger picture of the possibilities before you. Initial choices may be practical, such as the choice of medium or taking the general mood of the composition into account. In this case, you may choose to compose music that is optimistic and hopeful but may also have a sense of gravitas fitting for the overall concept.

Enjoy experimenting with ideas that you may discard but will nevertheless benefit from as your composing ability develops and matures.

Section 2
Learner set brief

In Composing Sections 1 and 3, there is a compulsory requirement to link with an Area of Study. Section 2 allows you to compose in a manner that is not specifically covered in the Areas of Study. You are free to make a link, however, if you wish to do so.

Even when we are composing a piece of music in our own 'style', we are very likely to hear echoes and influences of other pieces and composers in our own music. However hard we strive to be original, we are influenced by the music around us, and are inspired by the music that we love to perform and to listen to. Many great composers and songwriters have been inspired by other musicians while still writing in their own unique 'voice'. Beethoven was heavily influenced by Haydn, and Mendelssohn revered J. S. Bach, yet all these composers had their own distinctive style.

The apparent freedom of devising your own brief is hopefully exciting for you, but be sure to balance the love for your favourite styles and influences with a curiosity about the musical 'unknown'. Commit yourself to determined research; this is an important part of creative work.

The requirements for this composing task are laid out in the specification and are almost identical to those of the Board set brief.

Key words and phrases to remember are:

- Elements of music
- Musical devices
- Instrumental and compositional techniques
- Expression
- Development of musical ideas
- Understanding conventions and devices (of chosen style, genre, tradition)
- Conviction
- Sophistication
- Creativity.

Devising your brief

It is likely that your brief will change shape from your initial thoughts as you work on your ideas and this is to be expected. But the Board set brief provides a clear model of the ingredients you should aim to include in your final wording:

- A concise description of the music to be composed that may include references to style and/or structure. - romantic piano concerto, 2nd movement
- Mention of the purpose of composing, citing contextual possibilities such as a potential occasion and/or audience. -> e.g. [illegible] youth adult orchestra in Hertford.
- A statement about the musical forces to be used. -> full symphony orchestra & piano

Page 96 Tchaikovsky - 20:37 - 2nd movement key girl playing piano

This approach is underlined in the assessment criteria, where 5 marks are allocated for the effectiveness of your brief in enabling you to demonstrate your musical ideas.

To gain maximum marks your brief should contain sufficient detail to provide an 'excellent' starting point for a composition that will subsequently demonstrate technical and expressive control and coherence.

Contemporary songwriting

The importance of song is evident in all cultures and a study of the music in AoS2 will give you many opportunities to learn about techniques, structures, and the way the relationship between voice and its accompaniment can be explored.

Songwriting in a contemporary context can be an appealing possibility in constructing your own brief, whether you are building on the experience you already have as a songwriter or starting as a novice.

Understanding the 'family tree' of influences on established singer-songwriters could be instructive. Below is a list of artists and possible approaches that you could take.

Exercise 10

1. Bob Dylan is acknowledged by many as one of the greatest popular songwriters. Listen to some of his songs from across his career. Compare his performance of his song 'To Make You Feel My Love' with Adele's.
2. In addition to Ella Fitzgerald, which other singers/songwriters have inspired Adele?
3. Listen to some of the songs of significant songwriters such as Joni Mitchell, Burt Bacharach, Elton John, John Lennon, Paul McCartney, Holland-Dozier-Holland and Stephen Sondheim.
4. Can the writing of a song take place without a singer in mind?

Lyrics

Contemporary singer-songwriter Jack Garrett explained in a recent BBC radio interview that he often starts the songwriting process with a chord sequence - a musical idea - before thinking about the lyrics. This presents an alternative view to the commonly held belief that the songwriting process always starts with words.

Remember that you can write your own lyrics or use pre-existing words from a range of other sources.

You will forge your own independent way as you begin to test out your ideas.

Exam success

Some songs are unusual and technically sophisticated, while others can be profound in their simplicity.

It is always worth bearing in mind that the formula for commercial success may be somewhat different to that required for success at higher examination level. Harmonic language, instrumental writing, memorable melodies and rhythmic elements within a controlled structure all make an important contribution to this unique compositional expression.

Exercise 11

1. Why do we write songs? Create a study sheet that overviews the subject matter of songs from a range of artists.
2. What does the instrumental element contribute to a song? Evaluate the contribution of conventional instruments and technology resources in the music of Radiohead, for example.

LISTEN AND LEARN

There are many interesting online resources for songwriters but you should be wary of 'quick fix' solutions. Instead, learn from the music of other singers and songwriters whom you admire.

Other possibilities

You may want to consider a composition that combines elements of more than one Area of Study.

For example, you might consider writing an unaccompanied choral work using aspects of liturgical settings and structural devices such as those covered in AoS4, but with a more contemporary harmonic and rhythmic language. Or you might consider music for film or video games, music that reaches back to use elements from the Renaissance period, or instrumental music that captures a tightly focused soundworld.

Exercise 12

1. Choose five representative tracks that summarise some important aspects in creating an effective 'soundworld' in the work of the band Dream Theater or another progressive band of your choice.
2. Investigate the soundworld of Reich's *Music For 18 Musicians*, the original music composed by Philip Glass for *La Belle et la Bête*, or Arvo Pärt's *Fratres*.

Establishing a digital notebook of your investigations and potential ideas can help you keep track of your thoughts, and will provide source material should you wish to compile a brief commentary to accompany your composition.

The marimba features in *Music For 18 Musicians*

Section 3

Technical exercises

The three short technical exercises in this section are an option available to you if you want to specialise in composing (35%) at A Level.

- **Composing A (03)**
- **Section 3 (30 marks)**

The requirements are loosely framed in the specification to give you maximum flexibility in how you will approach the task of focusing on a specific technique.

A recommended methodology would be to research, construct and practise the techniques identified. You can then display a good level of understanding in your three relatively short final exercises completed later in the course.

Each final exercise should last no more than 40 seconds.

Relevance of the technical exercises to your overall portfolio

Thinking carefully about which area to focus on could help you develop the skills required for the other two compositions you will be working on.

An example of this might be the researching and writing of technical exercises in orchestral textures of the Romantic period with a link to AoS5. This could be highly relevant in preparing for and supporting a programmatic instrumental composition for your learner-set brief.

Examples suggested by the examination board

The choice of technique must be identified within **one** of the following areas:

- **Pitch organisation**
- **Rhythms and metre**
- **Texture.**

The technique you choose must be connected to **one** Area of Study. This may be an AoS that you are studying for Listening and Appraising. You are free to choose techniques, however, that link with any Area of Study.

OCR provides some examples of techniques and these are shown in the following table.

Technique	Focused examples	Area of study link
Pitch organisation	Modes in instrumental jazz	**AoS3**
	Serialism	**AoS6**
	Harmony and tonality in chorale writing	**AoS4**
	Harmonic language in Mozart's piano sonatas	**AoS1**
Rhythms and metre	Minimalism	**AoS6**
	Innovative approaches	**AoS6**
	Syncopation	**AoS3**
Textures	String quartet	**AoS1**
	Song accompaniments	**AoS2**
	Choral textures	**AoS4**
	Orchestral textures in programmatic music	**AoS5**
	Piano textures as found in Romantic period miniatures	**AoS5**

What will be assessed?

Understanding the three strands of the assessment criteria will help you as you consider your approach to the work of this section.

Language

Under this heading, credit is given for the range of exploration and for the imaginative, appropriate application of the chosen option (pitch **or** rhythm and metre **or** texture) in relation to the Area of Study (and its associated musical devices and conventions).

Technique

Under this heading, credit is given for the broader structural framing and techniques, within which the 'Language' of each composition is presented. Techniques of assembly, development, combining and connecting ideas are part of the assessment here.

Compositional coherence

Under this heading, credit is given for the relative success of combining together ideas and techniques and for the evidence of technical knowledge of the chosen medium.

Presentation of exercises for assessment

A recording, score, lead sheet or written account of the composition as appropriate must be provided for each exercise along with a completed coversheet.

The technique focus should be defined as clearly as possible.

Your composing exercises may be realised in performances with instruments/voices or through music technology.

A concise account of your research and working of the exercises might be described in a **short** written report as part of your submission.

This is not an OCR requirement but examiners can find it instructive to understand the context of your work.

A way of working – outlining a methodology

Four steps are suggested as a way of approaching this task.

They mirror suggestions for working on the two compositions:

- **Research**
  Investigating a range of uses of the chosen technique by composers in compositions taken from the Area of Study identified.
- **Construct**
  Thinking about the framework in which to present the techniques, and making choices about instruments/voices.
- **Practice**
  Enjoying the exploration of the chosen technique by composing a number of preliminary exercises on the way to formulation of the 'final three'.
- **Personal documentation**
  Keeping a record of the details and progress of all aspects of your work.

Pitch organisation

TECHNICAL EXERCISE

In this specific exercise, we are going to focus on Serialism. This connects with Area of Study 6: Innovations in Music, 1900 to the present day.

This would be an entirely appropriate area of pitch organisation to choose for technical exercises. It is not the role of this study guide to provide a manual for serial composing but some important texts are suggested for consultation:

- Perle, George. 1991. *Serial Composition And Atonality: An Introduction to the Music of Schoenberg, Berg, And Webern*
- Smith Brindle, R. 1968. *Musical Composition* (Chapter 6: Serialism)
- Whittall, Arnold. 2008. *The Cambridge Introduction To Serialism.*

The four versions of the row:

- Original or 'O' form; sometimes referred to as Principal or 'P' form
- Retrograde or 'R' form; the 'O' form backwards
- Inversion or 'I' form; all the intervals of 'O' are inverted
- Retrograde of the Inversion or 'RI' form; the 'I' version backwards.

The use of each of the 12 degrees of the chromatic scale (sounding in any octave) before any one of them is repeated is a guiding principle of serialism. The system avoids giving emphasis to any one note. The sense of a 'tonic' is avoided and the music will be evenly non-tonal. Although different versions of the 12-note row and their transpositions are available, in practice composers often limit the number of versions they use.

Serialism involves much more than the strict, methodical manipulation of 12 chromatic notes. Many composers believe it to be a very fruitful way of generating highly creative ideas; they would not consider the 12-note row and its associated techniques to be any more restrictive than the use of scales within the conventions of tonality.

It is equally important in serialism and tonality to give attention to textures, melodic shaping, harmonic possibilities, rhythmic invention and the use of instruments. This will be part of the framework within which you demonstrate your understanding of serialism.

Using online technology to generate a matrix of the various forms and transpositions of the 12-note row may have a time-saving appeal. In reality, this can encourage a mechanical way of thinking that can inadvertently distract you from understanding the fundamental importance of the shape, sound and character of the row itself.

A series of 12 letter names in a box may be 'matrix-represented' in the following way:

Webern: Symphony, Op. 21

F A♭ G F♯ B♭ A D♯ E C C♯ D B

On the stave, however, the shape of the sequence of notes is clearer because the intervals are represented visually:

Additionally, the symmetrical nature of this row is easier to detect with the eye.

The intervals of the first half are 'mirrored' in reverse in the second half.

Row notes	Interval
1–2 [12–11]	Ascending minor third
2–3 [11–10]	Descending semitone
3–4 [10–9]	Descending semitone
4–5 [9–8]	Ascending diminished fourth/Ascending major third
5–6 [8–7]	Descending semitone

The intervals between notes 4–5 and 9–8, though written differently, *sound* the same.

The bridging interval between notes 6 and 7 is a diminished fifth, or **tritone**, which ensures the two halves of the row are the maximum distance apart in tonal terms.

All these characteristics of the note row are more easily discerned in the staff presentation.

The works of three composers, collectively known as the Second Viennese School, demonstrate how serialism developed. Studying the use of serialism in the music of Schoenberg, Berg and Webern and completing short technical exercises could form one approach in this section of the unit.

Other composers who later used serialism when it was more established include Stravinsky, Stockhausen and Boulez.

Exercise 13

1. Using a notation programme of your choice, write out the three derived forms of the 'original', or 'O' form, which Schoenberg uses in the first movement of the Quintet, Op. 26.

2. Using the transpose function of a notation programme, produce the 11 transpositions of the 'I' form of the row in staff notation.

3. Listen to a performance of Schoenberg's Quintet, making notes about the texture of the music and how the composer uses the instruments **idiomatically** in each of the movements.

4. What structural forms does the composer use for each movement?

SEARCH ONLINE

You will find several recordings of Schoenberg's compositions on YouTube accompanied by an annotated score. For instance, search for 'Schoenberg Op. 26 Score'.

Researching the practice of the composers of the Second Viennese School as a preparation for your exercises might include:

- Listening to the highly chromatic music of Arnold Schoenberg's early compositions such as *Verklärte Nacht*, Op. 4 or his Chamber Symphony, Op. 9.
- Examining Schoenberg's compositions using serialism such as Variations for Orchestra, Op. 31 or Piano Pieces, Op. 33.
- Anton Weber – internal symmetries found in the row, use of canon, the principles of **Klangfarbenmelodie** and fragmentation producing **pointillism** in textures. Symphony Op. 21 is an important work; Three Songs, Op. 23 shows how the voice can be used in a serial context.
- In your own exercises you can demonstrate an understanding of the use of **Hauptstimme** and **Nebenstimme** to designate passages of principal and secondary importance, as demonstrated in the lower parts of the following example:

Preparatory exercises might include:

- Construction of different types of row: all intervals, symmetrical, a row containing small 'cells', rows with tonal 'areas' or whole-tone elements.
- Writing a 'melody' with conventional rhythmic and phrasing structure; writing a fragmented 'melody' of cells with rhythmic variety and shaping based on serial models you have studied.
- Constructing four-part chords using the row vertically, horizontally or freely distributed between the parts.
- Experimenting with imitation, canon and mirror images in two- and three-part writing.

Longer exercises

The assessment criteria for this part of the composing unit make clear that you should demonstrate a clear understanding of the technique you are using in the three exercises you submit.

Each exercise should be self-contained and coherent. You may find it useful, for example, to listen to some of Webern's shorter movements as a guide for the length and content of your own exercises. Five of the movements of the Six Bagatelles For String Quartet, Op. 9 last approximately 40 seconds or under, for example.

TECHNICAL EXERCISE

Rhythms and metre

In this exercise we will be focusing on syncopation. It connects with Area of Study 3: Developments in Instrumental Jazz, 1910 to the present day.

'Syncopation is, generally speaking, any deliberate disturbance of the normal pulse of metre, accent and rhythm.' ***Harvard Dictionary Of Music***

If syncopation places stress on the normally weak beats of a bar this can give rise to a sense of surprise or of the unexpected. It is found in abundant use in jazz and is often combined with other non-syncopated rhythms, creating polyrhythms.

In jazz, **swing** is quite different from syncopation found in other types of music. The notation of jazz syncopation is often only approximate and may not fully represent the nuance that is found in live performance. For this reason you may want to consider the possibility of a performance using instruments in the realisation of your exercises.

Some notated examples of syncopation commonly found in jazz are given in the appendix material of *Jazz Styles: History And Analysis* by Mark C. Gridley.

The suggested repertoire of AoS3 gives many examples of instrumental pieces within which ideas incorporating syncopation can be heard.

Exercise 14

1. Ragtime was something of a forerunner of jazz and popularised the use of syncopation. Listen to some music of the ragtime era (1890–1920) to hear how syncopated rhythms anticipate or delay the main beats of the bar.
2. Annotate this extract from 'Pine Apple Rag' to indicate the places where syncopation occurs and describe how it is being used.

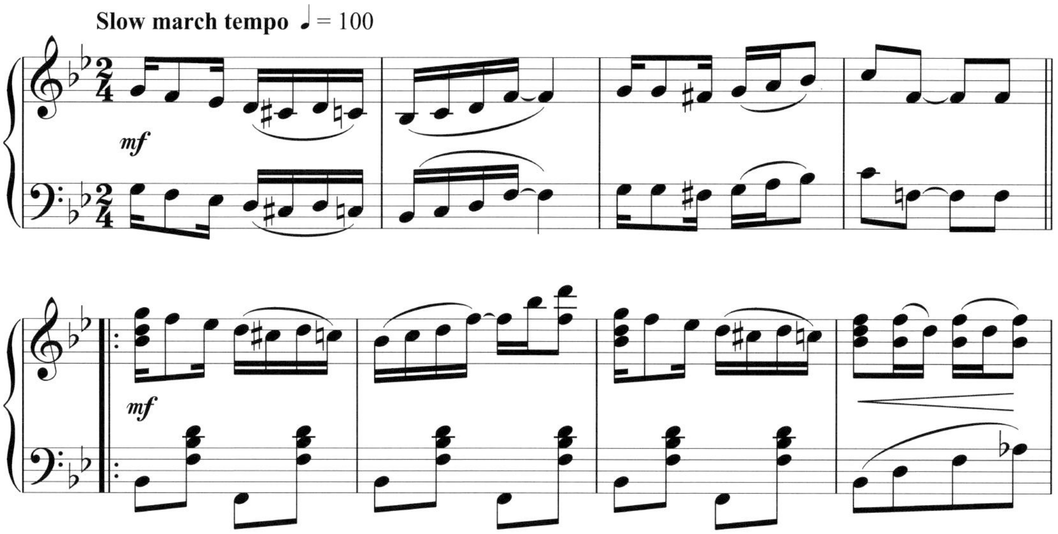

3. Compare John Coltrane's version of Rodgers and Hammerstein's 'My Favourite Things' with the original song version from *The Sound Of Music*. What role does syncopation play in the saxophone part and in the piano accompaniment?

Research in preparation for the construction of exercises will include contextual factors such as the use of instruments, textures and the effects of syncopation – for example, to push the music forward, providing a sense of energy or anticipation.

Listening example 1: Miles Davis, 'So What' from *Kind Of Blue*

There is a freedom and flexibility in the introduction to this iconic track but also some precise on-the-beat playing from both piano and bass.

The cymbal softly keeps the pulse steady as the bass riff commences, with the rest of the ensemble joining in the syncopation on the 'so what' motif.

The trumpet solo improvisation is a model of discreet use of anticipation in syncopation. The context in which the syncopation is framed includes layering of instrumental sound, call and response, transposition of motifs and a clear structure contrasting improvised material with the head.

Listening example 2: Herbie Hancock, *Maiden Voyage*

The piano chord pattern is played in the 2-bar rhythmic pattern below:

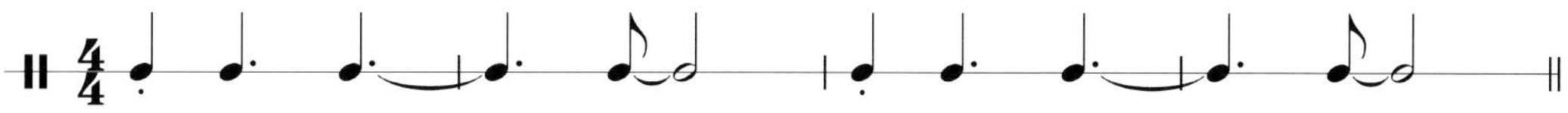

What are the other instruments contributing to the sense of on-beat pulse or syncopation?

Listening example 3: Duke Ellington, *Ko Ko*

Listen to Joe Nanton's trombone in the second and third choruses of the work.

The rhythmic music played by the instruments or groups of instruments can be categorised by their contribution to keeping the pulse or providing syncopation. Summarise this in the table:

Reeds	
Brass	
Trombone solo	
Piano	
Bass	

Preliminary and longer exercises

There are several different branches of jazz harmony. One of the easiest to get started with is modality, where melodies are taken from specific modes.

The Dorian mode – given below, starting on D – is used by Davis in 'So What'.

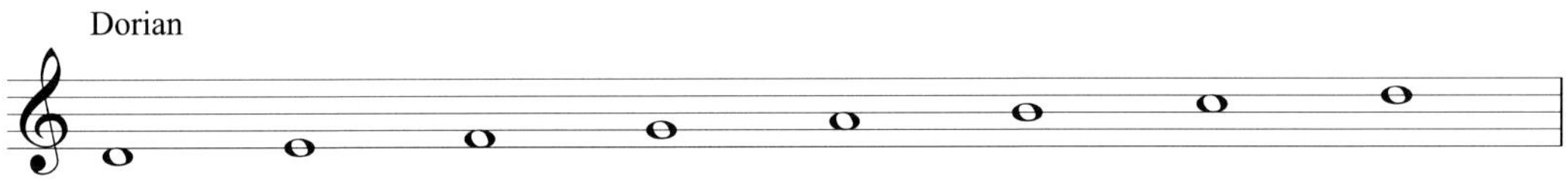

Play the mode, getting a good feel for the sound of its shape. Mark the interval between each pair of notes as a semitone or a tone.

a. Play and then write out a transposed version of the mode starting on E♭.

b. Using the D Dorian mode, shape an initial melodic idea that uses syncopation. Compose a contrasting section of equal length in E♭ or another transposition of your choice. Return to a slightly altered version of your opening idea to conclude the melody.

Syncopation is a defining aspect of jazz music. It is crucial to study jazz from a specific period or indeed study the music of particular artists. You can then closely identify and define particular traits of syncopation that you can demonstrate and develop in your own work.

Textures

TECHNICAL EXERCISE

The specific focus of this chapter is on piano textures in miniatures of the Romantic period, connecting with Area of Study 5.

This could be a fruitful approach to a technique under the descriptor of 'Texture'. It could be particularly relevant if your performing instrument is the piano, or if you are wanting to improve your understanding of how to write effectively for that instrument.

OCR makes it clear in the title and outline of Area of Study 5 that the emphasis is programme music, where a non-musical or narrative idea is communicated in the music.

When considering miniatures such as Schumann's *Scenes From Childhood* or Grieg's *Lyric Pieces* there is also an opportunity for connecting a performing perspective with compositional thinking. Some of these pieces are works that form part of the beginner piano repertoire and provide some clear, instructive examples of varied textures.

A MATTER OF INTERPRETATION

Compare performances of Grieg's *Lyric Pieces* on YouTube: Walter Gieseking, Emil Gilels and Stephen Hough provide a range of authoritative historical and contemporary interpretations.

Initial research will help you to understand the broader context within which textural writing is placed.

Exercise 15

1. Schumann indicated that the titles of the pieces in *Scenes From Childhood* were broadly based descriptions rather than detailed programmatic descriptors. Think of three 'titles' that you might choose as reminiscences of your own childhood.
2. Describe three musical devices (e.g. tempi, rhythms, harmony, texture) that appropriately reflect the broad suggestions of the titles in the following pieces from Schumann's *Scenes From Childhood*:
   - Blindman's Buff
   - Reverie
   - Child Falling Asleep.
3. Sometimes described as 'character pieces', these short piano solos often present a single mood. Listen to a range of Grieg's *Lyric Pieces* and describe the mood expressed in each one.
4. Many of the pieces are structured in ternary form. Identify the contrasting material in a range of pieces you listen to.

Learning about textures from the music

Grieg: *About Strange Lands And People*

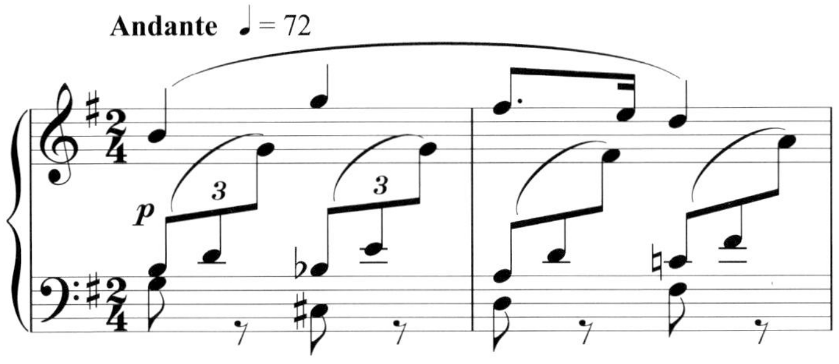

Texture

Optimistic, upward-reaching melody above a triplet accompaniment pattern notated between the staves/hands. Constant texture throughout helps to create a single mood.

Additional composing observations

'Strange' chord in bar 1, beat 2; contrasting descending minor section from bar 9; expressive use of tempo; ternary structure.

Grieg: *Watchmen's Song*

Texture

Strong octave unison between the hands followed by block chords: homophonic texture. In the contrasting 'B' section a septuplet flourish figuration over a tonic minor pedal alternates with block chord phrases.

Additional composing observations

How might the programmatic connection with Shakespeare's *Macbeth* be represented in the two textures? Ternary structure; dramatic contrast between ternary structure sections.

Grieg: *Berceuse*

Texture	Right-hand melody with repeating rhythmic pattern in the left-hand accompaniment. Drone-like texture of open fifth in the contrasting section in the tonic minor key.
Additional composing observations	How does the rhythmic element contribute to the musical effectiveness of this lullaby? The spread chords and use of upper piano register with both hands in the treble clef (e.g. b. 13–16) add to the delicacy and tranquil effect of the music.

Using these three examples as models, continue your research to identify other textural patterns. It will be useful to consider the spacing of left-hand chords, or the way in which melodies are placed at the bottom of a texture or weave between more contrapuntal lines, for example, so that the textures you write in your exercises are characteristic and typical of the period.

Exercise 16

For further research:

1. What musical and contextual justification is there for the popular naming of Chopin's Prelude in D♭, Op. 28, No. 15 ('Raindrop')?
2. What role do rhythm and texture play in Mendelssohn's 'Funeral March' Op. 62 No. 3, from his *Songs Without Words*?
3. What programmatic elements are supported in the textures used by Chopin in his nocturnes?

Preliminary and longer exercises

You will be able to show a good understanding of piano textures from this period if you do your research.

Remember to provide a title for each piece that demonstrates your programmatic intent in broad terms.

A brief, optional account of your research will help to demonstrate the preparation and compositional thinking that has informed your exercises.

The Classical period

OVERVIEW

This Area of Study focuses on the Classical period of music history and three of its musical giants.

What you need to know

You will be examined on this Area of Study in the Listening and Appraising examination paper at the end of your course. The questions on this Area of Study will be in Sections A and B of the Question Paper and are compulsory – you will need to answer all the questions related to this Area of Study, along with the compulsory questions on Area of Study 2.

For both Sections A and B a score of printed music will be provided in a separate insert, which you will need to use to help you to answer the questions. You will also be provided with a CD of the extracts of music used.

The examination will last two hours in total for AS Level and two-and-a-half hours for A Level.

Section A

This section will include:

- A piece of music you will probably not have studied.
- Short answer questions (between 1 and 8 marks each).
- Some multiple choice questions (one or two at A Level, more at AS Level) with a choice of four possible answers.
- General musical knowledge: writing part of a melody or bass line (i.e. dictation), identifying keys, chords, cadences, devices and techniques.
- Using what you know about the music of the period by Haydn, Mozart and Beethoven and applying it to other pieces of music.

Section A offers a total of 15 marks for A Level and 20 marks for AS Level.

Exercise 1 contains the kind of questions you might be asked in Section A.

Section B

This section will include:

- An extract from the 'prescribed work' you will have studied in detail.
- A full score in the insert.
- Comparison of two different performances of the same extract.
- Comparing the extract to similar passages later or earlier in the work.
- Relating the prescribed work to other music of the period or to the composer's overall output.

Section B offers a total of 20 marks – two questions of 10 marks each for both AS and A Level.

You may also choose to work on a composition brief related to this Area of Study.

Prescribed works

The piece of music you have to study in detail for Section B of the paper depends on which examination paper you are taking and when.

It is very important to check carefully that you are studying the correct piece:

AS Level	
June 2017	Mozart: Clarinet Concerto in A, K. 622, first movement
June 2018	Haydn: Symphony No. 100 in G, 'Military', first movement
A Level	
June 2018	Beethoven: Symphony No. 3 in E♭, Op. 55, 'Eroica', first movement
June 2019	Mozart: Piano Concerto No. 23 in A, K. 488, third movement

While the prescribed works are different for each level and year, all are excellent wider listening for the Area of Study and can be studied by the whole class, whatever final examination they take. For example, an A Level student studying Beethoven's 'Eroica' symphony may be asked to compare it with a symphony by another composer – Haydn's 'Military' symphony could then be used and comparisons drawn between the two.

It is important that you have at least one copy of a score of your prescribed work. Indeed, it can be useful to have two: one to write on and one to leave unmarked, so that as you become more familiar with the work you can practise answering questions about it without helpful notes written on the score. Scores are often available online for you to print out, but these should be used with caution as they vary in quality and reliability. Further information is given under each prescribed work.

In the examination you will have an insert. It will contain the extract of music from your prescribed work on which the questions are based. This full score will look slightly different from the score you will have studied, as it will have been created especially for the examination and may begin with a bar numbered 1, even if it is not from the start of the movement.

You will also need to listen to different recordings of your prescribed work and, again, many are available online. You should make sure that you listen to a variety of recordings, using both modern and 'period' instruments (instruments that were used at the time of Haydn, Mozart and Beethoven) and try to notice the differences and similarities. It is impossible to listen to your prescribed work too many times; ideally you will eventually be able to look at the score and to hear the music in your head!

Introduction

Meet the composers

Mozart, Haydn and Beethoven are closely linked together. All three composed music during the Classical period (c. 1750–1820), though Beethoven's later music may be considered to be part of the subsequent Romantic period (c. 1820–1910).

They all spent a considerable amount of time in the city of Vienna and are therefore sometimes known as the 'First Viennese School'.

Haydn's and Mozart's earliest works are often in **galant** style with very clear melodies, simple accompaniments and much ornamentation. Their later works are written in what is known as the 'mature' Classical style.

All three composers wrote a large amount of vocal music - not just instrumental music, which is what you will study here, but also sacred (religious) music, secular (non-religious) music and operas. For Haydn, Mozart and Beethoven, composing was very much something they did to earn money. Their works were always written for a particular reason, not just because they felt like it!

Scores are available for all of the works featured in this section - you should be able to purchase them or download them (for free) from online music libraries such as IMSLP.

Joseph Haydn (1732–1809)

1732	Haydn was born in the village of Rohrau in Austria. His parents were not particularly musical.
1740	Haydn's musical talent was recognised and he joined the choir of St Stephen's Cathedral in Vienna, also learning the violin and organ. He became familiar with Baroque music, including music written in counterpoint.
1745	On leaving the choir, Haydn remained in Vienna. He taught music, composed and performed, but struggled financially. He had some composing lessons, but mostly studied by himself, using textbooks and the work of other composers, particularly C. P. E. Bach.
1755	Haydn was invited to stay at a country house to perform and compose music for the musicians there. The musicians comprised two violinists, a viola player and a cellist, so Haydn produced his first string quartets.
1759	Haydn secured his first paid employment as a *Kapellmeister* (literally 'chapel master') for a Count Morzin. Haydn was in charge of the music-making at the Count's home, directing a small orchestra and writing instrumental, keyboard and sacred works.
1761	Haydn's big break: he was appointed second *Kapellmeister* to Prince Paul Anton Esterházy at Eisenstadt in Hungary. The prince was musical and had an orchestra. Haydn wrote much instrumental music and was eventually promoted to first *Kapellmeister*. Prince Paul Anton died in 1762. He was succeeded by his brother, Nikolaus.
1766	Haydn moved with the Prince to a new large palace, called Esterháza, which was remote from other cities. He wrote an enormous amount of music and experimented with new ideas. His fame spread and some of his music was published.
1781	On a trip to Vienna, Haydn met Mozart and the two became friends and admirers of each other's work, learning from each other's compositions.
1790	Prince Nikolaus died and his successor was not interested in music. The Esterházy orchestra was disbanded and Haydn was given a generous pension. He was free to move to Vienna and to visit London, to perform some specially written works.
1792	On his way back to Vienna from London, Haydn met Beethoven, who then came to Vienna for lessons with Haydn.
1794	Haydn undertook another extended visit to London, composing more music especially for the visit.

1809	Haydn died in Vienna, leaving a huge body of music, including over 80 string quartets, 104 symphonies, concertos, keyboard works and other smaller works.

To identify particular pieces, Haydn's works were given a number by Hoboken, who produced a catalogue. Works are given a Roman numeral to indicate the category (e.g. works in category I are symphonies) and then another number for the individual work.

Wolfgang Amadeus Mozart (1756–1791)

1756	Mozart was born in Salzburg. His father, Leopold was a violinist and composer.
1762	Mozart and his sister, who were both child prodigies, were taken to various European cities to perform to nobility and in concerts. This international childhood meant that Mozart encountered the work of current composers, including J. C. Bach (the brother of C. P. E. Bach) in London. Mozart had already begun composing and arranging music.

1769	Mozart was appointed *Konzertmeister* in Salzburg, in the service of the Archbishop, but continued to travel a great deal.
1781	Mozart arrived in Vienna, accompanying the Archbishop of Salzburg. Mozart was increasingly frustrated at being a servant and was eventually allowed to leave. For the rest of his life Mozart was what would today be called 'self-employed', working as a performer, teacher and composer to earn money. At times his financial position was rather precarious.
1786	Mozart visited Prague to hear a production of his opera *The Marriage of Figaro* and wrote more works for the city.
1791	Mozart died, leaving very little money to his widow Constanze, who published some of his scores. Famously his Requiem Mass was left unfinished, and was therefore completed by his former assistant, the composer Franz Süssmayr.

Although Mozart had a very short life he produced over 600 compositions. His works were catalogued by Köchel, who ordered the compositions chronologically, giving them a number such as K. 545. Many of Mozart's works were not published during his lifetime.

Ludwig van Beethoven (1770–1827)

Beethoven's life is often divided into three periods:

	FIRST PERIOD **In this first period he establishes himself as a composer.**
1770	Beethoven was born in Bonn into a moderately musical family. His father, himself a singer, was disappointed that Beethoven was not a prodigy as talented as Mozart. He had lessons on the piano, organ and violin and in composing.
1782	Beethoven's musical training lead to a position as an assistant organist.
1787	Beethoven briefly visited Vienna and met Mozart. He had to return home to Bonn as his mother was dying.
1792	Beethoven met Haydn in Bonn and followed him to Vienna. Beethoven had some lessons with Haydn, but these were not a great success. He earned money from teaching, performing and composing, sometimes dedicating his works to particular people who may have paid him.
1802	Beethoven began to go deaf and became very depressed. He produced a document now known as the *Heiligenstadt Testament* because it was written in Heiligenstadt, near Vienna, where Beethoven was staying for the summer. It was a letter of despair to his two brothers, but remained hidden until after his death.
1803	**MIDDLE PERIOD** This is the period in which Beethoven was most productive, when many of his most famous works were written.
1813	**LAST PERIOD** This is the period in which there were various problems in Beethoven's personal life and he produced a small number of very intense works.
1827	Beethoven died in Vienna. Thousands of people attended his funeral.

Beethoven's works are not as numerous as those of Haydn or Mozart, but they are often much more intense and of greater length. Like the other two composers he wrote sonatas, chamber music, symphonies, concertos and other orchestral works. Many of his works were published during his lifetime as a means of making money. Works were given Opus numbers in the order they were published, rather than the order in which they were written. You may occasionally come across works with a number such as WoO 59 ('Für Elise', for piano). WoO is an abbreviation for *Werke ohne Opuszahl* meaning works without an opus number.

Sonatas

Solo instrumental music

The word sonata means 'to be sounded' – it is a piece for instruments rather than singers. Sonatas had been written during the Baroque period, but earlier sonatas were rather different. In the Classical period the word sonata came to mean a piece for one instrument (or an orchestral instrument with an accompanying keyboard instrument) in three or four movements.

The structure and style of each movement usually followed a pattern:

- A fast movement in the tonic key.
- A slow movement in a different, but related key.
- If present, a minuet and trio (or later a scherzo), usually in the tonic key.
- A fast movement in the tonic key.

Sonata form

The first movement of a sonata was usually in (what is now called) sonata form. Confusingly this is the structure of just the first movement, not the whole sonata.

Sonata form is an extension of binary form but sonata form has three main sections:

Exposition		Key
First subject	A main tune	Tonic
Transition (sometimes called a bridge)	Music which changes key	Modulating to the dominant (for a piece in a major key) or the relative major (for a piece in a minor key)
Second subject	Another main tune	Dominant or relative major
Codetta	A short section to end the exposition	Dominant or relative major

The whole exposition is then usually repeated.

Development		Key
Melodies and motifs from the exposition are developed by being presented in different ways, sometimes in rapid succession		A range of keys, usually fairly closely related to the tonic
Recapitulation		**Key**
First subject	This may be an exact repeat of the first subject in the exposition, or there may be some changes	Tonic
Transition	This is different from the transition in the exposition, as it needs to end in the tonic	Tonic
Second subject	Since this is now in a different key there will be some changes, though further changes may be made too	Tonic
Coda		**Key**
A section to end the whole movement		Tonic

Classical composers did not call this structure 'sonata form'; it is a concept which was applied by later theorists. However, most of the first movements you will study (and some of the final movements and even slow movements) follow this pattern. Of course, what is most interesting is the way in which composers make changes to the expected structure.

Piano sonatas and the development of the piano

All three composers wrote solo piano sonatas, often as pieces for teaching their pupils. Mozart and Haydn usually wrote works in three movements, Beethoven usually in four.

Haydn wrote piano sonatas until the last ten years of his life, producing about 62 sonatas in total. His earlier works were not always called 'sonata', but were given that title when published. Although now not as popular as the sonatas of Mozart and Beethoven, Haydn's piano sonatas show his development as a composer through his lifetime.

When Haydn began composing, the piano was in its infancy and **harpsichords** and **clavichords** were more usual. What was exciting about the piano was its ability to play both quietly and loudly. Nevertheless, the early piano was very different from modern pianos: the keyboard was much shorter, the touch was lighter and initially there was no sustain pedal. To distinguish these early pianos from modern pianos they are often called **fortepianos**. It is likely that Haydn's early piano music was written for the harpsichord or clavichord and as the fortepiano became more popular he began to write more for this new instrument.

Haydn Piano Sonata in D major No. 50/ Hob. XVI: 37

- Written for the Auenbrugger sisters, Caterina and Marianna, who were excellent pianists in Vienna
- Published as part of a set of six in 1780
- I. Allegro con brio (sonata form)
- II. Largo e sostenuto (binary form)
- III. Finale. Presto, ma non troppo (rondo form)

You will probably notice the large number of ornament and articulation signs. While editors sometimes add these to music, many of the markings are Haydn's.

See Exercises 2, 3 and 4 for questions on this sonata (pages 102–103).

First movement

The transition in the exposition (bars 9–16) does not fulfil the usual role of changing key. Instead it remains in the tonic (D major), ending on the dominant chord, and the second subject simply begins in A major. This means that the transition can be virtually the same in the recapitulation (where the music remains in the tonic), although the first two bars are omitted (see bars 74–81).

Haydn uses some interesting chromatic chords in bars 28–35: a **Neapolitan 6th** and a **diminished 7th** (see below, where some notes have been omitted or simplified).

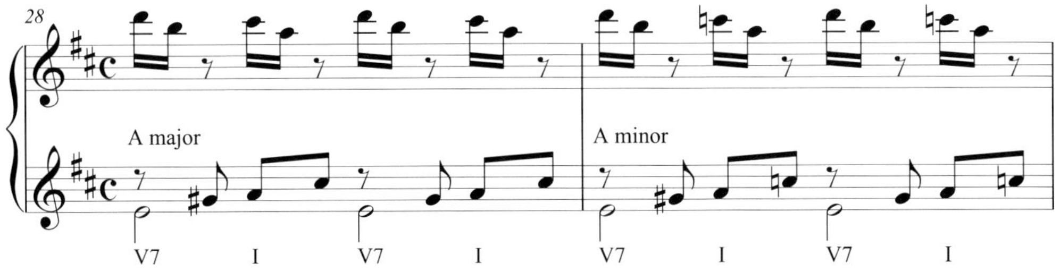

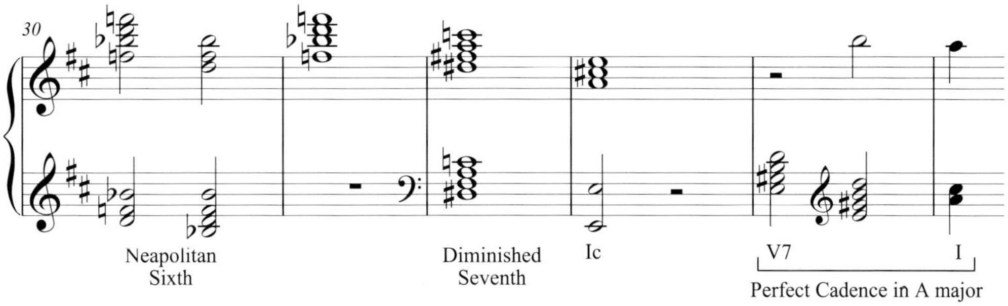

The development section begins where the exposition finished, in A major, with the first subject melody in inversion. It moves on to B minor by repeating bars 41 and 42 a 7th lower. Haydn then includes a descending chain of suspensions in the right hand over ascending left-hand semiquavers in bars 47–50. The suspended notes are found in the lower notes played by the right hand (e.g. the E at 47^1 and the held D on 47^3). Each time the suspension is prepared in the preceding beat and resolved on the following beat.

Second movement

The second movement is slow. It shows the influence of the sarabande (a type of dance often found in Baroque instrumental and keyboard music) with dotted rhythms, long held notes, triplet demisemiquavers and suspensions. As a chorister, Haydn would have been exposed to much Baroque music.

There are two sections with the first being repeated. The first phrase is a standard four bars, but the second is extended to five bars, meaning that the first section is nine bars in total. This is in contrast to the stereotype of Classical 'balanced' phrasing, where phrase lengths are equal.

Finale

This begins in D major and is in rondo form, with repeat signs and changes of key signature identifying where sections begin and end. The link passage (bars 81 to 93) ends with repetition of the note A. This is a dominant pedal and its function is to prepare for the return of the tonic.

For the final rondo theme statement Haydn writes out the first repeat, because the accompaniment to the first eight bars changes on the repeat. Instead of simple offbeat quavers Haydn writes a pattern found frequently in instrumental music of the Classical period: an **Alberti bass** (seen in the left hand of bars 102–108).

Mozart Piano Sonata in C major No. 16, K. 545

- **Composed 1788**
- **Mozart called this a sonata 'for beginners' and it is frequently played by people learning the piano now. It was published in 1805, after Mozart's death.**
- **I. Allegro (sonata form)**
- **II. Andante (G major)**
- **III. Rondo. Allegretto**

See Exercises 5 and 6 for questions on this sonata (pages 103–104).

Beethoven's sonatas

Beethoven composed 32 piano sonatas in his career, which now form part of any serious pianist's repertoire.

Many of the later sonatas were given evocative names, either by Beethoven or by others. The 'Moonlight' sonata (Op. 27 No. 2 in C♯ minor), which begins with a famous slow movement, is one such example.

Beethoven Piano Sonata No. 3 in C major Op. 2 No. 3

- **Written c. 1795, published 1796, dedicated to Haydn**
- **I. Allegro con brio (sonata form)**
- **II. Adagio (modified/abridged sonata form)**
- **III. Scherzo. Allegro (minuet and trio form)**
- **IV. Allegro assai (sonata rondo)**
- **Approximate performing time: 25 minutes**

Beethoven knew the piano sonatas of Mozart and Haydn. He stretched and extended the established forms, tonality and ways of combining different textures.

In this sonata Beethoven made some changes to the ways in which Mozart and Haydn tended to compose:

- There are four movements rather than three.
- It is considerably longer.
- There is a scherzo, not a minuet.
- It uses thicker textures (e.g. the opening of the first movement is in four clear parts).
- The first movement has a long development section, **cadenza** and coda.
- There is an augmented chord in bar 208 in the first movement.

Minuet and trio (or in Beethoven's case scherzo and trio) was a form often used for one of the middle movements of a sonata.

The structure is usually as follows:

A	Minuet	‖: a :‖ ‖: b (a) :‖	A binary- or ternary-form section.
B	Trio	‖: c :‖ ‖: d (c) :‖	A contrasting section (usually in a new key and with a change of texture) in binary or ternary form.
A^1	Minuet	a b (a)	The music of the minuet is played again, without repeats.

Though the individual minuet and trio sections are in binary or ternary form, the structure of the whole is ternary. Beethoven often added a coda at the end.

See Exercise 7 for questions on this sonata and Exercise 8 for some general questions (pages 104–105).

Sonatas for two instruments

The 'accompanied' sonata was very popular in the later 18th century, with many composers writing for solo keyboard/piano and an accompanying instrument such as the violin.

In his accompanied sonatas Mozart began to make the instrumental parts more balanced and equal, and Beethoven wrote for two equal performers. There is a noticeable contrast between Mozart's early sonatas for keyboard and violin (where the violin mostly accompanies the keyboard) and his later violin sonatas, where the two performers are equally important. Haydn did not write any accompanied sonatas. In the Romantic period composers began to write sonatas for an orchestral instrument with the piano taking a more accompanying role.

Mozart Sonata for Piano and Violin No. 11 in G, K. 379

- **Published in 1781 as part of a set of six sonatas**
- **I. Adagio (can be thought of as a separate first movement or a slow introduction)**
- **II. Allegro (modified sonata form)**
- **III. Theme and Variations. Andantino cantabile**

The final movement is a theme with five variations, followed by the theme again at the end of the work. Varying a theme is different from developing it; in a variation the music must be played in order, with the variance applied to each bar. When developing a theme, composers can select any material in any order.

See Exercise 9 for questions on this sonata (page 105).

Beethoven Sonata for Cello and Piano in A, Op. 69

- **Composed in 1808**
- **Dedicated to Baron von Gleichenstein (a patron of Beethoven's who played the cello)**

It is often claimed that this is the first example of a duo sonata, with the instruments on completely equal terms. The cello begins with the melody alone pointing to a more prominent role. However, the musical material is subsequently shared equally between both instruments.

See Exercise 10 for questions on this sonata (page 105).

Chamber music
Music for small ensembles

In the Classical period, chamber music is defined as music for a small group of players (usually three or more) with one player to a part. The term comes from earlier music played in a room (or 'chamber') in a palace or castle, rather than in a concert hall, church or theatre.

Haydn, Mozart and Beethoven wrote trios (for three performers), quartets (for four performers), quintets (for five performers) and beyond, with various combinations of instruments.

Certain combinations were fixed and had specific names:

- string trio: violin, viola and cello
- string quartet: two violins, a viola and a cello
- string quintet: usually a string quartet with an extra viola.

DECIPHERING DEFINITIONS

A piano trio is not for three pianos, but a piano, violin and cello; similarly, a clarinet quintet is for a clarinet and string quartet.

All chamber music from this era is essentially a sonata for a small group of instruments, with a sonata-form first movement and two or three other movements.

Haydn's string quartets

The string quartet was a new and important chamber music form in the Classical period and although probably not invented by Haydn, he was the person who shaped the genre; both Mozart and Beethoven studied his quartets.

Contemporary writers noted the 'conversational' style, in which all the instruments take part. In Vienna the string quartet was performed privately, giving the composers more freedom to write as they chose. The string quartet was the only genre of music Mozart and Haydn wrote for pleasure, to play at a 'quartet party' with friends.

The impetus for Haydn composing string quartets may have come from two directions:

1. The desire to compose music without the harpsichord (found in nearly all Baroque instrumental music), possibly so that the music could be performed outside.
2. His visit to a country house where there happened to be three other musicians, who, with Haydn, made a string quartet. Haydn wrote pieces for them to perform.

Haydn Op. 33 No. 2/Hob. III: 39 'The Joke'

- **Composed in 1781**
- **Published in 1782**
- **Dedicated to the Russian Grand Duke Paul**

Haydn wrote string quartets throughout his life and the Op. 33 quartets of 1781 were his first really successful ones, and are still played frequently today. The set of quartets were known as *Gli Scherzi* (because each one has a scherzo rather than a minuet) or the 'Russian' quartets (due to the dedication).

The score shows that Haydn had moved on a long way from the texture of his earliest quartets, where he used octave doubling. Here each instrument has an independent part, though there is sometimes doubling in 3rds, 6ths or 10ths. Often the 1st violin carries the melody, with the other instruments accompanying, but sometimes other instruments have the melody. Additionally, themes are developed both within and outside the development section.

This quartet is nicknamed 'The Joke' because towards the end of the finale, where the music sounds as though it is finished, the theme is then presented in fragmented form. This leaves the audience really not knowing when to clap!

See Exercise 11 for questions on this quartet (page 105).

Mozart String Quartet No. 17, K. 458 'The Hunt'

Haydn's Op. 33 quartets had a big impact on Mozart, who published quartets Nos. 14–19 in 1785 dedicated to Haydn. This is why they are now known as the 'Haydn' quartets.

The quartets were performed in Mozart's home over two different evenings at which Haydn was present. Haydn returned Mozart's compliment, saying to Leopold Mozart that his son was the greatest composer he knew.

This quartet from the set of 'Haydn' quartets was nicknamed 'The Hunt' (but not by Mozart or his publisher) as the opening bars sound like a hunting call and the first movement is in $\frac{6}{8}$. This nickname also helps to identify the work, as Mozart wrote another quartet in B♭ major.

See Exercise 12 for questions on this quartet (page 106).

At times the 'conversational' style of quartet writing is very clear; in bars 43–47 each instrument plays a short motif as a solo, as if commenting on it, before coming together again in bar 47. This short motif plays a large role in the rest of the movement.

At the start of the development we expect to feel unsettled, as composers dissect the music from the exposition and pass through several keys in quick succession.

Instead Mozart adds 16 bars of a stable melody in the dominant, before developing material from the exposition.

Beethoven's String Quartet No. 1 in F, Op. 18 No. 1

- **Composed 1798–1800**
- **Published 1801**

Perhaps overawed by Haydn and Mozart's achievements in the string quartet genre, Beethoven was 27 before writing his own, preferring to work out ideas in piano trios first.

The first movement of this quartet begins with a motif of just six notes, played in octaves by all instruments (bars 1–2). This was already a dramatic departure for Beethoven; though Haydn and Mozart were no strangers to using motifs, they would not have started the first movement of a piece in such a fragmented way. The use of the motif to build much of the material in the first movement gives a feel of continuous development.

Beethoven String Quartet No. 9 in C, Op. 59 No. 3

- **Composed and published 1808**
- **Dedicated to Prince Razumovsky, the Russian ambassador in Vienna (the set is often known as the 'Razumovsky' quartets)**

These quartets are long and difficult; it is likely that Beethoven was writing music for virtuosos to perform in public, not for amateurs to play at home. The cello part is fully independent, as in Beethoven's sonatas for cello and piano.

The first movement of No. 3 was inspired by Mozart's 'Dissonance' Quartet K. 495, with a slow introduction and many **dissonant** and ambiguous chords. Beethoven took the continued chromaticism and uncertainty to a new level. When the quartets were first performed in Vienna, audiences and critics were unconvinced.

See Exercise 13 for questions on this quartet (page 108).

Other forms of chamber music

Though the string quartet is often acknowledged to be the highest form of chamber music, it is not the only type of ensemble for which composers wrote.

Piano trios

All three composers wrote trios for piano, violin and cello. Haydn's earliest works are very much like accompanied sonatas, with a dominant piano and the other instruments accompanying or doubling; but his later works and Mozart's trios began to give the strings a little more independence, a development continued by Beethoven.

Beethoven's piano trios usually have four movements, while Mozart's and Haydn's generally have three.

Other chamber combinations

At Eisenstadt, Haydn wrote 126 trios for baryton, viola and cello, because Prince Nikolaus played the baryton. This stringed instrument is bowed and is similar to a viol, but there are extra strings which can either be plucked or left to vibrate sympathetically.

Mozart wrote six string quintets with an extra viola. Some argue that these are even better than his quartets, allowing for more depth of tone and for varying combinations of groups of two and three instruments. To accommodate the extra viola Mozart tended to write the 1st violin and cello parts further apart. Beethoven also wrote a few string quintets, but many were arrangements of other works.

Mozart was keen to write for the clarinet. He wrote his clarinet quintet K. 581 for the clarinettist Anton Stadler, for whom he wrote his clarinet concerto and a trio for clarinet, viola and piano. He also wrote some flute quartets and other compositions for various ensembles including wind instruments and sometimes piano. Beethoven also composed various pieces for wind ensemble, sometimes with piano, including a trio for clarinet, cello and piano.

A piano trio rehearsing

Symphonies
Works for orchestra

Developments within the orchestra during the Classical era were abundant. New instruments such as the clarinet were developed, and the number of instruments employed increased.

The symphony grew out of the Baroque Italian overture, a piece in three sections: quick-slow-quick. These overtures (sometimes called 'sinfonia') were originally written to precede an opera or oratorio performance, but were later played on their own. Haydn, often called 'father of the symphony', wrote at least 104, refining, enriching and expanding the form and creating a template used by other composers.

Mozart in his much shorter life wrote over 40 symphonies, taking the form from Haydn, but adding his own touches of orchestration and melody. Beethoven wrote nine symphonies, moving quickly from symphonies in the Classical style (Nos. 1 and 2), to large Romantic pieces, expanding both the scope and depth of emotion.

A symphony is really a sonata for orchestra, usually in four movements. The larger ensemble gave the composers even more opportunity to contrast timbres and to expand ideas.

OVERTURES AND SYMPHONIES

Do not confuse a symphony with an overture. An overture was initially a piece of music intended for performance before a larger work such as an opera. However, the instrumental overture was sometimes detached and played alone as an orchestral piece. This was especially true of Beethoven's music: his Coriolan and Egmont overtures are probably his most famous and are in sonata form, rather like the first movement of a symphony.

The orchestra

A symphony orchestra at the time of Mozart and Haydn was not the large ensemble of today. When Haydn began working for Prince Esterházy he had about 20 musicians, with the possibility of hiring more for special occasions.

The basis of the orchestra was the string section, with one or two players per part. To this were first added oboes and/or horns. Over time other wind instruments were added - one or two flutes and bassoons and then trumpets and timpani. The newly invented clarinet was also a possibility, but Haydn and Mozart viewed clarinets as an alternative to oboes and did not usually include both.

During Haydn's time working for Prince Esterházy the orchestra grew to about 25 musicians. Haydn first wrote for a large ensemble in his six 'Paris' symphonies, composed in 1785–1786. They were written for a masonic lodge orchestra, with up to 40 violins and corresponding large wind and brass sections. Haydn also had the opportunity to write for a larger orchestra in his London symphonies (numbers 93–104), performed during his visits there. By the end of the Classical period the standard orchestra comprised pairs of flutes, oboes, clarinets, bassoons, horns and trumpets, timpani and strings. This is the orchestra with which Beethoven began his career.

Instruments

The string section used instruments that were very similar-looking to the violins, violas, cellos and double basses played today, but with lighter and shorter bows and gut rather than metal strings.

The flutes at this time were made of wood, with holes covered by fingers, rather than pads, which were a later invention. Flutes had a smaller dynamic range and would be more difficult to keep in tune. Oboes, clarinets and bassoons at this time did have some keys, but not as many as on modern instruments. Clarinets in Classical music are usually transposing instruments 'in A', meaning that the notes they play sound a minor 3rd lower than written.

Brass instruments from a Classical orchestra were very different from those seen today. Both trumpets and horns would not have had any valves (used to alter the length of tubing and to play different notes) but would have been 'natural' instruments. This meant that they could play the notes of the harmonic series in a particular key by changing air and lip pressure, but other notes were unplayable. For this reason, brass instruments often do not play when the music has modulated or if a movement is in a different key. Sometimes brass players used crooks: sections of tubing inserted into the instrument to change the key. However, this took time and was not possible during a movement, only between movements or different pieces.

AS PRESCRIBED WORK 2018

Haydn: Symphony No. 100 in G, 'Military', first movement

- **Composed and first performed in 1794 in London**
- **I. Adagio–Allegro (slow introduction, sonata form)**
- **II. Allegretto (ternary form, in C major)**
- **III. Menuetto: Moderato (minuet and trio)**
- **IV. Finale: Presto (sonata-rondo)**
- **Instrumentation: two flutes, two oboes, two clarinets in C (second movement only), two bassoons, two horns in G, two trumpets in C, timpani (G and D) and strings**
- **Approximate performing time 25 minutes (complete work), eight minutes (first movement)**

Context

This symphony is one of the set of 12 known as Haydn's 'London' Symphonies, composed for his two visits to London.

After being freed from working full-time for the Esterházys on the death of Prince Nikolaus, Haydn was invited by the concert organiser Johann Peter Salomon to visit London. Symphony No. 100 was written for Haydn's second visit, in 1794. At the première, the symphony appeared with the first movement immediately after the interval and the other three movements after some solo items. The performance was directed by Salomon, with Haydn supposedly at the keyboard. However, there is no indication as to what he might have played! As with most of Haydn's 'London' symphonies, there is a slow introduction before the first movement.

The nickname 'Military' appears to have been in use from about 1795, and comes from the use of (for the time) a large number of percussion instruments in the second and fourth movements. In addition to the timpani there are a triangle, cymbals and bass drum.

Scores

There are many scores of this work available. Some editions have two flutes and some only one. All scores have the instruments in the same order:

- Woodwind at the top (flutes, oboes, clarinets, bassoons)
- Horns following from woodwind (as these were sometimes used with the woodwind)
- Other brass instruments (in this case trumpets)
- Percussion instruments are in the middle of the score
- The string section (1st and 2nd violins, violas, then cellos and basses sharing a stave) are at the bottom.

Instruments may be named in a language other than English, often Italian.

TROMBE

Remember that *trombe* are trumpets (not trombones).

Performances

There are a number of recordings of this much-loved symphony available, on CD and online. Some recordings will use whatever forces the orchestra happens to have: usually modern instruments and a relatively large orchestra.

However, you will also find 'historically informed' performances, in which the conductor and performers have tried to emulate how the music sounded when it was first performed. These latter recordings use 'period' instruments (i.e. found specifically at the time of Haydn), such as natural brass instruments with crooks rather than valves, wooden flutes and string instruments with gut strings and an orchestra of about 41 players – the size of the orchestra in the first performance.

The pitch of recordings can also vary. Today a^1 (the A above middle C) = 440Hz, but in Haydn's time there was no standard pitch and a^1 was generally a little lower, as in 'authentic' recordings. The tempo, dynamics and articulation used can be a matter of personal taste and again, will vary.

Monothematicism

Monothematicism means 'one theme' and was a technique used by Haydn and Mozart (in his later works). It can be seen in the first movement of this symphony. Below are the first two bars of the Adagio introduction and the first three bars of the Allegro.

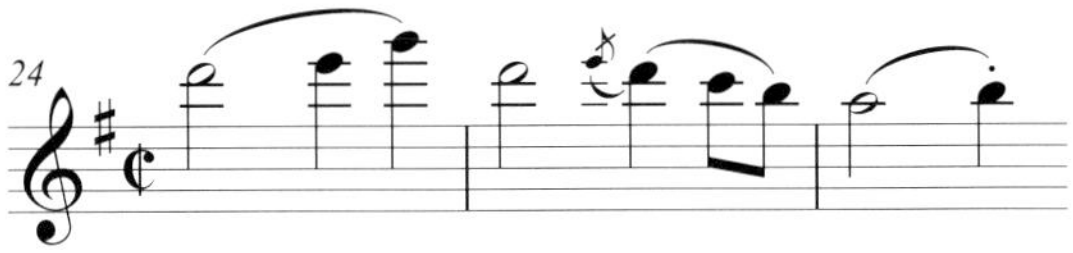

Both melodies have a rising 4th D–G (with an added note in bar 24), followed by stepwise descending notes and a rising major 2nd (accompanied by a prominent falling minor 2nd played by the bassoons). These motifs recur throughout the movement in various guises: in bars 3–4 the rising 4th followed by stepwise descending notes is heard again. Also bar 26 (repeated in bar 27) is simply a transposition of bar 24, the rising 4th again.

At the end of the transition the music reaches the dominant and the start of the second subject (bar 75). The melody and orchestration are familiar: this is the first subject transposed to the dominant! It is identical (except for the key) for five bars but ends with a different cadence. There is then another partial restatement of the first subject from bar 87 in D minor (the dominant minor). A new theme (which could be called the second subject second theme) appears in bar 94. Again, this contains a prominent 2nd interval, but this time rocking down and up.

Phrasing

When thinking of phrasing in Classical music it is often assumed that there are 'balanced' (i.e. equal) two- or four-bar antecedent-consequent phrases.

However, composers such as Haydn and Mozart delighted in writing unequal **antecedent-consequent** phrases and sometimes merged the end of one phrase with the start of the next. This can be seen at the start of this symphony: the first four bars, ending with a perfect cadence in the tonic (bars 3 to 4) are not simple two-plus-two bars, but really seven beats plus nine beats. Bars 5–8 begin exactly the same as bars 1–4, but there is a different answering phrase, over a perfect cadence in the dominant. The answering phrase still contains the important interval of a rising 4th.

The phrasing of the first subject is not quite so clear, though the two halves are clearly unequal. Some writers argue that the antecedent is just the first one-and-a-half bars and the rest is the consequent, resulting in one-and-a-half plus six-and-a-half.

Scoring and use of instruments

With clarinets in the second movement, Haydn has a complete double woodwind section at his disposal, and from the start of the symphony the new melodic independence of the woodwind can be seen.

In bars 2 and 5 the 1st bassoon (indicated by the use of '1' in the score) highlights the falling minor 2nd, doubling the violas, but by bar 9 the bassoon converts the interval to a rising minor 2nd, without any string doubling.

The woodwinds - flute(s) and oboes - are also given the task of beginning the Allegro at bar 24. They are completely alone for eight bars until the strings repeat the theme an octave lower, with changes from the sixth bar. This orchestration repeats from bar 75, but this time the melody is not repeated by the strings. This use of independent woodwind was still relatively new at the time Haydn was writing and can also be found in the development section, in bars 170–179. Here Haydn takes one bar from each of his themes (bar 170 from the first subject, e.g. bar 24 and bar 171 from the second subject second theme, e.g. bar 96) and puts them together. This idea is heard first from the woodwind, with the melody in the 1st oboe, before it is imitated by the strings. The pattern is repeated (this time with a flute melody in A minor) with the strings answering in the tonic key of G major. The final idea in bars 177–179 is played in imitation between the 1st oboe and 1st bassoon.

Bass instruments are also used as melody instruments, such as in bars 108–113, where the melody is played by bassoons (indicated by the use of 'a2' in the score), violas, cellos and basses. They are accompanied by held wind and brass chords and quavers in the violins. Similar passages include bars 183–187 and bars 192–193, where initially the cellos and 1st bassoon play an idea from the second subject second theme including held wind and viola chords and violin syncopations. They are joined by the basses in bar 184, and in the later bars the melody is also doubled by the violas at the octave and the 2nd violins in 6ths.

The horns and trumpets do not play a major role in this movement, because they were limited to the harmonic series on G. They first play from bars 14–16, helping to achieve a rapid crescendo. This is possible because, although the music has modulated, it is in the tonic minor, so many notes are available. Throughout the movement the brass plays a small number of pitches, mainly when the music is loud. The use of brass in the development section is limited to a few held or repeated notes. Brass is prevalent at the end of the movement where, from bar 239, they are able to play nearly continuously, because much of the music is based on tonic and dominant chords.

Building excitement

This first movement of the 'Military' symphony achieves a feeling of excitement in many ways:

- The use of rests creates a feeling of expectation. This can be seen in the short rests in bars 1 and 2 and nearly two whole beats of silence after the ***ff*** chords in bar 16. Haydn particularly uses silence to great effect at the start of the development section, with bars 125 and 126 completely silent. The sophisticated London audiences attending the first performances of this symphony would have expected the start of a new section, after the repeat of the exposition, so would have been wondering how this new section would begin. Haydn kept them waiting!
- In bar 8 Haydn introduces an accompanying figure of repeated quavers in the 2nd violins. These are also heard from bar 17 in the lower strings. This drives the music forwards and is used throughout the movement. The excitement builds when repeated quavers are heard as a reiterated tonic pedal in the cellos from bar 39. Melodic broken 3rds appear in the 1st violins from bar 49, followed by scalic passages from bar 62.
- Haydn also uses rhythmic effects. The rhythmic pattern of the two crotchets across the bar line from bar 49 creates a feeling of instability, driving the music forward. It reappears in bars 81–85, with greater force as now the cadence is heard in imitation between the wind and strings and twice in each bar rather than once.
- **Sequence** can also generate excitement and Haydn uses this device in the development section. In bars 134–139, a development of the rocking second subject second theme melody is heard in F minor, then repeated a tone higher, in G minor, from bar 147.

- From bar 157 the bass line drives the movement forwards. The violas, cellos and basses, sometimes joined by the violins and woodwind, have an ostinato pattern derived from the second subject second theme. This passes through different keys before falling a semitone to become a decorated dominant pedal of E minor. The dominant pedal prepares for the return of the tonic key and this can be heard near the end of the movement in bars 268–270, before many perfect cadences in the tonic.

Harmony and tonality (chords and keys)

In many ways the first movement of Haydn's 'Military' symphony fulfils expectations. It begins in G major, modulates to the dominant for the second subject, passes through other keys during the development and returns to the tonic for the recapitulation. However, there are subtler ways in which Haydn defies expectations.

The slow introduction makes a sudden move to the tonic minor (G minor) in bar 14. A dominant pedal from bar 19 prepares for the return of the tonic key. There is also a brief move to D minor in bar 87, when the first subject theme – now as the second subject first theme – is heard in this key.

Despite the exposition finishing with a clear perfect cadence in D major, the development begins in the unrelated key of B♭ major. From the distant opening the keys gradually move closer to the tonic, with D minor in bar 142 and G minor in bar 147.

Haydn saves his final key surprise for what some writers see as the start of the coda: bar 239. Bars 238–239 form an imperfect cadence to the flattened 6th, E♭ and the music continues in this key, with a tonic pedal and development of the second subject second theme. However, in bar 249 the bass moves down a semitone to D – the dominant – and from there quickly back to the tonic.

In terms of harmony, Haydn seems to prefer to use remote keys, rather than chromatic chords. However, some chromatic chords appear in this movement. Over the dominant pedal in bar 19 there is a **diminished chord** (G, B♭, C♯). Bar 139 features a **German augmented 6th** chord (B♭, D, F, G♯). Bar 146 has a false relation between the B♮ played by the cellos and the B♭ at the end of the bar played by the 2nd violins.

Diminished chord

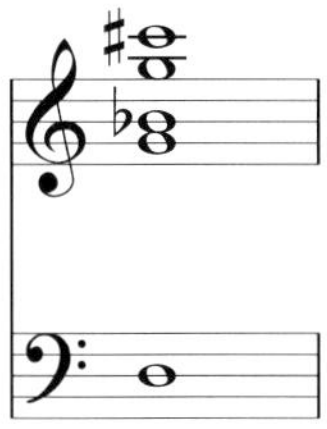

German augmented 6th

See Exercises 14 and 15 for questions on this work (page 108).

Mozart: Symphony No. 41 in C, K. 551 'Jupiter'

- **Composed in 1788 in Vienna**
- **It is not known if the symphony was performed in Mozart's lifetime – it was not published until after his death**
- **I. Allegro vivace (sonata form)**
- **II. Andante cantabile (sonata form, F major)**
- **III. Menuetto. Allegretto (minuet and trio)**
- **IV. Molto allegro (sonata form with fugal sections)**
- **Instrumentation: flute, two oboes, two bassoons, two horns in C, two trumpets in C, timpani (C and G) and strings**
- **Approximate performing time 35 minutes (complete work), 9 minutes (first movement)**

Mozart wrote symphonies throughout his career, with his symphonic style changing over the years. He was influenced by the music he encountered, and the size of the work and the instrumentation was usually dictated by where he was writing it for. Many of Mozart's early symphonies had three movements, but in his mature works there are usually four. The earliest symphonies had little development and over the years Mozart increased the dimensions of this section. By his last years Mozart's music had become more based on motifs and was sometimes monothematic.

Mozart's most famous symphonies are the last three, Nos. 39–41. Unlike most of his works, which were written for a clear reason – to be performed, as a **commission**, etc. – it is not obvious why he chose to write the symphonies in the summer of 1788.

This symphony is Mozart's longest and his last. The nickname 'Jupiter' does not appear until after Mozart's death. It was possibly first used by Salomon (who arranged Haydn's trips to London) to reflect the symphony's grandeur and majesty. The symphony includes music recycled from a comic opera aria composed earlier in 1788 at bars 101–110.

A LEVEL PRESCRIBED WORK 2018

Beethoven: Symphony No. 3 in E♭, Op. 55, 'Eroica', first movement

- **Composed in 1803–1804 (soon after the completion of Symphony No. 2)**
- **Dedicated to Franz Joseph Maximilian Fürst von Lobkowitz**
- **First performed in a private concert in summer 1804 at Eisenberg Castle in Bohemia for Lobkowitz**
- **I. Allegro con brio (sonata form)**
- **II. Marcia funebre. Adagio assai (march and trio form, C minor)**
- **III. Scherzo. Allegro vivace (scherzo and trio)**
- **IV. Finale. Molto allegro (theme and variations)**
- **Instrumentation: two flutes, two oboes, two clarinets in B♭, two bassoons, three horns in E♭, F and C, two trumpets in E♭ and C, timpani (E♭ and E♭) and strings**
- **Approximate performing time 45 minutes (complete work), 15 minutes (first movement)**

Beethoven is seen as the symphonic successor to Haydn and Mozart, as shown by his first two symphonies, which are similar in length to the later symphonies of Haydn and Mozart. Beethoven began to expand the symphonic form, but kept the outline structures standardised by Haydn and only slightly expanded the orchestra, sometimes adding piccolo, trombones or contrabassoon (until then only found in opera orchestras).

Context

This symphony is hailed as one of the most important works in Western music. It certainly marks a significant change in Beethoven's style and had a big impact on later Romantic composers. The composition of this symphony coincides with what is now called Beethoven's 'middle period', where he began to move away from the purely Classical style.

The symphony was published with the title 'Heroic Symphony, composed to celebrate the memory of a great man'. Heroic is the English translation of the Italian 'Eroica' and the great man is thought to be Napoleon. This is because on the title page of the manuscript score Beethoven has scrubbed out a direct reference to Napoleon. In 1804 Napoleon declared himself Emperor and Beethoven was apparently furious at this. However, there may also have been monetary considerations. Since Lobkowitz was a patron of Beethoven's and had paid to have six months' sole use of the symphony, Beethoven may have realised that he should not really dedicate it to anybody else!

The most striking difference between this symphony and those of Mozart and Haydn is that it is an emotional rollercoaster, with rapid movement between moments of great tension or drama and relaxation. Reviews of performances in 1805 refer to the symphony's great length and technical difficulty for the orchestra, describing it as 'lurid' and 'bizarre'. However, over the following years critical opinion became more positive.

Symphonic revolutions

In addition to the wide range of emotions expressed, this symphony is significantly longer than those of Mozart or Haydn. In the first movement Beethoven uses sonata form, but expands each section and writes a long development section and a coda, which is used as a kind of second development.

Beethoven was apparently concerned by the length of the piece and considered removing the repeat of the exposition, but decided the repeat would achieve musical balance.

Though the orchestra is only slightly expanded, the instruments are used differently:

- The cellos and double basses are no longer 'shackled' together, often having different music to play.
- The brass instruments are required to play much more difficult music; they are no longer tied to mostly tonic and dominant harmonies (e.g. the horn calls in the trio section following the scherzo are relatively difficult to play).
- The woodwind also has an independent role, often taking the melody while the strings accompany.
- Beethoven also writes for a full double woodwind section. The importance of the woodwind section is clear from bar 8 of the second movement: the 1st oboe has the melody, accompanied by the woodwind and horns, while the strings simply play a drum-roll effect.

Beethoven creates great moments of tension and drama in a variety of ways in the first movement. Rhythmically he leaves the audience feeling unsettled using syncopation and rhythms across the bar lines, creating metric ambiguity. This appears from bar 28: the ***sf*** accents every two beats directly contradict the triple metre. At the same time the full orchestra (tutti) is used together with dissonant harmonies. For an early 19th-century audience this must have been something quite shocking!

Beethoven also creates tension in terms of tonality. This is famously first used in bar 7, with the chromatic note of C♯ in the cello melody, creating a feeling of instability. Despite the two powerful E♭ major chords in the opening, the tonality of E♭ major is not yet firmly established and it is not until bars 14–15 that there is a perfect cadence in the tonic. This may have been Beethoven's signal that the audience were in for a rocky ride, as many different and sometimes very distant keys are visited during the course of the movement.

Structure

Beethoven uses sonata form for this first movement, though without a slow introduction, unlike his first two symphonies.

	Bar numbers	Keys
Exposition	1–153	
First subject	$1–15^1$	E♭ major
Transition	$15–83^1$	E♭ major–B♭ major
(Transition theme 1)	$45^2–57^1$	E♭ major–B♭ major
(Transition theme 2)	65–72	G minor–B♭ major
Second subject	83–99	B♭ major and minor
Development	153–397	Wide range of keys
Development theme	284–299	E minor and A minor
Recapitulation	398–550	
First subject	398–408	E♭ major–F major
Transition theme 1	$448–460^1$	B♭ major–E♭ major
Transition theme 2	468–475	
Second subject	486–497	E♭ major
Coda	551–691	Wide range of keys

All the themes in the preceding table are relatively short and often they are built from varied repeats of an even smaller motif. For example, Transition theme 1 is built from a three-note rhythm in a descending shape, passed between the flute, oboe, clarinet and 1st violins to create 10 bars of music. Similarly, Transition theme 2 is a motif of just three notes, repeated at successively lower pitches, until it leaps up high to start again.

The second subject is chorale-like, more a harmonic progression than a melody, with repeated chords. Again, Beethoven creates 16 bars from a four-bar idea. It is significant that this melody is not used in the development, only in the recapitulation.

Perhaps because the second subject is not developed, Beethoven introduces a new theme in the development, heard in the 1st oboe from bar 284. The cello and 2nd violin play a unison counterpoint to this melody, including the chromatic descent in bars 285^3–286 which is later used without the original melody (e.g. bars 326–327 in the 1st clarinet and 1st bassoon).

Between the clear statements of themes listed in the table (on the previous page), even in the Exposition and Recapitulation sections Beethoven extends the themes by sequence, in different keys and with different orchestration.

The new sections start later than the audience might expect because of the significantly greater length of this movement compared with its predecessors. Beethoven exploits this expectation. By bar 45 in a Mozart or Haydn symphony we would probably expect to be just about at the end of the transition section, to have reached the new key (dominant or relative major) and to be about to start the second subject. However, in this larger-scale symphony we are still in the transition and instead hear a new theme (Transition theme 1), but in the tonic of E♭ major. Similarly, in the long development section the key of E♭ major is achieved by bar 316, making it sound like the recapitulation is relatively close, but instead Beethoven twists into E♭ minor and has to bring the key back round to E♭ major again before the recapitulation can really start.

Harmony and tonality

Some mention has already been made of the far-reaching modulations Beethoven undertakes in this movement, far exceeding what contemporary audiences would have expected. Although the basic outline would be recognisable to Mozart or Haydn (tonic to dominant in the exposition, a variety of keys in the development and a return to the tonic for the recapitulation) Beethoven explores many side-streets in terms of keys.

Tritone

That the music might be adventurous in harmony and tonality is signalled right from the chromatic C♯ in bar 7. The note G played above it in the violins and violas creates a **tritone** (diminished 5th), the most **dissonant** interval in music. That the 1st violins are uncomfortable is reflected in their syncopated rhythm. By rising up a semitone again to reach D, the cellos help to form a 2nd inversion G minor chord in bar 9, followed by a dominant 7th in B♭ in 1st inversion in bar 10, and the harmony becomes more diatonic again for a few bars.

However, the dissonance soon reappears. There are diminished 7th chords in bars 25 and 26 over a dominant pedal (B♭) in the bass, resolving to the dominant chord in bar 27. A similar chromatic chord over a pedal is found in bar 147, at the end of the exposition. Here it is a **dominant minor 9th** (F, A, C, E♭, G♭) over a tonic pedal (B♭, as the music has now modulated to the dominant).

Beethoven indicates that the development section will be far-ranging in key by settling quickly on the dominant of C major at the start of the development (bar 160) and reaching

Dominant minor 9th (over B♭)

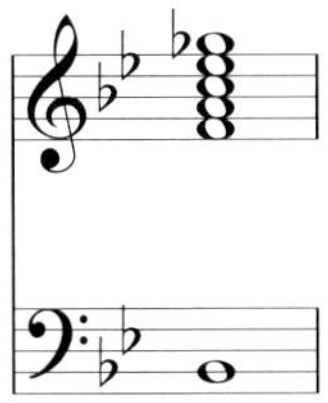

C major by bar 170. This is relatively far from E♭ major. However, C major quickly becomes C minor by bar 178, with the first subject motif of five notes heard in the minor key, an unsettling change of character. By sliding up a semitone each time, Beethoven reaches C♯ minor followed by D minor.

Beethoven changes mode a great deal in this movement – from the major to the minor version of a key and vice versa. The dominant minor, B♭ minor, is heard at bar 215, followed by a **French augmented 6th chord** in bar 219 (the notes F♭, A♭, B♭ and D) heading towards the key of A♭ major.

The climax of the development section is heard in the bars shortly before bar 280. These are preceded by strident, dissonant chords in B minor, a key very distant from the tonic. In bars 276–299 a very dissonant chord is scored for full orchestra at a forte dynamic, with the minor 2nd heard in the high flute parts. With the music in the key of E minor at this point, the chord is a 1st inversion 7th chord built on the flattened 2nd (i.e. F, A, C, E, with the E and F at the top of the texture). In bar 280 the harmony changes to a dominant minor 9th chord (B, D♯, F♯, A, C) and then a dominant 7th in bar 283, before the music continues with the new development theme in E minor.

In the development the tonic is reached by bar 316 and the recapitulation is assumed near, but instead the music dives into E♭ minor (another example of the major and minor versions of the same key). The harmony takes the scenic route back to the tonic, including a diversion via C♭ major in bar 362 (the flattened 6th of E♭ major).

Even the end of the development is not a straightforward move from the dominant to the tonic. At bar 392 the violin **tremolos** of A♭ and B♭ suggest the dominant 7th chord in E♭ major, as would be expected at this point. The 2nd horn plays over this the first four notes of the first subject theme, clashing with the accompanying harmony. However, this seems to have the effect of waking up the orchestra, who burst in with a loud dominant 7th chord ready to start the recapitulation two bars later.

In the recapitulation Beethoven explores a different solution to the dissonant C♯, originally heard in bar 7. Instead of sliding up to a D, it slides down to C♮ to move the music towards F major. As usual, this is not for long; by bar 416 the key is D♭ major. However, after this the recapitulation follows the outline of the exposition fairly closely.

After brief excursions into D♭ major, C major and F minor at the beginning of the Coda, this section stays mostly focused on the tonic and dominant. There are still moments of tension, particularly with the diminished 7th chord in bar 666. Even at the end of the movement the reiteration of the tonic chord is perhaps not as emphatic as might have been expected, with just three short chords. Perhaps Beethoven is signalling that the tonic key needs to be achieved in the other movements.

Orchestral textures

Some use of instruments has been detailed above. There are large tutti sections in this movement, with the whole orchestra playing, often very loudly. Though these are often points of tension, sometimes this texture is used for a point of relaxation. For example, in bars 37–45 the whole orchestra plays for the triumphant statement of the first subject theme, after at least 12 bars of uncertainty.

Looking at the score and sketches for the work, it appears that Beethoven spent much time deciding who should play exactly what at any particular point. Melodies are often passed between instruments: the cellos begin the first subject, but it is continued by the 1st violins. The second subject begins with the woodwind, answered by the strings.

From bar 186 Beethoven combines two themes heard earlier in the movement: the first subject theme is played by the violas, cellos and basses, while the 1st violins have the second transition theme from bar 65. Accompanying this counterpoint are wind and brass chords and 2nd violin syncopation.

Beethoven uses a **fugal** texture from bar 236, to indicate that a struggle is to begin again. The cellos accompany the first statement of the fugal melody in the violas, which is then heard in the 2nd violins, 1st violins and finally the cellos and basses. After this the polyphonic texture turns towards homophony with the chords from bar 248.

Markings in the score

There are many more markings in this score than in the symphonies of Mozart or Haydn. Beethoven carefully indicates the articulation (staccato and slurs) and the required dynamics (including *sf*, *fp* and *sfp*). The music changes dynamic quickly at some points and in some bars almost every note has a different marking (e.g. woodwind bars 83–86).

There are two significant markings near the start of the recapitulation. In bar 487 the 1st violins and violas have the only trills in the movement (other than the rolls on the timpani) and in bars 408 and 416 the first subject themes in the 1st horn and flute respectively are marked *dolce* (sweetly).

Questions relating to Beethoven's 'Eroica' may be found in Exercises 16 and 17 on page 108.

Adoption of expanded form

With the exception of Beethoven's Symphony No. 8, the rest of his symphonies used the expanded form of 'Eroica'.

Symphony No. 6, the 'Pastoral', has five movements, due to the programmatic content (the movements describe different countryside scenes). Beethoven's Symphony No. 9, the 'Choral', went further with the expansion of the form, with a chorus and soloists in the final movement – the symphony lasts approximately 65 minutes.

Concertos

Orchestra with soloists

A concerto is a work for a soloist (or a group of soloists) and an orchestra, where composers exploit the contrast between the different-sized groups. Concertos were composed throughout the Baroque period and by the early 18th century were standardised as works in three movements: fast–slow–fast.

The first movement and often the last movement were in **ritornello** form. This form is similar to rondo form in that there is a recurring theme, but unlike rondo form (where the theme always reappears in the same key) in ritornello form the theme may return in different keys. Between appearances of the theme are episodes, featuring the soloist. Episodes gave soloists the opportunity to display their virtuoso skills.

Towards the end of the 18th century many composers wrote concertos for both themselves and others to play. The solo concerto was much more common than a concerto with a group of soloists. In Vienna the prominence of the piano led to a large number of piano concertos being composed. The greatest concerto composer at this time was Mozart.

Mozart's concertos

Mozart began to explore the concerto form at a young age. He first took sonatas by other composers and adapted them as concertos, later writing his own. Mozart's five concertos for violin and orchestra were written in 1775, during his early career in Salzburg.

Mozart is famous for his 27 piano concertos, mostly written in Vienna. Here Mozart knew that performing a piano concerto would attract a large audience and earn him a substantial amount of money. Therefore, in Lent, when the theatres were closed, Mozart would arrange a series of 'subscription concerts', for which people would buy a ticket for the series. These concerts would include a new concerto, such as piano concertos Nos. 20 and 23.

Mozart also wrote concertos for wind instruments, including bassoon, flute, oboe and the clarinet concerto discussed later. These were written for patrons or renowned performers. Mozart's four horn concertos were written for his friend Joseph Leutgeb.

Mozart's concerto style

In his concertos Mozart took great care to write idiomatically for each instrument. This includes giving time to breathe for wind players. Though Mozart does write some very virtuosic passages in his concertos, this is never purely for display or at the expense of beautiful melodies.

Before Mozart the orchestra played a purely supporting role in the concerto, whereas Mozart elevated their position. Mozart's earliest concertos could be accompanied by just the string section, without detriment to the texture, but in his later concertos the wind section was increasingly important and independent.

Concerto structure

Classical concertos (and even concertos in the 19th century) continued to use the Baroque three-movement model of fast-slow-fast, rather than the four movements of the string quartet and symphony. However, in the first movements composers faced some difficulties.

Traditionally the opening music was played by orchestra, with the soloist entering later in the movement. However, this was not compatible with sonata form. If the orchestra and soloists both presented the exposition moving to the dominant for the second subject there would be a move to the dominant twice, which would not be satisfactory harmonically. There emerged a form specific to concerto first movements: a hybrid of ritornello and sonata form. This contained a 'double exposition' (rather like the exposition section of a string quartet or symphony being repeated) but with significant differences between the two exposition sections, not least the presence of the soloist in the second and the first remaining in the tonic. Composers found various ways of merging the two forms, but a basic outline is given in the table below.

Orchestral Exposition		
First subject/opening ritornello	Orchestra	Tonic
Transition (but remaining in the tonic)	Orchestra	Tonic
Second subject	Orchestra	Tonic
Codetta	Orchestra	Tonic
Solo Exposition		
First solo subject (which may or may not be the same as the first orchestral subject)	Soloist and orchestra	Tonic
Transition	Soloist and orchestra	Tonic-dominant or relative major
Second solo subject (which may or may not be the same as the second orchestral subject)	Soloist and orchestra	Dominant or relative major
Middle ritornello	Orchestra	Dominant
Codetta	Soloist and orchestra	Dominant or relative major

Development		
Development of some themes heard earlier (or occasionally a new theme)	Soloist and orchestra	Variety of keys
Recapitulation		
Some or all of the themes from the exposition	Soloist and orchestra	Tonic
Cadenza	Soloist	Over a tonic 2nd inversion chord
Final ritornello	Orchestra	Tonic

A LEVEL PRESCRIBED WORK 2019

Mozart: Piano Concerto No. 23 in A, K. 488, third movement

- **Composed initially from 1784, with oboes instead of clarinets, but then put aside and finished in March 1786 (entered into Mozart's own catalogue on March 2, 1786)**
- **Date of first performance is not known, but probably one of Mozart's Lenten Subscription concerts in 1786**
- **I. Allegro (sonata form)**
- **II. Adagio (ternary form, in F♯ minor)**
- **III. Allegro assai (sonata-rondo)**
- **Instrumentation: solo piano, flute, two clarinets in A, two bassoons, two horns in A, strings**
- **Approximate performing time 25 minutes (complete work), 7 minutes (third movement)**

Context

February and March 1786 was a busy time for Mozart: he was completing his opera *The Marriage of Figaro* and still found time to finish two piano concertos (K. 488 in A and K. 491 in C minor). Between 1782 and 1786 Mozart wrote 15 piano concertos, many of which he performed, and these were his main source of income at the time.

The autograph score was sold by Mozart's widow to a publisher and is now held in a library in Paris. Unusually for Mozart the autograph score includes a cadenza for the first movement; normally if he was performing a concerto he would improvise one. He did sometimes write down cadenzas separately if the work was to be performed by somebody else, such as a pupil. There is no cadenza in the third movement.

Scores and instrumentation

Though there are scores of this concerto online it is recommended that you acquire a miniature score as these are more reliable.

The orchestra does not include trumpets or drums, and has clarinets rather than oboes. This concerto and the ones written before and after this work (K. 482 in December 1785 and K. 491 in March 1786) are Mozart's first piano concertos to use clarinets. Both the clarinets and horns in this work are 'in A', meaning that they sound a minor 3rd lower than written (i.e. if they play the note C it will sound an A).

The score does not contain many dynamic markings; they are limited to ***f*** and ***p*** in the orchestral parts. Clearly Mozart knew how he wanted the music to be played and did not need to write dynamic indications into his part. It is likely that the orchestra would have also used crescendo and diminuendo, but these could either have been indicated by Mozart from the piano, or the performers would have known themselves where they would have been expected to put them in.

In some scores during the tutti orchestral passages the piano has the cello part notated in the left hand. This is found in Mozart's autograph, often with the abbreviation 'col basso', though sometimes Mozart writes out the bass part. Mozart probably accompanied the tutti passages on the piano, playing chords in the right hand, just as a continuo player would have done on the harpsichord in Baroque music. The autograph score does not contain any figures under the piano part, as Mozart would have known which chords to play, but the first published edition did include figuring.

Some older scores may contain indications of solo and tutti sections. In these scores the designation is not always helpful or reliable, but when written by Mozart in his scores it would sometimes indicate that the number of string players was to be reduced in the solo sections, perhaps to just one desk (two players) per part. This is because the fortepiano was not as loud as grand pianos today and may have been drowned out by a large string section.

Since this is one of Mozart's later concertos, the wind instruments are equal in importance to the string section. This can be seen very early in the third movement: in bars 20–24 the wind section alone answers the strings. It is striking how little the strings carry the melody in this movement. The 1st violins play the opening theme in bars 9–16 and alternate with the woodwind during the next 16 bars, but for most of the rest of the movement the strings simply accompany either the piano or the wind. The double basses and cellos nearly always play together in the third movement, but there are a few signs of the separation that was to come in Beethoven's works: bars 143–144 are for the cellos only (indicated by vcl. or violoncelli in the score) and the basses rejoin in bar 145 (with the indication 'bassi').

Style

This is considered to be Mozart's least virtuosic piano concerto; although Mozart never sacrificed beauty of melody for the sake of virtuosity, here there is less opportunity than usual for the soloist to display their technical brilliance.

Since Mozart was working hard to complete *The Marriage of Figaro* (K. 492) at the time this concerto was written, writers have pointed to the similarities in style between this concerto and operatic writing. Operatic arias are concerned with a solo singer accompanied by an orchestra; here a solo pianist is accompanied by an orchestra. Also, many of the melodies in this concerto have a lyrical quality, reinforcing the connection.

The third movement of this concerto seems to be full of energy and to be constantly driving forwards to the end. Mozart achieves this in many ways:

- The scalic runs and arpeggios in the solo piano part seem to want to run on and on.
- There are sometimes offbeat chords in the accompaniment, e.g. 1st violins bars 44 and 45 and a similar effect in bars 36–39, though they do play on every beat here.
- The joining of one melody to the next without a break. The music rarely comes to a complete stop (e.g. in bar 16 the end of the opening melody is cut down to half a bar, to allow the new melody to start). In this way the last note of one theme becomes the first note of the next.
- Use of tonalities and keys; e.g. dominant pedals, which want to resolve onto the tonic (bars 89–96), chromatic chords which seek resolution e.g. the Neapolitan chord in bar 297 (on the flattened 2nd of E major), modulation to keys other than the tonic, requiring a return to the tonic, in order to resolve.
- The repetition of melodies which lead in a different direction on the repeat, leaving the audience keen to know where they will go.

chromatic chords e.g. a napolitan chord in E maj (F, A, C)

Look for this in Mozart score →

Structure

Sonata rondo movements are a mixture of sonata and rondo form:

A	**Exposition**	First subject	Tonic
B		First episode/second subject	Dominant or related key
A		First subject	Tonic
C	**Development**	Development of existing ideas and/or new material	Variety of keys
A	**Recapitulation**	First subject	Tonic
B		Second episode/second subject	Tonic
A		First subject	Tonic

THEMATIC CLARITY

Mozart's third movement of K. 488 includes a huge number of themes; writers have pointed to at least 10, and even some of the transitional music has a thematic quality. Precisely what you identify as individual themes is not critical; however, you must be clear what you are talking about so that a reader can easily identify a place in the music. For example, when referring to parts of the third movement of Mozart's piano concerto, use standard labels (e.g. first subject, third theme) rather than just letter names.

bars 221–226 he toys between C# major & minor key using chord 7 with the addition of a tierce to brighten the music (opposite to Beethoven who would reinforce the key)

One possible interpretation of Mozart's movement is:

	Theme	Bar nos.	Instrumentation	Keys
Exposition				
First subject	A[1]	1–8	Solo piano.	A major
		9–16	Orchestral repetition of A[1].	
		16–39	Extension of A[1], strings and woodwind.	
	A[2]	40–61	Tutti, 1st flute/1st violin and horn dialogue.	A major
	A[3]	62–69	Solo piano.	A major
		70–77	Wind.	
Transition		77–105	Piano with string accompaniment.	Modulating to dominant
First episode/ Second subject	B[1]	106–113	Flute and bassoon with string accompaniment.	E minor
		113–129	Piano with string then orchestral accompaniment, extension of A[1].	
	B[2]	129–150	Piano with string or wind accompaniment.	E major
		151–175	Repetition of B[2] with variation, solo piano with light string or wind accompaniment.	
	B[3]	176–181	Piano with pizzicato string and horn pedal accompaniment.	E major
		182–202	Woodwind repetition of B[3] with piano countermelody, then piano extension of B[3] with woodwind accompaniment.	
First subject	A[1]	202–209	Solo piano.	E major–V in F♯ minor
		210–229	Tutti repetition of A[1] with modulation and extension.	

Development				
	C¹	230–237	Piano with string accompaniment.	F♯ minor
	C²	238–245	Wind.	F♯ minor
	C¹	246–254	Piano with string accompaniment.	F♯ minor
	C²	255–262	Wind, with modulation.	F♯ minor to D major
	C³	262–269	Wind with piano accompaniment.	D major
		270–277	Piano with string accompaniment.	
		278–285	Piano variation on C³ with wind accompaniment.	D major–V in A major
		286–312	Piano variation on bar 278–285 with string accompaniment, then extension and modulation.	
Recapitulation				
First subject	**A³**	312–319	Solo piano.	A major
		320–329	Wind then wind and piano dialogue on end of A³.	
Second episode/ Second subject	**B¹**	330–337	Wind with string accompaniment.	A major
		338–362	Piano with string accompaniment, extension and modulation, dialogue between piano and wind with string accompaniment.	A minor, interrupted cadence then modulation to V of A major
	B²	362–384	Piano with light wind or string accompaniment.	A major
		384–411	Piano with orchestral accompaniment, extended.	

	B³	412–417	Piano with pizzicato string accompaniment.	A major
		418–441	Wind with piano countermelody and string accompaniment, then tutti extension.	
Coda				
First subject	**A¹**	441–449	Piano with added woodwind accompaniment from bar 445.	A major
		449–456	Orchestral repetition of A¹.	
		456–480	Extension of A¹, strings and woodwind, piano added bars 464–472.	
Second subject	**B³**	481–488	Piano with pizzicato string and horn pedal accompaniment.	Hints of D major
		489–496	Wind melody with piano countermelody and string accompaniment.	
First subject	**A²**	496–524	Tutti, 1st flute/1st violin and horn dialogue with piano accompaniment at times. Extension to end the movement.	A major

Harmony and tonality

The preceding table shows that although Mozart stays mostly with the expected tonal scheme, he does make some changes. The second subject is heard first in the dominant minor (E minor instead of E major) from bar 106. This is mirrored in the recapitulation when the theme is heard in the tonic minor from bar 338. Both these slightly unusual keys are reached abruptly; there is little preparation for them.

Questions relating to Mozart's Piano Concerto No. 23 may be found in Exercises 18 and 19 on page 109.

AS PRESCRIBED WORK 2017

Mozart: Clarinet Concerto in A, K. 622, first movement

- **Composed in 1791 (Mozart's last instrumental work, two months before he died), dedicated to Anton Stadler, a clarinettist friend of Mozart's**
- **First performed in Prague in October 1791 with Stadler as soloist**
- **First published after Mozart's death in versions for the standard A clarinet**
- **I. Allegro (ritornello/sonata form)**
- **II. Adagio (ternary form)**
- **III. Rondo. Allegro (sonata rondo)**
- **Instrumentation: solo clarinet, two flutes, two bassoons, two horns in A and strings**
- **Approximate performing time 28 minutes (complete work), 13 minutes (first movement)**

Context

Mozart wrote this concerto for Stadler, a superb clarinettist of the Vienna Court orchestra. After Mozart's death Stadler pawned the autograph score of the concerto (which is now lost).

The concerto existed first as a sketch for basset horn, a member of the clarinet family, but longer and lower, with a bent neck. However, Mozart clearly decided that the clarinet would be a better option for this concerto and the sketch became the first movement. It seems highly likely that the concerto was intended to be performed on basset clarinet, an instrument developed by Stadler. It was a longer and fatter version of a standard clarinet, capable of playing four semitones lower, with a darker tone.

Mozart wrote for clarinets throughout his career; in childhood he had visited places such as Mannheim where the clarinet was well used. In Vienna the clarinet became closely associated with masonic music (both Stadler and Mozart were Freemasons) and was therefore sometimes seen as slightly rebellious.

Stadler's basset clarinet was in A, like standard clarinets of the time. Mozart's choice of A major for this concerto means that the clarinet part is written in C major (and therefore has no key signature), but will sound a minor 3rd lower, in A major.

Scores

The lack of Mozart's autograph score creates some difficulties, as some published editions include changes to the solo clarinet part so that it can be performed on a standard A clarinet. Whenever there were notes that were too low to be played on a standard clarinet, the music was transposed up an octave. There are therefore different scores available.

The Breitkopf and Härtel score (available at IMSLP) has the clarinet part in the treble clef. It is playable on a standard A clarinet. A reconstructed version for basset clarinet is published by Bärenreiter. This also has notes on the clarinet stave from the start of the movement, but at times the clarinet part moves into the bass clef. This is how Mozart wrote the clarinet part, indicating where the extra low notes were to be used. Bars such as 134–137 have low written Ds, which are unplayable on a standard clarinet.

Structure

The ritornello-sonata hybrid structure outlined on page 87 can be seen in this movement:

	Bar numbers	Key(s)
Orchestral exposition		
First subject/ritornello	1–16	Tonic
Transition	16–24	Tonic–dominant
First subject	25–49	Tonic
Codetta	49–56	Tonic
Solo exposition		
First subject	57–76	Tonic
Transition	76–100 or 103	Tonic minor (A minor)–dominant
Second subject	100 or 103–153	Dominant
Orchestral ritornello	154–164	Dominant
Codetta	164–171	Dominant
Development		
	172–250	Dominant, F♯ minor, D major, B minor, F♯ minor, E minor, D major, dominant
Recapitulation		
First subject	251–270	Tonic
Transition	270–287 or 291	Tonic
Second subject	287 or 291–342	Tonic
Orchestral ritornello	343–359	Tonic

This gives a basic outline of the main sections of the movement. However, there are many subtleties in this concerto, particularly the way in which Mozart uses his themes. The first significant point is the lack of a second subject in the orchestral exposition. Instead of introducing a new melody in bar 25, Mozart has the first subject in imitation; the 2nd violins are followed by cellos and then 1st violins. From bar 31 the first subject is then developed, with the addition of the wind. Here there are two points of imitation: the melody first played by the bassoons in bar 31 and the semiquavers first played by the 2nd violins.

The first subject continues to be well used throughout the rest of the movement. The solo exposition begins with the same first subject and from bar 128 it reappears in imitation, this time incorporating the soloist. Surprisingly, the development also begins with the first subject, though here it is soon extended with semiquaver figuration in the solo clarinet. The recapitulation also features the first subject theme, though it is some 70 bars shorter than the exposition in total. From bar 316 the first subject appears in imitation one final time, this time with the clarinet first.

The other important theme in this movement is the one first heard from bar 16. With the rising 7th in bar 17 (derived from bar 6) it is quite distinctive. Bars 16 and 17 are repeated in bars 18 and 19 and there is then a descending sequence of semiquavers leading into a rising scale and three E major (dominant) chords. This suggests to the listener that the music is leading towards something - perhaps to the second subject? Mozart confounds expectations with his restatement of the first subject.

The theme from bar 16 next appears in bar 154, the start of the middle orchestral ritornello (towards the end of the second exposition). Notice how the rising 7th has now become a falling 2nd. The falling 2nd version is used again from bar 239, beginning in D major and then changed from bar 242 so that it modulates to the dominant, ready to lead into the recapitulation in the tonic. The version with the rising 7th is heard one final time near the end of the movement, as the final orchestral ritornello from bar 343. However, the material is changed from bar 347, using material from bars 44–48, to lead into the codetta and to bring the movement to a close.

Orchestral textures

Many writers point to the intimate chamber music style of this movement, achieved in various ways:

- There are no trumpets or drums and no orchestral oboes or clarinets, resulting in a fairly small orchestra.
- Much of the material is for the solo clarinet and strings, with sparing use of full tutti textures, though these are used to make effective contrasts.
- There are times when the music sounds like the clarinet quintet (also in A major and also written for Stadler) - the start of the solo exposition is scored with reduced violin and viola accompaniment for the clarinet.
- Mozart also separates the cellos from the basses at some points (see bars 25–30 and bars 128–132).
- There are also examples of very thin texture, such as the solo clarinet with just 1st violin accompaniment in bars 86–88.

In this movement there is much use of consecutive 3rds and 6ths (the first subject in bars 1–8 is played in 3rds by the 1st and 2nd violins). There is also considerable use of imitation. The solo clarinet part is wide-ranging, from the lowest notes the basset clarinet is capable of playing to the high register – music such as that found at bar 70, where the clarinet has a leap of two-and-a-half octaves, demonstrates this.

The dialogue between both the clarinet and the other instruments – such as the music from bar 194–197 – also contributes to the chamber music feel. There is also dialogue within the wide-ranging clarinet part, between the low register (known as the **chalumeau register**) and the higher register (see bars 115–123). The clarinet also takes an accompanying role at times, such as the Alberti bass accompaniment in bars 134–137.

Harmony and tonality

The table on page 95 shows the keys Mozart uses in this concerto – a great deal of the tonic and dominant, with excursions to the tonic minor and relative minor.

Bar 93 features an augmented 6th chord on the first beat: C, E, G, A♯. Since this includes the perfect 5th above the root it is a German 6th chord. There is a Neapolitan 6th chord in the prevailing key of F♯ minor in bar 216.

Cadenza

In a first movement of a concerto Viennese audiences would have expected to hear a cadenza. The cadenza would occur just before the final orchestral ritornello: the orchestra would stop on a 2nd inversion tonic chord and then the soloist would take over. In the music it would be marked with a pause.

At the end of a cadenza the soloist would come to rest on a trill, under which the orchestra would play a dominant 7th chord, and then the orchestra would continue to the end of the movement.

There is no cadenza in the first movement of this concerto before the final orchestral ritornello (bar 342), just the trill over a dominant chord. However, there may have been other points at which Mozart would have expected some extra flourishes from the soloist. Bars 127 and 315 are marked with pauses in the score, and the soloist may have played a few extra notes (suggestions are given in the Bärenreiter score). Some writers have also wondered if Stadler would have played some kind of elaboration in bars 216–219.

Questions relating to Mozart's Clarinet Concerto may be found in Exercises 20 and 21 on page 109.

Haydn: Concerto for Trumpet and Orchestra in E♭ major, Hob. VIIe: 1

- **Composed in 1796 in Vienna (after Haydn's second return from England), first performed by Anton Weidinger in March 1800 at the Vienna Burgtheater**
- **I. Allegro (ritornello/sonata form)**
- **II. Andante (ternary form, A♭ major)**
- **III. Allegro (sonata-rondo)**
- **Instrumentation: solo keyed trumpet in E♭, two flutes, two oboes, two bassoons, two horns in E♭, two trumpets in E♭, timpani (E♭ and B♭) and strings**
- **Approximate performing time 15 minutes (complete work), 7 minutes (first movement)**

Haydn was not a virtuoso performer and concertos were not a requirement of his employment at Esterházy, so his contribution to this form of instrumental music is relatively small. He did write some keyboard concertos; these may have been for harpsichord, organ or piano and were sometimes named 'divertimento'. Today, Haydn's most famous and most frequently performed concertos are probably the two for cello and the one for trumpet.

Haydn wrote this work for his friend Anton Weidinger, a member of the Vienna Court Orchestra who had invented a keyed trumpet, able to play more notes than were available on the natural trumpets of the time. Weidinger's instrument had woodwind-style keys. This was not a success and was superseded by the valve system, invented around 1813.

Weidinger was clearly an accomplished trumpeter, as Haydn writes virtuosic passages at a fast tempo (e.g. bars 105–110 of the first movement). Use of the chromatic capability of the trumpet can be seen in passages such as bars 228–232 in the third movement. Since the trumpet is in E♭ the written music will sound a minor 3rd higher than written. This is true of both the solo and orchestral trumpets, which were presumably natural trumpets. However, the horns, also in E♭, will sound a major 6th lower than written.

In the first movement the similarity of the second subject (bar 60) to the first subject is clear with the initial stepwise ascending three notes. The development section is fairly short and begins in the relative minor (C minor). The pause towards the end of the recapitulation in bar 168 indicates that an improvised cadenza would have been performed here. Before this the orchestra has a standard chord progression, pausing on the expected 2nd inversion tonic chord. The end of the improvised cadenza would have been signalled by a trill played by the soloist. Though the autograph score is in a library in Vienna, no cadenza written by Haydn exists, so today soloists either perform their own or one written by somebody else.

Beethoven: Concerto for Piano and Orchestra No. 5 in E♭ major, Op. 73 'Emperor'

- **Composed 1809–1811 in Vienna, dedicated to Archduke Rudolf (who was a patron of Beethoven's and also one of his pupils)**
- **First performed in November 1811 at the Gewandhaus in Leipzig, with Friedrich Schneider as the soloist**

- **I. Allegro (sonata form)**
- **II. Adagio un poco mosso (ternary form, B major)**
- **III. Rondo: Allegro (sonata-rondo)**
- **Instrumentation: solo piano, two flutes, two oboes, two clarinets in B♭, two bassoons, two horns in E♭, two trumpets in E♭, timpani (E♭ and B♭) and strings**
- **Approximate performing time 37 minutes (complete work), 20 minutes (first movement)**

Like Mozart, Beethoven was a very accomplished pianist and wrote four of his five piano concertos for himself to perform. His earliest concertos are clearly Classical, but his later works, like his symphonies, are more Romantic, with significantly greater technical demands on the soloist. However, in terms of form, Beethoven followed the Classical concerto.

This is probably Beethoven's most famous piano concerto. Beethoven did not perform this concerto himself as he was too deaf by this stage. The nickname 'Emperor' was not given by Beethoven, but was probably added when the concerto was first published in England.

Though the tempo is allegro, the opening section functions in a similar way to a slow introduction, with the exposition beginning in bar 11. The pianist has a very virtuosic part right from the outset, with lengthy scales and arpeggios. These are interspersed with orchestral chords, with similar material recurring at the start of the recapitulation. This suggests a cadenza right at the start of the movement, which is perhaps why there is not a cadenza at the end of the first movement, only in the third.

The exposition contains three themes, two played by the orchestra and one (in the second exposition) by only the piano. The other theme in the second exposition is the orchestra's first subject, repeated with variation. The exposition also contains a brief move to the distant key of B major, perhaps as preparation for the second movement in this key. As expected, the first movement has a long coda.

The second movement is calmer and contains writing where the orchestra have the melody, with the piano accompanying. This movement is joined to the third movement by a held B on the bassoon, which then falls a semitone to B♭, the dominant of the finale.

The cadenza in the finale is not improvised, but was notated by Beethoven. Towards the end there is the expected trill, but this does not immediately precede the return of the orchestra. Instead the pianist pre-empts the return of the introductory theme, before the entry of the orchestra.

CONCERTI AND DIVERTIMENTI

Though the genres discussed in this chapter cover the main forms of instrumental music composed by Haydn, Mozart and Beethoven, you may come across other pieces with different names. In the Classical period the term 'divertimento' was used for a variety of works, for a small group of musicians or an orchestra, in a varying number of movements.

Haydn called many compositions 'divertimento' before they were later renamed sonata or concerto. Likewise, the music heard in Exercise 1 is part of a serenade – a piece for instruments in several movements to be played outside in the evening.

Exercise 1

Mozart: *Eine Kleine Nachtmusik*

This is a skeleton score of the beginning of the first movement from Mozart's *Eine Kleine Nachtmusik*. Follow the score while listening to a recording (there are many online). Play it as many times as you need to in order to answer the questions.

1. Which of the following instrumental families is heard in this extract?

   i. **brass** ii. **percussion** iii. **strings** iv. **woodwind**

2. Identify the key (tonality) at the beginning of the music.

   i. **E minor** ii. **F major** iii. **G major** iv. **A minor**

3. What is the correct term for the shape of the melody in bars 1–2?

   i. **broken chord** ii. **chromatic** iii. **modal** iv. **scalic**

4. Write the melody from bars 7–8 on the score. The rhythm of the melody is printed above the stave.

5. The small notes in bars 12 and 13 are appoggiaturas. Describe how they are played.

6. Identify the cadence at bar 17–18.

   i. **imperfect** ii. **interrupted** iii. **perfect** iv. **plagal**

7. Which bar of music is played again in bar 23?

   i. **bar 19** ii. **bar 20** iii. **bar 21** iv. **bar 22**

8. Identify the key (tonality) of the music in bars 26 and 27.

   i. **C major** ii. **D major** iii. **E major** iv. **G major**

9. What is the relationship of the key in bars 26 and 27 to the key at the start of the extract?

   i. **dominant** ii. **relative major** iii. **subdominant** iv. **tonic**

When you have answered all these questions, check your answers with a score and compare your answers with those given at the end of this study guide.

Exercise 2

Haydn: Piano Sonata in D major No. 50

Complete the table below with the bar numbers and keys of the main themes and sections in the first movement.

Section/theme	Bar numbers	Key(s)
Exposition		D major and A major
First subject	1 - 8	D major
Transition	9–16	D major
Second subject	17 - 35	A major
Codetta	35 - 40	A major
Development	41 - 61	A maj, B minor
Recapitulation	61 - 103	D maj
First subject	61 - 73	D maj
Transition	74 - 79	D maj
Second subject	79 - 98	D maj, D minor
Coda	98–103	D maj

Exercise 3

1. Identify an example of each of the following ornaments in the first movement of this sonata and find out how it would be played:
   - a. **acciaccatura** 1
   - b. **mordent** = lower mordent
   - c. **trill** 35
2. Identify an example of each of the following articulation markings in the first movement of this sonata and describe how each would be played:
   - a. **staccato**
   - b. **slur**
   - c. **staccatissimo**
   - d. **accent**

   = flattened turn
3. You may come across other ornaments in music you will study. Find out the sign for each of the following ornaments and how they are played:
   - a. **appoggiatura**
   - b. **turn**
   - c. **inverted/lower mordent**

4, 5 & 6.

hw

Exercise 4

Complete the table below, giving the bar numbers and main keys of each section of the third movement.

Section	Bar numbers	Total number of bars	Key(s)
A (rondo theme)	1-20	20	D major-A major-D major
B (Episode 1)	21 - 40	20	Dmaj. - F maj. - D minor
A	41 - 60	20	Dmaj. - Amaj. - Dmaj.
C (Episode 2)	61 - 80	20	G major
Link	81 - 93	~~12~~ 13	E minor - D major - A major
A	94 - 134	21	D major - A major - D major.

hw

Exercise 5

Mozart: Piano Sonata in C major No. 16

First movement (without using a score)

1. Use the rhythm given above the skeleton score to complete the melody in bars 1–4.
2. What is the name for the pattern in bars 1–4 in the left hand? Alberti bass
3. Describe in detail the shape of the melody in bars 5–8. Descending melody driven homophony
4. Identify the modulation at bar 10–12.
   i. **subdominant** ii. **relative minor** iii. **dominant** iv. **tonic minor**
5. What part of the structure of the music are bars 5–12? Transition

hw

Exercise 6

First movement (with a score)

1. What is the key at the start of the development section?
   i. **tonic** ii. **dominant** iii. **relative minor** iv. **dominant minor**
2. What is unusual about the start of the recapitulation? it is in the subdominant key
3. Identify an example of each of the following:
   a. **circle of 5ths** 19 - 21
   b. **melodic material based on arpeggios** 27
   c. **a perfect cadence** 28

Exercise 7

Beethoven: Piano Sonata No. 3 in C major

1. Complete the table below, giving the bar numbers in Beethoven's scherzo and trio.

A Scherzo	B Trio	Coda
a	c	Coda
b	d	
a	c	
Codetta		

(Instead of using repeat signs, Beethoven writes out the repeat of sections d and c, with changes at the end to lead to a different cadence. The scherzo is then repeated).

2. How does the trio section contrast with the scherzo?

Exercise 8

Having looked at three sonatas in some detail you may wish to compare these with other sonatas or piano pieces by Haydn, Mozart and Beethoven. When looking at a piece of music, have these questions in mind:

1. How many movements are there? What type are they (e.g. slow, fast, minuet, etc.)?
2. What is the structure of each movement?
3. What is the use of keys between and within the movements? Is this as expected?
4. Are there any other unexpected features?
5. How does the piece compare to other pieces by this composer and pieces by other composers?

Exercise 9

Mozart: Sonata for Piano and Violin No. 11

Describe in words how Mozart has varied the theme in each variation - what is the same and what has been changed?

Exercise 10

Beethoven: Sonata for Cello and Piano in A

1. Where does the cello demonstrate that it has an equal role in this sonata?
2. How does the role of the cello differ in this sonata from the role of the violin in Mozart's sonata?

Exercise 11

Haydn: Op. 33 No. 2, 'The Joke'

With a score, listen to Haydn's 'Joke' quartet and then answer the questions.

1. How many movements does the piece have? What types of movement are they (e.g. finale, slow movement, minuet/scherzo, etc.) and in what order do they appear?
2. What is the key of the quartet?
3. What is the key of the individual movements and how do they relate to the key of the quartet as a whole?
4. What is the structure of each of the movements? Is there anything unusual about the structure of a movement?
5. To which keys does each movement modulate? Is there anything unusual about the modulations?
6. Which instruments have the melodic interest at different times?
7. Describe the variety of textures found in each movement.
8. How does this work compare with earlier quartets by Haydn?

Exercise 12

Mozart: String Quartet No. 17, 'The Hunt'

Look at the skeleton score below and listen to a recording of the first 29 bars of the quartet. Then answer the questions.

1. Write the bass line in bars 3 and 4 on the stave. The rhythm is printed below the stave.
2. Write the melody from bar 5 to bar 6 on the stave. The rhythm of the melody is printed above the stave.
3. Name the cadences in bars 4 and 7–8.
4. Describe the structure of bars 1–8.
5. What is the name for the section of music from bar 9 onwards?
6. To what key does the music modulate in bar 20?
7. Name the ornament heard in bars 26–29.
8. Explain how Mozart uses the instruments in different ways during the extract.
9. Compare the stylistic features of this extract with those of another chamber work by Haydn, Mozart or Beethoven.

Exercise 13

Beethoven: String Quartet No. 9 in C

1. How does the music in bar 1 of the 1st violin part of the minuet relate to the music in bars 1–2 in the finale?
2. Trace Beethoven's use of this motif through the finale. You may wish to highlight on a score each time it is used and then list the different ways it is presented.

Exercise 14

Haydn: Symphony No. 100 in G, 'Military'

Listen to two different performances of bars 1–72 of Haydn's 'Military' symphony and comment on their similarities and differences. You may wish to refer to aspects such as articulation, tempo, balance between the sections of the orchestra or the overall sound of each recording.

Suggested recordings:

- The Royal Concertgebouw Orchestra conducted by Mariss Jansons.
- The Academy of Ancient Music, led by Christopher Hogwood.

(Both are available on YouTube.)

Exercise 15

Explain the concept of monothematicism. Refer to this work and to examples from other works in your answer.

Exercise 16

Beethoven: Symphony No. 3 in E♭, 'Eroica'

Trace how the first subject theme is used throughout the first movement of the 'Eroica' Symphony.

Exercise 17

Using examples, compare Beethoven's use of chromatic chords in the 'Eroica' Symphony with the music of Mozart and Haydn.

Exercise 18

Mozart: Piano Concerto No. 23 in A

Listen to two different performances of bars 1–77 of the third movement of Mozart's Piano Concerto No. 23, K. 488 and comment on their similarities and differences. You may wish to refer to aspects such as: articulation, tempo, balance between the sections of the orchestra and the overall sound of each recording.

Suggested recordings:

- Viviana Sofronitsky, piano; Musicae Antiquae Collegium Varsoviense, conducted by Tadeusz Karolak (begin at 16.33). → period instruments.
- Walter Gieseking, piano; Philharmonia Orchestra, conducted by Herbert von Karajan (begin at 17.57). → classic recording.

(Both are available on YouTube.)

Exercise 19

What features of this movement conform to the expectations of sonata form and what features conform to rondo form?

Exercise 20

Mozart: Clarinet Concerto in A

Compare and contrast two performances of Mozart's Clarinet Concerto in A major, K. 622 (bars 128–153), including similarities and differences in your answer. You may refer to articulation, instrumentation, tempo, balance between the sections of the orchestra and the overall sound of each recording.

Suggested recordings:

- Anthony Pay, clarinet; The Academy of Ancient Music, conducted by Christopher Hogwood (4.25–5.17).
- Jack Brymer, clarinet, The London Symphony Orchestra, conducted by Sir Colin Davis (4.19–5.07).

(Both are available on YouTube.)

Exercise 21

Compare this concerto with another concerto you know by Mozart, Haydn or Beethoven.

The legacy of Tin Pan Alley

OVERVIEW

This Area of Study covers popular song from the era of recorded sound. It focuses on the repertoire from the **early years of recording**, including blues, jazz and the 'standards' – a repertoire of songs which is sometimes known as 'The Great American Songbook'.

Much of the focus is on the singers who sang the songs, but you should also study the accompaniment, composers, lyricists and arrangers.

The invention of recording completely transformed the idea of a popular song. In the early years of the 20th century there had been plenty of popular songs, but these had made their way around the world in the medium of printed music.

In the United States publishers vied with each other to sell the newest songs. The competition between them produced thousands of songs, good and bad. The successful ones were performed, recorded and broadcast. As Irving Berlin (who composed 'White Christmas') said, 'A good song is a song that sells'.

The centre of the publishing industry was Tin Pan Alley (officially West 28th Street, New York), which got its name from the cacophony of music coming from the windows of the various publishers as they tried out, bought and sold the songs. At a time when many homes owned a piano and singing and playing songs was a popular form of home entertainment, there was a huge market for easy-to-play songs.

Songs were often sold in arrangements with separate parts for bands, suitable for public entertainment in theatres, **vaudeville** or other public places (see page 188 for their use in connection with Jelly Roll Morton in Storyville, New Orleans).

Once you had your song accepted, publishers could be ruthless in their demands. A publisher might insist on changes (extra verses, new lyrics or structure) in line with their view of the business of selling the music. Publishers employed 'pluggers', salesmen whose job was to get the song performed in as many places as possible. If it became popular with the public, sales of the published song would increase. In 1917, two billion copies of sheet music were sold in the United States.

Many of the songs are still performed to this day. Popular artists such as Robbie Williams, Lady Gaga and Annie Lennox have performed and recorded songs from this repertoire, and they also inform the work of contemporary jazz musicians.

Opposite: The Andrews Sisters

What you should know

There is a summary of the requirements for this Area of Study in the OCR specification. Both AS Level and A Level have their own prescribed works which you must study.

In addition, you and your teachers should choose a programme of listening to suit the requirements. This may include the songs suggested in this study guide.

You should find examples to cover the following:

- Styles of popular song – blues, jazz, swing and big band
- Musical elements
- Conditions and context.

The prescribed songs are:

- **A Level (2018)**
  Ella Fitzgerald: *The Cole Porter Songbook* (Verve Records, 1956)
  i. 'Anything Goes'; **ii.** 'Too Darn Hot'; **iii.** 'Let's Do It'; **iv.** 'Ev'ry Time We Say Goodbye'.
- **A Level (2019)**
  Frank Sinatra: Classic Sinatra 1953–1960 (Capitol, 2000)
  i. 'I've Got The World On A String'; **ii.** 'They Can't Take That Away From Me';
  iii. 'I've Got You Under My Skin; **iv.** 'Come Fly With Me'
- **AS Level (2017)**
  Sammy Davis Jnr.: *Greatest Hits Live* (available on Curb Records, 1995)
  i. 'Mr. Bojangles'; **ii.** 'What Kind Of Fool Am I?'; **iii.** 'The Birth Of The Blues'.
- **AS Level (2018)**
  Nina Simone: *I Put A Spell On You* (Philips, 1965)
  i. 'I Put A Spell On You'; **ii.** 'Tomorrow Is My Turn'; **iii.** 'Feeling Good'.

You need to study:

- The music and the performance of the prescribed songs.
- Interpretations of the songs by other performers.
- How popular songs are composed, including differences in style and structure.
- How singers perform popular songs, including vocal techniques and expression of the lyrics.
- The accompaniment and how it is used.
- The background to the songs and their recordings.
- How to use your listening skills and technical language to analyse and explain the music, and to make critical judgements.

About the recordings

All the songs for the prescribed works are available on CD, MP3 or a similar format. Check that you have the correct recordings. The details of album titles are also printed in the OCR specification.

For the suggested alternative versions of the prescribed songs, these are also audio recordings. These are chosen because the sound quality is usually better. The title and year of the album is given to help you to match the discussion and timings with the correct recording. You must study the prescribed recordings, but you are also free to use any comparative recordings that you (or your teacher) find.

LISTENING TO THE MUSIC IS VITAL

There are thousands of recordings available. Get to know the work of the great singers. The prescribed works and the examples in this book are a starting point. Much of this repertoire has been recorded many times and continues to be performed today. Listen to recordings, and find scores and lead sheets to sing, study and play. If possible listen to live singers performing blues, jazz or other standards. Better still, develop your own skills in performing, either as a singer or accompanist (or both), and try to work with a group.

The examination questions

There are questions on this Area of Study in both Section A (unfamiliar music) and Section B (prescribed music).

- **Section A**
  Short questions on details of the composition and performance of a song from any aspect of the Area of Study. The CD for the examination will have a recording of a complete song (or an extract from it). The Insert will contain a lead sheet - a notated copy of the vocal melody and chord symbols.
- **Section B**
  Two questions on one or more of the prescribed songs and their background.

Sheet music

You may already have found that scores of music by Haydn, Mozart and Beethoven exist in different versions. Many of their scores are now available in scholarly editions (sometimes known as Urtext editions).

Modern editors study the original manuscript score (if available) and other sources, such as early printed scores and parts. By comparing all the sources, scholars can produce a final score which reflects the composer's intentions as far as possible.

The situation with popular music is much more complicated. Often many changes will have been made to an original song:

- The publisher may have simplified the music to produce easy-to-read sheet music for the public to buy.
- Singers may change the lyrics or reinterpret the printed melody (e.g. to suit their vocal range or their preferred style of performing).
- Arrangers and jazz musicians regularly reharmonise songs.
- New versions develop over time with changes, such as an introduction or a new bridge section. If these catch on they can become the accepted version of the song.

Some popular songs therefore exist in a number of published versions. When it comes to songwriting, in general there is less concern for the composer's intentions.

In the examination there may be clear differences between the recorded song on the CD and the printed lead sheet in the Insert. You should be aware that changes are part of the process of performing and recording popular music. You may be asked to compare printed and recorded versions.

Singers often transpose a song so that it suits their voice. Arrangers usually know the range of the singers they are writing for. A professional backing band can play songs in a different key on demand. Frank Sinatra's song 'Love Walked In' (on page 177) is an example of a question where the lead sheet and the performance are in different keys.

Chord symbols

You should be familiar with the shorthand notation for chords. In the exam any printed music for this Area of Study will be in the form of a lead sheet – the vocal line (with the words) and the chords indicated in letter style. The Roman notation will not be used in this section.

Chord notation is not completely standardised, but there are some common features:

- The root of a chord is indicated by a capital letter. A single letter only is a major chord.
- Minor chords are indicated by adding 'm' or 'min'. In older jazz notation you may see a minor chord indicated by a '–' sign (e.g. C– is C minor).
- Numbers refer to the pitch above the root. C6 = C major with the note A added.
- Accidentals (sharp, flat, natural) refer to the pitch of the number which comes after it. C(♭6) = C major with a flattened 6th (A♭).
- Inversions are indicated as 'slash chords': a slash (/) followed by the pitch in the bass (as a capital letter).
- Major 7th chords can be written Cmaj7 or (in more old-fashioned notation) C△.
- Diminished chords can be written Cdim or C°.

Singers and voices

The terms 'chest voice' and 'head voice' are used to describe the area of resonance in the singer's voice when pitching lower and higher notes.

The physical process required to produce the voice is complicated, but for a singer the terms describe how it feels to sing in that part of your range or register.

In popular music the chest voice generally refers to the low and middle ranges of the voice. The middle of the voice communicates powerfully and most directly with the audience. Here the voice can be controlled, diction is clearest, and tone and expression can be varied.

The head voice is the high end of the voice. Here the voice is bright and exciting, allowing it to carry easily. It is more difficult to control in tone and accuracy, or to be expressive with the words and expression.

The **passaggio** is the part of the voice between the chest voice and the head voice. It is sometimes called the 'break'. Singers aim to move smoothly between registers, achieving consistency of tone in the passaggio.

For power and consistency of tone singers aim to develop a mixture of chest and head voice. A full chest voice used loudly at a pitch above the natural passaggio is sometimes known as a 'belt'.

Male singers have a **falsetto** register, which goes higher than the head voice. The female version of this is the **flageolet** (or flute) register.

Accompaniment

You should be familiar with the sound of standard instruments and their main techniques.

A big band from the 1930s would be grouped in three sections:

- Woodwind/reeds - clarinet, alto saxophone, tenor saxophone
- Brass - trumpet, trombones
- Rhythm section - piano, guitar, drum kit, (double) bass.

Some arrangers use standard orchestral instruments, such as strings and French horn. String-based orchestration is common in arrangements for film and musical theatre. Orchestral instruments such as flute, oboe, harp, French horns and tuba can also be found.

Also make sure that you can recognise less common instruments:

- Accordion
- Alto flute
- Banjo
- Baritone saxophone
- Celesta
- Cor anglais
- Hammond organ
- Harmonica
- Mandolin.

Copyright

Composers and lyricists were paid by the publishers for every copy sold, and after 1908 they were also paid for each copy of their music sold as a **piano roll.**

Income from radio and recordings generated enormous sums for the writers of successful songs. It became important to be included on the credits for a popular song. Some agents or publishers took advantage of their position to take a share of the credit for songs to which they had made only a minor contribution.

Recording, radio and microphones

The invention of the gramophone transformed popular song. Singers continued to perform live, even to tour. But with recording and the radio, their singing could become famous to listeners who had never been to their live performances.

From the 1920s, radio stations multiplied in the United States. Unlike Britain, where the BBC was a national broadcasting organisation, in America anyone could set up a radio company in their own city. Soon there were dozens of stations, each competing for advertising revenue by attracting listeners with the best shows. Companies would become involved in sponsoring radio shows (and later television) as a form of advertising.

Recording technology was rudimentary to start with. The development of microphones improved the sound quality. The competition between radio stations helped to spur improvements in the technology of recording sound. Radio engineers developed their equipment to record from a variety of venues, including outdoors. Recording companies benefited from the advances made in radio.

Before the 1950s, records were limited to three minutes of playing time. The disc format involved a playback speed of 78rpm (revolutions per minute), so the disc ran out of space quickly. In the 1950s the speed reduced to 33rpm, allowing up to 30 minutes of playing time on one side of a 12-inch disc - known as the LP (the long-playing record). The new disc was manufactured in vinyl, achieving a much higher sound quality than the brittle shellac that had been used for the 78s.

The LP allowed for longer songs, and also allowed record companies to sell more songs on one disc. A 78rpm disc contained just two songs: a Side A song and a Side B song. Companies still released records in this format (although from the 1950s these were on smaller 45rpm vinyl discs), giving rise to the 'single'. The single became the cheapest, standard format for the most popular songs, and could be easily stacked in **jukeboxes**. The hit song would be on Side A, with another 'bonus' song on Side B.

Structure

The most common structural pattern used in songs from this era is the 32-bar song form. In letters this structure is represented as AABA.

This is made up of two **A** sections of eight bars each, a **B** section of eight bars based on new material and harmony (sometimes known as a bridge), followed by a final **A** section.

THE AABA STRUCTURE

This structure was memorable and satisfying. Check which of the prescribed songs you are studying use this form.

Other forms are also used, some of them 32 bars long (e.g. **ABAC**, **ABCD**), others using different lengths and different proportions.

Blues

The blues queens

In the 1920s and 1930s the most popular blues performers were women: Ma Rainey, Bessie Smith, Marion Harris, Mamie Smith, Ida Cox and others. The blues queens made much of their stage personality, with the costume and jewellery part of the performance.

In 1920 Mamie Smith featured on the first records aimed at the African-American public. They were released on the Okeh label by the General Phonograph Corporation, which had developed a line in records tailored for American immigrant communities. Smith's first blues recording, 'Crazy Blues', sold 75,000 copies in the first month of its release and quickly reached a million sales. The restricted quality of the recording is obvious today: the trombone is too prominent, and the voice too far back, competing with the band to be heard. Nevertheless, it was very successful, and soon record companies were signing up black artists to record blues and jazz, known as 'race records'. They were being bought by black and white audiences alike.

Gertrude 'Ma' Rainey's recordings (over a hundred from 1923–1928) set a fashion for a rougher vocal sound. Rainey had been in a touring company and had considerable stage presence as a singer. Her style and example influenced another member of the company, Bessie Smith, with Rainey the most significant of the blues queens.

For an example of Rainey's singing listen to her 1928 recording of Louis Armstrong's 12-bar blues 'Hear Me Talking To You' (with her Tub Jug Washboard Band). The Paramount recording is poor even by the standards of the 1920s but her performance has presence and character. Paramount terminated her contract in the same year, deciding that the style was out of fashion. She made no further recordings.

Ma Rainey with her band

Country blues

The roving acoustic guitarist

The country blues singers favoured the acoustic guitar. Many earned a living as travelling, busking musicians, including a number of blind musicians.

Country Blues (sometimes known as folk blues) developed in many regional variations. One was Delta Blues, which came from the Mississippi Delta. The songs tended to have simple lyrics, often personal, intense and rhythmic. Musicians include Robert Johnson, who began to record his music in 1936, only two years before his death at the age of 27, but who went mostly unnoticed at the time. 'Come On In My Kitchen' (1936) is an 8-bar blues, an intimate, soulful lament which has a powerful effect, although his record company did not agree and made him record a faster second take.

Another variation was Piedmont Blues, based in the Piedmont Plateau from Virginia to Georgia and Florida. Its style was quicker, syncopated in the ragtime manner, with finger-picked guitar playing both melody and bass. Musicians include Fulton Allen, ('Blind Boy' Fuller), who made 130 recordings before his death at the age of 33. Listen to 'Step It Up And Go' (recorded in New York in 1940), a fast piece that was taken up by other musicians, black and white.

Blind Boy Fuller

AMPLIFICATION

In the 1940s amplification became available for guitars, with blues musicians taking up the semi-acoustic guitar for ease of projection.

As rural black populations looked for work in the great cities, regional varieties were adapted and the music was taken outside its places of origin.

Texas blues

Texas Blues used improvised guitar melodies, closer to jazz in its swung rhythms and the interplay between the voice and the guitar.

Musicians include: Blind Lemon Jefferson and later T-Bone Walker (see the questions on page 178) and Lightnin' Hopkins. Hopkins recorded a huge number of songs in his career, from R&B hits in the late 1940s and 1950s to blues recordings in the 1960s and 1970s, when interest in the blues revived and he was in demand for folk festivals and folk clubs. 'Coffee Blues' (1952) is a good example of his improvising skills.

Memphis blues

Memphis Blues was a cheerful, syncopated style, suitable for dancing and often used in local vaudeville.

One famous Memphis musician was Memphis Minnie. She ran away from home at the age of 13, busked in Memphis and joined the circus as a band musician. Discovered by Columbia Records in 1929, she made a successful career as a blues musician. She took up the amplified semi-acoustic guitar when she moved to Chicago. 'Me And My Chauffeur Blues' (1941) was her biggest hit.

The later Memphis Blues style featured heavier use of the electric guitars. Musicians include B.B. King (1925–2015), who was brought up in the Mississippi Delta and later lived in Memphis. Listen to 'Every Day I Have The Blues' (1955), which shows the influences of jazz and blues guitarists on his playing style and of gospel in the warmth and directness of his singing.

B.B. King with his famous electric guitar, 'Lucille'

Jazz

The influences of blues in jazz

The blues was an important influence on jazz musicians. Jazz singers such as Ella Fitzgerald and Billie Holiday used key features of the blues style in their performances.

FURTHER INFORMATION

There is more information about jazz and its instrumental style in Area of Study 3: Developments in instrumental jazz (pages 182–221).

Singers have always played an important role in jazz. Many bands would have a singer, useful for slower ballads or faster novelty numbers. In the 1920s, when one of the main functions of the band was to provide music for dancing, a song might be performed as a largely instrumental number, with only one or two verses for the singer. There was a large following for instrumental jazz soloists and the bands. People would know the names of bands and individual soloists.

In the 1930s the singer's role grew in importance. As the technology of putting a soundtrack to a movie developed and improved, songs and their singers featured much more in Hollywood film musicals. The record-buying public bought more songs and the concept of hit songs developed. By the 1940s, hit songs were beginning to be the most profitable part of the record industry.

Key features of the jazz style included:

- **Swing** and syncopation
- Blues intonation and timbre
- Improvisation
- Scat
- Rhythm section
- Walking bass
- Woodwind (known as 'reeds') and brass instruments.

Bing Crosby and Frank Sinatra

The most important characters in the development of 'star' singers were Bing Crosby (1903–1977) and Frank Sinatra (1915–1998).

Bing Crosby was the older of the two:

- He was the first singer to successfully develop a singing style for recording, cultivating a natural, relaxed and unforced tone, and showing a real understanding of microphone and recording technology.

Bing Crosby and Louis Armstrong in a scene from *High Society* (1956)

- His early repertoire included witty, syncopated jazz pieces and more romantic numbers.
- His singing communicated the meaning of the lyrics, conveying emotion without exaggeration or sentimental melodrama. His singing adopted the style and techniques of jazz, particularly from working with Louis Armstrong. Armstrong's scat singing was very influential and Crosby adopted this technique.
- In a long career of over 50 years, Crosby had a major part in the recording, film and television industries.

Frank Sinatra continued Crosby's pioneering work for the next generation of audiences:

- He became one of the first teen crazes, similar to the later hysteria over Elvis Presley.
- He sang with Tommy Dorsey's band from 1940, learning a legato style and smooth phrasing from singing in long breaths, rather than dividing a line into several short phrases, as 1930s singers tended to do.
- His singing was immediate, natural and intimate. It told a story and invited the audience to follow the meaning of the words.
- Sinatra went solo in 1942, and developed his own lush, romantic style (with the help of arranger Axel Stordahl). Many of his songs employed a large group of strings to create a rich, opulent sound.
- He performed and recorded the standards by the great song composers of the 1920s and 1930s. Other singers followed his lead in the choice of material to sing.
- After a decline in his popularity in the early 1950s, Sinatra varied his approach. He recorded a series of albums for Capitol (1953–1961), developing the idea of the concept album to suit the new technology of the LP. The idea of arranging songs in a sequence that made sense as a whole became a model for later recordings artists.
- He had a huge repertoire of songs, including faster numbers, displaying a wide, expressive range.

A LEVEL PRESCRIBED WORK 2019

Ella Fitzgerald and The Cole Porter Songbook

The First Lady of Song

Ella Fitzgerald

Ella Fitzgerald (1917–1996) made her first recording in 1935, singing 'I'll Chase The Blues Away' with Chick Webb and his orchestra. Brought up in Yonkers, New York, she was 15 when her mother died.

She learned to sing from performing gospel music in church and from the popular artists of the day. She features on the syllabus for A Level 2018.

Louis Armstrong's jazz solos on trumpet and vocals and the hard-driven swing of the Boswell sisters (often in partnership with Bing Crosby) were regularly heard on record and on the radio. Modelling her singing on Connee Boswell, Ella Fitzgerald entered and won a talent contest at the Apollo Theater in Harlem at the age of 17. Work with the Chick Webb Orchestra followed.

Her vocal contributions became important to the band's success. While the instrumental swing numbers were popular with dancers, there were plenty of similar bands in a competitive market. It was Fitzgerald's singing which made the band stand out and gave it more than a local profile. In addition, recordings with vocals sold more than instrumental recordings. At a young age she became a leading figure in popular music. She stayed with the band for six years, becoming its leader when Webb died.

Her stand-out hit with Chick Webb was 'A-Tisket, A-Tasket' (1938), a hard-swinging arrangement of a nursery rhyme from Fitzgerald's childhood. It sold successfully to both white and black audiences, who responded to its combination of child-like simplicity and emotional depth. It set a trend for other female vocalists to look for simple melodies in order to top the charts, and perhaps signalled a move away from the sophisticated artistry of the successful song composers of the 1920s and 1930s.

After 'A-Tisket, A-Tasket' Fitzgerald did not often make the Top Ten singles charts, but her recordings always sold reliably. She was often referred to as the First Lady of Song. In 1954 Decca claimed that their recordings of her had sold 22 million copies. She regularly topped the *Down Beat* magazine readers' poll for Best Female Vocalist until 1971.

'LADY BE GOOD'

Listen to Fitzgerald's 1947 version of 'Lady Be Good', from the album *Lullabies Of Birdland*. This shows her virtuoso technique and the influence of bebop on her singing in the 1940s. The long chorus in scat style sounds completely natural and holds the audience's attention in a way that few other singers could manage. In true bebop style, she includes a musical quotation as part of the high-paced delivery, in this case from 'A-Tisket, A-Tasket'.

Management

Since early in her career Fitzgerald was managed by Moe Gale. The industry was dominated by white businessmen, and opportunities for black singers were limited.

White singers could have their own radio shows, but black singers - however well known - relied on guest appearances. Gale's strong connections with the broadcasting company NBC were useful in increasing Fitzgerald's public profile. She also performed at Norman Granz's Jazz at the Philharmonic concerts, which were earning her $50,000 a year by 1953. Gale negotiated her fees, but it turned out that he was overlooking the need to pay taxes. Fitzgerald was shocked when the US tax authorities demanded back payment. When Gale's contract as Fitzgerald's manager expired that year, Granz took over her management and paid the tax bill out of his own pocket.

Granz wanted Fitzgerald as the vocal star of his new record label, Verve. He was determined to prise Fitzgerald away from her longstanding contract with Decca.

Ella's Cole Porter LP

As the LP became established, the album format was developing. Frank Sinatra had achieved success with albums which grouped songs under themes.

Record producer Norman Granz had recorded the pianist Oscar Peterson for albums focusing on specific jazz composers. He was satisfied that an album of Cole Porter songs would be a commercial success. He laid the groundwork with extensive publicity, making it known that Cole Porter had admired Fitzgerald's diction.

The album format suited Fitzgerald. She was very experienced in delivering a full set in live performance. She had a huge repertoire of songs and could set down a recording with the minimum of rehearsal. There were enough of the Cole Porter songs available to take the unusual step of recording a double album.

The recording sessions took place in the Capitol Melrose Studios in Los Angeles. The arrangements were by the 25-year old Buddy Bregman, whom Granz had appointed Verve's Head of Artists and Repertoire (A&R). A few numbers (including 'Let's Do It') were recorded with her accompanist Paul Smith and a small group of players.

The format of the *Cole Porter Songbook* was influential. Record companies that had struggled to find new material for a 50–60-minute LP, filled up their albums with recordings of the standards. Other singers recorded albums of standards, teaming up with an arranger to create new versions of well-known songs. Fitzgerald herself followed up with a series of albums devoted to particular songwriters, including Duke Ellington (1957, recorded with Ellington himself), Irving Berlin (1958) and George and Ira Gershwin (1959).

Cole Porter

Cole Porter (1891–1964) was born into a wealthy Indiana family who intended him to follow a career in law. At Yale University he studied English and music, before attending Harvard Law School.

Mostly he was writing music and lyrics for songs and shows. When the United States joined the First World War, Porter went to France. He stayed there after the war, married and maintained a lavish social life. He continued to write with mixed success for Paris, London and Broadway. In 1928 he had his first Broadway hit, *Paris*, which included the song 'Let's Do It'. The show ran for 195 performances and was made into a film.

Porter became one of the leading song composers in the United States. The other prescribed songs from Ella Fitzgerald's *The Cole Porter Songbook* are also taken from his shows:

- 'Anything Goes', the title song of his 1934 musical
- 'Ev'ry Time We Say Goodbye', from *Seven Lively Arts* (1944)
- 'Too Darn Hot', from *Kiss Me, Kate* (1949).

Singing style

When listening to Ella Fitzgerald singing, pay attention to the following char

- An accomplished technique – she maintained the quality of her voice for a of over 50 years.
- Her voice has presence and warmth, and a bright, youthful character.
- She has a wide range, spanning over three octaves.
- She has a very accurate sense of pitch, both in low and high registers.
- Her voice is agile and flexible, moving easily between registers and singing fast pieces without straining in tone and intonation.
- She has a sure sense of swing and a lightness of rhythm. Syncopation and the anticipation or delay of notes and phrases are natural and precisely placed.
- Composers liked her truthful approach to their music. She lets the melody speak for itself without adding exaggerated touches.
- She was an excellent scat singer, using her experience as a band singer and her knowledge of bebop to perform extended scat sections in her performances.

A LEVEL PRESCRIBED WORK 2018

'Anything Goes'

'Anything Goes' was written for Ethel Merman, a popular Broadway singer. She starred (with Bing Crosby) in the 1936 movie of the same name, and also in a 1954 live television version with Frank Sinatra.

Her bold tone, clear diction and strong personality were ideal for musical theatre, where singers had to project their performance without the help of microphones.

Ella Fitzgerald's version is sung in the key of G, with the introduction in G minor.

There are two verses, in 32-bar song form (**AABA**). After the band break at the beginning of the second verse, Fitzgerald repeats the words of the first verse.

The harmonic movement is simple in the **A** sections – basically a tonic chord to subdominant and back to the tonic. The **B** section is more active, with the chord changing in every bar.

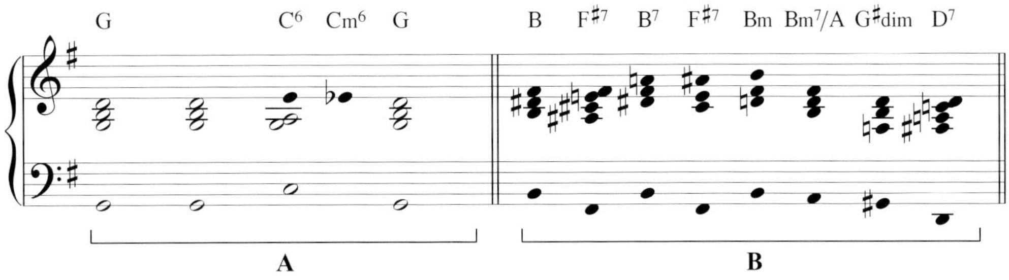

Ella Fitzgerald: 'Anything Goes'

0:00 Introduction

The mock-seriousness of the introduction ('Times have changed') is set up in the minor key. By contrast, sections about modern times ('If today') switch to the major key.

The orchestration is carefully handled to reflect the two halves of the lyrics:

- The opening violin quavers are taken from the vocal line in the introduction.
- An oboe countermelody fills in between phrases.
- Trombone chords (with vibrato) mark the change of mood. The violins now take up the oboe's role.
- Spread harp chords are prominent throughout the introduction.

0:46 Verse 1, **AA**

The opening phrase of the melody repeats three pitches in a changing syncopated rhythm. Note how the syncopated beat occurs in a different place in the bar each time:

- 'Stocking' over beat 3
- 'On' over beat 2
- 'Shocking' on beat 1.

The answering phrase uses long notes, allowing the singer to broaden out to the tag 'anything goes'. The flute/woodwind fill is based on the three-note figure from the melody.

1:19 **BA**

The bridge (B) section is more complex harmonically, beginning in the **mediant** major key of B major. It returns to the dominant (D7) by means of a switch from B major to a chord of B minor. The melody and rhythm outline are simpler: a repeating one-bar pattern with its first note climbing higher each time.

1:54 Verse 2, **AA** (instrumental)

The first half of the second verse is taken by the full band. Bregman uses the instruments in sections. The reeds take the lead at the beginning, answered by the trombones in unison and then the trumpets, which take the second section. A hard-swinging style is adopted, with unexpected strong accents on fourth beats.

Note some of the instrumental techniques in use:

- **Smears** in the saxes
- **Fall-offs** in the trombones
- **Shakes** on the trumpet chords.

2:27 **BA**

The voice returns, repeating the words from Verse 1.

Comparative versions

Frank Sinatra

From *Songs For Swingin' Lovers* (1956), arranged and conducted by Nelson Riddle. Key: E♭ major.

Frank Sinatra recorded *Songs For Swingin' Lovers* in the same year as Ella Fitzgerald recorded *The Cole Porter Songbook*. Sinatra's partnership with arranger Nelson Riddle was very successful commercially and artistically. Norman Granz wanted Riddle for his series of songbooks, but he had to wait until Riddle was out of contract.

His 'Anything Goes' has the following distinctions:

- Moderate swinging tempo, slightly faster than the Fitzgerald version.
- No introduction section; four bars then into the main melody.
- Two verses of music, repeating the words. No band break.
- Reharmonised accompaniment, richer chords, modulation to take second verse into higher key (a semitone higher, E major).
- Swinging bass rather than crotchet walking bass (Fitzgerald) or tonic-dominant (Paige, see below).
- Studio recording, building a relationship with the audience via the microphone, with an intimate, relaxed style. Speaks directly to the audience with the added words at the end, 'May I say before this record spins to a close, I want you to know...'.
- Rich texture in accompaniment to first verse: flowing quavers in celesta, single flute, fills in muted trumpets. **B** section has fall-offs in flutes.
- Second verse has fuller accompaniment. Alternating high-low chords in sax/trumpet fills. **B** section has ascending semiquaver chords, crescendo in violins and trumpets, building to the end of the phrase.

Elaine Paige

From *Songbook* (2007).

Elaine Paige (b. 1948) was first known for creating the role of Eva Perón in *Evita* and became one of the most significant figures in British musical theatre.

She recorded 'Anything Goes' in front of a live audience. Her version has the following:

- Faster, up-tempo **Charleston** feel. Two beats in a bar, tonic-dominant bass.
- A slow start, then an accelerando into the tempo.
- A more forceful and projected tone - more musical-theatre style (closer in style to the song's first interpreter, Ethel Merman).
- Strong personality and humour, bringing out the meaning of the words even at a fast tempo, engaging with the live audience.
- The voice sings throughout, with no band break.
- Two full **AABA** verses, then **BA** again, each time with different words.
- **Stop-time** treatment for **B** sections (second and third times) reinforces the 1920s feel.
- Electric piano, bass guitar. Rhythm section for the first verse, full band enters towards the end of the verse.

A LEVEL PRESCRIBED WORK 2018

'Too Darn Hot'

Recorded by Ella Fitzgerald and the Buddy Bregman Orchestra, February 7, 1956.

'Too Darn Hot' is from Porter's musical *Kiss Me, Kate* (1949), based on Shakespeare's *The Taming of the Shrew*. It was one of Porter's most successful musicals. 'Too Darn Hot' is the opening number of Act 2, sung by a male character, Paul. In the 1953 movie the song was allocated to a female character, sung and danced by Anne Miller.

Cole Porter's risqué lyrics take advantage of a sensational item of contemporary news: The 'Kinsey report' refers to the controversial study of male sexual behaviour by the biologist Alfred Kinsey, published in 1948. For the movie many of the lyrics in the show were toned down to avoid being censored, and in this song the reference to Kinsey was omitted.

Structure

The irregular pattern of 20 bars is made up of two melodic ideas:

- 'x', the descending minim figure, 'It's too darn hot.'
- 'y', the syncopated figure, with its ascending 4th anacrusis (upbeat), 'I'd like to sup with my baby tonight.'

The first 12 bars divide into a neat 'xyy' pattern of three four-bar phrases. Ella Fitzgerald's version is sung in C minor.

The remaining eight bars extend the verse in a breathless ascending sequence of the 'y' motif, now shortened to two-bar units. The change to C major (the tonic major) brightens up the mood to match the playfulness of the words. In these eight bars the harmonic movement is faster. It returns to C minor for the 'x' motif, ''cause it's too darn hot', at the end.

The example summarises the changes in harmony:

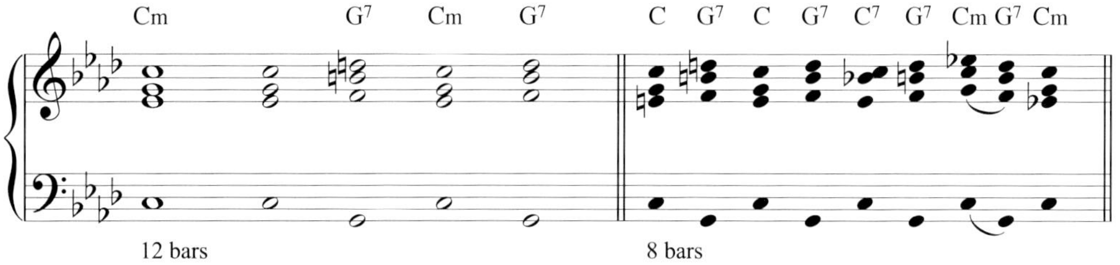

The bridge is more regular: 16 bars of four-bar phrases, leading in to repetitions of 'It's too darn hot.'

Ella Fitzgerald: 'It's Too Darn Hot' (1956)

0:00	**Introduction**	Saxophone melody, answered by trombone chords.
0:05	**Verse 1,** 'It's too darn hot'	Characterful singing, accurate and musical. In the last line of the verse it slides up to the 3rd of the scale, there's a darkening of tone, and the blues intonation brings out the humour. Saxes give an answering two-note motif, in close harmony. There's a pizzicato walking bass.
0:35	**Verse 2,** 'It's too darn hot'	The rhythm section keeps the music moving forward. Listen out for the descending minim countermelody in the second half and the trumpet hits on the fourth beat of the bar.
1:04	**Bridge,** 'According to the Kinsey Report'	The melody moves higher, continuing the swinging, jazz feel. There's a lighter texture in the band, a decorative piano backing with rhythm section. Brass accented chords used to respond to rhyme at the end of short lines, e.g. Mister Pants * for romance * is not * (* asterisk indicates a chord).
1:28	**Refrain,** 'Cause it's too, too, too darn hot'	Longer hits in the brass, with trumpet shakes.
1:39	**Verse 3,** Band break	Full band, more intensive swing feel. Melodic material exchanged between the sections: final trombone melody in close harmony, accent (with cymbal) on the syncopated chord at the top of the phrase.
2:04	**Verse 4,** 'I'd like to coo with my baby tonight'	Muted trumpet takes the beginning, improvising a melody to replace 'Too darn hot'. Voice returns for the 'y' motif.
2:34	**Bridge-extended,** 'According to the Kinsey Report'	Fitzgerald slides up to the final note of the short lines – 'Gob, squab, marine, queen'. 'Gob' is a slang word for sailor; 'squab' is a young pigeon, here used as a term of endearment.
3:02	**Refrain,** 'Cause it's too, too, too darn hot'	The muted trumpet returns as the repeats of 'too darn hot' get quieter.

Discussion

How effective is this version? Compare with faster versions (such as Tormé or Gazarek).

What are the advantages of a slower tempo? What is gained or lost in the faster versions? Which of the versions do you prefer and why? *Kiss Me, Kate* remains one of Porter's most performed shows – how different would a staged performance be? How does Bregman's arrangement contribute to the success of this recording?

Comparative versions

Mel Tormé

From *Mel Tormé Swings Shubert Alley* (1960). Arrangement by Marty Paich.
Key: E♭ minor.

Mel Tormé (1925–1999) was from Chicago. *Mel Tormé Swings Shubert Alley* is one of a series of albums made in partnership with the arranger Marty Paich and his Dek-Tette (but named on the album as the Marty Paich Orchestra). A child prodigy, Tormé had his first hit as a song composer at the age of 16. As a solo singer he was one of the leading male singers after Sinatra. He picked up the nickname 'the Velvet Fog', intended as a compliment, but one he did not appreciate. He had a huge knowledge of music and song arranging. You may find a video of him introducing this song for a television programme, in which he introduces the unusual instruments in the band.

His interpretation includes:

- A very fast swing tempo.
- A tuba and French horn in the band, giving a smooth blend to the harmonies and power to the bass.
- The melody rearranged to begin with 'I'd like to sup'.
- The phrase 'Too darn hot', repeated and developed at the end of verses, e.g. in Verse 1 and Verse 2 repeated four times with a syncopated rhythm (matched by the chords in the band).
- Multiple key changes: up a semitone to E minor for Verse 2, and again to F major for the bridge.
- Trombone solo after Verse 1, alto saxophone solo after Verse 2.
- Full band after the bridge, back in E♭.
- Verse 3 in E♭ minor. Uses sequence, then repeating the words on one note.
- Varied harmonies for the second bridge.
- Descending chromatic sequence for 'Too darn' (five times), modulating through a series of perfect cadences. Chords are: Am7 – D7 – Gm7 – C♯7 – F♯m7 – B7 – Fm7 – B♭7 – E♭.

Sara Gazarek

From *Live At The Jazz Bakery* (2006). Accompaniment: piano trio. Key: C minor.

PIANO TRIOS IN CONTEXT

In jazz a 'piano trio' is piano, bass and drums. In AoS1 (for example Haydn) it usually means piano, violin and cello.

Sara Gazarek (b. 1982) is an American jazz singer. This album, her second, was recorded live in Los Angeles for the Native Language label.

Her interpretation includes:

- Fast movement.
- Intimate atmosphere of a jazz club, light voice, swinging style.
- No introduction. The voice begins with the opening line, as if in the middle of a set.
- Syncopated accompaniment, filling in the crotchet beats between the minims of 'too darn hot'. Piano and bass in octaves.
- Walking bass and swing feel from the eight-bar section at the end of the verse.
- Harder swing for the bridge section. Rhythmic swing stops dramatically at the 'thermometer' – ascending chords in minims in the piano for the temperature rising.
- Instrumental breaks, two full choruses with solos each for double bass and piano. The solos are part of the performance: the audience applauds Erik Kertes for his bass solo. Josh Nelson's piano solo has a wide-ranging melody in the right hand, with light chords in the left.
- Voice returns for the second bridge.
- Coda uses repetitions of 'too'. The section is performed twice, unaccompanied the second time.

A LEVEL PRESCRIBED WORK 2018

'Let's Do It'

The song is a hit from the 1920s. It can be heard on a recording by B. A. Rolfe and his Lucky Strike Orchestra, dating from about 1929–1930.

The band was named after its sponsors, a leading brand of cigarettes. The unknown singer takes only one verse, using the racial stereotypes of the original lyrics (which Porter later replaced with the lines heard on the Fitzgerald recording). His singing style is typical of the understated 1930s style of male singing. The main attention is on Rolfe's orchestra, playing in the fast, energetic dance style of the time.

By contrast, Ella Fitzgerald's performance is much slower. Ella Fitzgerald's version is sung in F major. The song is in 32-bar song form (**AABA**). The **A** section has diatonic harmonies, with a perfect cadence to end. The **B** section modulates through the subdominant (B♭) and flattened mediant (A♭), with chord V7 (an imperfect cadence) leading the music to the return to the tonic. A simplified outline is:

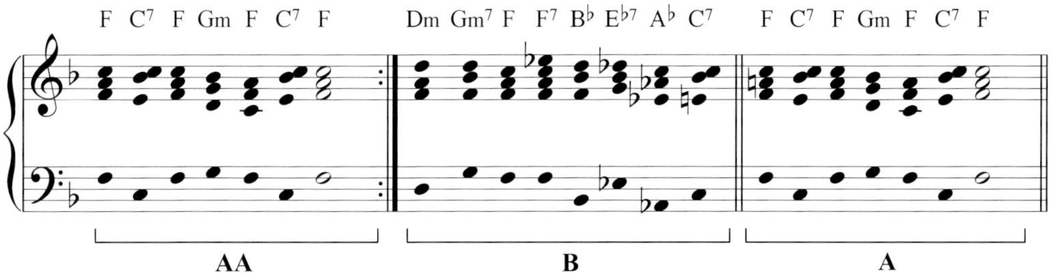

Ella Fitzgerald: 'Let's Do It' (1956)

0:00	Introduction	The small group used to accompany this song is very different from Bregman's rich, string-based orchestral arrangements. The four instruments can be heard clearly: a guitar solo in 3rds, pizzicato bass, drums (played with brushes) and a few notes on the piano. The guitar solo is prominent but once Fitzgerald starts to sing the volume is brought down to the same level as the piano.
0:12	Verse 1, **AA**	Fitzgerald's performance of the first verse is simple and direct. She omits the chromatic notes in the melody, resulting in a largely diatonic version of Porter's song. For example, the opening motif is sung on D and C, two pitches a tone apart. Compare this to Eydie Gormé and Diana Ross (see the next page), both of whom sing the chromatic passing note (as found in the published version of the song). The bass moves in a slow minim beat. The piano's bright, constantly moving countermelody lies above the range of the voice, filling in between the phrases of the melody.
0:58	**BA**	The bridge has more sustained phrases, with the piano more chordal in style. The humour is brought out more. The band stops so that 'Think of Siamese twins' is sung unaccompanied, and the singer emphasises the internal rhyme of 'Argentines without means'. She begins 'People say' on the second crotchet beat and has to hurry through 'in Boston even beans' to get the extra syllables of the line in time.
1:47	Verse 2, **AA**	Each beat of 'Ro-man-tic' is decorated with a lower auxiliary note. The slow pace of the song allows Fitzgerald to decorate the repeat, giving the song more swing. The melody now has its chromatic passing notes, sometimes stretched out to a crotchet rhythm (as in 'Sponges, they say). Note how resourceful she is in varying the pitch, rhythm and phrasing so that the repeated double meaning of 'do it' remains interesting.
2:37	**BA**	The volume increases as the song reaches the end, with the piano and guitar becoming more prominent. A 'shad' is a fish found off the east coast of the United States; 'shadroe' was a delicacy served in expensive restaurants.

Comparative versions

Eydie Gormé

From *Eydie Gormé Vamps The Roaring Twenties* (1958). Conducted and produced by Don Costa. This version includes the original 16-bar introduction, with piano, omitted by Fitzgerald and by Diana Ross (see below).

Eydie Gormé (1928–2013) first became popular in the 1950s as a young television star. Many of her solo albums are themed selections of songs – *Eydie Swings The Blues*, *Eydie In Love*, *On Stage* and so on.

Her version of 'Let's Do It' is from a selection of hit songs from the 1920s and includes:

- Full introduction, with its twee references to nature. Gormé sings in a simple style with a clear, bright tone. For 'fall in love' at the end, she slides up to each note, anticipating a change in mood and style.
- The opening of the main melody is delivered in a softer, suggestive style. She avoids a full tone and slides under the notes. She controls and varies the vibrato, adding little bursts to shape and colour the end of notes.
- 'Outer atmospheric pets' is a reference to Laika, the first dog in space in the Russian Sputnik rocket.
- Verse 2 is a semitone higher in G♭ major.
- The first two sections of Verse 2 feature an exchange between the full band and the voice. The band is used in groups of saxophones (with a smear into the notes) and the brass (adding shakes on some longer notes).
- The voice takes over fully at the bridge (**B**) section.
- A coda is added with new words to create a big finish.
- The mechanical fade at the end was a common recording practice at the time.

Diana Ross

From *The Blue Album* (1971–1972). Released as *Blue* (Motown Records, 2006). Conducted and arranged by Gil Askey.

Diana Ross was born in Detroit in 1944. She was the lead singer of The Supremes, who rivalled The Beatles for popularity in the 1960s. She recorded *The Blue Album* following her success in *Lady Sings The Blues*, the film based on the life and music of Billie Holiday.

Her distinctive recording includes:

- She sings the first verse complete.
- Saxophone and vibraphone improvisation in the background. Held chords in the strings begin when the voice enters.
- For the repeat Ross omits the **AA** beginning. She sings twice through the bridge and final section (using the words of Verse 1 from 'The Dutch in old Amsterdam': **AABA**-**BABA**.
- Sets up the repeat of the bridge with an unexpected treatment of 'love' – ritardando, accompaniment reduced to piano only, into the drum fill and the repeat.
- After the build-up of the second bridge, the final line is taken softer and slower. Ross holds the final tonic note while the accompanying chords change.
- Vocal performance shows plenty of flexibility with rhythm, anticipating and delaying notes with a clear feeling of swing.

A LEVEL PRESCRIBED WORK 2018

'Ev'ry Time We Say Goodbye'

This version is sung in B♭ major.

The structure is a 32-bar **ABA**^{1}**B**^{1}. All the sections are an equal eight bars in length. The printed version of the song includes a few lines of introduction (sung by neither Fitzgerald nor the two singers compared on the next page). There is a full repeat of the main song to the same words. The last line is repeated (extended and varied) as a coda ('Ev'ry single time we say goodbye').

A simplified harmonic outline is given here, showing the main chords and leaving out changes between similar chords.

- There are fewer changes of harmony in the **A** sections. **B** is more active - here notated as one new chord in every bar.
- **A** and **A**^{1} are the same chords, except **A** ends with E♭ minor ('I wonder why a little') and **A**^{1} with E♭ major ('begin to sing about it'). This is a good example of Cole Porter's subtle use of harmony to match the meaning of the words.
- **B** ends with an imperfect cadence, with chord V7 leading back to the tonic. **B**^{1} ends with a perfect cadence.

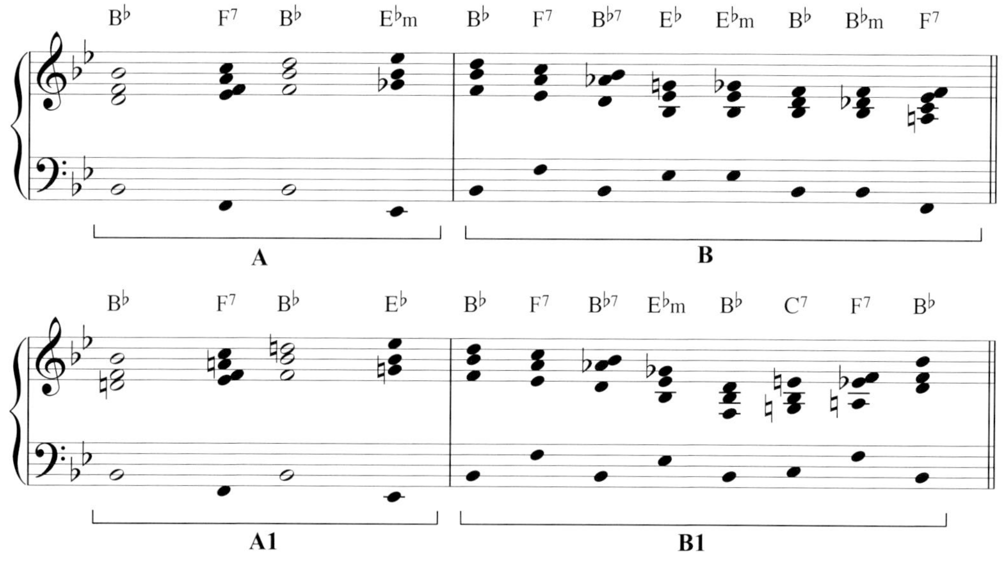

Ella Fitzgerald: 'Ev'ry Time We Say Goodbye' (1956)

0:00	Verse, **AB**, 'Ev'ry time we say goodbye'	The cellos lead the four-bar introduction (with string tremolo and a harp chord). They continue with a countermelody in the **A** section, joined in counterpoint by the violins in the **B** section.

The song moves at a steady, moderate pace. Fitzgerald sings with an expressive, even tone, shaping the phrases. She sings 'Ev'ry time we say goodbye' in one breath. Note the slight darkening of tone and the intonation on the G♭ for 'think so little of me'.

1:00	**A¹B¹** 'When you're near there's such an air'	The second half is warm and involved. She sustains the repeated notes. She takes her time with phrases, using a natural rubato in extending phrases, then quickening the rhythm for 'from major to minor'.
1:45	Repeat, **AB**, Instrumental	The violins take up the melody, beginning Fitzgerald's last note. The richness of the sound comes from playing **sul G** (on the lowest string). In contrast a solo flute picks up the **B** melody, joined in 3rds and 6ths by the oboe.
2:32	**A¹B¹**, 'When you're near there's such an air' (reprise)	The voice returns, sustained and expressive, the accompaniment slightly fuller. 'Major to minor' has a richer tone this time. She allows the music to speak for itself, with only a slight rallentando at the end.

Comparative versions

Dinah Washington

From *The Swingin' Miss 'D'* (1956). With Quincy Jones and his Orchestra. Key: A♭ major.

Dinah Washington (1924–1963) was the stage name of Ruth Lee Jones, one of the most popular of the female black pop singers of the 1950s. She was mainly a jazz singer, but she adapted easily to other styles. She died from a drug overdose at the age of 39. She was known for singing 'torch songs', a type of slow song about a lost or unrequited love. 'Ev'ry Time We Say Goodbye' can be considered as such. The album is an early example of the work of producer Quincy Jones, who was 23 years old at the time, before he rose to prominence for his work with Michael Jackson and as a highly influential record producer.

Her interpretation offers the following:

- A once-through version with no repeat. A coda is added: 'I feel so sad ev'ry single time we say goodbye.'
- Sustained singing, with controlled, fast vibrato on longer notes, but focused and projected.
- A bright, penetrating timbre, secure in tuning, persuasive in subtle pushes into pitches, (e.g. the treatment of repeated notes); also 'There's no love song finer' has a mordent on the first note, then a smear on each note of 'love song finer', with an upward inflection on 'change'.

- Washington moves into the higher octave for 'we say goodbye' – a direct, powerful, highly expressive finish.
- Slow swing tempo, bass pizzicato in minims, brushes on snare.
- Piano filling with elaborate decoration, e.g. rapidly descending scales. Later at **A^1** this role transfers to vibraphone, with the piano playing chords.
- A rich texture of soft, sustained chords on reeds, with countermelody in muted trumpets. Powerful, accented chords in trumpets and trombones, adding depth and seriousness.

Cheryl Bentyne

From *Let's Misbehave: The Cole Porter Songbook* (2012). Arranged by Corey Allen (piano), with James Moody (tenor saxophone) and L. A. Jazz Trio. Key: G major.

Cheryl Bentyne (b. 1954) is best known as the soprano lead of the vocal group Manhattan Transfer, which she joined in 1979.

This version is from her recent solo album of songs by Cole Porter:

- Introduction for unaccompanied tenor sax sets a solitary mood.
- Soft dynamics for the voice throughout the song.
- Concentrated and sustained, the intimate atmosphere draws the listener in. This is the longest version, aiming for a particular emotional effect.
- Bentyne uses considerable variety in tone, for example in the way she begins the notes and allows them to end. The slow tempo gives her time to be very detailed with the expression, e.g. the change of tone for 'die'. She varies the vibrato, occasionally adding a gentle swell on a long note, sometimes adding it at the end of a sustained note.
- Reharmonisation of melody, with richer chords in the piano.
- Very slow tempo, swing rhythm played by cymbal with brushes. Piano fills, slow bass.
- The final 'goodbye' is sung unaccompanied before the final chord in the band.
- Verse 2 saxophone solo, matching the expression of the voice, then extending into a more decorative elaboration. The saxophone continues as a countermelody as voice joins in.

Discussion

Which of these versions do you prefer? What are the challenges of singing this song slowly? How does Fitzgerald's faster, more flowing approach affect the emotion in the song? Compare the arrangements by Buddy Bregman and Quincy Jones, recorded in the same year.

A LEVEL PRESCRIBED WORK 2019

Frank Sinatra

Four hit songs

One of the most popular entertainers of his generation, Frank Sinatra's relaxed crooning style belied a meticulous attention to the interpretation of a song. 'Ol' Blue Eyes' was one of the leading members of the Hollywood Rat Pack and is remembered almost as well for his film roles as for his singing.

Frank Sinatra (1915–1998) was from Hoboken, New Jersey. He was an only child of Italian parents. He started singing as a teenager and idolised Bing Crosby. After being expelled from school, Sinatra worked as a delivery boy and at a shipyard, while also singing in clubs or on local radio. Despite her doubts about his choice of career, his mother - Dolly, a forceful personality - helped get his first break in singing with a vocal group, the Hoboken Four. By 1939 he had a contract with the Harry James band, earning $75 a week. Sinatra had his mother's drive and self-confidence. He was determined that he was going to get to the top. After a few months he left the James band to join Tommy Dorsey, with a new contract of $125 a week.

Sinatra's job was to sing the vocal sections of dance numbers. Typically, in a three-chorus structure, the song melody is introduced by the band, followed by a solo of 32 bars for the singer, before the band takes the final chorus. (Ivie Anderson's version of 'I've Got The World On A String' with the Ellington band is an example.)

Tommy Dorsey's long, lyrical trombone solos became a model for the young Sinatra. Dorsey was famous for playing his solos in one breath. Even before he joined the band, Sinatra had wanted to develop a legato style that was very different from the short-breathed phrases of earlier singers. He made a conscious effort to avoid taking a breath mid-phrase. The smooth shaping of the vocal line generated a powerful expressive effect. Even in a short solo, Sinatra was able to create a narrative, unfolding the story from beginning to end in a natural, conversational singing style. Audiences were transfixed. Dorsey allowed him to record ballads, with arrangements by Axel Stordahl.

Going solo

Sinatra eventually left the band in 1942 so that he could go solo. Unlike Harry James, who had released Sinatra from his contract amicably, Tommy Dorsey was reluctant to let his star singer go.

Their contract specified that Sinatra had to pay 43% of his lifetime earnings to Dorsey. It took a long court case (reputedly Dorsey was threatened at gunpoint by Sinatra's criminal connections) to settle the matter.

As he began his solo career, young women mobbed his concerts and screamed at his every appearance. In New York fans refused to leave after a Sinatra concert, preventing ticket holders for his next show from gaining admittance. A riot ensued and police had to be called.

Sinatra's repertoire of songs was based on the standards of the 1920s and 1930s. Most singers concentrated on newly composed songs. The best-selling songs were often 'novelty songs' - catchy tunes, often humorous or childlike, with undemanding lyrics or musical content. Examples include Ella Fitzgerald's 'A-Tisket, A-Tasket' and Edyth Wright singing 'The Dipsy Doodle' with Tommy Dorsey (1937). Sinatra sang novelty songs, but he also explored the music of composers from the Tin Pan Alley generation, such as George Gershwin, Cole Porter and Harold Arlen.

In the 1950s the development of the LP - the long-playing record - meant that recording companies were releasing albums of songs rather than singles. LPs could total 40 minutes of music or longer. When Sinatra recorded for Capitol Records (1953–1961), he thought carefully about the choice of songs on an album, creating a balanced programme rather than a random collection. The success of his recordings of standards and their presentation in a concept album set an example that was followed by other singers and their recording companies.

The four prescribed songs are taken from albums that Sinatra recorded for Capitol in the 1950s.

Song	Album	Date
'I've Got The World On A String'	*This Is Sinatra!*	**1956**
'They Can't Take That Away From Me'	*Songs For Young Lovers*	**1954**
'I've Got You Under My Skin'	*Songs For Swingin' Lovers!*	**1956**
'Come Fly With Me'	*Come Fly With Me*	**1958**

A LEVEL PRESCRIBED WORK 2019

'I've Got The World On A String'

- **Music by Harold Arlen, lyrics by Ted Koehler.**
- **Arranged and conducted by Nelson Riddle.**
- **First released as a single (Capitol Records, 1953). Included on the album *This Is Sinatra!* (Capitol, 1956).**
- **Sinatra's version is sung in D.**

'I've Got The World On A String' was one of the first of Sinatra's recordings for Capitol. It was the beginning of a musical comeback for him. Despite developing a successful acting career and attracting attention for his private life, he was making little impact on the record-buying public. It was widely thought that a new contract with Capitol would make little difference to a singing career in decline.

Unknown to Sinatra, Capitol executive Alan Livingston had managed to replace Axel Stordahl, Sinatra's usual arranger, with a brilliant young unknown called Nelson Riddle, who had been doing arrangements for Nat King Cole. Livingston felt that Sinatra needed a new sound, with less emphasis on romantic strings. Recording 'I've Got The World On A String' at Capitol's 5515 Melrose Avenue Studio in Los Angeles, Sinatra was led to believe that the arrangement was by Billy May, a well-known arranger whom Sinatra could not turn down. In fact the arranger – and conductor – was Nelson Riddle.

Born Hyman Arluck, composer Harold Arlen (1905–1986) was the son of a Jewish cantor. He left school at the age of 16 and formed his own band. He tried to make it as a singer, but he teamed up with lyricist Ted Koehler and wrote a series of shows for the Cotton Club in Harlem. At a time when prohibition was still in force, wealthy white patrons were able to enjoy the entertainment and the illegal liquor. The club had a new show every year. Arlen and Koehler wrote 'I've Got The World On A String' for the 1932 *Cotton Club Parade*. It was sung by Cab Calloway, who recorded it with his band. After the Cotton Club, Arlen wrote songs for several Hollywood musicals, most notably MGM's *The Wizard Of Oz* (1939).

Nelson Riddle (1921–1985) developed a long and successful partnership with Sinatra. His work with Sinatra gave him a high public profile as an arranger. His technique of arranging a song included:

- Reducing the accompaniment to allow the voice to be heard.
- Introducing new material or interesting ideas as fills, between the vocal phrases.
- Building up the music to a climax about two-thirds of the way through a song, matching the way Sinatra preferred to pace his singing.
- After the highpoint of the song, reducing the volume and intensity while looking for opportunities to be interesting and inventive with the ending.

The song is in the standard 32-bar song form (**AABA**). The **A** section has faster harmonic movement, mostly changing chords at every minim. The **B** section is more static, with long-held chords changing at intervals of two bars.

A (8 bars)

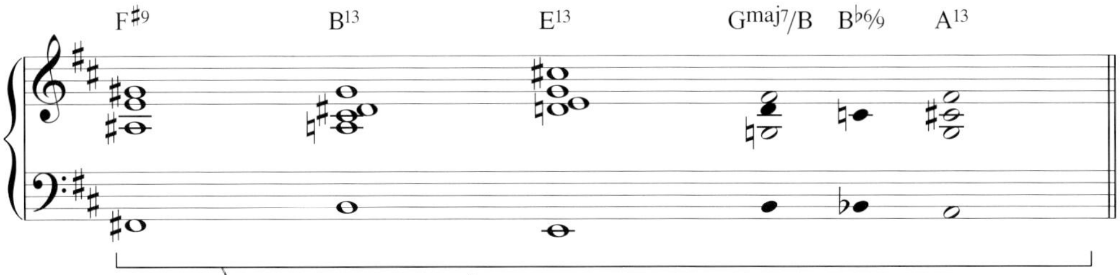

B (8 bars)

0:00

The two-bar instrumental opening begins with a cymbal stroke.

0:07 AA$_1$

Sinatra is much more flexible with the tempo and pitch of the opening lines. Compare the published version of the melody with Sinatra's interpretation (see the example below). The opening line is slow, taken at the speed of an introduction. Only at 'what a world' does the song's bright swing tempo begin.

Published version (transposed into D major, original in F major)

Transcription of Sinatra's version

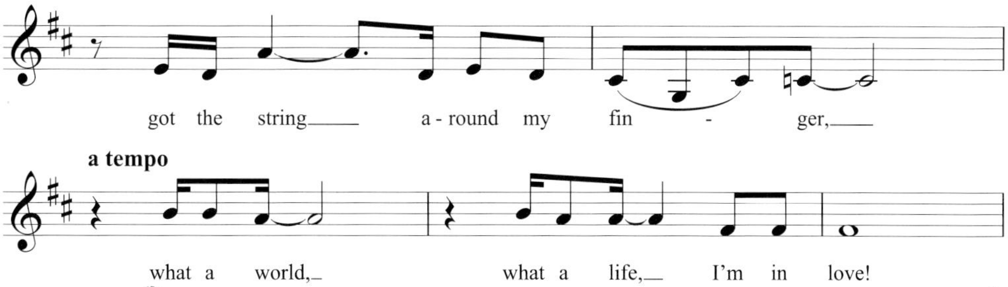
got the string___ a - round my fin - ger,___
a tempo
what a world,_ what a life,_ I'm in love!

Riddle & Sinatra changed this so every member of the orchestra would have had to change the key if it hadn't been decided on before - you can't transpose an orchestral arrangement like you can just a piano.

- The choice of key – a minor 3rd lower – suits Sinatra's baritone range.
- The slower tempo for the introduction introduces the subject of the song directly. Changes to the rhythm of the words (e.g. the faster semiquavers of 'sittin' on a rainbow') make the introduction more of a direct conversation with the audience.
- Sinatra avoids the agile leaps of the original, preferring more conjunct movement. The awkward arpeggio opening over the range of a 10th is reduced to its upper pitches, covering a 3rd.
- 'What a world' is sung an octave higher – easier for the singer to project and in a brighter part of his range.

Frank Sinatra: 'I've Got The World On A String' (1953)

0:46 **B** The bridge has the simplest of melodies, almost all on F♯ and G♯. The pizzicato bass rhythm changes from the dotted crotchet-quaver pattern to even crotchets. The melody's dotted rhythm is answered by the trombone chords in the same rhythm. Accents on the syncopated notes provide an extra feeling of swing. The slide is used to create the vibrato on the held notes. The trumpets provide a bright sound for the final phrase.

1:02 **A$_2$** The dotted rhythm returns in the bass. The band stays in the background, as Sinatra takes the song to its conclusion for the first time. There is a brief link to the repeat for the full band, with the trumpets leading the melody. → Riddle was a trumpetist in his early career so understood brass especially.

1:21 **B$_2$** The song returns to the bridge. This time Sinatra varies the second and fourth phrases with a leaping melodic shape. The orchestration is muted trumpets, then reeds. There is a touch of humour in the full band link: the trumpets' climb to the final, highest note is interrupted by a descending octave leap by the saxophones before the final brass **sforzando** chord. (saxaphones)

Wah - wah played by trumpets, only a skilled session player would be able to play. 'Wah' played by saxaphones.

1:37 **A$_3$** The final A section is extended to 12 bars. The full band – especially the bright, powerful sound of the trumpets – keeps out of Sinatra's way, allowing his melody to be heard over the soft saxophone harmony. The ending alternates four short vocal phrases and the full band: 'what a world, ... man, this is the life, ... hey now! ... I'm so in love!'

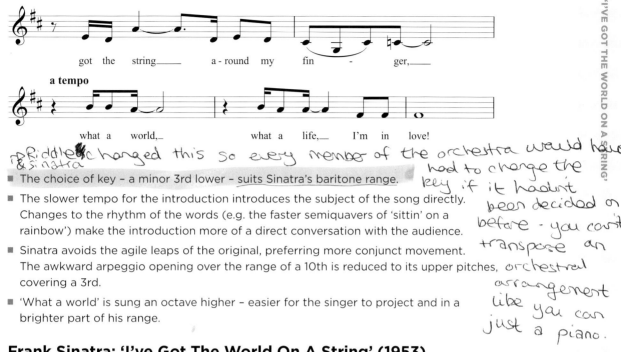

Trumpets here are used to lead the melody as trombone is too loud & raucous & later used to provide colour & harmonies instead are

Comparative versions

Ivie Anderson (1933)

Recorded with Duke Ellington Orchestra, available on the album *Ivy Anderson: I've Got The World On A String* (One Media, 2002). Key: F major.

Another early recording was Ivie Anderson's with the Duke Ellington band. Ivie Anderson (1905–1949) – sometimes spelt Ivy Anderson – joined the Ellington band in 1931, just as the band was ending its residency at the Cotton Club. She recorded this song in New York before the band's first European tour. It was only released in Europe. The recording shows the singer's status as only part of a band, taking her turn between instrumental solos. Although Anderson received prominent billing in the Ellington band's publicity, the instrumental soloists were regarded as the stars. Anderson was highly regarded by Ellington and she stayed with his band until illness forced the end of her career.

- Melody first heard as a muted trumpet solo by Cootie Williams.
- This is followed by Anderson's vocal.
- The third time, the melody is performed as a trombone solo (Lawrence Brown) for **AAB**, then trumpet for final **A**.
- Anderson's solo is in clipped, short phrases. She uses faster movement at the beginning of phrases (e.g. 'sittin' on a rainbow'), so the final notes of a phrase anticipate the beat.
- Listen for slides up to notes and down at the end. There is some vibrato on sustained notes.
- Anderson's voice is clear, focused and restrained. There is some warmth is the lower registers.
- The voice is accompanied by crotchet bass and strummed chords in guitar. Ellington is playing soft piano chords and countermelodies in the background.
- The clarinet has elaborate arpeggio figuration in the **A** sections. In the bridge (**B**) it has a more melodic fill between the vocal phrases.

Diana Krall

From the album *Only Trust Your Heart* (GRP Records, 1995). Key: F major.

Diana Krall (b. 1964) is a Canadian singer, pianist and songwriter. Her second album, *Only Trust Your Heart,* was produced by Tommy LiPuma and recorded in New York. The jazz piano trio format – with Krall playing piano as well as singing – gives more flexibility than the 1950s' orchestral arrangements.

- 16-bar introduction: trading four-bar phrases in piano, then bass, drums and back to piano.
- Four choruses of **AABA**.
- Chorus 1: Voice introduces the melody. Krall has a similar contralto range to Anderson (both their versions are in F major).
- Krall is much freer in improvising around the melody in jazz style.
- The small band allows a more intimate style, which suits her voice, e.g. suddenly soft for 'what a life', followed by the delayed 'ooh, I'm in love', decorated in quavers and leading into the next phrase without a break.
- Chorus 2: Piano solo.
- Chorus 3: Double bass solo by Christian McBride.

- Chorus 4: **AA** has four-bar phrases in piano answered by drums. The voice returns for the bridge (**B**) – 'Life is a beautiful thing.'
- Ending alternates between voice and piano chords. Ends with a playful repetition of 'I'm in love' on a single pitch before the final chord.

A LEVEL PRESCRIBED WORK 2019
'They Can't Take That Away From Me'

- **Music by George Gershwin, lyrics by Ira Gershwin.**
- **Recorded 1953. Arranged by George Siravo. Conducted by Nelson Riddle.**
- **From the album *Songs For Young Lovers*.**
- **Sinatra's version is sung in the key of D major.**

The collaboration between the Gershwin brothers produced many songs now regarded as standards. George Gershwin had left school at the age of 15 and got his first job working as a 'song plugger' for a music publisher on Tin Pan Alley.

In the 1920s, George Gershwin began writing a series of musicals for Broadway. A period of study in Paris helped him to develop his knowledge of classical music. Attempts to get lessons from respected classical composers such as Ravel were rejected. Gershwin's partnership with his brother Ira continued with the musical *Porgy and Bess* (with DuBose Heyward). The subject matter was revolutionary for its time, but Gershwin's openness to the influence of black American musicians is clear. In the Thirties he was beginning to get invitations to write for Hollywood musicals. 'They Can't Take That Away From Me' was written for the RKO film musical *Shall We Dance*, featuring Fred Astaire and Ginger Rogers.

Fred Astaire is an important figure in the development of American song. Many of the standards were first sung by him in his films. Often the songs were part of an elaborate and virtuosic dance sequence for Astaire and his partner Ginger Rogers. Long instrumental breaks would be added to the songs for this purpose. Astaire's singing was competent and stylish, but it was largely his dancing that was popular.

The movie has a light, romantic plot. Astaire's character, the ballet dancer Petrov, is rumoured to be secretly married to tap dancer Linda (Ginger Rogers). They marry and immediately divorce to stop the rumours. 'They Can't Take That Away From Me' is a vocal solo for Astaire in which Petrov lists the things that he will miss about his wife now that they are divorced. It has an 18-bar introduction ('Our romance won't end on a sorrowful note...'), which Sinatra replaced with a shorter introduction and later performers omit altogether. There is no extended dance sequence, but when Astaire and Rogers performed the song again in *The Barkleys of Broadway* (1949), it was treated as a full dance number.

The song was nominated for an Academy Award in the 1937 Oscars, but by then Gershwin had died from a brain tumour at the age of 38.

Songs For Young Lovers was Sinatra's first album for Capitol Records. Most of the arrangements were by George Siravo (not credited on the album), who had been arranging faster numbers for him. There was a smaller band than usual, and Nelson Riddle was conducting. At less than two minutes long, Sinatra's performance is short. He sings the material once only - without repeats or an instrumental break. The album was released in a 10-inch format, with eight songs. At less than 22 minutes, this was longer than could be recorded using 78rpm discs. The later LP release would have 12 songs.

The structure of the song is **AABA**. Each section is eight bars, but the repeat of the last line makes the final A section 12 bars. The harmony moves around tonic and dominant chords in the A section, ending with a perfect cadence on the repeat. The B section is in F♯ minor (the mediant), modulating to E major as a preparation for the tonic.

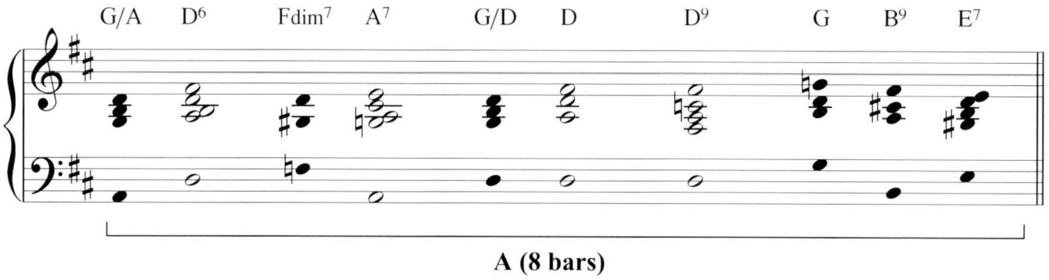

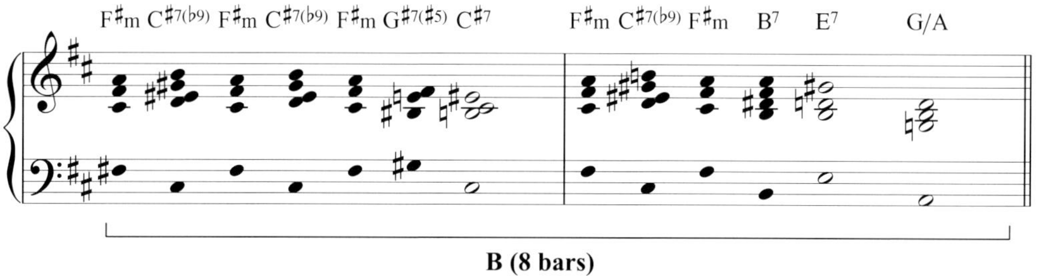

Frank Sinatra: 'They Can't Take That Away From Me' (1953)

0:00	Instrumental introduction	
0:13	Vocal introduction/ Verse	The slow vocal introduction is based on the music of the bridge (B section). With only piano accompaniment, the singer gives a clear and simple introduction to the song, with new lyrics: *There are many, many crazy things that will keep me loving you, And with your permission, may I list a few.*

0:30	**A**	The music picks up tempo for the beginning of the song. The eight-bar section begins with the strong beat where the bass and drums begin. The five-syllable anacrusis in the melody is an unusual feature. George Gershwin originally wrote three notes, but he was persuaded by Ira to allow five, giving more flexibility and character to the lyrics. Sinatra handles the words with natural-sounding sensitivity and relaxed authority. He varies the repeated phrases with rubato, delaying some notes before pushing the music forward to complete the phrase in time. For example: ■ He holds back 'the way you sip your tea'. ■ 'No, no, they can't...' is behind the beat, and 'take that away from me' is quicker to compensate. The accompaniment has a two-beat feel, for example in the strong tonic-dominant pattern in the pizzicato bass. There is more crotchet movement towards the end of the section. The answering melodic phrases in the saxophone provide a contrast with the repeated single notes of the vocal line.
0:47	**A**	Sinatra gives added warmth to his tone and expression in singing the first line ('The way your smile just beams'). The warmer sound of the strings is added to the saxophone.
1:05	**B**	The regular crotchets of 'never, never meet again' in the printed song are interpreted freely. The shorter first syllable of the first 'never' is closer to the natural rhythm of speech. Note the musical way he shapes the phrase, sustaining the high C♯s on the second 'never' and on 'again', then using a glissando on 'road' to reach the C♯ an octave lower. The arrangement (unlike Gershwin's harmony shown on the previous page) has the chords over a tonic pedal (F♯) in the bass at the beginning of both halves of this section.
1:21	**A**	Sinatra begins the repeat of the melody by adopting the style of the saxophone answering phrases. He gives a warmer, intense tone to 'the way you've changed my life', bringing out the importance of the line.

Comparative versions

Billie Holiday

Available on *Lady Day: The Complete Billie Holiday On Columbia 1933–1944*, Vol. 3.

Original recording on the Vocalion label (News York, April 1, 1937), by Billie Holiday and Her Orchestra. Key: B♭ major.

Billie Holiday (1915–1959) recorded her first version of the song soon after the movie was released. Born Eleanora Fagan, her singing style was strongly influenced by blues and instrumental jazz. Her way of improvising, using rhythmic displacement and her bluesy tone and intonation, reflected the popular jazz solos of performers such as Louis Armstrong. While other singers had richer voices, a wider range or more technical skills, Holiday's tone, phrasing and expressive control often made a direct connection with the listener. Her memorable and powerful interpretations led to a string of hit songs in the 1930s and 1940s. These were much admired and imitated by other singers.

The backing is by the Teddy Wilson band, for contractual reasons recording for Vocalion as Billie Holiday and Her Orchestra. A few months later Holiday performed the song again for a live radio broadcast from the Savoy Ballroom with the Count Basie Orchestra.

- Slower, four-beat feel.
- No vocal introduction. Instrumental intro, two melodic phrases on muted trumpet (anticipating the repeated notes of the song).
- Holiday's interpretation is reflective and regretful. There is a clear feeling of loss. Compare this with her Basie recording, which is more defiant and assertive, with a fuller brass sound in the band.
- It is expressively sung in a gentle swing style, following the pitch of the Gershwin melody, with some variation on the second time (e.g. into a higher register).
- The music is played twice through first time with voice (**AABA**), instrumental for the repeat (**AA**), voice returns at the bridge (**AB**).
- The instrumentation is a small jazz band, with Teddy Wilson on piano, and strummed guitar chords.
- Buster Bailey plays elaborate clarinet countermelodies and fills. He takes the solo on the repeat.
- Poor recording quality, with a thin tone and hiss.

Steve Tyrell

From the album *This Guy's In Love* (Sony, 2003). Key: E♭ major

Steve Tyrell (b. 1944) has spent most of his career as a music producer. His solo contribution to the film *Father Of The Bride* led to his late development as a singer. From the release of his first album, *A New Standard* (1999) he has specialised in recordings of standards, including *Songs Of Sinatra* (Hollywood Records, 2005) and his fourth album, *This Guy's In Love*.

His style in 'They Can't Take That Away From Me' includes:

- No sung introduction.
- A syncopated chordal figure in the instrumental intro (see example), used to harmonise the repeated note of the A melody.
- A darker, rougher timbre in the vocals than Sinatra. Longer notes tend to be cut short with a little vibrato. It is expressive, characterful singing.
- The B section changes to a walking bass, while the band plays a more regular four-beat swing, with sustained string chords.
- A repeat that has a tenor saxophone solo by Michael Brecker, breaking into double time.
- An extended ending by singing 'they can't take that away' three times before the final 'from me'. Note the changes in harmony, the continued role of the solo saxophone, and the return of the chordal riff for the outro.

Discussion

Which performance of the song do you prefer? Is that because of the singer's technique or expressive qualities? Does having an older, more mature sounding singer change your understanding of the song? Why is Sinatra such a significant figure in popular song? How does his role compare with earlier figures such as Fred Astaire or Bing Crosby? Is it important for singers in this repertoire to avoid copying Sinatra's interpretations? What should a new performance try to achieve?

A LEVEL PRESCRIBED WORK 2019

'I've Got You Under My Skin'

- **Music and lyrics by Cole Porter.**
- **Recorded 1956. Arranged and conducted by Nelson Riddle.**
- **From the album *Songs For Swingin' Lovers.***
- **Sinatra's version is in D♭ major.**

Cole Porter wrote 'I've Got You Under My Skin' for the MGM film musical, *Born To Dance* (1936), sung by Virginia Bruce. Her singing is clear and expressive, in the musical theatre style of the day, featuring a string-based orchestral accompaniment with little suggestion of swing. The slower tempo and extended rallentando (at the end of the song) make musical and dramatic sense in the context of a film musical. Later performers tend to choose a faster pulse.

Most published editions of this song use Porter's original harmonies (e.g. in *Cole Porter: The Definitive Songbook*, Faber Music), but you can also find Sinatra's version in D♭ major (available online).

James Kaplan's biography *Sinatra: The Chairman* tells the story of the recording. Having recorded the album, Capitol decided they wanted an extra three songs on the LP. Riddle had a day to arrange them. Sinatra usually gave some guidance as to the treatment he wanted for his songs: for this song it was 'a crescendo'.

It was the last song to be recorded for the album. Riddle said he was simply glad to have finished it on time. He was writing the score in the car as his wife drove him to the studio. While other songs were being recorded, a team of copyists was preparing the parts for the band. Sinatra - who usually disliked multiple takes - insisted on 22 takes before he was satisfied.

The basic structure of the song is 56 bars long, through-composed rather than in a standard form. It takes an AAB shape:

- **Intro** 6 bars
- **A** 16 bars four phrases of four bars each
- **A[1]** 16 bars
- **B** 24 bars six phrases of four bars each.

Riddle's arrangement adds:

- **Link** 10 bars Band crescendo based on the riff from the Intro
- **A**^{1} 16 bars Full band with trombone solo
- **B** 24 bars Voice returns
- **Outro** Repeat of last line, followed by instrumental coda.

Frank Sinatra: 'I've Got You Under My Skin' (1956)

0:00 Intro of six bars.

0:11 A The two-bar ostinato in the bass continues. The harmony of the first eight bars alternates chords over a tonic pedal D♭.

The ostinato stops at 'so deep in my heart', and the harmony is more varied.

0:41 **A**^{1} The ostinato returns for the second **A** section, again for the first eight bars. At 'I said to myself', the minor chord (E♭m7♭5 with a D♭ in the bass) disturbs the mood, responding to the doubt expressed in the lyric.

1:12 **B** After six bars of tonic pedal, the harmonic movement is faster as the bridge works towards the climax. Note the chromatic descent in the bass, then decisive movement in 4ths and 5ths.

1:58 **Link** Riddle took inspiration for the arrangement from Maurice Ravel's orchestral showpiece *Boléro* (1928), which features a hypnotic ostinato over a tonic pedal and a famous trombone solo.

2:16 **A**^{1} Full band/trombone solo.

The full band takes the melody in the repeat, with an improvised solo by trombonist Milt Bernhart. The second half of the band break swings harder. There is a stronger feeling of four crotchets in the rhythm section (e.g. the walking bass and loud drums and cymbals) and in the countermelody of repeated notes in unison saxophones.

2:45 **B** The voice continues with a fuller treatment of the **B** material. The short phrases of syncopated brass chords are kept in the background, allowing Sinatra's voice to dominate.

- He varies the melody with more daring higher notes at the beginning of phrases – the sustained F♭ on 'Don't you know', and the E♭ on 'But each time'.
- He inserts extra lyrics to build the excitement: 'Why not use your mentality, step up, wake up to reality.'

The lyric 'stop before I begin' prompts a variety of musical treatments by different singers and arrangers. Sinatra sings the line as 'stop just before I begin', the extra syllable allowing an even triplet rhythm. The band stops, then reduces the volume with the return of the opening riff for the last line.

Comparative versions

Anita O'Day

From the album *Anita O'Day Swings Cole Porter With Billy May* (Verve, 1959).
Key: A♭ major.

Anita O'Day (1919–2006) had a long and successful career as a jazz singer. She recorded a series of albums for Verve. She blamed a botched medical procedure in her childhood for being unable to do vibrato, and she developed a more rhythmic style to compensate. Her tough, outgoing personality and her lifestyle (she had a number of drug convictions, which led to spells in prison) contrast with other singers who projected a more wholesome image.

Verve Records had already recorded a whole album of Cole Porter songs with Ella Fitzgerald under the direction of Buddy Bregman. This set a trend for themed albums featuring songs by a single composer. O'Day's Cole Porter album was arranged by Billy May (who arranged 'Come Fly With Me' for Sinatra). May was well enough known to be credited alongside O'Day in the title of the album.

Her version of 'I've Got You Under My Skin' includes the following features:

- Fast tempo, Latin-American dance-style accompaniment, e.g. syncopated bass/chords on opening riff, trumpet melody intro and outro, ride cymbal.
- Short (1:50), once through the music, no repeated sections, no band break. The last line is sung three times.
- Voice enters unaccompanied.
- O'Day sings comfortably down to E♭ below middle C. Range of a 12th up to B♭.
- Relaxed, warm tone, intimate in expressing emotion.
- Opening accompaniment figure used throughout the A section, then (except for a fill at the end of A^1) not used until the end of the song.
- Accompaniment to B section has more regular crotchets in bass, swing rhythm in drums, contrasting with Latin feel of the A sections.
- The treatment of 'stop' – singer and band stop suddenly, silence, pause, then band resumes at tempo with the opening riff.

Gloria Gaynor

Short (3:48) version, released as a single (Polydor, 1976), available on the album *Gloria Gaynor: The Collection* (Spectrum Records, 1996). The long version (8:14) is featured on the album *Gloria Gaynor - I've Got You* (Polydor, 1976). Arranged by Charles Calello and Lance Quinn. Key: C major.

Gloria Gaynor (b. 1949) was at her most popular in the 1970s, following the release of her first disco-style album, *Never Can Say Goodbye* (1975). Her albums were aimed at audiences in clubs. Audiences wanted longer stretches of music for continuous, energetic dancing. The LP version of this song is over eight minutes long. Producers used studio technology to create medleys of songs over a strong 'four-to-the-floor' crotchet beat.

Layers of accompaniment were added, including backing singers and orchestral countermelodies, similar to the richly textured arrangements in soul music:

- Introduction material: swirling chromatic figure in strings, descending bass guitar motif, backing voices whisper 'Ssskin' and sing chordal 'I've got you, baby'.
- There is a once through of the song, followed by variations of the A section.
- Gaynor's singing is powerful and direct. She uses smears to slide into pitches, and varies the melody to introduce more dramatic higher pitches (e.g. 'I tried so...', and 'But why should I try to resist').
- Typical features of disco textures: four-to-the-floor bass drum (even crotchets); active, funky bass guitar part; trumpet riff (every two bars in **A**, pitches change with the chords).
- **B** section features a high violin countermelody. Backing voices are more active in repeating the end of the solo lines.
- Treatment of 'stop': four-beat rhythm stops (replaced by bass drum on beats 2 and 4), reverb in voice on 'stop'.
- Repeat of **A** led by backing singers, with solo answering in high register, improvising powerful soul-style melodies.
- At 2:46 the repeat of **A** has a cross-rhythm ostinato for the backing singers ('I've got you' - sung three times every two bars, on the pitches G–C–A).

A LEVEL PRESCRIBED WORK 2019

'Come Fly With Me'

- **Music by James Van Heusen, lyrics by Sammy Cahn.**
- **Arranged and conducted by Billy May.**
- **From the album *Come Fly With Me* (Capitol Records, 1957).**
- **Sinatra sings the song in B major.**

'Come Fly With Me' is the title song from an album of songs on the theme of travel. Sinatra had planned the selection of songs carefully. He wanted a specially written opening song with the title that he had chosen for the album, *Come Fly With Me*. Van Heusen and Cahn had written other songs for Sinatra, including 'Love And Marriage' (1955). Their published version of 'Come Fly With Me' includes a sung introduction ('When Dad and Mother discovered one another...'), omitted by Sinatra.

Band leader and arranger Billy May (1916–2004) had been a trumpeter and arranger with big bands, including the Glenn Miller Orchestra. After a period with NBC, he joined Capitol, writing for Nat King Cole and other singers. A fast worker, he could turn out a score at the last minute. Sinatra's choice of Billy May for this album represented a change from the partnership with Nelson Riddle. Following the success of the format, May and Sinatra collaborated on two follow-up albums, *Come Dance With Me!* and *Come Swing With Me!*

A young Sinatra in the recording studio

The song has an irregular AABA structure of 56 bars:

A	12 bars
A[1]	12 bars
B	16 bars
A[2]	16 bars

The harmony moves faster in the **A** section. Section **A** ends with an imperfect cadence, while **A**[1] has a perfect cadence.

The bridge (**B**) divides into two halves of eight bars each. It can be described as **BB**[1]. The tonality changes to G major (the flattened submediant). This is a distant key from the tonic B major. At the end of the bridge the music ends with a dominant F♯ major chord ('angels cheer') to get back to the tonic. This involves an awkward modulation via F♯maj7 ('you so near') and C♯7 ('You may hear').

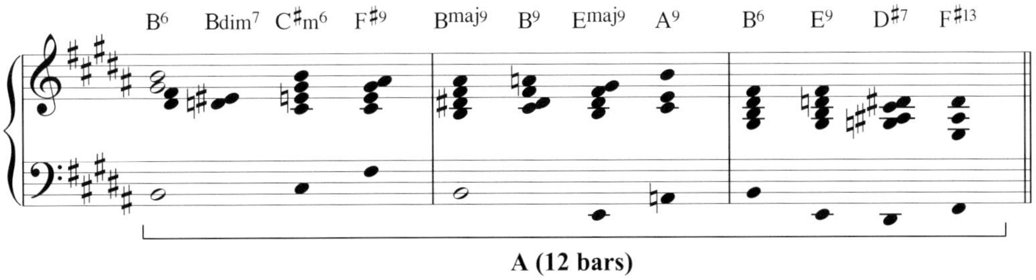

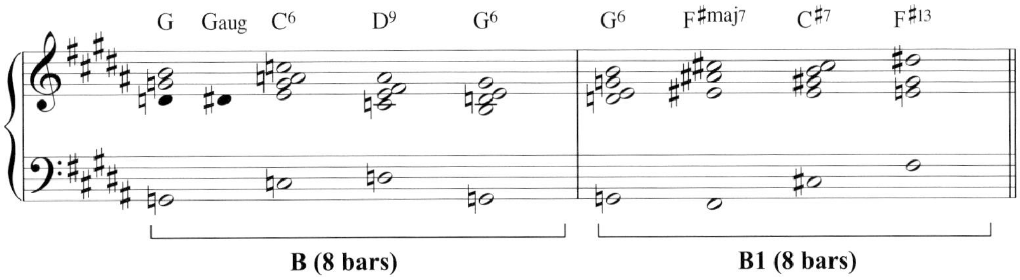

Frank Sinatra: 'Come Fly With Me' (1957)

0:00	**Introduction**	(Instrumental), four bars. A short introduction with trills in the violins and syncopated chords in muted trumpets. The contrary motion of the ascending tremolo and the descending glissando in the lower strings suggest a plane taking off.
0:07	**AA^1**	The A sections consist of three phrases of four bars each, ending with an imperfect cadence ('Let's fly, let's fly away'). The repeat (**A**^{1}) ends with a perfect cadence ('Let's take off in the blue'). The accompaniment has four distinct strands: ■ Rhythm section: pizzicato bass in crotchets, drums ■ Countermelody in low unison saxophones ■ High staccato chords in muted trumpets, flute, xylophone ■ Close harmony in trombones. Strings are added for the **A**^{1} repeat of the melody.
0:49	**B**	Sinatra takes the swooping melody in long, smooth phrases. He takes a breath after 'rarified' but not at the next rhyme ('starry-eyed'), continuing in one breath into 'Once I get you up there'. The romantic humour of the last line ('Angels cheer because we're together') is lightly scored: high string chords for the descending chromatic harmonies and a bell-like use of glockenspiel for the angels.
1:19	**A^2**	The final A section is extended to 16 bars by adding a new ending phrase ('Come fly with me, let's fly, let's fly away.').
1:47	**A^1**	Instrumental. The full band takes the repeat, shortened to 12 bars. The powerful sound of the full band contrasts with the saxophones in 3rds, a characteristic feature of May's arrangements.
2:08	**B**	Voice. The repeat of the bridge is more relaxed. Sinatra takes longer over some of the notes. The accompaniment is based on sustained string lines and staccato, syncopated chords in the trombones.
2:38	**A^2**	The final section is extended to 20 bars by a two-bar band break on the last line. Sinatra's 'Pack up, let's fly away' is a forceful and rhythmic finish.

Comparative versions

Shirley Horn

From the album *Close Enough For Love* (Verve Records, 1989), available on the album *15 Tones* (UMG, 2012). Performed by the Shirley Horn Trio, with Buck Hill (tenor saxophone). Key: C major.

Shirley Horn (1934–2005) founded her trio in the 1950s. She made a few albums as a standalone singer but – inspired by musicians such as Nat King Cole and Ray Charles – always returned to the trio format in which she sang and played the piano. Based in Washington DC throughout her career, the jazz trumpeter Miles Davis invited her to New York in 1961 after hearing an early recording.

Horn's version of 'Come Fly With Me' comprises the following:

- It is a piano trio with tenor saxophone. Horn plays piano herself. The tenor sax player is Buck Hill. Compare his sax solo with the flute solo in the Rawls version (see below).
- It has no instrumental introduction: the voice begins.
- Horn's voice is relaxed and understated, avoiding a full tone. She uses a wide range, with a rich lower register. She freely interprets the printed melody, using syncopation and shifts of register.
- Horn is skilled at maintaining the independence of the piano part from the voice.
- Listen to the use of a bass pedal on A♭ in the B section.
- The solo tenor saxophone takes a full AABA chorus.
- The voice returns at 'Weatherwise'. The vocal section is extended by varied repeats of the last line, including a scat version, in duet with the sax.

Lou Rawls

From the album *Rawls Sings Sinatra* (Savoy Jazz, 2003). Key: B♭ major.

Lou Rawls (1933–2006) was a Chicago-born singer. He was a member of a gospel group in Los Angeles until he joined the United States Army as a paratrooper. After returning to Los Angeles to continue his gospel singing, he was injured in a car crash in 1958 and took a year to recover. After being discovered by a Capitol music producer at a Los Angeles club, he made a number of highly successful albums for the company in the 1960s.

***Rawls Sings Sinatra* comes from the end of his career and features 'They Can't Take That Away From Me' as well as 'Come Fly With Me', which includes the following characteristics:**

- Band introduction of four bars – dramatic ascending chromatic chordal brass, flute fills. No strings in the band. A busy texture of brass and reeds.
- Rawl's voice is strong, projected and has more bass range than the lighter Sinatra sound. It is a relaxed, mature sound of a highly experienced singer.
- He varies the lyrics, adding occasional extra words: e.g. 'we will just glide' and at the end 'Let's go, Baby.'
- The melody is varied at times, e.g. the rhythmic repeated note on 'Weatherwise it's such a lovely day.'
- Longer than Sinatra's version: Rawls has a full repeat of the **AABA** structure – **A** (full band), then **A** (flute solo), then **B** with voice (as in Sinatra).
- Rawls is more adventurous in varying the melody and rhythm for the final time, e.g. higher register and rhythmic swing of 'down to Acapulco Bay.'

Discussion

What are the differences in the arrangements of Nelson Riddle and others, such as Billy May? Which qualities are useful in a successful arranger? How does the writing for band in Sinatra's Fifties recordings contrast with earlier or later recordings? How are changes in recording technology reflected in Sinatra's recordings? What is the role of Capitol Records? What do you learn about business practices in the music industry at this time?

AS PRESCRIBED WORK 2017

Sammy Davis Jr.

Sammy Davis Jr. (1925–1990) spent his whole life in show business. He toured as a child entertainer with his father in the Will Mastin Trio.

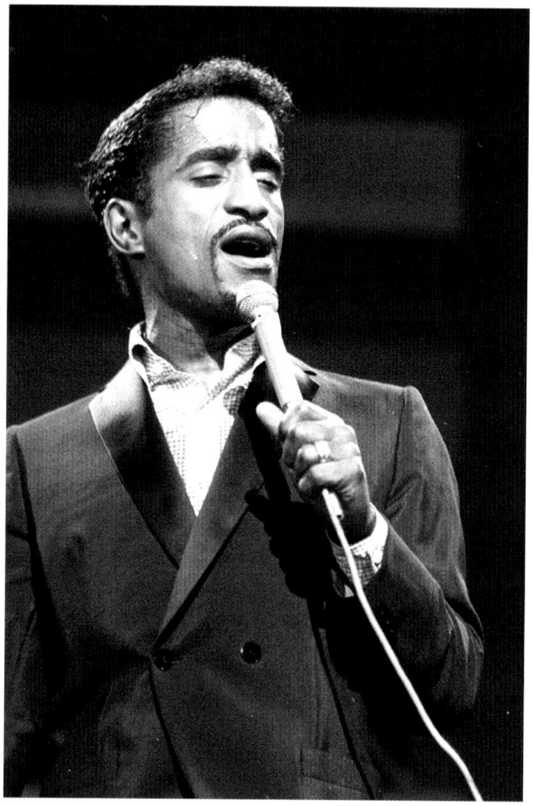

During World War Two he joined an integrated army unit, in which white and black soldiers served together. In his autobiographies he writes at length about encountering racism for the first time. He realised that when he was a child his father had protected him from the racist attitudes that were common at the time.

Rejoining the Will Mastin Trio after the war, he developed as a versatile performer who could sing, dance and act. He lost an eye in a serious car accident in 1954. During his recovery he was introduced to Judaism and he converted a few years later. In the 1950s and 1960s he appeared in leading roles in Broadway shows. Movie roles included *Ocean's 11* (1960), made with fellow members of the 'Rat Pack', a group of singer-actors which included Frank Sinatra and Dean Martin.

Davis's singing was influenced by Frank Sinatra's style. From his recordings certain characteristics stand out:

- Davis has a warm, powerful voice, with a wide range. He is able to sustain his tone and sing sensitively and strongly.
- He has a very good sense of timing. He is able to judge phrasing, knowing when to delay or anticipate a phrase, or interpret a melody to suit his own vocal range.
- He communicates well through the lyrics. He is fully engaged in his performance, colouring the notes to reflect the meaning, and holding the audience's attention.

GREATEST HITS, LIVE (1977)

The three prescribed songs for AS Level 2017 were recorded live by RCA Victor in two concerts at the Sydney Opera House, Australia in August 1977. They were released by Warner Bros. on the album *Greatest Hits, Live*. The conductor and arranger was George Rhodes, Davis's musical director for 30 years. When Davis launched the Sammy Davis Jr. Show on NBC in 1966, Rhodes became the first black musical director on a major American TV network.

By the 1970s Davis was recording more popular numbers in an attempt to appeal to a younger audience. He continued to sing his earlier hits, and he was particularly associated with 'Mr. Bojangles', 'What Kind Of Fool Am I?' and 'The Birth Of The Blues'. He made studio recordings of them, but the live performances show his affinity with the audience, as well as his intensity and ability to take risks during performances.

AS PRESCRIBED WORK 2017

'Mr. Bojangles'

This song references two people who went by the same name: Bojangles was the nickname of Bill Robinson, a black entertainer and dancer. Sammy Davis Jr. credited Robinson with having taught him to tap dance. Robinson broke down some of the colour barriers that existed in vaudeville and became the highest earning black performer before the war.

Jerry Jeff Walker, the song's original singer, wrote the song after a chance encounter in a New Orleans jail with a white street performer who used the name Bojangles (presumably as a tribute to Bill Robinson). In the song Bojangles is an alcoholic; he performs in local fairs and mourns the loss of his dog. This is quite different from the biography of Bill Robinson (who died almost 20 years prior to the song's composition).

This version is sung in E♭ major.

The original song had five verses and a chorus, as in the Neil Diamond and Jerry Jeff Walker versions discussed later. Davis sang the full version often, but for the Sydney performance he cut the song down to three verses, with the chorus sung twice at the end.

The verse is an **AAB** form. Each section ends on a dominant chord (with a IV–V imperfect cadence), so there is always a feeling of wanting to move on to the next section.

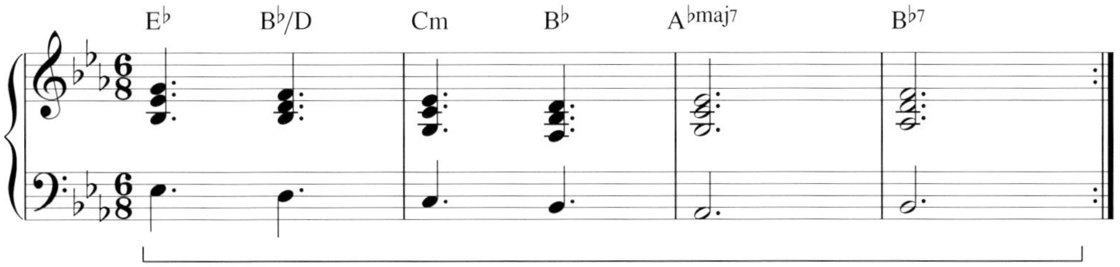

AA - 4 bars (x2)

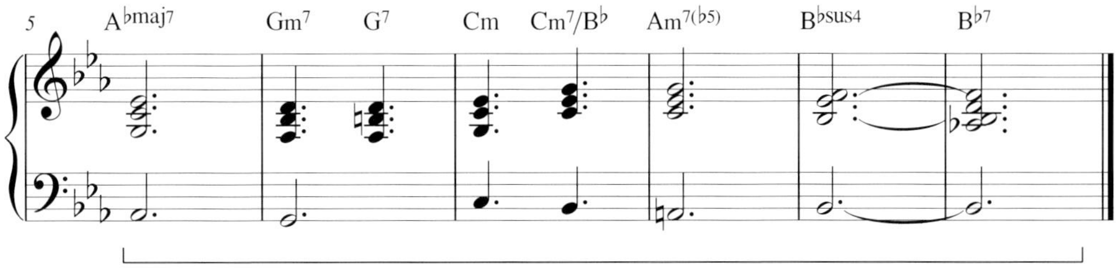

B - 6 bars

The chorus is eight bars long. It repeats the phrase 'Mister Bojangles' in three two-bar phrases (Cm–B♭ chords), finally arriving at the tonic chord (E♭) on 'dance'.

Sammy Davis Jr.: 'Mr. Bojangles'

0:00 Davis begins with a bar of vocalised rhythm, then the guitar and bass introduction begins, playing over the two-bar pattern five times. The audience recognises the song immediately and applauds in anticipation. Davis adds a whistled countermelody.

0:30 Applause again as Davis begins to sing. He tells the story simply, in short phrases, as if remembering what happened. The phrasing is smoother on 'He jumped so high', accompanied by soft strings. He delays 'touched down' as long as he can, making his picture of the dancer more enthralling.

1:10 Another storytelling effect comes with the hesitation and repetitions of 'with' and 'how his' to suggest a spontaneous narrative. The accompaniment is fuller: the cymbal is added in the drums and there is a piano countermelody in 3rds and 6ths. At the **B** section there are soft brass chords and a countermelody in the saxophones, with a crescendo as the song tells of the death of the dog.

1:49 Bojangles tells his story in his own words, characterised by Davis in a hoarse voice. The texture is reduced for the story, building up again from the **B** section. This time the crescendo continues into the chorus.

2:26 The bass and drums break into quavers for the chorus. Davis is quite free with the lyrics in the interests of storytelling: 'That's Mister Bojangles. Call him Mister Bojangles.'

2:47 The repeat of the chorus allows Davis to improvise, going into the top of his range (touching B♭ on the first 'Mister Bojangles' and a sustained A♭ on the second).

3:08 The Outro reduces the band and returns to the mood of the opening over the guitar accompaniment. Davis repeats phrases from the chorus: 'Come back and dance again', 'Please Mister Bojangles'. He ends with the whistled melody of the introduction.

Discuss the effectiveness of Davis's version.

- His performance is emotionally charged. It covers a wide range: the understated, narrative feeling of the opening, the energy and power of the chorus, and the wistful sadness of the ending.
- How effective is the arrangement of the song? Compare this with longer versions. Why did Davis opt for the shorter version for this performance? Discuss the use of the extended introduction and outro.
- Some find the song exploitative and insensitive in its attitude to Mr. Bojangles and his alcoholism. Discuss whether Davis manages to avoid this.

- Did Davis's personal connection with Bill Robinson – like him, the most famous black singer and tap dancer of his day – allow him to show empathy and understanding for the subject of the song? Or is his approach sentimental and overdone? Or is this song nothing to do with Robinson at all?

Comparative versions

Neil Diamond

From *Touching You, Touching Me* (Uni, 1969). Arranged by Lee Holdridge. Key: C major.

Singer-songwriter Neil Diamond included 'Mr. Bojangles' on his fifth album, which otherwise mostly included his own songs. Brought up in New York, he left college for a 16-week job writing songs for a publishing company. Although the job did not work out, he went on to a highly successful career, selling over 100 million records worldwide.

His version of 'Mr. Bojangles' is notable for the following:

- Full version in five verses, with the chorus after Verses 2, 4 and 5.
- Instrumental introduction (two guitars, bass).
- Faster tempo, more direct performance, longer phrases in the verses.
- Neil Diamond's singing is in a natural, folk style, linking with the country music origins of the song.
- Chorus is simpler in rhythm, less movement, bass only on the first beat of the bar: guitar countermelody to 'Mister Bojangles', repeated with second guitar in 6ths, cymbal rhythm.
- Organ chords are added in Verse 2, strings in Verse 3.
- Full orchestra in Verse 4, including trumpets. Suddenly softer, brass drops out at the dog's death.
- Outro features a 'dah lah' vocal line with violin countermelody. Fade out at the end.

Jerry Jeff Walker

From *Gypsy Songman* (Ryko, 1986). Walker first recorded his song in 1968, but this is a later recorded version. Key: D major.

His recording displays:

- Brisk tempo, faster than Davis and Diamond.
- Full five verses, with the chorus after Verses 1, 3 and 5.
- Guitar solo between the second chorus and Verse 4; also in the Outro.
- Walker's vocal performance is characteristic of country and western style, clear storytelling, melodic and rhythmic, clipped ends of phrases with few sustained notes. Occasional use of yodelling (a quick shift to falsetto) for a few notes, e.g. at the end of the final chorus.
- Consistent in mood and expression; maintains an even pace and volume, e.g. the episode of the dog is little different in style and expression from the other verses.
- Strong, regular rhythm in bass and drums, decorated chords and countermelodies from guitars (with country 'twang' of steel strings).

AS PRESCRIBED WORK 2017

'What Kind Of Fool Am I?'

Words and music by Leslie Bricusse & Anthony Newley.

Davis sang many songs by the British songwriting duo, Bricusse and Newley. 'What Kind Of Fool Am I?' is from their first musical *Stop The World – I Want To Get Off*, which had a successful Broadway run in 1962. Davis recorded the song in the same year, released as a hit single and in an album, *What Kind Of Fool Am I And Other Showstoppers*. The song was popular with other artists from the beginning.

Londoner Anthony Newley (1931–1999) left school at the age of 14 and worked as an office boy while he learned to act. He was cast as the Artful Dodger in David Lean's film of *Oliver Twist* (1948). He developed a career as a singer and teamed up with lyricist and composer Leslie Bricusse (b. 1931) so that he could star in his own stage musical.

Newley sang 'What Kind Of Fool Am I?', the closing song of the show, in the original British and American productions. He played the role of Littlechap, who enjoys a lifetime of success before he realises his own selfishness. You can hear his brisk, Cockney-accented version of the song for Decca on the album featuring the original Broadway cast. The line 'I don't give a damn' could not be broadcast, so he later made a further version that was suitable for radio.

Let's look at the 'standard' version of the song. This is in the key of B♭ major.

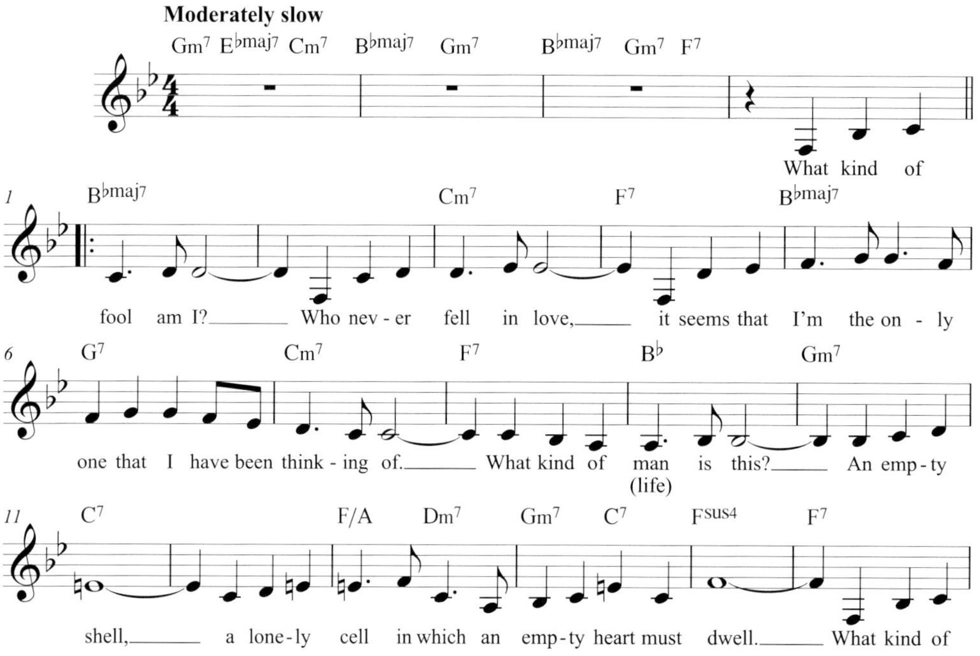

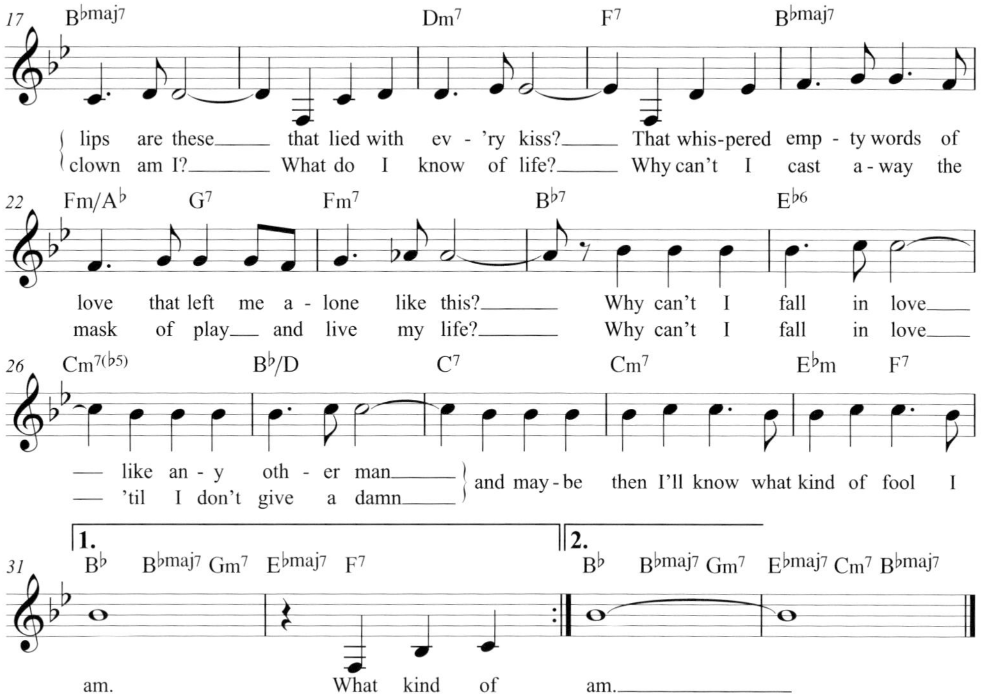

Sammy Davis Jr.: 'What Kind Of Fool Am I?'

Bars	Phrasing	Shape of melody	Harmony
1–8	2+2+4	Low register. Each phrase climbs higher than the previous one.	Ends with imperfect cadence.
9–16	2+2+4	Ascending shape. 'Shell' on the leading note of the new key (A), reaches the B♭ on the last note 'dwell'.	Modulates to the dominant (F).
17–24	2+2+4	Repeats bars 1–8. Changes last two bars to go higher.	Modulating to subdominant (E♭). Imperfect cadence to end on B♭7.
25–32	2+2+4	Highest part of the melody. Alternates between tonic and supertonic (B♭ and C).	Return to tonic, using chromatic chords.

In the final section (bars 25–32) the melody is very simple – in the printed version it is only two notes. Davis is much freer in arranging the vocal line to suit his vocal qualities, such as choosing higher notes or whole phrases instead of continuing in a low register. The piano accompaniment is richer and more elaborate than the original.

Much of the expressive effect of this passage comes from the chromatic movement in the strong original harmonies (see the upper note of each chord):

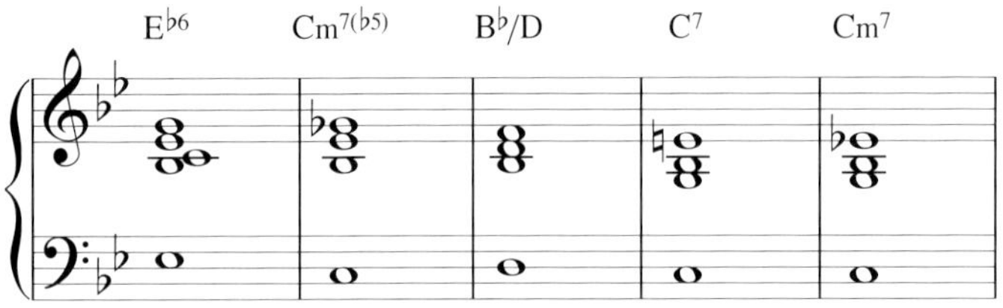

Each section has broadly the same rhythm and phrasing (two short phrases of two bars, followed by an extended four-bar phrase). The similarity between the four sections of the song makes it difficult to label the structure in the usual A, B method.

For example, each of these tells you something about the structure of the song:

AAAA

A - A^1 - A - A^2

ABAC

A^1 - A^2 - A^3 - A^4

Discuss how clear and useful these are. Are there better alternatives? The following section uses **A^1 - A^2 - A^3 - A^4**.

Now let's look at our prescribed work, the live version of the song taken from Sammy Davis Jr.'s album, *Greatest Hits, Live.*

Sammy Davis Jr.: 'What Kind Of Fool Am I?'

0:00 **A^{1}A^2**

There is no introduction. In the Sydney performances the song formed part of a medley with another Bricusse & Newley song, 'The Candy Man', which it followed without a break. The first three notes are sung unaccompanied.

The romantic piano textures, with decorative arpeggios and countermelodies, keep the music moving. The piano fills in between phrases and during longer notes in the voice. Davis pauses for a quip with the audience. His singing is light in tone, relaxed and conversational, as if in a club or cabaret. The pianist is used to adjusting to the singer's spontaneity: after Davis's 'Excuse me' the piano repeats a few notes of the accompaniment so that the song continues without a break.

0:58 **A^{3}A^4**

'What kind of lips are these...'

The second half of the song continues with the piano accompaniment. The singing is more concentrated, with more expressive treatment of the words:

- A break (a pause in both voice and piano) before 'empty' makes the word sound more bitter.
- A diminuendo and straight tone (without vibrato) on 'alone'.
- A decoration on 'other', then continuing into the next phrase ('and maybe then I'll know') with a crescendo in one breath.

1:52	**A³A⁴** 'What kind of clown am I?'	A tone higher, in C major, repeating the music of the second half to new words. The full orchestra enters, with even quavers in the cymbals. The first five bars have a tonic pedal C in the bass, with a rich, reharmonised texture of high piano chords (C–C(♯5)–Am/C) and sustained notes in reeds and brass. **A³** keeps mostly in tempo, with a clear rhythmic pattern in the bass and clear countermelodies in unison saxophones. **A⁴** is freer in rhythm, with the band following Davis as the music slows. He extends some notes with pauses, e.g. the high A on ''til'. He takes the melody up to a high G to finish the song, with a slow dramatic slide to repeat the pitch. The brisk fanfares in the tag bring the music to a rousing conclusion.

Comparative versions

Nancy Wilson

From *Today, Tomorrow, Forever* (Capitol, 1964). Arrangements by Kenny Dennis (drums). Key: B♭ major.

Born in Ohio in 1937, Nancy Wilson began as a jazz singer. She moved to New York at the suggestion of alto saxophonist Julian 'Cannonball' Adderley. In the 1960s she recorded a succession of R&B and jazz albums for Capitol Records. *Today, Tomorrow, Forever,* recorded in only two days with her husband Kenny Dennis, is a selection of best-selling songs of the period.

Her version of 'What Kind Of Fool Am I?' includes:

- Light, fast-moving, jazz waltz version, $\frac{3}{4}$ time signature.
- The celesta takes the role of the piano, adding playfulness and grace to the dance feel of this version. Plays the melody in the introduction and then a jazzy countermelody in the first half of the song (**A¹** and **A²**).
- Pizzicato bass, drums and guitar.
- Similar structure to Davis: **A¹** - **A²** - **A³** - **A⁴** - **A³** - **A⁴**.
- Guitar has quietly strummed syncopated chords, then takes over the solo countermelody at **A³**.
- Longer note values for the last line, but keeps the tempo until the end.

Regine Velasquez

From *Listen Without Prejudice* (PolyGram/Mercury, 1994). Key: B♭ major.

Regine Velasquez (b. 1970) is one of the most successful singers from the Phillipines. *Listen Without Prejudice* was her first album with a major international label and became a best-selling album on the Asian market. Although less popular in America and Europe, she has sold millions of albums in Asia, appeared in films and sponsored charitable causes.

Her version of 'What Kind Of Fool Am I?' includes:

- A very slow, hesitant and soft beginning, with phrases broken up to create a breathless, vulnerable picture.
- The full melody sung twice through.
- Dynamic contrast, with the first time very quietly, synth strings added for **A³** and a crescendo to forte on the final note.

- A key change to E♭ major the second time. Strings play the **A**[1] melody. The voice returns for **A**[2], while the orchestra drops out. She sings to piano accompaniment only, suddenly softer. She crescendos to forte on 'dwell'.
- A sharp contrast at **A**[3]: change of key to C major, voice in power-ballad style – strong, forceful, highly charged with emotion.
- A leap to F on 'then' and 'kind'. Long pause on 'fool' (with fill in the accompaniment). Leap up to E for the final note.

AS PRESCRIBED WORK 2017

'The Birth Of The Blues'

Words by B. G. DeSylva & Lew Brown. Music by Ray Henderson.

'The Birth Of The Blues' was published in 1926 and first performed in George White's *Scandals*, a Broadway comedy revue. Its composer and lyricists were responsible for updating the songs in the show as the script changed from year to year.

The words offer an idealised version of the origins of the blues, suitable for a white New York audience rather than a true historical account. Its inventors are 'some people long ago' (or an alternative, offensive version of this line). The notes and 'weird melodies' are taken from the breeze, the poor and imprisoned, and the sound of a whippoorwill – a North American bird with a distinctive, musical call that sounds like its name.

The song has an introduction and a 32-bar **AABA** structure: the **BA** is repeated and the final **A** extended into a coda.

Davis's version is sung in C major. The harmony of the eight-bar **A** sections has a chromatic ascending bass, moving in 3rds with the voice and the harmony (in the strings). This creates a strong progression from tonic to dominant chords in the first four bars. Below is the published version of the song – notice how Davis alters both the pitch and rhythm of the melody.

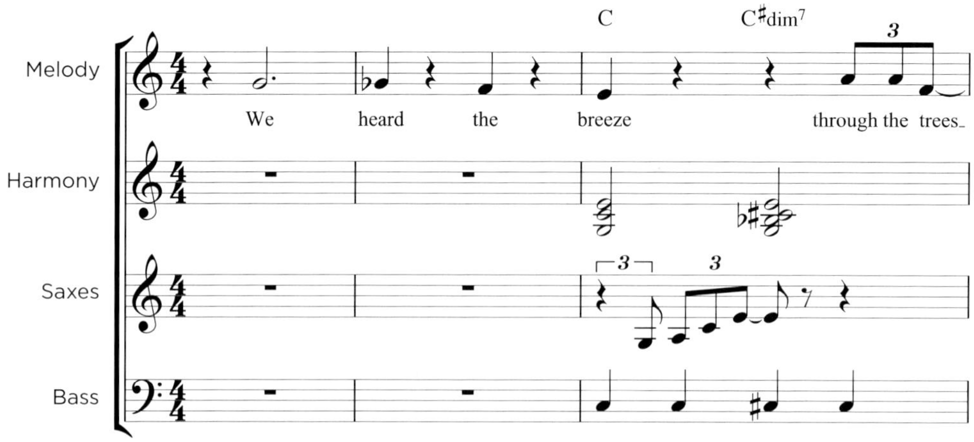

Sammy Davis Jr.: 'The Birth Of The Blues'

0:00	Introduction	Voice and piano. 16 bars. Sammy Davis Jr. takes ownership of the song, changing 'some people' to 'my people' and 'they' to 'we'. The piano plays a decorative blues accompaniment. Davis takes the introduction at a moderate tempo, with some rubato when he wants to bring out the expression in a line (e.g. 'swayin' to and fro'). He adds semi-improvised interjections to the original melody: ■ 'We didn't have nothin' but some soul' ■ 'I said the blues' ■ 'Oh yeah' – an octave leap down to C at the very bottom of his range, a deliberately amusing touch.
0:56	**AA**	The band enters for the song, with a strong crotchet beat in the bass and drums. The saxophone's four-note figure answers the voice in an ascending sequence. Note Davis's expressive treatment of 'weird': a break before the word and a sudden leap up to a high-register A.

1:33	**BA**	The **B** ('bridge') section has a new riff on E7 (see example), moving to A7 for the second half. The piano has high repeated triplets. The voice sings mostly repeated high Es (going up to G♯ for 'high'), descending on ''til it was worn'. Syncopated hits in the brass and drums punctuate the ends of phrases (after 'horn' and 'worn'). The ascending saxophone riff returns for the **A** section:

2:07	**BA**	The full band leads a repeat of the **B** section, swinging the riff louder and harder than before. Davis breaks off after the first line to encourage the audience to clap along ('like we did in the old days'). The final return of **A** features a call and response between trumpets and trombones, repeating a two-note minor 3rd figure (C descending to A), at first at every half bar, then speeding up to every beat. In the stereo recording the trumpets are in the right channel and the trombones in the left to reproduce the **antiphonal** effect of the live performance. An interrupted cadence (G7–A13, with a blues-style clash of C♮ and C♯) leads into a coda.
2:42	Coda	The last line is repeated. The final chord (played three times) is C13(♯11) – a tonic 13th chord with B♭ and F♯.
3:11	**BA** (reprise)	The reprise of the final section begins during the applause. Davis encourages the audience to keep clapping ('Don't let me down now!'). He varies the vocal line, adding more exciting ideas as the song comes to an end.
3:44	Coda (reprise)	The final three chords are more extended, separated by Davis's improvised lines.

Comparative versions

Frank Sinatra

78rpm version, for Columbia (1952) released in *Frank Sinatra Sings His Greatest Hits* (Sony, 1997). Conducted by Axel Stordahl. Key: B major.

In Sinatra's version:

- Six bars are added before the introduction ('These Are The Blues').
- It begins with a forceful big-band sound, full chords with trumpet shake on sustained notes. Accompaniment reduces for the main introduction and song.

- Sinatra is slower than Davis with this song. A steady, moderate pulse throughout, including both introductions.
- Sinatra draws out each note leading to the **A** section ('They heard the...') with a ritardando. He does the same later after the bridge (**B**) section ('And then they...')
- The main 16-bar introduction has strummed guitar and bass keeping time in crotchets.
- The solo alto saxophone answers the voice in the introduction. The reed section continues the dialogue after 'They heard the breeze'.
- A solo trumpet (with a **plunger** mute) takes over for the second **A** section ('And from a jail came the wail...').
- Sinatra's vocal performance is smoothly phrased, and consistent in tone and expression, allowing the melody and words to come through naturally.
- The **AABA** is sung once only, followed by the coda.

Shirley Bassey

From *Born To Sing The Blues* (Philips, 1957), released in *The Complete 1950s Masters* (NFM, 2011). Key: A major.

Dame Shirley Bassey (b. 1937) is one of the best loved of popular British singers. *Born To Sing The Blues* was her first album, released when she was only 20 years old. Born in Cardiff, she had worked in a factory, sung in clubs and had a child. Obviously talented, producers did not quite know what to do with her and tried her on blues arrangements by Wally Stott.

These were released as a 10-inch LP, with four songs on each side. Her version of this song highlights:

- Brief lead-in for full band, followed by introduction with piano only.
- Free tempo in the introduction. Bassey sings pairs of quavers as short-long (e.g. the first line: 'say some', 'people') – a **Scotch snap/Lombard** rhythm, giving character to her delivery of the words.
- Piano, accompanying in block chords (e.g. parallel 9th chords), with some arpeggio fills. Only limited use of idiomatic blues style, more conventional song features (e.g. descending straight quavers and a mordent on the final note to the end of each section).
- Same tempo as Sinatra, same structure as Davis: **AABABA** (coda). Trumpet solo for the second **B** section.
- Clear, powerful tone. Controlled phrasing (e.g. 'breeze' is delayed to the second beat, then sung with 'through the trees' in one breath. Goes up to C♯ in the **B** section ('from a whippoorwill') without breaking into head voice.

Discussion points

Which of these versions do you prefer? Sinatra and Bassey were recorded early in their careers. Davis delivers the performance of a mature and experienced artist, recording a song that he had performed many times. How does the presence of an audience influence the performance? Does performing the song slowly give it depth and meaning? What are the strengths and weaknesses of Davis's approach? Compare the three arrangements of the song.

AS PRESCRIBED WORK 2018

Nina Simone

I Put A Spell On You

Nina Simone was one of the most controversial recording artists of all time. Her aggressive championship of the American Civil Rights movement and her intolerance of inattentive audiences led to her reputation as a singer who demanded to be taken seriously.

Nina Simone (1933–2003) was born Eunice Waymon in Tryon, North Carolina, the sixth of seven children. As a child she was obviously gifted as a classical pianist. She moved to New York and trained briefly at the Juilliard School. She took up singing, found that she could get work in clubs with a repertoire of popular music and adopted Nina Simone as a stage name. She recorded her first album in 1957 and achieved a commercial hit with Gershwin's 'I Loves You Porgy', released as a single.

Her early recordings up to the late 1960s tend to be of jazz standards, including an album of Duke Ellington's songs, but mostly she avoided concept albums. *I Put A Spell On You*, the title song of which is a prescribed work for AS Level 2018, was one of seven albums recorded for Philips. By now her repertoire was becoming broader in style, mixing in popular songs from a variety of sources.

The elements of her performing style include:

- A rich **contralto** voice, with distinctive, sensuous timbre in low registers.
- She tended to sing from the piano and accompanied her own singing, sometimes including extracts of Bach, whose music she revered.
- An intense feeling and a serious approach to her songs, restrained and expressive.
- An individual vocal style which shows the influence of jazz, soul, blues and gospel.
- A consistent style of singing applied to all the material she sang, including jazz standards, popular songs and folk songs.

Simone developed a reputation as a complex, talented but difficult artist. She alleged that she was being exploited by those around her, which was sometimes true. Her relationship with her manager/husband, Andrew Stroud, was turbulent and abusive. She was also highly valued by her recording companies and built up an enthusiastic following with audiences. She used her position as a famous singer to express support for civil rights and against racial discrimination in the United States. A strong identification with her African heritage led her to incorporate traditional songs into her programmes. Today she is thought to have been affected by bipolar disorder, a condition which was little understood at the time.

AS PRESCRIBED WORK 2018

'I Put A Spell On You'

Screamin' Jay Hawkins (1929–2000) wrote and recorded 'I Put A Spell On You' in 1955 and again in 1956 (for Okeh Records, the version usually heard).

The wildness of his performance created a sensation and gave him his nickname. A stage act was developed in which he wore a cape and rose out of a coffin (later supplemented by live snakes, fire and a skull). It became a popular song, with later arrangers and singers creating more restrained performances.

Nina Simone's version is in F♯ minor.

The song has a 16-bar structure, divided into four phrases of four bars each. The basic harmony is simple in outline:

- Bars 1–4, F♯ minor
- Bars 5–8, B minor–C♯7 (imperfect cadence)
- Bars 9–12, F♯ minor–B minor
- Bars 13–16, F♯ minor–C♯7 (imperfect cadence)

Hal Mooney's arrangement adds:

- A descending bass at the beginning of the first and last phrases.
- A suspension (sus 4) to the C♯7 chord at the end of the first half.
- He uses a secondary dominant (F♯7) to move to the B minor chords in bars 4–5 and 10–11.
- He adds new chords to create a 'turnaround' (a chord progression at the end of a verse, leading to the repeat of the verse).

Nina Simone: 'I Put A Spell On You' (1965)

0:00	Introduction	Four bars in slow $\frac{12}{8}$ (compound time). The melody in the strings emphasises the blue note C♮ in bars 1 and 2.
0:17	Verse, 'I put a spell on you'	The slow pulse is maintained, with sustained chords in the strings and a sparse but rhythmic bass line on the double bass. An acoustic guitar (which is mixed louder as the song progresses) plays chords. The piano has a decorative countermelody, with blues figurations and tremolos. Simone's singing is dark toned, with intense short phrases and long rests. An intricate scat fill adds to the drama. The melody is built around the minor 3rd between F♯ and A – heard in a low register at first, then an octave higher. 'You know, I can't stand it' begins an insistent argument in alternating minor 3rds, until 'I put a spell on you', with the minor 3rd repeated an octave lower.
1:22	Tenor sax solo	The tenor saxophone takes the first half of the repeat. It picks up immediately on the minor 3rds, gathering in pace and intensity. The rapid repeated notes are played with a double-tonguing technique. The middle section of the solo is shaped in more legato phrases, returning to the shorter motifs at the end. Tremolo strings build up to the return of the voice.
1:55	Coda	Simone imitates the saxophone's motifs from the end of its solo, scatting on the repeated F♯ and repeating 'I love you'. At the final cadence she adds an unaccompanied scat cadenza. The saxophone repeats B in the final F♯13 chord.

Discuss the effectiveness of Nina Simone's version of this song:

- How does her singing style suit the music? The album is often marketed as a jazz album. Is this music jazz? Are there any other influences?
- Some writers link the power of her performance to her unhappy personal life. Is this justified? Or is it because she is a highly professional musician at the peak of her powers?
- How does her version compare with others? Does the song work equally with a male or female singer?

Comparative versions

Arthur Brown

From *The Crazy World Of Arthur Brown* (1968).

Arthur Brown (b. 1942) is an English rock singer and performer. Having studied drama in Paris, he specialised in shock performances with theatrical gestures, such as heavy make-up and his signature burning metal helmet. Brown used a powerful voice and screams in his singing. Some of his approach anticipated the stage performances of later artists such as Alice Cooper and Marilyn Manson. His only album with his band *The Crazy World Of Arthur Brown* had one side of original material in a psychedelic rock genre, while side two had more commercial cover versions of other songs, including this track.

It includes:

- Similar tempo to Simone, but active, fast-moving organ riffs. More exciting, forward movement.
- Three verses. Organ solo at the beginning of Verse 2.
- Powerful, controlled singing. Firm tone, baritone timbre, range up to A (repeatedly slides up to this in Verse 2). Some wilder declamation included at the beginning of the final verse.
- Louder, heavier, rock style of drumming, with fills at the end of phrases.
- Harmony follows the same outline: varied descending bass pattern (G-F-C-D), used as an ostinato to link the end of verses with the beginning of the next.
- Descending chromatic movement over the subdominant chord (chord IV - see bars 5-6 and 11-12 of example): Gm-Gm(maj7)-Gm7-Gm6.

Joss Stone

From *Jeff Beck: Emotion & Commotion* (2010). Guitar solo by Jeff Beck. Key: F♯ minor.

Joss Stone (b. 1987) is an English soul singer, whose first album, *The Soul Sessions* (2003), was very successful in the United Kingdom and in the United States.

Her performance of 'I Put A Spell On You' is one of her two guest tracks on an album by veteran guitarist Jeff Beck, for *Emotion & Commotion*:

- Longer version than Simone's: two complete verses.
- Stone's singing is highly expressive. She communicates the story in the lyrics, using variety of dynamics and tone, and stylish soul inflections.
- Repetition at the end of the song (e.g. 'Because you're mine') builds up to climax, then breathy, sighing. Dramatic, communicates a range of emotions.
- Jeff Beck's guitar is featured in the short introduction, a solo break at the beginning of Verse 2, then in duet with the voice until the end.
- Intro begins with the triplet rhythm of the repeated chords in piano. Heavy backbeat in drums. Crescendo to staccato chord, dramatic silence before the voice enters.
- Legato melody in violins at the end of the verse, linking into the next verse.

AS PRESCRIBED WORK 2018

'Tomorrow Is My Turn'

Original song 'L'amour c'est comme un jour' by Charles Aznavour, Marcel Stellman & Yves Stephane, arranged by Horace Ott.

'Tomorrow Is My Turn' is an arrangement of 'L'amour c'est comme un jour', the title song of the 1960 French film *Le Passage du Rhin*. Its composer is Charles Aznavour (b. 1924), one of the best known of French popular singers. Aznavour had the lead acting role in the movie, a wartime drama about the escape of French labourers forced to work in Germany. The film was released in the United States under the title *Tomorrow Is My Turn*.

Like the United States, France went through a golden age of popular song in the mid-20th century. Some of the singers gained an international reputation – Édith Piaf, Yves Montand and Charles Aznavour. French songs could appear in America in English-language cover versions. For example, 'La Mer' by Charles Trenet (1946) was adapted in the same year by Jack Lawrence as 'Somewhere Beyond The Sea'. The song became famous after Bobby Darin's 1959 recording.

Listen to Aznavour's recording of 'L'amour c'est comme un jour' in French (see below) and to versions by other French singers, for example Nara Noïan. Aznavour also recorded the song in English and made a duet version with the British rock musician Sting.

As a guide, Aznavour's original waltz melody (adapted with English words) is printed below.

The melody is made up of four eight-bar phrases, moving at a crotchet pace. The chords change every two bars. The chorus is more intricate, a quaver-based chorus of 28 bars. There is a faster harmonic rhythm (chords changing every bar). The use of descending sequence and the strong harmonic progression gives the chorus a distinctive and memorable forward momentum.

The 28 bars of the chorus divide into two unequal halves:

- Bars 33–44 (12 bars). It begins on the subdominant chord of F minor. Note the use of perfect cadences.
- Bars 45–60 (16 bars). The second half of the chorus is longer. While the first half descends by step only as far as F (in bar 43), the second half continues the sequence in order to end on the tonic D.

Nina Simone's version is in G minor.

Nina Simone: 'Tomorrow Is My Turn' (1965)

0:00	Introduction	The metre has been changed from the original $\frac{3}{4}$ waltz to a regular four-beat jazz pattern with a pizzicato walking bass and swing quavers. Although the key is G minor (transposed to exploit Simone's rich low register), the introduction deceptively suggests B♭ major, the relative major. The first chord is E♭/F – the F in the bass is the dominant of B♭. After six bars the piano melody begins in B♭ major, setting up the sound of the accompaniment for the first verse.
0:19	Verse 1, 'Though some may reach for the stars'	Simone's singing is relaxed, with a gentle jazz swing. The melody is arranged in four-bar phrases in a $\frac{4}{4}$ time signature. For example, bars 1–8 of the $\frac{3}{4}$ melody become bars 1–4 of Simone's version. All that remains of the waltz metre are a few sung triplets. Simone is syncopated and flexible with the rhythms: each phrase is sung differently. There is a firm four-beat feel in the pizzicato walking bass, pushing the music forward. The piano countermelody fills in the texture. Staccato trombone chords in a syncopated rhythm.
0:47	Chorus, 'Tomorrow is my turn, no more doubts, no more fears'	The faster pace of this arrangement provides a challenge in the chorus. Each phrase is quickly followed by the next. There are few opportunities to snatch a breath. Simone has to articulate the words and phrase the melody in a musical way. Backing singers (singing 'Ah') and violins accompany the opening phrases (and their repeat).
1:11	Link	The eight-bar link uses chromatic changes of harmony involving a rising semitone (Gm – E♭/G – Gm6), a pattern known for its use in the 'James Bond Theme', particularly when heard on brass instruments.
1:25	Verse 2, 'When the summer is gone, there's another to come'	Simone begins the verse on a sustained A ('When') as the link is ending. She varies the melody slightly, occasionally selecting higher notes. The message of the final lines ('But, honey, it's too late to regret, what is gone will be no more') is underlined by returning to her rich lower register.
1:53	Chorus	Simone continues to vary the melody. Backing singers respond with short motifs: 'Tomorrow, my turn'. She pauses on a low A for 'concern'. Her scat cadenza on the dominant chord expressively repeats the semitone E♭ – D, then up to another semitone B♭ – A, ending on the held G of the final perfect cadence.
2:26	Coda	The chord progression from the link is repeated, a tempo, until the fade.

From the album *I Put A Spell On You*. Recorded in 1965 for Philips Records.

Comparative versions

Charles Aznavour

'L'amour c'est comme un jour', from *Aznavour: Best Of 40 Chansons* (recorded 1962; album by EMI Music Netherlands, 2013). Original version (sung in French). Key: D minor.

Aznavour's recording has the following characteristics:

- Moderate waltz tempo.
- Lyrics are for a love song. The opening lines are: 'Le soleil brille à pleins feux, Mais je ne vois que tes yeux.' (The sun burns brightly, but I only see your eyes).
- Aznavour is flexible with the printed crotchet rhythm. Example: he changes the rhythm to follow the natural rhythm of the words in bars 1–2. After a short crotchet 'Mais', he delays the rest of the line, then uses faster movement in quavers to complete the phrase. He creates a relaxed, spontaneous response to the words - tender, thoughtful, sincere.
- Orchestra is mostly strings - also harp, glockenspiel. Pizzicato bass notes on the strong beats of the waltz.
- Countermelody in violins, in duet with the voice: expressive ascending intervals, sighing motif (on beats 2 and 3), fills out the quavers in the waltz rhythm. Fuller string lines in the chorus, e.g. lower opening lines in the violas, answered by violins, then into harmony.
- Lengthens the last few notes to establish the ending. Soft violin melody to finish in D minor.

Rhiannon Giddens

From *Tomorrow Is My Turn* (Nonesuch, 2015). Key: A minor.

Rhiannon Giddens (b. 1977) is from North Carolina. A singer, violinist and banjo player, she has worked mostly with her folk band, Carolina Chocolate Drops. *Tomorrow Is My Turn* is her first solo album.

The track includes:

- Slow waltz tempo. Plucked bass and brushes on snare drum keep the beat.
- A clear, bright tone from Giddens, consistent through her range, with clear diction. Confident, expressive phrasing at the slow tempo. Begins unaccompanied, no introduction.
- Rearranged words, e.g. last lines of Verse 1 are taken from Verse 2.
- Solo strings - violins, cello - beginning with tremolo in Verse 1, low cello phrases, add to reflective mood. Brighter violin countermelodies, in 3rds.
- Verse 2 change to pizzicato violins at 'When summer is gone'. Role of strings becomes more intricate in chorus: rich string texture, overlapping melodies, interchange between violins and cello.
- A change of mood in the ending: strings stop, slower; Giddens sings a short descending phrase on 'concern'; last line is unaccompanied; brief, restrained instrumental finish.

Discussion

- Which of these versions do you prefer?
- What are their strengths and weaknesses?
- How do the choices of metre and tempo affect each song?

- What does Nina Simone add in the $\frac{4}{4}$ version that is missing in the waltz versions? What is lost?
- Compare the role of the strings in the three versions.
- What do the English words mean? How do Simone and Giddens interpret them?

AS PRESCRIBED WORK 2018

'Feeling Good'

This song was written for the English musical *The Roar of the Greasepaint – The Smell Of The Crowd*, first performed in Nottingham in 1964. The following year the show reached the New York stage.

'Feeling Good' was sung by Gilbert Price, whose manager, Andrew Stroud, was also Nina Simone's husband and manager. Price's recording (on the recording by the original Broadway cast) is surprisingly different from Simone's.

You may also find a version sung by Anthony Newley, the song's co-writer. Both show 'Feeling Good' as it was originally conceived for musical theatre. The partnership of Leslie Bricusse and Anthony Newley also wrote Sammy Davis Jr.'s hit song 'What Kind Of Fool Am I?' (see page 158) and went on to collaborate on the film of *Willie Wonka And The Chocolate Factory* (1971).

Nina Simone sings the song in G minor.

Harmony

Nina Simone: 'Feeling Good' (1965)

0:00	Introduction 'Birds flying high'	Unaccompanied first 12 bars, in free time, acts as an introduction to the song. Her distinctive low register comes across clearly. The range is from D below middle C to the B♭ nearly two octaves above. The silences between the short phrases make each phrase have an impact.
0:38	Verse 1 'Fish in the sea'	The band enters with a heavy descending bass riff, dominated by the sound of trombones. The example shows the unusual length of 11 bars for this phrase. Gm/B♭–Am–D7 in bar 8 sets up a perfect cadence, but the unexpected C in the bass of the next chord (Gm/C) delays it until the bars 9–10. The instrumental link uses the same chord progression as the link passage in 'Tomorrow Is My Turn'.
1:19	Verse 2 'Dragonfly out in the sun'	The repeated quavers are replaced with sustained chords, allowing Simone expressive flexibility with the rhythm of her melody. The pitches outline a blues scale of G minor, for example in the ascending opening phrase.
1:48	Verse 3 'Stars when you shine'	The highlight of the verse is 'Freedom in mine', suddenly going up to B♭ in the higher register.
2:18	Coda	Vocal cadenza in free time, accompanied by sustained chords. The mood is tense and dramatic, building up the suspense for the final chord. The 'mechanical fade' at the end of the recording was a common studio device in the 1960s.

Words and music by Leslie Bricusse and Anthony Newley. Recorded in 1965 for the album *I Put A Spell On You* for Philips Records.

Comparative versions

Michael Bublé

From *It's Time* (Reprise Records, 2005). Key: E♭ minor.

The Canadian-born singer Michael Bublé (b.1975) has made a very successful international career from singing the standards. For this album he worked with Canadian arranger David Foster (also from Canada). The $\frac{12}{8}$ repeated chords and the bass riff in Simone's version are carried over into this arrangement.

- Large orchestra, big-band sound dominated by trumpets, trombones and saxophones.
- The arrangement carefully matches Bublé's interpretation. He repeats lines in a pre-planned way, with the accompaniment making way.
- The Introduction is accompanied from the beginning (tremolo strings). 'New dawn... new day' is separated with detached chords in synthesised strings. It is shortened, with no repetition of the words, as in the original Newley version. 'Good' is sung unaccompanied, before the band enters.
- Verse 1 introduction extended to four bars, voice repeats 'I'm feeling good'. Band stops before the voice enters.
- Changes of key, climbing a semitone higher each time; band section in E minor (abrupt change of key), Verse 3 in F minor (the band passage is used to modulate to the new key, building up to entry of voice on a top F).
- Extends last verse with three repetitions of 'It's a new dawn, it's a new day, it's a new life'. Builds higher each time: final time the voice repeats a high A♭ with answering band chords (high F in trumpet). Suddenly quieter for the voice to end 'for me'.
- Coda: 'for me', diminuendo to ***pp***, riff continues for eight bars, then final chord. Bublé makes the most of the contrast, pushing the sighing, expressive repetitions.

Jennifer Hudson

From *I Remember Me* (Arista Records, 2011). Key: C♯ minor.

- Unaccompanied introduction (string tremolo added on 'Breeze'), strong delivery, dramatic pauses between phrases.
- Shortened lyrics, leaving out 'new dawn', so words are: 'It's a new day, and I'm feeling good.' Last note 'good' sung and sustained up the octave.
- $\frac{4}{4}$ feel to the main song (e.g. in the drums), faster tempo. $\frac{12}{8}$ in brass riff and melody but a squarer feel, with melodic phrases starting on the first beat of each bar.
- Verse 2 accompaniment moves in crotchet beats. Studio-created echo effect, repeating the sung words (e.g. 'sun', 'know'). Ends with 'And I'm feeling good'.
- Coda uses layering of voice tracks, with improvised decoration of the final lines. Added string lines to build up texture. Tempo keeps going to the strong final chord.

Discussion

- There are similarities between each of these arrangements. Which of these do you prefer?
- Can Nina Simone's version be related to external events, e.g. the civil rights movement? Does this make it more powerful?
- Compare the treatment of the introductions. How effective are the modulations in Bublé's version?
- How does Hudson's version demonstrate changes in studio technique since Nina Simone's?

Section A

Unfamiliar music

'Love Walked In'

(By George and Ira Gershwin), sung by Frank Sinatra. Duration 2:20.

The song was published in 1937. The recording was made in 1961. The singer is Frank Sinatra. The performance is in D♭ major, a tone lower than the original key.

Lyrics

Love walked right in and drove the shadows away;
Love walked right in and brought my sunniest day.
One magic moment and my heart seemed to know
That love said 'Hello',
Though not a word was spoken.

One look and I forgot the gloom of the past;
One look and I had found my future at last.
One look and I had found a world completely new,
When love walked in with you.

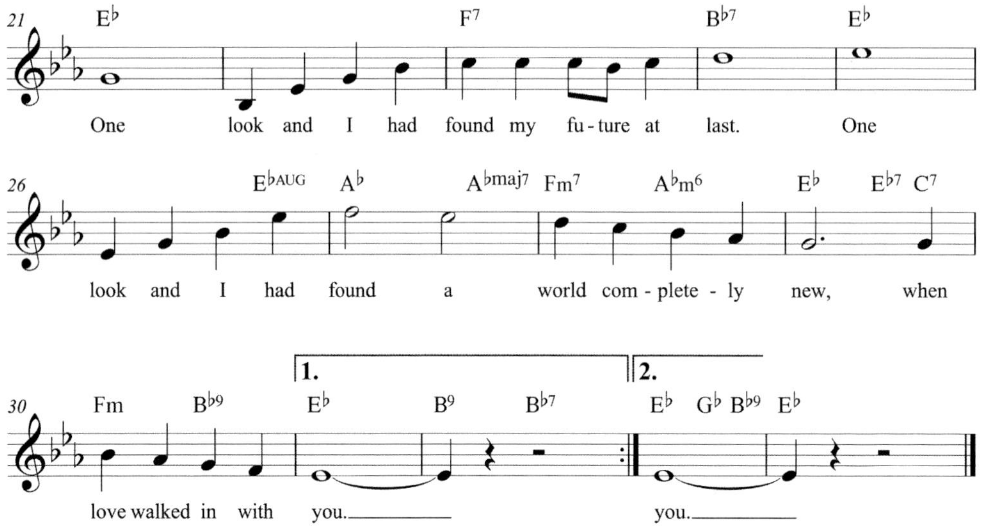

a. Identify the performing technique used to play the double bass part in the accompaniment. (1)

b. Identify the type of bass part played in this recording. Underline your answer. (1)

i. **ground bass** ii. **ostinato** iii. **root notes** iv. **walking bass**

c. Compare the musical treatment of the word 'Love' in bar 1 and in bar 5. (3)

d. Describe TWO other ways in which the singer in the recording interprets or varies the rhythm of bar 1 to bar 8 as it is printed in the lead sheet. (2)

e. Identify the group of instruments that first plays at bar 12. (1)

f. Explain the arranger's treatment of the 1st and 2nd time bars (bars 31–32 and bars 31a–32a) in the recorded version of the song. (2)

g. When the music is repeated the melody is varied. On the stave below, write the pitch and rhythm of the final phrase of the song, **'love walked in with you'** (bar 30, bar 31a and bar 32a), as performed by Sinatra. (4)

h. Identify the instrument that plays the final chord in the recorded performance. Underline your answer. (1)

i. **glockenspiel** ii. **harp** iii. **vibraphone** iv. **xylophone**

'Call It Stormy Monday (But Tuesday Is Just As Bad)'

Words & music by T-Bone Walker. Duration: 3:03.

The song was composed sometime before 1947. This recording was made in 1961. The singer is T-Bone Walker.

Lyrics

The lyrics divide into three verses.

1 **They call it stormy Monday, but Tuesday's just as bad. (x2)**
Wednesday's worse, and Thursday's also sad.

2 Yes, the eagle flies on Friday*, and Saturday I go out to play.
Sunday I go to church, then I kneel down and pray.

3 Lord, have mercy, Lord, have mercy on me.
Lord, have mercy, my heart's in misery.
Crazy 'bout my baby, yeah, send her back to me.

* 'the eagle flies on Friday' refers to payday at the end of the week.

a. Comment on the vocal performance in the song and explain how the singer uses his skills to reflect the meaning of the words. (5)

b. Briefly compare T-Bone Walker's singing in this song with that of one other blues singer of your choice. (4)

c. Explain how the use of instruments in this song is characteristic of blues of the mid-20th century. (6)

Section B

Familiar music

Aim to write each answer in a single page.

A Level (2018)

Ella Fitzgerald: *The Cole Porter Songbook*

1. Explain the circumstances behind the making of Ella Fitzgerald's recording of this music.
2. Comment on the qualities of Cole Porter as a writer of songs.
3. Compare Ella Fitzgerald's performance of 'Anything Goes' with that of any other artist of your choice.
4. Discuss how harmony and tonality is used to support the lyrics in any two of these songs.
5. Assess the skills needed to sing 'Ev'ry Time We Say Goodbye' and their use in performances of this song by at least two artists.
6. Explain to what extent the issue of *The Cole Porter Songbook* represented a new approach to selling records in the 1950s.

A Level (2019)

Frank Sinatra: *Classic Sinatra 1953-1960*

1. Discuss the role of the arranger Nelson Riddle in Frank Sinatra's recordings.
2. Explain Frank Sinatra's technique as a singer, with examples from one of the prescribed songs.
3. Outline some of the techniques of harmony and tonality used in the big band arrangements made for Frank Sinatra.
4. Assess Frank Sinatra's contribution to popular vocal music.
5. Briefly compare performances of 'They Can't Take That Away From Me' by Frank Sinatra and one other singer. Explain which version communicates most vividly with the audience and give your reasons.
6. Describe the business of producing and selling recordings of popular music to the public of the 1950s.

AS Level (2017)

Sammy Davis Jr.: *Greatest Hits, Live*

1. How would you assess Sammy Davis Jr.'s qualities as a singer?
2. Comment on the effectiveness of the arrangement and accompaniment in Davis's performance of 'What Kind Of Fool Am I?'
3. Listen to another version of 'Mr. Bojangles' and compare it with the version recorded by Sammy Davis Jr.
4. Explain the challenges for an African-American singer in developing a career in recording, radio and television during the mid-20th century.

AS Level (2018)

Nina Simone: *I Put A Spell On You*

1. Outline the differences and similarities between Nina Simone's 'Tomorrow Is My Turn' and that of another singer of your choice.
2. Explain the role of recording and record companies in the early career of Nina Simone.
3. Discuss the use of instruments in the arrangement of 'I Put A Spell On You'.
4. How would you explain Nina Simone's success as a performer?

From Jelly Roll Morton to Courtney Pine

OVERVIEW

From its emergence in the bars and brothels of downtown New Orleans, jazz music has had a long and varied history. Alongside its rhythmic innovations, it has always relied heavily on the harmonic language of traditional Western classical music.

Players often came from poor backgrounds with a self-taught approach to music education – some didn't read music. At its core there is a sense of equality and fair play, with band members often getting an equal chance to take their turn in the spotlight.

The Count Basie Orchestra

The term 'jazz' was hardly known in 1910. There were many other recognised popular styles of music, such as ragtime, which popularised the use of syncopated rhythms, and vaudeville, the popular music-hall style of the time. When the sheet music for W. C. Handy's 'Memphis Blues' was published in 1912, the blues began to reach a wider audience in America, paving the way for jazz a few years later.

Many critics credit New Orleans as the birthplace of jazz. 'Jelly Roll' Morton published his 'Jelly Roll Blues' there in 1915, and the recording company Victor released the first commercial recordings made by The Original Dixieland Jass Band in 1917. The cornet player and bandleader Joe 'King' Oliver and his pupil Louis Armstrong left New Orleans and took their musical style north to the cities of Chicago and New York around this time, as did many other jazz musicians.

In the 1920s and 1930s, jazz was in huge demand. Live bands supported dance socials, which were a very popular activity. Bandleaders and soloists became famous through recordings and radio broadcasts. Commercial opportunities generally favoured white musicians, but many of the outstanding jazz musicians of the time were black Americans, and their music enjoyed considerable popularity.

During the Second World War, swing bands came under financial pressure and many of them folded. Musicians such as Dizzy Gillespie, Charlie Parker and Thelonious Monk pioneered bebop, a fast-paced, virtuosic style of playing which made more demands on audiences.

In response, musicians such as Miles Davis developed slower, more thoughtful styles, such as cool jazz, which started in the 1950s. The link with dance had weakened: jazz remained popular, but it was intended for listening rather than dancing, and was competing with other styles for commercial attention. **Jazz-rock fusion** became one way for jazz to respond to the newer styles of the 1960s and 1970s.

Opposite: Miles Davis, photographed in 1959

Although bebop provides much of the standard language of recent and present-day jazz, modern jazz is hugely varied. Performers, arrangers and composers now train and work not only in the United States but all over the world.

What you should know

There is a summary of the requirements for this Area of Study in the OCR specification. There are also two lists of suggested listening, but you and your teachers are free to choose your own suitable programme of listening. You can use the suggested pieces in the specification or in this study guide.

You must find examples to cover the following:

- Styles of jazz
- Musical elements
- Conditions and context.

For A Level you need to know about all the styles listed, explain the music (using examples from your chosen listening) and be able to discuss the background from 1910 to the present day.

For AS Level in 2017 you need to know about early jazz and swing, explain the music (using examples from the prescribed pieces by Duke Ellington) and be able to discuss the background to early jazz and swing.

For AS Level in 2018 you need to know about cool jazz and bebop, explain the music (using examples from 'So What' by Miles Davis) and be able to discuss the background to cool jazz and bebop.

LISTEN, LISTEN, LISTEN

Listening to jazz music is a vital part of understanding it, and the examples in this book are a starting point. Find other jazz works, listen to recordings, and find scores and transcriptions to help you. If possible, listen to live jazz. Better still, develop your own skills in improvising and try to work with a group.

Keep a notebook or folder with details of your jazz listening. For the essay question in the examination you will need to show that:

- You are **familiar with the music**. Aim to learn the music well enough to be able to discuss it confidently.
- You can **listen carefully** to it and can **analyse** the music. This means being able to explain overall features and discuss details of the music and the performances.
- You know the **technical language** to discuss jazz convincingly. Reviews of jazz are sometimes aimed at fans, and don't give much musical detail. Look for information aimed at students and musicians, including materials from academic publications.
- You know the **background** to the music and its performers. Some of the information is given in this study guide. Find out more about these topics. Conduct your own research.
- You are able to make **critical judgements**. This means using your knowledge of the music and the background to express an opinion. You must be able to discuss change over time, strengths and weaknesses, and successes and failures. You have to be able to support your opinions with reason and evidence.

Important features of jazz

Improvisation

Professional jazz musicians must be able to make up music spontaneously, playing in any key as required. Some arrangements are notated or have notated sections, but by and large, instrumental solos are improvised. Musicians can rely on familiar melodic shapes or 'licks' to help build their improvisations.

Changes

Many jazz pieces use a set pattern of chords or 'changes', such as a 12-bar blues or 32-bar song form (**AABA**). Players are often expected to know the most familiar tunes, or 'standards', and be able to play them in any key.

Tone and timbre

Jazz instrumentalists use a variety of ways to alter the sound of a note. Vibrato can be fast or slow. A rough or breathy tone can be used deliberately. There are different types of mutes to vary the sound of brass instruments. Variety of attack and decay – how notes begin and end – is also an important characteristic of jazz.

Blues intonation

A blue note is usually the flattened 3rd, 5th or 7th of the scale. Because the scale derives from African vocal music, the tuning of these notes is often microtonal (you'll hear this on guitars and wind instruments), and is often emphasised with a bend or a growl.

Walking bass

Early jazz bass parts were frequently march-like, based around tonic and dominant notes. The walking bass (on a plucked double bass) emerged in the 1930s and 1940s. The bass line keeps the beat, but it also rises and falls, improvising around chords in a combination of scale and broken-chord patterns. It has a sense of shape and direction.

Rhythm section

This is usually made up of piano, guitar, double bass and drums. Early jazz often used banjo, with a tuba for the bass. Later jazz (e.g. Miles Davis's later works) has electric alternatives for acoustic instruments: bass guitar, electric guitars and keyboards.

Front line

The instruments playing the melody line. New Orleans style (also known as 'Dixieland') featured trumpet (or cornet), clarinet and trombone. The big bands used saxophones as the basis of the reed section and for solos.

Swing

The jazz style of the 1930s and 1940s is often known as 'swing'. However, swing is also used to describe the rhythmic feeling of the jazz music from this era. Ragtime was known for using syncopation. Jazz gave the straight eighth-notes of ragtime (eight even quavers in a four-beat bar) a lilting feeling by lengthening the first quaver of every pair, and shortening the following note. Anticipating or delaying beats against the steady beat of the rhythm section adds to the feeling of swing.

JAZZ INSTRUMENTAL TECHNIQUES

Jazz uses a wide range of instrumental techniques for varying the sound, and it is a good idea to find out about these to help deepen your understanding of the genre. Try finding out about techniques for varying the sound of a trumpet. You could draw a chart to show different sounds and the techniques used by the player.

Search for pitch bends on YouTube:

- **Fall** (fall-off or drop)
- **Doit** (pronounced 'doyt')
- **Scoop**
- **Smear**.

You could also research different trumpet mutes:

- **Harmon mute** (with/without stem)
- **Plunger**
- **Straight**
- **Cup**.

DEFINING JAZZ

Having a working definition of what jazz is can really help when analysing it. However, many people disagree about what constitutes jazz. Does jazz have to swing? Does it have to be improvised? Is having jazzy timbres and rhythms enough? Keep these questions in mind throughout this chapter.

Origins of jazz

Ragtime

In the 1890s there was a craze for ragtime music in the United States of America. Scott Joplin was the leading composer, writing and publishing piano 'rags' at a time when playing the piano was a popular form of home entertainment. Many other composers followed suit to cash in on the new fashion.

Ragtime arrangements for ensembles were published, and there was a huge demand for music for dancing. As ragtime became popular, dance bands adapted melodies to the new style by 'ragging' well-known melodies – in other words, they played a syncopated version.

Features of ragtime include:

- A march-style accompaniment, with a strong tonic-dominant bass and off-beat chords.
- A syncopated melody, contrasting rhythmically with the strict beat of the accompaniment.
- Several sections, each with its own theme. Bridge passages could be used to modulate between keys.

Joplin disliked fast performances of his ragtime music. He preferred moderate speeds and an elegant style, reflecting the values of the respectable, educated black middle class. By contrast, the younger generation of New Orleans musicians, such as Jelly Roll Morton and Sidney Bechet, were playing in the 'hotter', syncopated style preferred in New Orleans.

New Orleans

New Orleans lies at the mouth of the Mississippi river. It was sold by Napoleon in 1803 to the United States as part of the Louisiana Purchase. It had been in Spanish and French hands and retained much of its French character, language and customs throughout the 19th century. There was a large community of Creole people (people of French ancestry), many living in the prosperous French Quarter of the city. They looked to Europe as a model for music in the opera houses and for popular dance entertainment.

While Downtown was largely French-speaking, the large black and American immigrant population of Uptown New Orleans spoke English. The music of the black population who lived in the Uptown districts was more outgoing and rhythmic in character, more closely related to the music of the plantations. King Oliver, Louis Armstrong and other significant early jazz musicians came from this part of New Orleans.

King Oliver's Creole Jazz Band. King Oliver (seated); Louis Armstrong (third from right); Lil' Hardin (far right)

Stories of the beginnings of jazz are sometimes linked to an area of 38 blocks known as Storyville (locals called it The District). From 1896 the local politicians attempted to restrict prostitution to this part of the city. Some Storyville establishments hired a 'professor' (a pianist) to entertain clients on the piano or to organise a small band, playing until the early hours of the morning. Visitors from other parts of the country heard jazz there for the first time, but the role of Storyville as the birthplace of jazz is sometimes exaggerated. Storyville was 'closed down' in 1917, after a public outcry against the frequent violence and perceived immorality of the district.

Early jazz

The early New Orleans style

From New Orleans to Chicago, jazz was an unstoppable phenomenon in the 1920s. Recordings from the early years of jazz have a raw energy reflecting the one-take speed at which they were recorded.

The main features of early jazz were:

- Small groups. → from where they originally came from small bands in small venues
- Polyphonic texture: e.g. trumpet melody, elaborate clarinet countermelody in a higher register, and a trombone countermelody of more sustained notes. This form of collective improvisation is sometimes known as 'New Orleans polyphony'. all improvising together.
- A rhythm section (because it was loud): piano/banjo to play chords ('comping'), a bass on either plucked double bass, or brass such as trombone or tuba, and simple percussion – the drum kit had not been developed yet.
- A chorus structure, with the music improvised around the chord changes.
- Blues was popular for slower music, with faster music in ragtime or march styles, often responding to the dance fashions of the 1920s (e.g. the **Charleston** or the **Black Bottom**).

Jelly Roll Morton

Jelly Roll Morton (1890–1941) grew up in New Orleans in a Creole family. As a young man he worked in Storyville, both as a musician and as a pimp and gambler. After Storyville closed down, he worked in California before settling in 1923 in Chicago.

Demand for jazz was high during this period. Morton's publishers paid for the recording sessions and (unusually) for the rehearsals. He recruited the best New Orleans players, called them the Red Hot Peppers and paid fixed fees: $5 per rehearsal and $15 per recording. He preferred working with players who could read music, often Creoles like

→ often educated, unlike most African Americans, but most Creole's considered themselves a cut above African Americans though & more were educated

himself. Some sections would be notated, but he allowed improvised solos. He demanded high standards and this resulted in some of the best recordings of early jazz.

Jelly Roll Morton's 'Black Bottom Stomp' is based on two sets of changes, labelled here as **A** and **B**.

A (B♭ major, 16 bars)

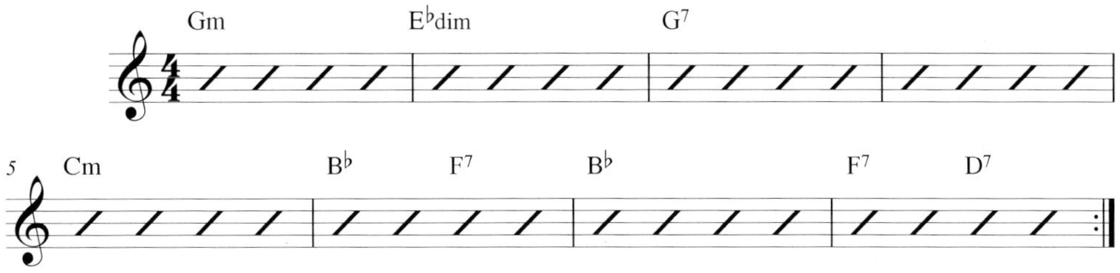

B (E♭ major, 20 bars)

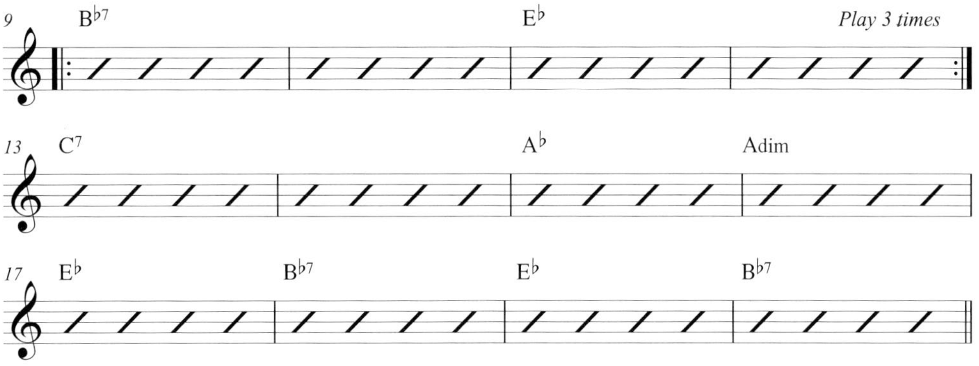

'Black Bottom Stomp' combines sections of collective improvisation (typical of the New Orleans style) with short instrumental solos (such as the piano solo, halfway through the piece). The three **A** choruses in B♭ major seem like an extended introduction. Three of the choruses in the E♭ major section are in the New Orleans polyphonic style, i.e. for full band with multiple melodic lines. The section starts with one chorus in this style (chorus **B**^{1}), then a few solos (choruses **B**^{2} to **B**^{5}), and ends with two choruses for the whole band.

Jelly Roll Morton: 'Black Bottom Stomp' (1926)

0:00	Intro	Ensemble	Slides for trumpet and trombone, answered by clarinet.
0:07	**A**^{1}	Ensemble	Front line in the same rhythm: semibreves in first four bars, then a faster syncopated motif. Trumpet and clarinet fills keep the music moving forward between phrases.
0:23	**A**^{2}	Trumpet and ensemble	Four bars of trumpet melody answered by the syncopated motif. Faster movement in bass in second half of the chord pattern.

0:38	**A**^{3}	Clarinet solo	Rhythmic figure in high clarinet and strummed banjo.
0:52	Link	Ensemble	Descending chromatic phrase ending on B♭ – dominant preparation for change of key to E♭ major.
0:56	**B**^{1}	Ensemble	Polyphony, typical of the New Orleans style. Trumpet melody, counter-melodies in clarinet (wide range, rapid descending arpeggios) and trombone (note the use of glissando, e.g. in the break at bar 8).
1:15	**B**^{2}	Clarinet solo	Solo in the clarinet's lower **chalumeau** register. Secondary rag rhythm (a repeated pattern of three quavers creating a cross-rhythm) is a common feature of ragtime and dance music of this period.
1:33	**B**^{3}	Piano solo	Jelly Roll Morton's piano solo uses **stride** technique: piano left hand alternates between bass and chords.
1:51	**B**^{4}	Trumpet solo	Trumpet is muted. **Stop-time** accompaniment is untidy, but recording the track again was not the practice at this time.
2:10	**B**^{5}	Banjo solo	A secondary rag pattern. No front line instruments. Bass plays 'slap' pizzicato: the string is allowed to hit the fingerboard.
2:28	**B**^{6}	Ensemble	New Orleans polyphony. Break on cymbal with the player using a hand to stop the sound.
2:48	**B**^{7}	Ensemble	New Orleans polyphony. Final chorus adds excitement with off-beat snare drum. Elaborate trombone countermelody in **tailgate** style.

Jelly Roll Morton & His Red Hot Peppers Vol. 1, Chicago Days 1926/27, EPM Jazz Archives

The players on this recording are:

- Kid Ory, trombone
- Omer Simeon, clarinet
- Jelly Roll Morton, piano
- Johnny St. Cyr, banjo
- John Lindsay, double bass
- Andrew Hilaire, drums
- George Mitchell, trumpet.

Louis Armstrong

The Hot Five and Hot Seven recordings

→ small groups of early jazz.

Like Jelly Roll Morton's Red Hot Peppers, the Hot Five only worked together in the recording studio. Originally from New Orleans, Louis Armstrong (1901–1971) had moved north to Chicago, following his mentor King Oliver. Armstrong became a successful soloist with the Fletcher Henderson Orchestra in New York.

Lil Hardin, Armstrong's wife and an accomplished jazz pianist, composer, arranger, singer and bandleader in her own right, persuaded him to work in Chicago with a promise of a job at Bill Bottom's Dreamland Cafe for $75 a week. Together they worked on the music for the recording contract with the Okeh Phonograph Corporation.

The 'Hot Five' and 'Hot Seven' recordings were commercially very successful. Armstrong's solo trumpet playing was the main selling point. Later recordings featured more of his work and fewer ensemble choruses. Some of the discs were sold with a free photograph of the star soloist.

Louis Armstrong's solos were published so that trumpeters could play them, and his playing style was much imitated. It featured:

- A powerful tone over a wide range, colouring individual notes with vibrato, shakes, rips and falls.
- Inventive improvisations shaped to give a bold, dominating presence in the group.
- The replacement of straight quavers of ragtime with swing quavers.
- Much more freedom with rubato, syncopation, cross-rhythms and rhythmic displacement (playing a whole phrase behind or before the beat).
- 'Scat', a new vocal style in which the soloist improvises using nonsense syllables.

Lil Hardin: 'Hotter Than That' (1927)

0:00	Intro	8 bars	
0:09	Chorus 1	32 bars	Trumpet solo.
0:45	Chorus 2	32 bars	Clarinet solo.
1:21	Chorus 3	32 bars	Vocal solo.
1:56	Duet	16 bars	Voice and guitar.
2:14	Link	4 bars	Piano.
2:18	Chorus 4	32 bars	16 bars: Trombone solo. 16 bars: Ensemble.
2:51	Coda	10 bars	Voice and guitar.

Louis Armstrong: 25 Greatest Hot Fives & Sevens, ASV

The original Hot Five line-up was:

- Louis Armstrong, trumpet
- Lil Hardin, piano
- Kid Ory, trombone
- Johnny Dodds, clarinet
- Lonnie Johnson, guitar.

Louis Armstrong: 'West End Blues' (1928)

0:00	Intro	Trumpet solo	A trumpet cadenza is a bold way to begin. Covers over two octaves. Arpeggio-like at the beginning, then descends in double time to the dominant of B♭.
0:15	Chorus 1	Trumpet solo	12-bar blues structure. Trumpet solo begins simply, then elaborates with faster movement. Piano and banjo play detached chords on each crotchet beat.
0:49	Chorus 2	Trombone solo	The solo is simpler in style, high in register. Tremolo chords in piano, banjo continues to keep time. Rhythm in a bock-a-da-bock (small cymbals arranged as tongs).
1:24	Chorus 3	Duet clarinet and voice	Call and response between clarinet and scat voice.
1:59	Chorus 4	Piano solo	Earl Hines' solo in stride style. He was known for his 'trumpet style' of piano playing (e.g. the strong melody and right-hand octaves in the middle of this chorus).
2:32	Chorus 5	Trumpet solo	Armstrong sustains a high B♭ for 16 beats. Followed by a virtuosic double time passage based on the notes of the introduction.

Louis Armstrong: 25 Greatest Hot Fives & Sevens, ASV

By 1928 the Hot Five line-up had completely changed, with Lil Hardin and Louis Armstrong drifting apart. The line-up was:

- Louis Armstrong, trumpet and vocal
- Fred Robinson, trombone
- Jimmy Strong, clarinet
- Earl Hines (who replaced Lil Hardin), piano
- Mancy Carr, banjo
- Zutty Singleton, drums.

Swing

Big bands and tea dances

By the end of the 1920s there was growing public demand for the new style of jazz known as swing. An important element in swing was the use of a much larger band (a big band or swing band) than in early jazz, because the music often accompanied dancing at venues of considerable size.

The size of the band meant that arrangements became important. In the 1920s, bandleaders such as Paul Whiteman, Fletcher Henderson and Jimmie Lunceford established the sound of the swing band:

- Sections of instruments, usually brass (trumpets and trombones) and reeds (saxophones and clarinet). The sections could play riffs in unison or in harmony, one player to each note of a chord, with the melody in the highest part.
- Sections could be used for antiphonal effects, e.g. answering each other (known as call and response) or playing fills between phrases.
- The rhythm section becomes more important in providing the rhythmic momentum and creating the background for swing. The pizzicato double bass uses a variety of rhythms, including the walking style. The strummed chords in rhythm guitar style and the addition of hi-hat to the drums.
- Solo improvisation remains important, with rich harmonies and a range of timbres available to accompany the soloist.

SWING AND STRIDE

Listen to the Fletcher Henderson style in his recording of 'Henderson Stomp' (1926). The **stride** style piano solo is by Fats Waller. Benny Goodman's 1940 version of 'Henderson Stomp' features a virtuosic Goodman clarinet solo.

The popularity of the bands continued into the 1930s and 1940s. They were separated racially: the climate of the time made it very difficult for white and black players to play in the same club or concert. Commercial opportunities were greater for the white bands. Paul Whiteman is sometimes criticised for smoothing over the rougher edges of jazz in order to appeal to a mass market. Benny Goodman consciously incorporated some of the 'hotter' characteristics of the black bands, and was leader of the first racially integrated band. Goodman bought up the arrangements of Fletcher Henderson and employed him as an arranger and pianist.

Count Basie

One of the outstanding bandleaders was William James 'Count' Basie (1904–1984). He was originally from Kansas City, Missouri, where the popular style had a more relaxed feel, compared with New York jazz, and used riffs more often.

Count Basie: 'Jumpin' At The Woodside' (1938)

0:00	Intro	8 bars	Rhythm section.
0:08	Chorus 1	32 bars **AABA**	Ensemble. Alto sax solo for **B** section (0:24).
0:39	Chorus 2	32 bars **AABA**	Ensemble. Basie's piano solo in **B** (0:55).
1:09	Chorus 3	32 bars **AABA**	Trumpet solo (Buck Clayton). In **B** (1:26) trombones drop out, sustained chords in saxophones. The final **A** section riff quotes the opening of 'Lester Leaps In', highlighting what Lester Young is about to play.
1:40	Chorus 4	32 bars **AABA**	Tenor sax solo (Lester Young). His style of improvisation develops interesting melodic lines, sometimes away from the chord (anticipating techniques in bebop).
2:14	Chorus 5	48 bars **AAAAAA**	Duet for clarinet and trombone, then clarinet solo. No **B** section.

Count Basie 1937-1943, Giants of Jazz, ASIN: B000UCH95M

Basie was one of the most successful and long-lasting of the bandleaders. When the big bands folded after the 1940s, Basie (like Duke Ellington) managed to keep a band going until his death.

- BBC in England - 192
- 1928 it becomes a corporation (run by national government) not just company.

Duke Ellington

→ He came from an upper-middle class

Edward Kennedy 'Duke' Ellington (1899–1974) was from Washington D.C. and was introduced to classical piano by music-loving parents. The teenage Ellington modelled his playing on the stride pianists such as James P. Johnson.

He moved to New York, where his band, the Washingtonians, performed at the Kentucky Club, toured dance venues. He made his first recordings with this band and broadcast on local radio.

→ nightclub

Early broadcasting days

Duke Ellington (left) and his orchestra

→ Very populated area by elite white people who would go despite being a black ghetto area.

From 1927 to 1931 Ellington's band was at the Cotton Club in Harlem. He came to national attention through weekly radio broadcasts from the club on NBC. His manager Irving Mills was a shrewd publicist. He ensured that Ellington had more exposure than other black bands. Mills promoted Ellington as a serious artist while also making sure that he was turning out commercially successful hit songs. Recordings of the band's music were being distributed all over the world. In 1933 the band toured Europe, where Ellington's work as the leading composer of jazz was being compared with contemporary classical composers.

– Stravinski said Ellington was "one of the most important composers of the 20th century" ⚠

running 10th's in the base, quick LH → stride piano

Following a 1939 tour of Europe, Ellington and Mills split. Ellington made a series of recordings as part of a new contract with RCA Victor. Fresh from its European success, the band was at a peak. It was a settled band: most of the players had been with Ellington a long time.

It was a balanced group – its 15 players divided into:

- Three trumpets
- Three trombones
- Four reeds
- A rhythm section – including Ellington on piano
- Singer Ivie Anderson
- New additions Ben Webster on saxophone and Jimmy Blanton on bass gave Ellington new sounds and techniques to work with.

As a composer he was very sensitive to each member's qualities as a player. He crafted solos and ensemble parts which exploited their individual tone or style of playing. He took up their ideas from rehearsal and integrated them into the music before finalising the written score. Ellington's sound was very personal to him and to his players. Arranger Billy Strayhorn, who joined Ellington at this time, called this method of working 'the Ellington effect'.

Jimmy Blanton's virtuosity and rich tone on bass had an immediate effect on the band. Unusually for the time he was given solos, rather than being restricted to timekeeping – in 'Concerto For Cootie' the bass is used with the horns, for example, to bring out the descending chromatic quavers in the introduction. His playing influenced the other bass players in jazz. Blanton died from tuberculosis in 1941, at the tragically young age of 23 years.

Duke Ellington's orchestra consisted of:

- Johnny Hodges and Otto Hardwick, alto sax
- Barney Bigard, clarinet
- Ben Webster, tenor sax
- Harry Carney, baritone sax
- Wallace Jones, Cootie Williams and Rex Stewart, trumpets
- Lawrence Brown, Joe Nanton and Juan Tizol, trombones
- Fred Guy, guitar
- Duke Ellington, piano
- Jimmy Blanton, bass.

SWING ERA COMPARISONS

Compare Ellington's recordings from the 1940s with examples of earlier Ellington, e.g. 'Creole Rhapsody' (1932) and 'East St Louis Toodle-Oo' (1926 version, performing as Duke Ellington and his Kentucky Club Orchestra).

AS PRESCRIBED WORK 2017

Duke Ellington: 'Ko-Ko' (1940)

0:00	Intro		The four-note repeated E♭ in the baritone sax is the main rhythmic figure of the whole piece.
0:12	Chorus 1	Valve trombone solo	Juan Tizol's solo opens with the four-note rhythm on the pitches B♭–C♭–A♭–G♭, answered by 7th chords in the saxes. Syncopated octave B♭ tones in the piano towards the end of the chorus.
0:32 **0:51**	Chorus 2 Chorus 3	Trombone solo	Joe 'Tricky Sam' Nanton has two choruses, using a 'ya-ya' effect. This technique was his own invention, and involved using a combination of a growling plunger mute and another mute fixed inside the trombone, to create a vocal-like sound. The four-note riff is in the saxes, answered by a brass 'du-wah' (alternating repeated notes quickly between closed and open plunger.) In Chorus 3 the solo starts with the restricted sound of a tight plunger, before returning to the 'ya-ya'.
1:08	Chorus 4	Piano solo	The riff repeats every bar, so the answering 'du-wah' is shorter. The fourth note of the riff, D♭, makes the 7th of the E♭m7 chord.
1:26	Chorus 5	Full ensemble	The riff moves to unison trumpets, back to two-bar phrases, with sustained chords in saxes and trombones. The fourth note of the riff, F, is a more dissonant 9th of the chord, adding to the tension.
1:44	Chorus 6	Double bass and ensemble	A 'chase chorus' between double bass and the band, alternating two-bar phrases.
2:03	Chorus 7	Full ensemble	Final 'shout chorus'. Melody in unison saxophones, with clarinet on the highest note of the sustained chord in brass.
2:22	Coda		Return to the music of the introduction.

Duke Ellington & His Orchestra: *Never No Lament: The Blanton-Webster Band*

The approach to harmony in 'Ko-Ko' is complex:

- The minor key (E♭ minor) is less common for a blues.
- There is a feel of the **Aeolian** mode in the regular use of C♭ and D♭.
- Blue notes are used to create dissonance in chords (for example, the clash of D♭ and D♮ in the saxes in the first riff of Chorus 1).
- Ellington uses whole-tone chords and scales in his piano solo.
- There is more use made of chord extensions in later choruses (for example, 9ths and 11ths in Chorus 7), creating a dissonant effect.

The dark, brooding sound is characteristic of Ellington's 'jungle' style, which he originally developed for the exotic African-style floor shows of the Cotton Club. Despite its origins as entertainment for white audiences, he took his African-American identity seriously. 'Ko-Ko' was intended as part of an opera called *Boola*, which he never completed.

AS PRESCRIBED WORK 2017

Duke Ellington: 'Concerto For Cootie' (1940)

0:00	Intro	8 bars	F major. Opening solo phrase answered by close harmonies in reeds over a descending chromatic bass. Reeds and bass begin in straight eights, then into swung quavers with crescendo to full band.
0:17	**A**	10 bars	Cootie Williams's trumpet solo, closed plunger mute over pixie mute. Answering trombone chords. Pizzicato walking bass in second half leads into an extended band passage (in saxes, one trombone on lowest note of chords).
0:41	**A**^{1}	10 bars	Answering reeds on the repeat, with brass added in the last two bars.
1:07	**B**	8 bars	Trumpet growl, plunger half open. Walking bass, more of a swing feel.
1:25	**A**^{2}	8 bars	As opening **A**, with trombones reharmonised.
1:45	Link	4 bars	Loud descending chromatic figure on unison trombones, syncopated chords in band, modulating to a new key.
1:56	**C**	16 bars	D♭ major. Bright, open tone on solo. Three variations on the same phrase in middle and high registers (up to a top B♭, concert A♭).

2:34	Link	2 bars	Return modulation to F major over quavers in the bass.
2:38	**A**^{3}	6 bars	F major. Return of **A** melody, with inverted second phrase. Reeds accompany.
2:53	Coda	10 bars	Ascending scale (beginning on the dominant C) brings in the final section in full band. Repeated high notes in trumpet answering. Reduced instrumentation to finish quietly.

Duke Ellington & His Orchestra: *Never No Lament: The Blanton-Webster Band*

'Concerto For Cootie' was later rearranged as a song, 'Do Nothing 'Til You Hear From Me', first recorded by Woody Herman in 1943. This version has more usual eight-bar sections, more suitable for a vocal hit.

AS PRESCRIBED WORK 2017

Duke Ellington: 'Harlem Air Shaft' (1940)

0:00	Intro	12 bars	12 bars. Antiphonal use of sections: brass begin, saxophones lead the middle 4 bars, trombones at the end. Strong rhythm section: Sonny Greer plays drums with brushes, guitar, walking bass, Ellington adds piano fills.
0:15	Chorus 1	32 bars **AABA**	Melody in unison saxes, answered by muted trumpets in chords. In **B** chordal saxophones in call and response with trombone solo from Joe Nanton (growl technique, as in 'Ko-Ko').
0:55	Chorus 2	32 bars **AABA**	Rhythm section stops for four bars. Saxes in harmony, sliding up to high sustained notes, then more intricate riffs. Cootie Williams improvises on solo trumpet.
1:35	Chorus 3	32 bars **AABA**	Trombones melody in harmony (trumpets added for the sustained chords in **B**), countermelody in saxes. Barney Bigard improvises clarinet solo. Jimmy Blanton on bass and Sonny Greer on drums drive the music forward.
2:14	Chorus 4	32 bars **AABA**	Drops to piano, then crescendo to a loud conclusion. Clarinet solo continues quietly, then stops for the muted trumpet, returning again for the **B** section and the end. Overlapping short repeated motifs create excitement in final **A** section.

Duke Ellington & His Orchestra: *Never No Lament: The Blanton-Webster Band*

Ellington later described 'Harlem Air Shaft' - which portrays noises and smells sensed through a ventilation shaft - in terms of a programme. Opinion is divided about whether he made up the background story after the music was written. Some say that he often linked music with images and that the programme came before the music. For example:

- During the intro the different sections in different keys suggest the groups of people living their own lives.
- The high saxes in Chorus 2 and the drums re-entering represent the high aerial's fall and crash.
- The quiet clarinet and muted trumpet at the beginning of Chorus 4 represent the 'intimate gossip'.

THE HOT BACH

'...So much goes on in a Harlem air shaft. You get the full essence of Harlem in an air shaft. You hear fights, you smell dinner, you hear people making love. You hear intimate gossip floating down. You hear the radio. An air shaft is one great big loudspeaker. You see your neighbor's laundry. You hear the janitor's dogs. The man upstairs' aerial falls down and breaks your window. You smell coffee... I tried to put all that in "Harlem Air Shaft".'

Duke Ellington, quoted in Richard O. Boyer's column, 'The Hot Bach' for *The New Yorker* (1944).

Bebop

Jazz after the Second World War

The Second World War had an extremely disruptive effect on big bands, many of whose members enlisted or toured Europe, performing for Allied troops.

Many singers (like Sinatra) left to begin their own solo careers. Although Count Basie and Duke Ellington successfully kept their bands going, big bands declined in popularity as people thirsted for something new. Enter bebop!

Charlie Parker

Bebop developed in New York in the 1940s. The trumpeter Dizzy Gillespie and pianist Thelonious Monk experimented with the new style in small groups. Soon they were joined by Charlie Parker on alto saxophone.

They shared an interest in experimenting with what jazz could do. They explored new scales and new chord formations using harmonic developments by classical composers, such as Ravel and Bartók. With the recording industry suspended because of strikes, there are few recorded examples of the beginning of bebop. By the time Parker recorded 'Ko-Ko' in 1945, the new style was well established.

The main features of bebop were:

- Small groups of players, but also some larger bands.
- Theme (the **head**) at the beginning, followed by improvised solo choruses, with the head repeated at the end.
- Fast solos, mainly on trumpet or saxophone. Unpredictable melodies, irregular phrases, covering a wide range.
- Timekeeping by walking bass and ride cymbal. 'Chattering' drums respond more to the solos, with unexpected accents or **bombs**.
- Reharmonisation of standard chord changes, e.g. chord substitutions, flattened 5ths, chromaticism, unusual scales.

Audiences found bebop challenging. Bebop came to be regarded as music to listen to rather than for dance. It was strikingly different to commercially successful swing, which was dominated by white bandleaders. The intellectual approach to jazz reinforced the sense of identity and artistic achievement of African-American musicians.

ie Parker: 'Ornithology' (1946)

0:00	Intro	Drums	
0:05	Theme	Ensemble	
0:39	Chorus 1	Alto sax solo	Charlie Parker
1:16	Chorus 2	Trumpet solo	Miles Davis
1:13	Chorus 3	Tenor sax solo	Lucky Thompson
2:20	Theme	Ensemble	

Charlie Parker: Ornithology (1945-1947), Naxos Jazz Legends

'Ornithology' is set to the chord progression of 'How High The Moon'. Each chorus is 32 bars long. The more relaxed tempo and accessible melodic style make it an easier introduction to bebop than 'Ko-Ko'. Parker recorded this in Los Angeles for his new contract with the Dial label.

It also features the 19-year-old Miles Davis on trumpet. The players are:

- Miles Davis, trumpet
- Charlie Parker, alto sax
- Lucky Thompson, tenor sax
- Dodo Marmarosa, piano
- Arvin Garrison, guitar
- Vic McMillan, bass
- Roy Porter, drums.

Parker had not rehearsed with the group before the recording session – with an addiction to heroin he was less than reliable. The recording session also included 'A Night In Tunisia' and 'Moose The Mooche'.

Charlie Parker: 'Ko-Ko' (1945)

0:00	Intro	32 bars	**A** Alto saxophone and trumpet melody in octaves **A** Trumpet **B** Alto saxophone **A** Alto saxophone and trumpet in 3rds.
0:25	Chorus 1	64 bars	At the beginning of the first bridge section, the repeated notes which begin the phrase are played by alternating different fingerings of the same note.

1:16	Chorus 2	64 bars	A phrase from the clarinet showpiece 'High Society' at the very beginning of the chorus. The bridge section has a highly syncopated broken chord variation on the notes of 'Tea for Two'.
2:07	Drum solo	32 bars	
2:30	Coda	28 bars	Repeat of the head

Charlie Parker: Ornithology (1945-1947), Naxos Jazz Legends

Charlie Parker's Reboppers were:

- Charlie Parker, alto saxophone
- Miles Davis, trumpet
- Dizzy Gillespie, trumpet and piano
- Curly Russell, double bass
- Max Roach, drums.

'Ko-Ko' - not to be confused with Duke Ellington's piece of the same name - is based on the chord changes of 'Cherokee', a song written by British bandleader Ray Noble. Its distinctive feature is its use of the **circle of 5ths** in the bridge section: F♯13 - B9 - E9 - A - D13 - G9 - C9 - F9.

BRIDGE THE GAP

Listen out for the bridge (the B section of an AABA shape) - it will help you understand the structure of the solo choruses.

Parker had a huge influence on young musicians. He set new standards of virtuosity for the next generation of performers. The features of his style were:

- A light, dry saxophone tone, avoiding long vibrato sustained notes.
- Huge variety of melodic ideas packed into an agile, fast-moving solo part in double-time quavers. He had a stock of melodic phrases for use in fast improvisation.
- Some use of quotation, recognisable fragments of music which are inserted into an improvisation.
- Unexpected accents, emphasising the unpredictable and varied phrase lengths. His phrasing cuts across the four-bar or eight-bar phrases implied in the accompaniment.
- Improvising using notes which suggest chord extensions (9ths, 11ths, 13ths) or new interpretations of the accompanying chords. Accenting dissonant notes in the solo part.

STUDYING CHARLIE PARKER

A transcription of Parker's solo is printed in Barry Kernfeld's *What To Listen For In Jazz* (Yale University Press).

Cool jazz

The chilled approach

The significance of Miles Davis and Gil Evans in developing the concept of 'cool jazz' cannot be underestimated.

Miles Davis

Miles Davis (1926–1991) was significant in the development of cool jazz for a number of reasons:

- He was the leader of various groups, and worked closely with other pioneers.
- As a soloist he explored new trumpet sounds and techniques.
- He left an extensive recorded legacy, which has become a model for others.
- He experimented with modal jazz, e.g. his *Kind Of Blue* album.
- His album *Bitches Brew* is a seminal work of **jazz-rock fusion**.

Davis had a distinctive trumpet style:

- He used a Harmon mute without stem, and performed close to the microphone.
- His style was economical: he used silence effectively as well as pace and timing of melodic phrases and has fewer double-time passages.
- He allowed himself a freedom of rhythmic style, able to improvise freely without feeling restricted by bar lines.
- Softer in tone than other trumpeters, he favoured the middle register. Davis and arranger Gil Evans' arrangements often have a smooth, sustained sound, using carefully spaced chords.

AS PRESCRIBED WORK 2018

Miles Davis: 'So What' (1959)

0:00	Intro	Bass and piano	Slow intro, with a flexible tempo (called 'rubato'). Use of unrelated major chords, creating impressionist mood.
0:34	Chorus 1	Bass theme	Paul Chambers plays the theme on double bass. Piano responds with two chord motif ('so what'), later with saxophones/trumpet added.

1:31	Chorus 2	Trumpet solo	Miles Davis begins with short phrases separated by silences. Cymbal splash marks the start of the chorus, then Jimmy Cobb (drums) switches to sticks.
2:29	Chorus 3		Tonic pedal D in bass for eight bars, then resumes walking bass. Solo covers a wider range (two octaves). Davis uses some ghost notes and half-valving. He returns to the short phrases of the opening for the final **A** section.
3:25	Chorus 4	Tenor sax solo	John Coltrane begins with short modal phrases separated by silences. Moves into double-time arpeggios. Piano matches the urgent mood of the solo. **B** section in upper register, then dark tone of low register for **A**^{3}.
4:21	Chorus 5		Decorated D minor arpeggios over a dominant pedal in the bass. Walking bass resumes for **A**^{2}. Each phrase goes a step higher, until the highest notes in **A**^{3}.
5:16	Chorus 6	Alto sax solo	Cannonball Adderley **A**^{1} Rapid ascending scale, descends more slowly. **A**^{2} Melodic, longer note values, breaking into more virtuoso display. **B** Anticipates change of chord by beginning the new phrase a bar before the change of chord in the piano. **A**^{3} Slower motif begins and ends this section.
6:10	Chorus 7		**A**^{1} 'So what' motif in piano. **A**^{2} Motif of repeated crotchets, played three times in a descending pattern. **B** Piano moves faster at 6:37 (staccato upper notes, sustained lower notes). A snare drum roll and detached piano chord marks the change back to the Dm7 chord. **A**^{3} Refers to slower motif from the end of Chorus 6.
7:06	Chorus 8	Piano solo	Return of 'so what' motif in trumpet and saxes. Bill Evans's solo is chordal (not the usual melody in right hand). Dense chord clusters in the **B** section, reducing to parallel 2nds for **A**^{3}.
8:16	Chorus 9	Bass theme	
8:59	Coda		

Miles Davis Sextet. From the album *Kind Of Blue*. Recorded in New York for Columbia, March 2, 1959.
Timings refer to the 'Legacy Edition' of the album.

Members of the Miles Davis Sextet were:

- Miles Davis, trumpet
- Julian 'Cannonball' Adderley, alto sax
- John Coltrane, tenor sax
- Bill Evans, piano
- Paul Chambers, bass
- Jimmy Cobb, drums.

'So What' uses an **AABA** structure (32-bar song form) for each chorus. The chord pattern is very simple: Dm7 for the A sections, shifting up to E♭m7 for B.

The Dorian mode

In the 1950s, Miles Davis was interested in the possibilities of modal jazz. The opening phrases of his solo use only the notes of the Dorian mode - a scale of D, using only the white notes on a keyboard. The structure is:

Tone - semitone - tone - tone - tone - semitone - tone.

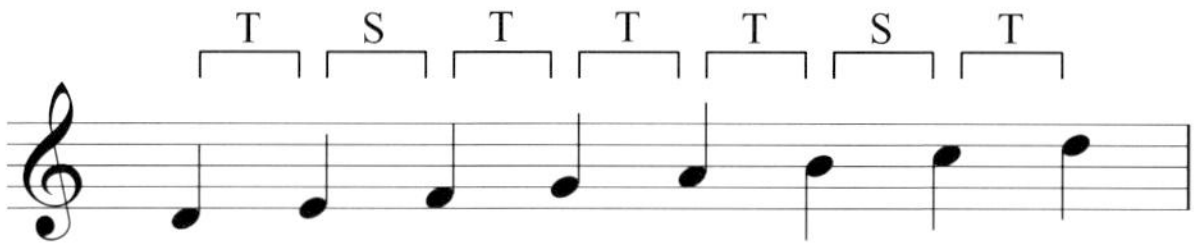

Davis wanted to focus more on developing melodic ideas. He thought that the fast chord changes of bebop caused soloists to rely frequently on familiar licks - the melodic ideas that they used most often. The static chord pattern in 'So What' aimed to free the soloists to be original with the melody.

Gil Evans

Canadian composer and arranger Ian Ernest Gilmore 'Gil' Evans (1912–1988) worked in the 1950s on three albums with Miles Davis. These included *Porgy And Bess* (1958), a rearrangement of George Gershwin's 1934 opera. It was the biggest-selling of Davis's early albums.

Evans made his reputation with his arrangements for the Claude Thornhill Band, which featured unusual textures of French horns, tuba and flutes. His preference for large ensembles limited his chances to work for recording companies, who usually wanted to keep their costs down.

Porgy And Bess was recorded in four sessions of three hours each - not enough time to do complete justice to the complex writing of the arrangements. Gil Evans conducted, but the band had not played or rehearsed the arrangements before the sessions. Davis later said that it was the most difficult thing he had ever done, while Gil Evans wished he had insisted on enough time to get it perfect.

The band was unusually large for a jazz recording. Flutes, alto flutes, clarinets and a bass clarinet provide the main reed sound (there was only one saxophone, instead of the standard large reed section of saxophones). The players were expected to be able to double on more than one reed instrument as required. Three French horns are added to the brass. The tuba gives a focused depth to the bass sound of the brass section. The large forces are handled with skill and imagination, creating rich layers of sound to support the soloist.

Hard bop

The aftermath of bebop

The style known as 'hard bop' grew out of bebop. While cool jazz was relaxed and soft-toned, following the lead of Miles Davis, hard bop continued the fast pace and dark, urgent style of Dizzy Gillespie and Charlie Parker.

In hard bop, drums became louder and bolder in responding to solos. Art Blakey's Jazz Messengers became well known for their hard, driving style, inspired by their leader, who was a drummer himself.

'CRANKY SPANKY'

Listen to Art Blakey's 'Cranky Spanky', from the album *Hard Bop*, recorded in 1956. The breathtaking pace is maintained throughout over a fast walking bass. Art Blakey is very active throughout, doing much more than merely keeping time.

Much of hard bop was simpler and easier for listeners to follow:

- It had more singable melodies.
- It had more of a blues feel. It was closer to gospel and soul music.
- It used funky or Latin rhythms.
- It featured repetitive figures in the accompaniment.

An example of the more popular style is Horace Silver's 'Song For My Father' ('Cantiga Para Meu Pai'). Silver was the original pianist with the Jazz Messengers. He had a few popular hits with his own quintet at a time when bebop and hard bop struggled for recognition with the general public.

'Song For My Father' has a $\frac{4}{4}$ **bossa nova** style beat in tribute to his father, who originally came from Cape Verde and who is photographed on the album cover.

Hard bop bandleader Art Blakey

Horace Silver: 'Song For My Father' (1964)

0:00	Intro	Bass	Bass riff (tonic-dominant), doubled by piano left hand.
0:08	Theme	Melody in trumpet and tenor sax	The repeating chord pattern is Fm–E♭7–D♭–C11–Fm9. Rhythm section stops abruptly on the C in the bass before going on to the last two chords.
0:53	Theme	Repeated	Piano adds extra chordal fills.
1:40	Chorus 1		Melody line is in right hand in single notes, with 3rds at the break. Richer chords in left hand: Fm9–E♭9–D♭9–C9.
2:25	Chorus 2	Piano solo	Right hand begins in parallel 4ths, fuller texture, funkier rhythm.
3:10	Chorus 3		Right hand uses repeated notes in the upper voice, lower voice has the melody.
3:54	Chorus 4	Tenor saxophone solo	Piano continues with full, rhythmically active chords.
4:41	Chorus 5		Ending is extended before the return of the theme.
5:44	Theme	Ensemble	Repeat of the theme.
6:30	Coda	Piano and bass	Improvised piano over the Fm riff.

Horace Silver Quintet. From the album *Song For My Father*. Recorded in Van Gelder studio, Englewood Cliffs, New Jersey, for Blue Note, October 26, 1964.

The Horace Silver Quintet members were:

- Horace Silver, piano
- Carmell Jones, trumpet
- Joe Henderson, tenor saxophone
- Teddy Smith, bass
- Roger Humphries, drums.

Joe Henderson's tenor sax solo is inventive and varied. The three-note figure (bracketed in the examples) occurs throughout the piece. Duke Ellington used a similar rhythmic figure in 'Ko-Ko'.

Theme

Theme: 'B' section

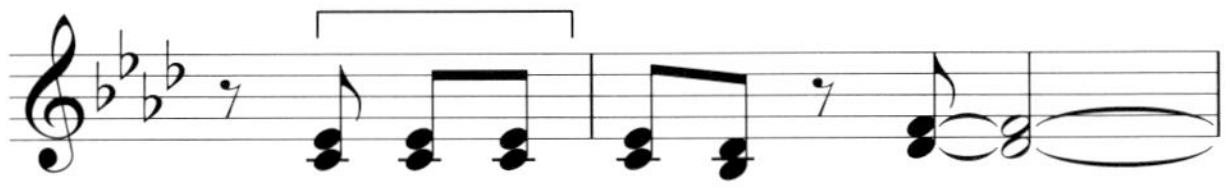

Chorus 1 – Piano solo

Chorus 4 – tenor sax solo (A[1])

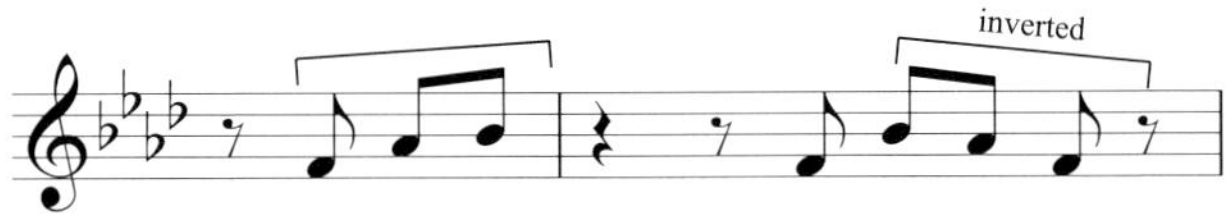

Chorus 4 – tenor sax solo (A[2])

Chorus 5 – tenor sax solo (A[2])

Henderson develops his melodic ideas in an interesting and imaginative way while also controlling the overall structure of the solo.

Chorus 4:

- **A**[1] includes short motifs, inverted, then extended into longer phrases, rising to a bluesy C♭, staying within a narrow range.
- **A**[2] has faster repetitions of the motif (see example). At the break it changes into triplets, ascending and descending through two octaves.
- **B** has more use of double time, before a rapid climb to the highest note, with a sustained, blues feel.

Chorus 5:

- The **A**[1] motif moves into a higher register for this chorus. It works in double time, with an ascending phrase based on the triplet rhythm from the theme.
- **A**[2] continues to build up tension by using the motif with repeated B♭s. It moves into shorter note values (demisemiquavers, very fast triplets).
- **B** is the fastest section, but begins to return to double time. The ending is extended, over variations of the motif in the middle register. There is considerable use of trilling. A downward slide from dominant C to tonic F is notable.

Avant-garde and free jazz

Jazz of the 1960s and 1970s

When Ornette Coleman launched his album *Free Jazz* it was the first LP of extended and continuous free improvisation. This wasn't just a new style of music, but a whole new approach to performing and composition.

Ornette Coleman

In 1959 when the Ornette Coleman Quartet began their two-week run at the Five Spot in New York, opinion was divided. Already well known from the release of two albums, there was huge interest and coverage in the press. While some walked out, others were struck by the controversial new style of jazz. The run was extended to two months.

Previously dismissed by leading figures in jazz, Coleman (1930–2015) began to gain support and respectability. His alto saxophone playing had a similar influence as Charlie Parker's had on an earlier generation. His albums were released with titles that emphasised the newness of his brand of jazz: *The Shape Of Jazz To Come*; *The Change Of The Century* and *Free Jazz*.

The term 'avant-garde' is often used to describe the experimental jazz styles of the 1960s and 1970s. Literally French for 'advance guard', it is used for cultural styles that push the boundaries. Musicians associated with this style include Cecil Taylor, Charles Mingus, Sun Ra, and The Art Ensemble of Chicago.

'Avant-garde' was also used for classical musicians of the same period, such as Boulez, Stockhausen and others (see Area of Study 6, pages 290–327).

Ornette Coleman: 'Civilization Day' (1971)

0:00	Theme	Very fast. Trumpet and alto sax play the theme twice.
0:14		Unaccompanied duet between trumpet and sax. Bass and drums enter at 0:27, setting the backing for the solos. Walking bass in repeated pairs of quavers. Swing rhythms in ride cymbal, with active snare drum.
0:33	Trumpet solo	Don Cherry's solo begins with a melodic phrase, and is then improvised in fast, energetic phrases. Melodic phrases in longer note values at 1:51 and 2:14. Note the use of repeated figures an octave apart at 2:28, with the bass climbing chromatically to build up tension. The drums are more active as the solo reaches the end, then drop out when the alto sax begins.
2:53	Alto sax solo	Ornette Coleman begins with a sequence of virtuoso phrases, climbing as the bass descends. The alto sax is full of melodic ideas, occasionally settling into slower melodic phrases, e.g. at 4:07. At 4:35 there are 10 bars of cymbal crashes in dotted crotchets, with the bass working in groups of three quavers. The music goes back to crotchet beats at 4:51, with intense repeated quavers in bass and cymbals. From 4:59 the sax and bass (now in a quaver walking pattern) are more relaxed and melodic. The drums take over.
5:17	Drum solo	Billy Higgins' solo maintains the fast pace.
5:47	Theme	

From the album *Science Fiction*. Recorded by Columbia Records in New York, September 9, 1971.

The Ornette Coleman Quartet were:

- Ornette Coleman, alto sax
- Don Cherry, pocket trumpet
- Charlie Haden, bass
- Billy Higgins, drums.

The pocket trumpet is a small version of the trumpet, sometimes used as a practice instrument.

Ornette Coleman was an influential figure on alto saxophone playing:

- He freed jazz from the necessity of chord changes.
- He managed to be dissonant but still swing.
- There is a sense in his music that the melody is evolving as it is played. There is very little in the way of repetition.
- He had a very fertile melodic imagination.
- Coleman also developed his own philosophy of 'harmolodics', to explain his approach to improvisation and composition.

Coleman's playing style developed as an extension of bebop. Once he was performing there were changes to the bebop style:

- More fragmented phrases.
- No piano, so no chords to guide the melodic improvisation.
- Timbre and texture become more important than the relationship between the melody note and the accompanying chord.
- More variety of tone, including rough tone, shrieks and gurgles, and very high (*altissimo*) register. Unusually, Coleman often performed on a plastic saxophone, which has a more 'shrill' timbre.

Despite the label 'free jazz', not everything was freely improvised. The group rehearsed at length, building a strong sense of ensemble through listening intently to each other. The rhythm section is not merely accompanying. Charlie Haden's firm bass tone and Billy Higgins' urgent polyrhythmic drumming partner the soloists in shaping the music.

The melodies were often written down. Note how the alternate take of 'Civilization Day' (re-released on Ornette Coleman: *The Complete Science Fiction Sessions*) is very similar to the original track. The walking bass and swinging ride rhythms in a consistently fast tempo and $\frac{4}{4}$ metre are similar in style to the rhythm section in bebop.

FURTHER LISTENING

In Britain the leading figure in free jazz was Jamaican-born Joe Harriott. Both alto saxophone players, Harriott is often compared to Ornette Coleman. Listen to the album *Abstract* (1962), which shows Harriott's distinctive and original style.

Jazz-rock fusion

Cultural expansionism

Increase in commercial aviation and the subsequent expansion of interest in the cultures of many continents led to the fusing together of musical styles.

In the mid-1960s Miles Davis began introducing elements of rock and funk music into his bands:

- Electric guitar and electric piano/keyboards.
- Electric bass began to replace double bass.
- More ostinato patterns in the bass (instead of walking bass).
- Drum patterns of straight quavers instead of swung quavers.
- More percussion sounds and rhythms of music from Latin America or Africa.
- More penetrating solo sounds, such as soprano saxophone or amplified trumpet.
- Use of synthesised sounds and electronic effects, e.g. reverb and delay pedals.

The best known of his later albums is *Bitches Brew* (1969).

John McLaughlin

The album *Birds Of Fire* (1972) by the Mahavishnu Orchestra is a good example of the jazz-rock or jazz-funk fusion style.

The band was led by British guitarist John McLaughlin (1942–), who played with Davis on *Bitches Brew*. The other members of the group came from a variety of backgrounds. Jan Hammer was Czech, Rick Laird was Irish-born but began his career in New Zealand. Only Billy Cobham and Jerry Goodman were American – an indication that jazz was opening up to new international influences. McLaughlin played an instrument with two necks, one with seven strings, the other with twelve.

Indian musical techniques and its philosophy were popular at this time. McLaughlin was profoundly influenced by both. He gave up taking drugs, set up a pre-performance meditation for the band, performed all in white and burned incense on stage. Some of the other musicians found this approach difficult to take, and the band broke up in acrimony. The influence of Indian music can be heard in the long improvisation over a drone, on the final track 'Resolution' and the irregular time signature $\frac{19}{8}$ during 'Celestial Terrestrial Commuters'.

Birds Of Fire was unusually successful for a jazz album, rising to number 15 in the U. S. Billboard Pop Album charts in 1973.

John McLaughlin/Mahavishnu Orchestra: 'One Word' (1972)

0:00	Intro	Drum roll, crescendo
0:20	Theme	Dramatic motifs with long held chords: D♭ major - D major/D♭ major - E major/D♭ major. Drums play fast semiquavers on the held chords, with fills.
0:54		Guitar plays semiquaver repeated note riff, then with violin. Repeated G quavers in the bass. Broken chord melody in octaves, triplet rhythm. Chord of A major to end.
1:39	Bass solo	Rick Laird's solo begins quietly, gradual crescendo. Synthesiser drone on bass A and E.
4:12		Trading phrases between electric guitar, synthesiser and violin. Longer phrases to begin with, then shorter and overlapping.
6:04	Drum solo	Band stops for Billy Cobham's solo. Note use of polyrhythms (different rhythms in each part of the drum) and variety of dynamic.
8:13	Band	Band returns with the theme. Drum fills, continuing the style of the solo.
8:36		New material in $\frac{13}{8}$ time signature. Four-bar phrase played seven times. Very fast semiquaver riff in octaves, descending A–G–F♯–G in bass.

From the *Birds Of Fire* album. Mahavishnu Orchestra. Composed by John McLaughlin. Recorded in New York and London, for Columbia, August 1972.

Members of the Mahavishnu Orchestra were:

- John McLaughlin, guitar
- Jerry Goodman, violin
- Jan Hammer, keyboard/Moog synthesiser
- Rick Laird, bass
- Billy Cobham, drums.

Contemporary jazz

Style fragmentation

Since the 1980s the public profile of jazz has declined. Few musicians (if any) have been able to dominate the jazz scene or capture the public imagination in the same way as Miles Davis, Duke Ellington or earlier jazz giants.

The variety of styles in contemporary jazz makes it impossible to choose typical examples. Among the diversity of styles and trends, you may find:

- Classically influenced jazz, improvised but not swinging.
- Smooth jazz and soulful saxophone melodies.
- Acid jazz and hip-hop jazz, influenced by dance music, including electronic sampling, DJ techniques, etc.
- Latin jazz and other 'world music' influences.
- Neo-classical styles, referencing the jazz style of an earlier era.

You are not expected to know about all these styles, but you should investigate a few examples of contemporary jazz.

Gonzalo Rubalcaba

Gonzalo Rubalcaba (1963–) was brought up in Cuba. His music shows the influence of his training in classical piano and his familiarity with Cuban music.

The 2007 album *Avatar* takes its title from the Avatar Recording Studios in New York, where it was made.

Gonzalo Rubalcaba: 'Hip Side' (2007)

0:00	Intro	Six bars bass riff. Unusual $\frac{6}{4}$ metre.
0:17	Theme	Chord structure is: Dm7 (eight bars) – G7 (two bars) – E♭7 (four bars). Melody begins in unison, dividing at the end of phrases. Contrasting ideas: rhythmic semitone figure with octave leap at 0:33, followed by slower melody. Last four bars: hi-hat semiquavers and syncopated piano/bass riff.
0:54		Theme repeats.

1:42	Chorus 1		The solo begins in the third bar. Short phrases, separated by rests. Very little left hand – two-note chords on E♭7 at the end.
2:19	Chorus 2	Piano solo *Gonzalo Rubalcaba*	Free use of dissonant notes, e.g. B♭ and A♭. Modal scales and playing outside the chord.
2:56	Chorus 3		Listen for detached notes ascending in 3rds (outlining a 13th chord). This takes the piano right hand into this higher register for the first time.
3:33	Chorus 4		Repeated chords. Listen for repeated notes at the beginning of phrases.
4:11	Chorus 5	Alto sax solo *Yosvany Terry*	Descending chromatic notes, relaxed expressive phrasing. Piano plays chords. Solo into double time at the end of the chorus.
4:47	Chorus 6	Trumpet solo *Mike Rodriguez*	Solo begins with an ascending scale in even quavers. Staccato repeated chords in piano. Legato phrases at the end of the chorus, with sustained chords in the piano.
5:23	Chorus 7		Sax and trumpet take half a chorus each. Sax solo ends with rapid repeated notes on alternate fingering. Trumpet responds with repeated notes.
	Chorus 8	Sax and trumpet	Exchange of shorter phrases in double time, building up excitement and tension.
	Chorus 9		The trading becomes faster, ending with overlapping repeated notes and the end motif from the theme.
7:09	Theme		
7:55	Coda		Diminished 7th chords, shifting chromatically, with extended drum fills.

From the album *Avatar* by Gonzalo Rubalcaba. Composed by Yosvany Terry Cabrera.
Recorded in the Avatar Studio in New York, 2007, for Blue Note.

You may be able to find a video performance of this piece with more extended solos. The recording represents only one version of this piece. There is also an article in the magazine *Keyboard* from May 2008, including a transcription of the first part of Rubalcaba's solo. You may be able to find this online.

The *Avatar* album was recorded by:

- Gonzalo Rubalcaba, piano
- Yosvany Terry, alto saxophone
- Mike Rodriguez, trumpet
- Matt Brewer, bass
- Marcus Gilmore, drums.

Maria Schneider

American composer and big band leader Maria Schneider (1960–) began her career as an assistant and copyist to Gil Evans towards the end of his life. Her carefully orchestrated writing shows the influence of Duke Ellington and Gil Evans.

Much of the album *The Thompson Fields* is inspired by the rural landscape and sense of community of her native Minnesota. However, 'Arbiters of Evolution' comes from the courtship rituals of birds-of-paradise in New Guinea, where the female selects a mate by its ornate plumage and elaborate dance-like movements. The two rival males, strutting in turn, are represented by the solos for the tenor and baritone saxes.

The pre-composed sections are 'through-composed'. There is no repeating chorus structure. The first 32 bars are structured as **AABA**, but then the music develops, continuing and extending the first material.

Maria Schneider: 'Arbiters of Evolution' (2014)

0:00	Theme	The repeated notes of the theme (see example) are accompanied by four ascending detached syncopated chords in the bass. A strong $\frac{4}{4}$ feel. At 1:15 listen for the pedal D in the lowest trombone. The rest of the band climbs higher in four-bar sections, each with a different dissonant extension of D minor. Complex contrapuntal texture of brass and reed figures.
2:03	Tenor sax and band	The underlying repeated chords stop for a $\frac{6}{8}$ passage, with tenor sax solo. Alternates between $\frac{4}{4}$ and $\frac{6}{8}$.
3:30	Free time	Extended improvisation, ascending 5ths in bass, accordion, piano. Glissandi in piano, crashes in drums – marked 'like a big wave'.
5:09		$\frac{4}{4}$ beat returns, now very slow, giving plenty of room for the improvised sax solo. From 5:49 there is a very slow build-up of tempo, over the D minor chord extensions used at 1:15.
7:05	No time. Baritone sax solo	Band stops. Piano, bass and guitar only. Extended improvised duet between Scott Robinson (sax) and Frank Kimbrough (piano). Atmospheric bird music, soft, with sax phrases answered by repeated piano chords.

9:37	Band re-enters	Slow tempo. Baritone sax solo continues.
10:33		Gradual accelerando. Melodic phrases from the opening return.
11:14	Theme	A tempo – almost at the opening speed. Repeats much of the opening music. The baritone sax continues its solo as a countermelody with the full band. The tenor sax joins in at 12:14.
13:22		Band begins to diminuendo to a fade out.

From The Thompson Fields by the Maria Schneider Orchestra. Donny McCaslin (tenor saxophone), Scott Robinson (baritone saxophone). Recorded in August 2014 in New York for ArtistShare.

There is a large band of 18 players:

- Five reeds (clarinets and saxes)
- Four trumpets
- Four trombones
- Accordion
- Guitar
- Piano
- Bass
- Drums.

The band's music is precisely notated, allowing the complex writing to be controlled. The improvised element comes in the elaborate saxophone solos, and in the free-time sections for the soloists and rhythm section.

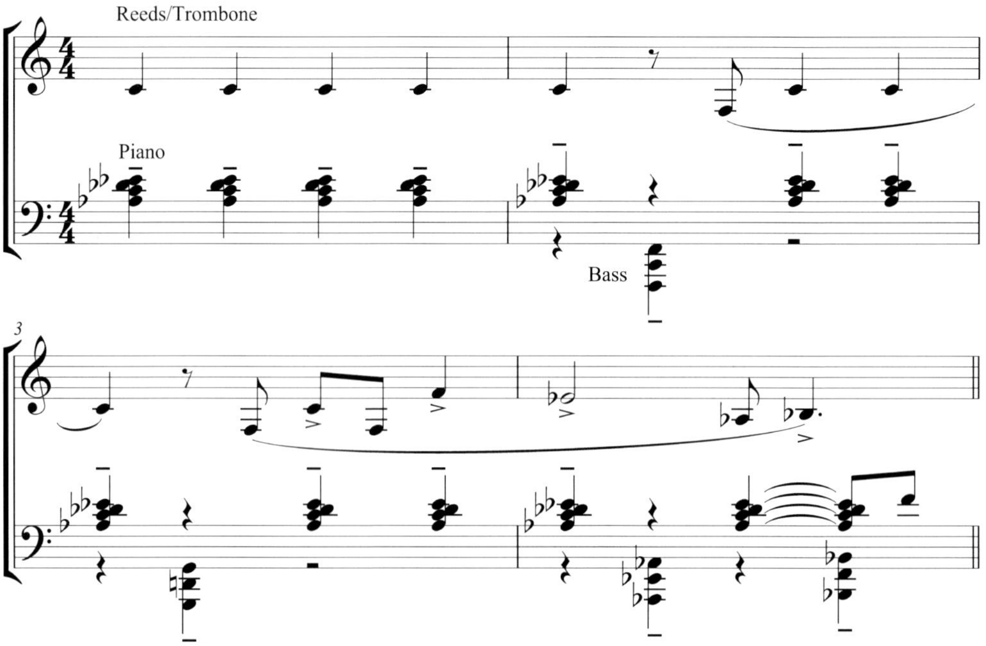

Courtney Pine

Tenor saxophonist Courtney Pine (1964–) is one of the leading personalities in British jazz. Born and brought up in London, his first album *Journey To The Urge Within* appeared in 1986. His saxophone playing shows the influence of John Coltrane.

In addition to the standard bebop style, his music has its roots in hip-hop and the sounds of the West Indies, such as ska and reggae. He has actively encouraged a new generation of black jazz musicians in this country through the Jazz Warriors and the Abibi Jazz Arts organisation.

Transition In Tradition, released by Destin-E in 2009, is less diverse than some of his albums. Its subtitle, *En Hommage À Sidney Bechet* refers to the great New Orleans clarinet player from the early years of jazz, a key figure in the development of the genre. Bechet (1897–1959) pioneered the use of soprano saxophone, which Pine plays on the album.

The *Transition In Tradition* album outlines a narrative from the past in Haiti and New Orleans, via the title track to the present day. The music is engaging, energetic and inventive, with a variety of styles and moods in pre-composed and improvised sections.

The titles of the 10 tracks in the album reference New Orleans and Haiti as origins of a musical tradition:

- Haiti
- New Orleans a.k.a. (Crescent City Rise)
- Le Matin Est Noir
- Transition In tradition
- Toussaint L'ouverture
- The Tale Of Joe Harriott*
- The Sound Of Jazz?
- Creole Swing
- Afropean**
- Au Revoir.

The album was recorded by:

- Courtney Pine, bass clarinet, alto flute, soprano saxophone
- Omar Puente, violin
- Alex Wilson, piano
- Harry Brown, trombone
- Stefon Harris, vibraphone, marimba.

* 'The Tale of Joe Harriott' is a tribute to the Jamaican-born British alto saxophone pioneer of free jazz in Britain. Pine plays the alto flute on this track.

** 'Afropean' is defined as 'to be part of African descent and to exist in Europe, culturally, spiritually or, in this case, musically. In 2007 Courtney Pine hosted a concert with this title at the Barbican Centre to mark the bicentenary of the abolition of the transatlantic slave trade. The concert was recorded and released as an album by the same name the following year.

DISCUSSION

Take some time to get to know the music of this album. It was critically acclaimed when it was first released. If possible, discuss and share your views with others (for example, in your A Level class). Issues you might want to consider include:

- To what extent is this jazz?
- What musical influences do you hear in the music?
- What do you understand about the programme or story of the music?
- Does the diversity of the material make the album more interesting or less coherent?
- In what ways does Courtney Pine's use of bass clarinet enhance the music? Would tenor saxophone have been better?
- Which tracks appeal to you the most? Why?
- How convincing or successful is the album?
- What is meant by postmodern jazz? Is this album an example of it? In what ways?

FURTHER READING

- Gridley, *Jazz Styles: History And Analysis.* (Pearson, 2008). Detailed, illustrated text book for American students. Useful bullet-point summaries of styles and important figures.
- Kernfeld, Barry. *What To Listen For In Jazz.* (Yale University Press, 1997). A helpful introduction, with chapters on rhythm, form, arrangement, composition, improvisation. Includes a CD.
- Shipton, Alyn. *A New History Of Jazz.* (Continuum, 2009). A readable history, including British and European jazz.

Section C
Essays

AS Level (2017)

Duke Ellington, early jazz and swing

1. Identify the distinctive features of Duke Ellington's style as a composer.
2. Explain the contribution of the instrumental soloists in Duke Ellington's band. Refer to examples from at least one of the prescribed recordings.
3. Outline the reasons for Ellington's success as a bandleader in the years leading up to 1940, the year when the prescribed recordings were made.
4. What was the role of the rhythm section in early jazz and swing?

AS Level (2018)

Miles Davis, cool jazz and bebop

1. Explain the importance of Miles Davis in the development of jazz in the Fifties.
2. To what extent is 'So What' cool jazz?
3. Compare and contrast the performances of two of the soloists in 'So What'.
4. Describe the circumstances surrounding the recording of the album *Kind Of Blue*.

A Level

Jazz history

1. Explain the continuing influence of jazz musicians from New Orleans in the 1920s and 1930s.
2. Explain the reasons for the decline of the big bands after 1945.
3. Which British or European musician deserves to be widely known for his or her contribution to jazz?
4. What challenges faced a musician attempting to make a living from jazz in the first half of the 20th century?
5. Assess the influence of the music of Latin America on jazz. Use examples from the work of at least one jazz composer.
6. Evaluate one work that might be considered as free jazz.

The music of Divine Office

OVERVIEW

For this Area of Study you will investigate sacred music from France, Roman Catholic Italy, Lutheran Germany and Anglican England, composed as part of the service within a church setting and for performance at other venues or occasions.

In music the Baroque period is generally said to be from about 1600–1750, following on from the Renaissance period. Like many musical periods, the Baroque period saw a decisive move away from what had gone previously. Complicated polyphony was often replaced with monody (a single melodic line with accompaniment), though composers still wrote polyphonic music.

- The system of modes was superseded by the major-minor key system.
- Contrast became very important: timbres, textures and terraced dynamics (abrupt changes in dynamics) were exploited both within and between movements of a work.
- Some pieces were written to exhibit one mood throughout.
- Even religious music began to have secular influences: folk melodies and rhythms from dance were sometimes incorporated.
- Viols were replaced by violins.

The orchestra began to come together, with a string section as the basis, though other instruments were sometimes added (oboes, bassoons, trumpets and timpani). New forms also appeared including **opera**, **oratorio**, and **cantata**. All involved movements known as **arias** and **recitatives** in addition to the choral forms found in Renaissance music.

The Baroque period saw much musical activity across Europe. Italian and French influences spread to Germany and England. Though the Church was slightly less important than during the Renaissance, it was still significant and composers had to write music acceptable to those in religious positions of power. In Italy this was the Roman Catholic Church. However, in the 16th century, there were Reformations in both Germany and England (and in other countries in Europe), a reaction against the Roman Catholic church.

Opposite: St Thomas Church, Leipzig

In Germany this was led by Martin Luther, who was uncomfortable with the power of the church leaders and the hierarchical nature of the church. Lutheran services were in German (rather than Latin) and included simple music so that the congregation could take part, rather than just listening to the choir. The congregation would join in with **chorales** (hymns), initially sung in unison, but later in four-part harmony, with the melody in the top part. The Bible became much more important, though the Mass remained, but was renamed the Lord's Supper.

Similar reforms took place in England, though here they were led by Henry VIII, who broke with the Catholic church so that he could divorce his first wife and remarry. This led to the establishment of the Anglican church, with services in English and music for the congregation to participate in.

The Counter-Reformation was the Roman Catholic church's response to the Reformation. Rules and regulations were made about what was acceptable (including the place of music in church services). These were discussed at the Council of Trent and finalised in 1563. The Counter-Reformation actually led to a musical style not unlike that of the Reformation: simpler music in which the words could be clearly heard.

What you should know

Requirements for this Area of Study may be found in the OCR specification, along with two lists of suggested listening. Some of the pieces listed are discussed here. However, you do not need to stick to the listed pieces – there are many more you could choose to study.

For A Level you should study music from Italy, Germany, England and France, including the conditions in and context for which the music was written.

For AS Level in 2017 you will study the set work J. S. Bach: Cantata No. 140, *Wachet auf, ruft uns die Stimme* and will need to be able to discuss the Lutheran background in Germany.

For AS Level in 2018 you will study the set work Purcell: Coronation Anthem No. 4, *My Heart Is Inditing* and will need to be able to discuss the Anglican background.

Much information is given in this study guide, but you should listen to as much religious music from the period as possible and, even better, go to hear it in context, in a church service or in a concert performance.

SATB

Musicians often use the acronym 'SATB' (Soprano, Alto, Tenor, Bass) to list the different voice parts used to perform a musical work. The acronym changes depending on the voices used (e.g. SSAA means that there are two Soprano and two Alto parts).

The cantata

Lutheran Leipzig

After periods of employment in Weimar and Cöthen, the German composer J. S. Bach (1685–1750) spent the last 27 years of his life as a church *Kantor* (director of music) in Leipzig.

Here he wrote an enormous amount of music for the city's two main Lutheran churches: St Thomas and St Nicolai. In addition to teaching at the attached school and directing the choir and orchestra from the organ, Bach was required to provide cantatas for performance on Sundays and church festival days.

CANTATA

The word cantata literally means 'to be sung'. In the Baroque period it referred to a piece of sacred or secular music in several movements involving soloists, a choir and an orchestra.

Although music was not used in services during Lent and Advent, Bach would have performed about 60 cantatas per year. Bach wrote many sacred cantatas. Some have been lost, but over 200 have survived.

AS PRESCRIBED WORK 2017

J. S. Bach: *Wachet auf, ruft uns die Stimme*, BWV 140

- Composed 1731
- Assumed first performed 25th November 1731
- Seven movements
- For STB soloists, SATB choir and orchestra.

Context

Music was very important to Lutherans and the main Sunday service included a cantata, appropriate to the particular Sunday. The cantata would make reference to the two Bible passages which were read to the congregation and discussed during the sermon. The cantata was performed just before the sermon.

This cantata takes themes from the two readings assigned to the 27th Sunday after Trinity, which only occurs when Easter falls extremely early in the year. The two readings (2 Corinthians 5: 1–10 and Matthew 25: 1–13) refer to the assurance of salvation, and the second reading refers to the second coming of Christ as the arrival of a 'bridegroom', coming to claim his bride (the human soul).

Wachet auf is a chorale cantata, meaning that it takes the music of an existing chorale and uses it as the basis for some of the movements. In this case the chorale is *Wachet auf* by Nicolai, written in 1599. The chorale melody and words are used in the first, fourth and seventh movements, while the other movements set words by an unknown poet, which again refer to the content of the readings.

Instruments

This cantata requires some instruments specific to the Baroque period, which are not found today. In addition to two oboes, there is a part for taille, which was a tenor oboe, sounding a 5th lower than a standard oboe, rather like the modern cor anglais. A horn doubles the sopranos in the choir.

The string section includes a part for violino piccolo, a 'small violin', sounding a 3rd higher than a standard violin. Although not specifically mentioned in the score, bassoons may have joined the cellos on the bass line, as was often the case when oboes were present. The string players would probably have been one or two per part.

Bach would have directed this cantata from the organ. Together with the cello (and possibly double bass and/or bassoon) they would have formed a group known as the **basso continuo** (or just continuo). This group was extremely important in Baroque music: the cello played the bass line while another instrument - usually a harpsichord or organ - played both the bass line and improvised chords above. Figures written below the music (known as figured bass) indicated which chords were to be played.

All the voices used would have been male as at this time only men sang in church. The high-pitched vocal parts would have been sung by treble boy choristers.

THE RIGHT SCORES

It is important that you acquire a full score of this work, not a vocal score, which reduces the orchestral parts to a piano part. Older scores retain Bach's use of the soprano, alto and tenor clefs for the respective voice parts, making them harder and more time-consuming to read. Both the Bärenreiter and Eulenburg scores have the vocal parts using standard clefs.

J. S. Bach: *Wachet auf, ruft uns die Stimme*, BWV 140

1. Choir: 'Wachet auf, ruft uns die Stimme' ('Awake calls the voice to us')

- In ritornello form – the ritornello is built on two motives: a repeated dotted note figure, heard **antiphonally** between oboes and strings at the start and a scalic figure with syncopation (e.g. bar 5, 1st violins).
- Bar 9 – 1st oboe has a chain of suspensions.
- Bar 17 – sopranos enter with Verse 1 of the chorale sung in dotted minims (compare this with the melody in the final chorale). This part is known as the **cantus firmus**, around which the other parts weave their music. The chorale cantus firmus means that this movement is a 'chorale fantasia'.
- Bar 19 – other voice parts begin to enter: altos with a rising figure, then tenors and basses in imitation. Throughout the movement the lower voice parts have a polyphonic texture, singing music which fits with, but is not related to, either the cantus firmus or the orchestral music.
- Bar 29 – a similar pattern for the second line of the chorale: sopranos first, with the other voices entering later, a rising phrase in imitation.
- Bar 43 – the third line: all the voices enter together, the lower parts singing the exhortation 'wake up' ('wachet auf'), followed in bar 45 by much closer imitation, just a beat rather than a whole bar apart.
- Bar 53 – the music is repeated from the beginning, though it is written out, as the voices have different words.
- Bars 105 to 117 – a ritornello statement, modulating to the dominant with a perfect cadence in bars 116–117. For the next two vocal entries, the lower parts start before the soprano cantus firmus.
- Bar 135 – the most exciting passage in the movement, a **fugato** on the word 'Alleluja'. Though this looks like the start of a real fugue, the fact that the voices do not enter at the traditional intervals (here the altos begin on G, tenors on B♭ and basses on E♭) means that it isn't.
- Bar 137 – altos have the syncopated motif from the orchestral ritornello. The sopranos do not appear with the cantus firmus until bar 150.
- Bar 161 – the voices begin at the same time as the cantus firmus, in imitation as usual, but by bar 165 the lower parts are singing homophonically, giving emphasis to the words 'mach euch bereit' ('make yourselves ready'), together with a modulation to the subdominant (A♭). The importance of these words is further emphasised in the following phrase: the sopranos move on to new words, but the lower parts repeat the words of the previous phrase, again moving to a homophonic texture in bar 173.
- The dal segno at the end indicates that the work is to be repeated from the sign (bar 2). The movement ends after the final ritornello with the pause on the chord at the start of bar 17.

2. Recitative (Tenor): 'Er kommt, der Bräut'gam kommt!' ('He comes, the bridegroom comes!')

The tenor soloist acts as a narrator. The words are sung quickly, with no repetition and with rhythms reflecting the pattern of speech. This is typical of Baroque recitative and such movements carried the action forward. There is a very disjunct melody, with some wide leaps. There is also use of rapid modulation (the movement begins in C minor but this is followed by perfect cadences in G minor, and B♭ major, before returning to C minor) and of dissonant chords: over the tonic pedal in bars 1–3 there is chord VII (a diminished chord) at the start of bar 2 and a diminished 7th chord is heard at the start of bar 11.

3. Aria (Duet, Soprano and Bass): 'Wann kommst du, mein Heil?' ('When will you come, my Saviour?')

This is a kind of love duet or conversation between Jesus as the bridegroom (bass) and the soul as his bride (soprano).

There is an **obbligato** part for the violino piccolo, which is as important as the vocal parts. It is a flowing virtuosic melody with continuo accompaniment.

As in the first movement, there is a dal segno marking but only the opening instrumental introduction is repeated, so this is not a da capo aria (in which the whole of the first section of vocal music would be repeated).

4. Chorale (Tenors): 'Zion hört die Wächter singen' ('Zion hears the watchmen sing')

This is the second verse of the chorale, sung by the tenors, in the chorale rhythm. It is accompanied by a countermelody, played by the violins and violas and the continuo.

The upper string part consists of a number of motives:

- A (bars 1–2, repeated in bars 3–4)
- B (bars 5 repeated in sequence in bar 6)
- C (bars 7–8)
- D (bars 12 – a cadential motif).

The whole movement is built from these small fragments, presented over the chorale melody in a seemingly random order! The tenor chorale does not start and finish each phrase with the string melody; they overlap.

The key of this movement is the same as each of the chorale movements: E♭ major. Bars 22 to 33 are a repeat of the opening ritornello.

5. Recitative (Bass): 'So geh herein zu mir' ('So come into me')

The bass describes the unity of Jesus as the bridegroom with his bride, the soul. It begins in E♭ major, but like the previous recitative, passes through several keys in a short space of time (F minor, B♭ minor and A♭ major), ending in B♭ major. It links the key of the previous movement with the key of the following movement. There are frequent diminished 7th chords (bars 2, 8 and 12) and uses of secondary dominants.

6. Aria (Duet, Soprano and Bass): 'Mein Freund ist mein!' ('My friend is mine!')	This duet is again between Christ and the soul (or the bridegroom and bride). It also has an obbligato part, for solo oboe, with continuo accompaniment. Here there are more occasions on which the two voices sing together (e.g. in bar 11 they sing together in 10ths) and some have described it as a love duet. This movement is a da capo aria. The 'da capo dal segno' indication at the end means that the music from bar 1 is played again and the movement finishes in bar 46. It is therefore in ternary form: **A** (bars 1–46), **B** (bars 47–73) and A again at the end. In the repeat of the **A** section the soloists would have added ornamentation.
7. Chorale: 'Gloria sei dir gesungen' ('Let Gloria be sung to you')	This is a four-part homophonic choral setting of the third verse of the original chorale, with instruments doubling the vocal parts. It is not known whether the congregation would have joined in. This setting of the chorale makes the irregular phrase lengths very obvious; they vary between two and five bars in length.

Later Performances

In the Lutheran church this cantata would not have been sung again until 1742, when there was another 27th Sunday after Trinity. Since no other cantata by Bach exists for this particular Sunday in the church's calendar it is likely that *Wachet auf* was performed.

After Bach's death most of his music ceased to be performed, though this cantata may have been an exception. There was a revival of Bach's music from the mid-19th century, but unfortunately by this time much of the music had been lost. Bach's cantatas are now very popular with recording artists and several have undertaken to record every single extant example, often combined with some kind of pilgrimage.

FURTHER LISTENING

Bach wrote many more cantatas, including *Christ unser Herr zum Jordan kam*, BWV 7, which uses the first verse of a chorale by Martin Luther as a cantus firmus in the chorale fantasia first movement and the final verse harmonised in four parts in the last movement.

Anthems and motets

The use of biblical texts

Due to the civil war and the ensuing Commonwealth period, there is a gap of about 15 years when no English church music was composed. As a Puritan leader, Oliver Cromwell allowed no music in church and theatres were closed. At the Restoration in 1660, when church music was permitted again, choirs initially sang older music in the pre-Restoration style. However, composers were quick to write new works, including new ideas from France and Italy.

Henry Purcell (1659–1695) began his musical training as a chorister in the Chapel Royal in London, composing some short pieces during this time. By the age of 20 he was organist at Westminster Abbey and in 1682 was appointed organist at the Chapel Royal.

During his last year as a chorister Purcell was under the care of the composer Pelham Humfrey, who, from 1672, was Master of the Children. Some writers suggest that Humfrey influenced the style of Purcell's compositions. Purcell wrote much music for the church, along with secular vocal music and instrumental pieces.

Anthems

An anthem is a piece of choral music, setting a religious text in English to music, so is specific to the Anglican church. A similar work with Latin or German words, for the Roman Catholic or Lutheran church, is called a motet.

Early English anthems were known as full anthems as they were sung by the full choir throughout in a polyphonic texture, unaccompanied. During the 17th century composers began to write verse anthems, which explored the new Baroque ideas of contrast, homophony and tonality (rather than modality). The new-style anthems also contained verses, sung by soloists rather than the full choir. Anthems were found in the services of morning and evening prayer (also known as evensong) and followed the Third **Collect**.

AS PRESCRIBED WORK 2018

Purcell: *My Heart Is Inditing*, Z30

- **Composed and first performed 1685**
- **Verse anthem**
- **For eight-part choir, eight soloists, strings and organ**
- **Approximate duration: 15 minutes.**

Context

Purcell was asked to write two anthems for the coronation service of James II in 1685. *My Heart Is Inditing* (meaning overflowing with happiness) was performed towards the end of the long service, after the crowning of James's wife Mary of Modena as Queen. The anthem therefore brings out references in the text to the Queen. The text was taken from Psalm 45 and Isaiah 49.

This grand occasion allowed Purcell to compose for far larger forces than he was used to; though strings were used in the Chapel Royal when the King was present, for the coronation the choirs of Westminster Abbey and the Chapel Royal were combined, together with a large group of instruments and a new organ.

Purcell had already composed many anthems, some in the older polyphonic full style, but from 1682 all his anthems were in the verse-anthem format. The anthem is continuous, with no break between the different sections.

Modern editions vary as to the voice parts required for this work. Purcell used a variety of clefs in his autograph: treble, soprano, mezzo-soprano, alto, tenor, baritone and two basses, but some editions suggest two each of sopranos, altos, tenors and basses.

In this context 'inditing' means overflowing or bubbling over (with happiness), so is appropriate as a coronation text!

Purcell: *My Heart Is Inditing*, Z30

1. Symphony

The anthem begins with an instrumental section known as a symphony, for strings and organ. There are two sections, both of which are repeated, with similarities to a French overture since the first section is slower, featuring dotted rhythms, and the second section would have been played faster and is polyphonic, with imitative entries.

We can see use of both the older modes (in this case the **mixolydian** mode, with its flattened 7th) and the newer tonality of the C major scale. References to this are found throughout the anthem: the dominant major is not firmly established and the dominant minor is found.

The start of the anthem is bright, partly due to the register of the cellos; they play relatively high until bar 18. Though there is not a great deal of use of sequence in this section, there is a sequence in bars 21–22 in the 1st violin.

The imitative entries of the second section are not exact enough to form a strict fugue. The dotted rhythms continue and there is a dance-like feel to the music. This section features more use of sequence (e.g. bars 42–44 and 46–47 in the bass, bars 46–47, 56–57, 59–60 and 63–66 in the 1st violin). There are suspensions in the 1st violin in bars 31–32 and 2nd violin bars 50–51. The second section follows a broad I–VI–II–IV–I plan, not emphasising the dominant major at all (the dominant minor is heard in bar 36).

2. Chorus: 'My Heart Is Inditing'

The voices, accompanied by the strings and organ, enter independently, in an imitative texture, building until all eight parts are present in bar 78. Though the strings often support the voices by playing with them (e.g. the viola begins with the alto, at the same pitch) they sometimes have independent parts (e.g. the 1st violin at the start of this section) and sometimes double the voices one or two octaves higher, giving a brighter sound.

Use of the flattened 7th at times gives rise to false relations: in bar 72 the 1st violins have a B♮ at the start of the bar while the 2nd violins (and sopranos) have B♭ at the end of the bar. There is a similar effect in bar 98, together with a suspension (the note C in the top voice part). A false relation is characteristic of English early-Baroque composers.

At bar 85 the texture changes with the change of words. It is now homophonic with antiphony between the upper and lower voices. At bar 97 the third voice from the bottom (in most scores designated 2nd tenor) is the lowest part in the texture, below the two bass parts. The chorus ends with a short instrumental ritornello, repeating the music from bar 93.

3. Chorus: 'At His Right Hand'

Like the previous chorus, this begins with the voices entering in imitation, supported by the strings and organ. There is word painting on the word 'glorious', which Purcell sets to a jaunty dotted rhythm, performed by voices usually in pairs, singing in 3rds or 6ths. From bar 138 the melisma is extended to two bars. Again, there is a change of texture with the start of the new words: to reflect the richness of the Queen's clothing of 'wrought gold' all eight parts sing in homophony.

4. Verse and Chorus: 'She Shall Be Brought Unto The King.'

In the verse section only seven soloists are used; the first bass is silent. The accompaniment is also reduced to just continuo. The verse begins with trios of voices, first an upper group, answered by a lower group, and joining together from bar 147. In bar 151 the 2nd alto and 1st tenor have a different rhythm for 'needlework' from the rest of the group, so that they can begin the new imitative texture for 'the virgins that follow her'. The use of imitation and a stepwise descending shape reflects the meaning of the words.

The verse begins in E minor, passing through D major, G major and A minor, with a chromatic section including a diminished 7th in bar 159, before reaching G major in bar 160. The move to a major key in bar 160, together with the dotted rhythm for the word 'joy', again reflects the meaning of the words. The 2nd bass also joins the soloists at this point.

When the chorus enter (with full string accompaniment) in bar 193 they repeat the words from the verse, but in a full homophonic texture in C major. A brief ritornello is followed by the return of 'joy and gladness', with the same again from bar 212. For each repetition the chorus entry is more polyphonic. At bar 221 the alto 'and shall enter' is imitated in inversion by the 1st sopranos and 1st tenors.

5. Symphony

At the middle of the anthem the symphony is repeated, with a change to the final two bars.

6. Verse: 'Hearken, O Daughter'

Four soloists are answered by the four other soloists; this pattern continues for some bars. The meaning of the words, that the Queen is to forget her own family and think only of her new duties to the King and the country, is reflected in the use of minor keys, chromaticism and the false relation between the 1st soprano F and 2nd tenor F♯ in bar 259.

The new triple-time section from bar 262 begins with the antiphonal effect heard earlier: a lower trio answered by a higher trio. Throughout this section the 2nd bass is silent. At bar 269 the words from bar 241 are repeated, but now in triple time rather than duple. The contrasting trios of voices are still used. The poignancy of this section continues in the concluding ritornello, in the key of A minor with suspensions.

7. Chorus: 'Praise The Lord'

Though this section begins in F major there is no B♭ key signature, reflecting the dual use of modality and tonality. The praise is presented in homophony in as many as 12 different parts (voices and instruments), but from bar 332 becomes polyphonic with imitative entries, returning to a homophonic texture at bar 350. Again the section concludes with an instrumental ritornello, ending in C major.

8. Chorus: 'Alleluia'

The chorus begins with two contrasting ideas presented in imitation: a long held 'amen' and 'alleluia' in shorter note values. However, by bar 392 the alleluias dominate the texture. Bar 403 features a simultaneous false relation in the 1st soprano and 1st bass.

The anthem ends with grand homophonic alleluias, with the range of notes (from 2nd bass to 1st violin) extending to over three octaves.

Bar numbers and names of voice parts in this commentary refer to the 1948 Schott edition of the work, edited by C. F. Simkins.

Extended listening

Purcell's anthem *Hear My Prayer, O Lord* is just one movement for SATB choir and continuo. It was apparently intended to be the start of a larger work written about 1682, which Purcell did not complete. The existing movement, with words from the first verse of Psalm 102, has a bleak text in which the word 'crying' is sung to a chromatic melody. The anthem gradually builds to a climax very near the end, with a huge discord.

Purcell's childhood teacher Pelham Humfrey wrote a number of anthems, only two of which were in major keys. His anthem *By The Waters Of Babylon* explores the misery of captive Jews, from Psalm 137.

Handel later wrote an anthem, also called *My Heart Is Inditing,* for the coronation of George II some 40 years later in 1727. Like Purcell's anthem it was used while the Queen was crowned. Some parts of Handel's text are different and there are differences in instrumentation. At the same service Handel's famous anthem *Zadok The Priest* was also performed; it has been used at every coronation service since.

Handel also wrote 11 anthems as house composer for the 1st Duke of Chandos, now known as the 'Chandos anthems'. No. 9, *O Praise The Lord With One Consent* was composed in 1717–18. Although it uses a small group of musicians (STTB soloists, chorus, oboe, two violins and basso continuo) it is a grand piece of music, with eight movements.

Motets

All the composers covered in this Area of Study wrote either motets (in German or Latin) or anthems (the English equivalent). In France, motets were classified either as *petits motets*, with only basso continuo accompaniment, or *grand motets*, with more instruments:

- Rameau's motet *Quam Dilecta Tabernacula* – a setting of Psalm 133 in Latin, for soloists, chorus, flutes, strings and continuo, lasting about 20 minutes – is a *grand motet.*
- Schütz's *Symphoniae Sacrae I* is a collection of 20 motets, setting various psalms in Latin, for soloists, various instruments and continuo. It was published in Venice in 1629.

Music for Mass

The Mass is the most important service of the Roman Catholic Church. It reminds the congregation of the last supper of Christ, his crucifixion and resurrection. A similar service is found in the Lutheran and Anglican churches, known as the Divine Service/Eucharist/Holy Communion/Lord's Supper.

This service followed a plan, which included both sections that were the same every time (known as the Ordinary) and sections which varied according to the time of year or particular saint who was being celebrated (the Proper). A Mass would have looked something like this:

Ordinary	Proper
	Introit
Kyrie (Lord, have mercy, Christ have mercy)	
Gloria (Glory to God in the Highest)	
	Gradual and Alleluia
Credo (The Creed: I believe in one God)	
	Offertory
Sanctus (Holy, Holy, Holy) Osanna (Hosanna) Benedictus (Blessed is he that cometh in the name of the Lord)	
Agnus Dei (Lamb of God)	
	Communion

The Mass would end with the words 'Ite, missa est' (Go, ye are sent forth) and it is from these words that the name 'mass' is taken.

The cantatas and anthems above related to the parts of the service which changed with the day and season. Composers also set the Ordinary parts of the Mass, either a complete setting of all the sections, or a setting of one section, such as the Gloria.

Vivaldi: *Gloria* RV589

- **For SSA soloists, SATB choir, oboes, trumpets, strings and basso continuo**
- **Composed c. 1716**
- **12 movements**
- **Approximate performing time: 30 minutes.**

Context

Having been ordained but never practised as a priest, Vivaldi was employed at the Ospedale della Pietà in Venice as a violin tutor. The Ospedale was an orphanage and school for girls. While there, Vivaldi produced many concertos for the girls to perform.

Up to the 20th century it was thought that Vivaldi had not composed any sacred music, but scores were discovered and relate to the time Vivaldi had to stand in as *maestro di coro* because the incumbent was ill. Vivaldi was in this post for several years and wrote music to be sung in the church, though much is now lost.

The tenor chorus part is reasonably high and would have been sung by some of the girls; the bass parts may have been sung as written or an octave higher (as they were doubled by instruments this wouldn't have caused a problem).

Each sentence of the Gloria becomes a movement, and Vivaldi's prowess as an opera composer is evident in the variety of the movements. It is likely that the work would have been preceded by an *Introduzione,* a kind of motet.

Antonio Vivaldi (1678–1741)

Vivaldi: *Gloria*

1: 'Gloria in excelsis Deo' ('Glory be to God on high')	In this movement the orchestra has the melodic material, using two different motifs: octaves with repeated notes and a quaver-semiquavers pattern. In contrast the choir have a homophonic (and homorhythmic) chorale-like setting of the words. Like much of Vivaldi's music it sounds deceptively simple, but Vivaldi explores a range of keys, including the relatively remote C♯ minor in bar 48. The penultimate chorus 'Quoniam tu solus sanctus' is a simplified and shorter version of this opening movement, with different words and without any modulation.
2: 'Et in terra pax' ('And on earth peace')	This work completely changes in mood between movements; here there is a different time signature, texture, key (the relative minor of B minor), tempo and mood. In contrast to the first movement, where the orchestra took the melodic lead, the strings provide a continuous background for the voices. The music passes through many keys, though not all are established with perfect cadences. In bars 64–65 the move from C minor to B minor is achieved by the dominant 7th in C minor in 3rd inversion being reinterpreted as an augmented 6th chord (with the bass as E♯ rather than F♮), resolving up to the F♯ (the dominant of B minor). Bar 11 uses a Neapolitan 6th chord.
6: 'Domine Deus' ('O Lord God')	This movement, for solo soprano, includes an obbligato instrumental part. Vivaldi suggested violin or oboe for this.
12: 'Cum Sancto Spiritu' ('With the Holy Spirit')	This fugue is not actually by Vivaldi! He arranged a movement from a 1708 work by Ruggieri and used it here (and in his previous Gloria, RV 588). This type of plagiarism, so heinous today, was not frowned upon in the Baroque period. This is a double fugue with two subjects.

FURTHER LISTENING

Gregorio Allegri (c. 1582–1652), based in Rome, wrote a number of Mass settings (items of the 'Ordinary' of the Mass), including *Missa Vidi turbam magnam (I saw a great multitude).*

Bach wrote a famous setting of the Mass over a period of about five years, known as the 'B minor Mass'. However, this was not performed in his lifetime and does not reflect Lutheran practice, which was to compose the parts of the Ordinary separately and to use only the Kyrie and Gloria.

Music for Vespers

Monteverdi's *Vespers* and J. S. Bach's *Magnificat*

In addition to Mass, the Roman Catholic Church had eight services every day known as the Divine Office, beginning with Matins very early in the morning and ending with Compline at night.

Vespers, or Evensong as it is known in English-speaking churches, is sung in the evening. These services would often have been fairly simple, with a hymn, psalms and prayers.

Claudio Monteverdi (1567–1643) began his musical study as a choirboy at Cremona cathedral. He then went on to employment at the court in Mantua, where he composed a great deal of secular music and performed as a singer and viol player.

Monteverdi: *Vespers*

- For SSATTBB soloists, two choirs (singing in up to 10 parts) and instruments, including recorders, cornetti, trombones, strings and basso continuo
- Published 1610 in Venice
- 13 movements
- Approximate performing time: 90 minutes.

CORNETTI

This is not to be confused with the modern cornet. The cornetto (or cornett) has a brass mouthpiece, but a woodwind-style body, creating a sound somewhere between a modern trumpet and an oboe.

Context

Monteverdi's *Vespro della Beata Vergine* were published together with a Mass. Since Monteverdi was not required to compose religious music, scholars have wondered if the work was meant to help him gain future employment. It may have been successful, as he became conductor at the famous church of St Mark's in Venice in 1613.

The service of Vespers is the seventh Divine Office, known as Evensong in the Anglican Church. Monteverdi's publication includes an enormous amount of music and it was probably not designed to be performed all in one service, but was a portfolio, showing how well Monteverdi could compose, and a resource from which choir directors could select pieces. There are 13 movements for varying numbers of singers and instruments and two alternative versions of the Magnificat, the hymn in praise of Mary. Some of the pieces are motets and some set words of psalms. Many movements have a cantus firmus.

Monteverdi's music, rather like Purcell's, contains old and new elements, referred to by Monteverdi as 'prima prattica' – first (older) practice – and 'seconda prattica' – second (newer) practice.

From the older style he used:

- A cantus firmus in many movements
- Modal rather than tonal harmony
- Complex polyphonic textures.

From the newer practice he explored:

- A freer treatment of dissonance
- Madrigal-style writing in flowing vocal lines
- Simple accompaniment
- Examples of word painting.

Monteverdi: *Vespro della Beata Vergine*

1: 'Deus In Adjutorium'/'Domine Ad Adjuvandum' ('Make haste O God' / 'Make haste O Lord')	This opening movement requires large forces: there are six different instrumental parts (for 12 different instrumentalists), together with continuo and a six-part choir. After a simplified **plainsong** opening, Monteverdi reuses music from his 1607 opera *Orfeo,* demonstrating immediately his intention to bring secular influences into sacred music. While the choir sings in a homophonic and homorhythmic texture, the instruments, particularly the 1st and 2nd cornettos/violins, play in canon.
3: 'Nigra Sum' ('I am a black')	This motet is a solo song with a relatively simple continuo accompaniment, allowing for a more ornamented vocal line. The word 'surge' ('arise') in bars 14–15 uses a long ascending scale, reflecting the meaning of the word. Bar 20 has an example of a biting dissonance: while the bass line has E, the vocal line moves to F♮, a compound semitone above.
11: Sonata sopra: 'Sancta Maria Ora Pro Nobis' ('Holy Mary, pray for us')	The title 'sonata' suggests an instrumental piece and, until bar 64, this is a piece for eight instruments. However, the 1st sopranos enter with the cantus firmus melody, a plainsong phrase repeated many times, with differing rhythms and occasional accidentals. Over the top are heard different accompanying instrumental melodies.

Editions of this work vary considerably, particularly in bar numbers. Bar numbers here refer to the Philharmonia Score No. 470 (Universal Edition) and to the score published by Möseler.

Extended listening

Monteverdi's *Beatus vir* is a setting of Psalm 112. It was probably for Vespers at St Mark's in Venice and was published in a collection of sacred music in 1641.

St Mark's was a very important church in the early-Baroque period – composers from all over Europe came to hear the music that was performed there and took ideas back to their own countries. The church was famous for its use of cori spezzati – choirs spaced apart in the building, singing alternately (or 'antiphonally'). Two of the composers associated with St Mark's, Antonio and Giovanni Gabrieli (uncle and nephew) also wrote for separated groups of instrumentalists in concertato style (in the style of a concerto, i.e. with opposing groups of voices and/or instruments).

St Mark's, Venice

J. S. Bach: *Magnificat in D*, BWV 243

- **For SSATB soloists, SSATB choir and orchestra (flutes, oboes, oboes d'amore, trumpets, timpani, strings, continuo)**
- **12 movements**
- **Approximate performing time: 30 minutes.**

Context

J. S. Bach's *Magnificat* originated in a version in E♭ major, written in 1723, shortly after he moved to Leipzig. Bach returned to the setting 10 years later, making some changes (including changing the key to D major, a key more suited to trumpets) for a performance on July 2, 1733, at the feast of the Visitation.

At Evensong the *Magnificat* was usually sung in German, but on six important occasions each year (including Christmas and Easter) Latin was used. The words are from Luke 1: 46–55 and the **Doxology**, with each verse from the Bible being a movement, except for verse 48 which is spread across two movements. There are no recitatives, just choruses and arias.

J. S. Bach: *Magnificat in D*, BWV 243

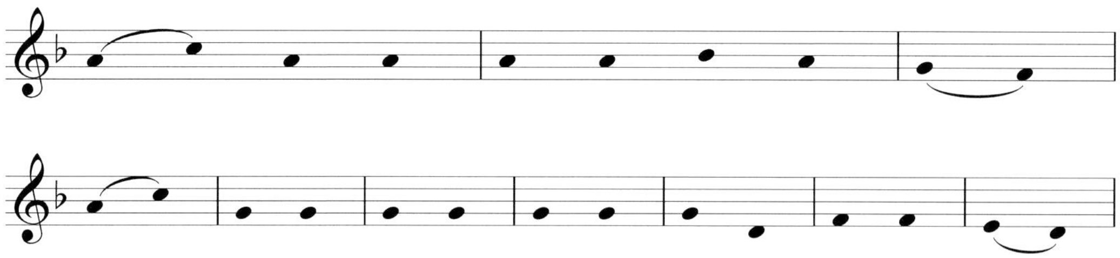

'Magnificat anima mea' ('My soul proclaims the greatness of the Lord')	After a long instrumental section, including trumpets and drums, pointing to the festal nature of the work, the choir sings motifs heard on the oboes at the beginning. The texture is polyphonic throughout, ending with a purely instrumental section. The opening music returns in the final movement, at bar 20, followed by the choir singing the words 'Sicut erat in principio' ('as it was in the beginning'), a kind of joke as the music returns to the beginning!
'Quia respexit' ('Because he has regarded')	This soprano aria features an obbligato **oboe d'amore**. Humility is reflected in the descending vocal lines, which ascend for 'ecce' ('behold'). There is no break between this movement and the following chorus, which sets the last two words of the Bible verse 'omnes generationes' ('all generations'), with the chorus reflecting the group of people.
'Fecit potentiam' ('He has shown strength')	Elements of the first movement are used again. The opening rhythm is the same as bar 33 in the first movement; it is for full choir and orchestra and ends in D major. 'Strength' is shown by the vocal lines outlining chords in bars 1 and 2, using a dotted rhythm at the end of the bar and the repeated five-note figure in the instrumental bass line. In bar 28 the choir stops on a diminished 7th chord (E♯, G♯, B, D), followed by silence. A short coda uses some striking harmonies: bar 29 is an augmented chord in first inversion, followed by a diminished 7th in the second half of bar 30, leading to a cadence in B minor. The same diminished 7th chord (with the E♯ rewritten as F♮) is used in the second half of bar 33, but this time leads to a cadence in D major. The harmony reflects the words - the conceit in the hearts of the proud.
'Suscepit Israel' ('He has taken Israel under his protection')	This movement features a cantus firmus in the oboe. It is the melody to which the German Magnificat was traditionally set, known as the *tonus peregrinus*. This was a psalm tone - plainsong to which the Magnificat was sung in the Lutheran church. The name refers to the fact that it has a different main note in each half of the music.
'Sicut locutus est' ('In accordance with what he said')	Since the words of this movement refer to Abraham (from the Old Testament) and 'forefathers', Bach refers to his musical forefathers, with a movement that begins as a strict and predictable fugue.

FURTHER LISTENING

Schütz (1585-1672) wrote several Magnificat settings, both in Latin and German. One of his German versions is included in the collection *Symphoniae Sacrae II (Meine Seele erhebt den Herren)*, first published in 1647 in Dresden. Vivaldi's most famous Magnificat is RV610, for SSAT soloists, SATB choir, two oboes, strings and continuo in nine movements.

Oratorio
Sacred concert music

Unlike the religious music discussed so far, oratorios were not performed as part of a church service. They began in Italy around 1600 in an oratory - a prayer room - in Rome. It grew into a form similar to opera, with soloists, a choir and instrumental accompaniment, performing recitatives, arias and choruses, with various characters represented.

Unlike opera, oratorio was not staged and was performed in a concert setting without costumes, scenery, props or acting. Oratorios generally made more use of the chorus than operas. Oratorio thrived in Italy, particularly during Lent when opera performances were not permitted, so audiences attended oratorio performances instead.

Early Baroque Italian oratorio came in two types: *oratorio latino* - with a text in Latin prose - and *oratorio volgare* - with a poetic text in Italian. From its beginnings in Rome, oratorio spread throughout Italy and beyond, to Germany and eventually to England.

Early oratorio: Carissimi's *Jephte*

The Italian composer Giacomo Carissimi (c. 1605–1674) was one of the most significant early-Baroque oratorio composers, with an international reputation.

He was responsible for the music at the Oratorio del Santissimo Crocifisso in Rome, where many oratorios were performed.

Jephte (sometimes called *Historia di Jephte*)

- Oratorio latino
- Composed c. 1645
- For six voices and continuo: soloists and chorus SSSATB (or sometimes SSATTB)
- Approximate performing time: 30 minutes.

Context

Jephte is probably Carissimi's best-known work. The story of Jephte (known in English as 'Jephthah') comes from the Old Testament book of Judges, with additions by an unknown writer. As a typical oratorio latino, it is in one section (many performances last about 30 minutes), with a significant role for the chorus. Although scores have just organ continuo accompaniment (the autograph score has been lost), performances sometimes use violins and cello, as in other works by Carissimi.

The chorus represents the crowd commenting on the scene and sometimes takes the role of the narrator (historicus in Latin), telling the story. The soloists also sometimes act as narrator and are the characters Jephte and his daughter. The plot tells of Jephte's victory over the Ammon armies and his promise to sacrifice the first person he sees on his return home if he is victorious. On returning he is met by his daughter, who discovers she is to be sacrificed. The oratorio ends with a lament from Jephte's daughter and the chorus.

A baroque organ

Carissimi: *Jephte*

Nos. 1 and 2: Solos. 'Cum vocasset in proelium' ('When called to battle') and 'Si tradiderit Dominus' ('If You will give')	Much of the oratorio uses the new Baroque style of monody, developed by Monteverdi. This can be seen in the first two numbers, in which an alto soloist as narrator sets the scene and a tenor soloist takes the role of Jephte in a recitative-like style.
No. 3: Chorus. 'Transivit ergo Jephte' ('So Jepthe crossed over')	This begins in a homophonic texture, moving to polyphony after the first line.
No. 4: For two soprano parts. 'Et clangebant tubae' ('And the trumpets sounded')	Begins with an entirely appropriate fanfare-type melody.
No. 5: Solo bass. 'Fugite, fugite, cedite, cedite impii' ('Flee and give way, godless ones')	Aria style, with a wider-ranging vocal melody and a livelier accompaniment. The soloist is telling the armies of Ammon to flee ('fugite') and Carissimi uses word painting with a fast-rising scale.
No. 6: Chorus. 'Fugite...' ('Flee...')	Repeats the words from the earlier bass aria, with antiphonal effects and word painting on 'corruite' (fall down) as the melody falls each time. There is very little repetition of words in this oratorio.
No. 8: For chorus sopranos and altos. 'Et ululantes filii Ammon' ('And the children of Ammon howled')	Carissimi uses chromatic harmony to heighten the words, with the continuo descending the full chromatic scale. There are also suspensions, such as the double suspension at the start of bar 8 in the two sopranos. Harmony is also used to great effect in the final chorus lament section of the movement, with a **Phrygian cadence** in bars 3–4 and many single, double and triple suspensions, such as the double suspension in the 3rd soprano and alto part in bar 22. Jephte's daughter's preceding version of this lament also features chromaticism and dissonance (e.g. bar 9), together with some awkward intervals.
No. 10: Soprano solo. 'Incipite in tympanis et psallite in cymbalis' ('Strike the timbrels and sound the cymbals')	Carissimi was fond of repeating a short phrase transposed a 4th or 5th higher or lower. Bars 22–23 are repeated a 4th higher in the following bar, while the accompanying bass line is transposed down a 5th. Most words are set syllabically; however, there are occasional examples of melisma, e.g. 'cantenus' ('sing') and 'et' ('and').

No. 15: Tenor solo. 'Heu, heu mihi filia mea, heu!' ('Alas my daughter, you are undone!')	Jephte's lament features chromaticism and dissonance.
No. 23: Soprano solo. 'Plorate, plorate colles' ('Mourn, you hills, grieve, you mountains')	Filia's solo features echoes from the other two sopranos, reflecting the acoustics of the mountain landscape.
No. 24: Chorus. 'Plorate, filii Israel' (Weep, you children of Israel')	Melismas are also here. The move away from strictly syllabic writing reflects the celebratory nature of the words.

FURTHER LISTENING

Handel's oratorio *Jephtha* is based on the same Bible passage, together with material from the play 'Jeptha or the Vow' by the Scottish playwright George Buchanan (1506–1582). Handel uses Buchanan's name for Jephtha's daughter: Iphis. It was Handel's last oratorio, written in 1751, for six soloists, chorus and orchestra in three acts. It begins with an orchestral overture, and the ending is changed so that an angel intervenes to prevent the sacrifice of Jephtha's daughter.

Sedecia, re di Gerusalemme (Zedekiah, King of Jerusalem) was composed by Alessandro Scarlatti in Rome in 1705. It is in Italian, in two acts for six soloists and orchestra. A sinfonia is followed by many arias and recitatives and a very brief second sinfonia, with a chorus at the end, sung by the soloists together. Fabbri's libretto was taken from the Bible (Jeremiah 39:1–10).

English oratorio

Handel's *Messiah*

The theatrical nature of Handel's oratorios caused a sensation in 18th-century London.

George Frideric Handel (1685–1759) was born in Germany, but spent some years in Italy before moving to England in 1712, where he remained for the rest of his life. While in Italy Handel met most of the leading composers, encountered a number of styles, and had become a truly cosmopolitan composer by the time he moved to England. Handel's composition of Italian oratorio began in 1707 in Rome, when he composed his first, with his second, *La Resurrezione*, written the following year.

The oratorio in England

English audiences had a taste for Italian opera so Handel composed a number of these. However, in the 1730s various musical entertainments began to appear in English and opera in Italian lost favour.

Handel created a new form, combining elements of Italian opera and oratorio, English anthems and German Protestant oratorio, initially almost by accident. In 1732, he presented private performances of an earlier work, *Esther*, and wanted to stage it publicly in an opera house. However, this was not permitted by the Bishop – it was thought immoral to stage a biblical work in such a venue. Handel therefore presented a concert version, which was a resounding success.

Handel created a form with the following features:

- Sung in English
- Soloists, a chorus (with a significant role) and an orchestra
- Religious subject
- In three acts
- Performed in a theatre or concert hall.

Unlike Italy, in England opera performances were permitted during Lent, so Handel's oratorios competed with these. Handel composed over 20 English oratorios, eventually abandoning opera.

Messiah (HWV 56)

- **Composed in 1741, first performed in Dublin 13th April 1742**
- **Oratorio in three parts**
- **Libretto by Charles Jennens, taken from the King James Bible and the Psalms as found in the Book of Common Prayer**
- **Orchestra: Oboes, bassoon(s), two trumpets, timpani, strings and continuo**
- **Approximate performing time: 3 hours.**

Context

This is Handel's most famous work, and is still performed frequently today. Having been sent the libretto by Jennens, Handel is said to have completed his composition in just 24 days! In the winter of 1741–42 Handel visited Ireland to give some concerts, including a charity concert in which *Messiah* was performed.

The work was given a very warm welcome, though when Handel performed it in London it was not so well received. Unlike nearly all Handel's other oratorios, *Messiah* is not a dramatic work; there is no real plot and the chorus and soloists do not take on the role of characters.

It is also one of only two of Handel's oratorios in which all the words are taken from the Bible:

- Part I concerns the prophecies about the arrival of Jesus and extends to Jesus' birth
- Part II covers Jesus' passion (crucifixion)
- Part III covers the expected second coming of Jesus.

Handel made numerous revisions to *Messiah;* often due to different singers taking the solo roles and Handel wanting to provide music suited to their voices. When it was first published in 1767 (after Handel's death) most of the later revisions were not included.

Handel: *Messiah*

Sinfonia/ Overture

The work begins in E minor, with an overture for wind, strings and continuo. It is in the style of a French overture: a slow section with dotted rhythms followed by a fugal faster section. Although the faster section features all four instrumental parts there are only three entries of the fugue subject (1st violin, 2nd violin and cello). There are two dominant pedals: on D when the music is in G major (the relative major) and on B when it has returned to E minor.

There is one other instrumental movement in *Messiah:* 'Pifa', also in Part I. This is a pastoral interlude, introducing the shepherds who are about to hear of Jesus' birth. It follows tradition in being in $\frac{12}{8}$, with pedal notes to imitate the sound of the shepherds' bagpipes.

Tenor: 'Comfort Ye' and 'Ev'ry Valley'

The vocal music begins with an accompanied recitative (strings and continuo) in E major. At the start the strings play nearly continuously, stopping briefly so that the tenor can be heard. However, later in the movement ('the voice of him'), the accompaniment becomes much sparser, with occasional string chords. This reflects that the tenor is a lone voice in the wilderness. In bar 14 Handel plays with expectations by repeating the opening music an octave higher for one-and-a-half bars. However, the music then changes course with new material. The opening music is heard in the dominant from bar 27. Since this recitative is accompanied, it would have been performed at a fairly regular tempo. It has some aria-like features, with a lyrical melody line, held notes and repetition of some words. However, the word setting is nearly all syllabic.

The recitative ends with a perfect cadence in A major and is followed by the tenor aria 'Ev'ry valley', also in E major. Handel repeats the echo effect heard in the recitative (bar 4) in bars 10–11 of the aria. In bars 15–19 the word 'exalted' is itself exalted with a long melisma, involving an ascending sequence. Further examples of word painting are the wide range of pitches used when singing about hills and valleys compared with 'the rough places plain' on one repeated note, and 'low' in bar 25 sung to a low note.

Chorus: 'And The Glory Of The Lord'

This joyful chorus is in A major, at a brisk tempo, accompanied by the woodwind, strings and continuo. Within the $\frac{3}{4}$ metre Handel uses hemiolas, where six beats feel like three groups of two beats (rather than two groups of three beats) – the first is found in the orchestral introduction in bars 9–10.

Handel builds the entire chorus from just four ideas:

- The opening alto melody, outlining the tonic triad.
- 'Shall be revealed', with a descending sequence and a short melisma.
- 'And all flesh' where the same descending pattern is repeated three times.
- 'For the mouth' with long repeated notes.

Chorus: continued

Interest is maintained by presenting the melodic ideas in a variety of textures and keys. The first idea is heard from the altos alone, then by the chorus in a homophonic texture. From bar 22 it is used as part of a polyphonic texture, before a triumphant homophonic statement in the dominant from bar 33, ending with a hemiola. There is a further homophonic statement from bar 76 in B major. The phrase is also used at the point where the highest note of the movement appears, from bar 106 in the tonic, reaching a high A in the sopranos in bar 110. It is possible to trace the use of the other three melodic ideas through the movement in a similar way.

Alto: 'Behold, A Virgin Shall Conceive'	This is the first example of a secco recitative in *Messiah,* with just continuo accompaniment.
Alto: 'He Was Despised'	This is a da capo aria (from Part II), where the first section of music is repeated at the end. Section A is from bars 1–49, followed by a contrasting B section from bars 50–67. Baroque soloists would have varied the repeat of section A by adding ornamentation. Despite the melancholy subject, Handel writes in E♭ major, with a modulation to the dominant at bar 21. The solemn mood is reflected in the falling melody (e.g. 'a man of sorrows' in bars 14–15), suspensions, particularly in the bass line (bars 22–23), and awkward intervals (e.g. 1st violins in bar 22). The orchestra sets the mood in the opening ritornello, with a three-note descending figure played in 3rds (heard throughout the A section, between the soloist's phrases) and a minor 3rd (G♭) and flattened 6th (C♭) in bars 6 and 7. The flattened 3rd in the vocal line emphasises the word 'grief' (bar 18). In bars 41–42 the orchestral accompaniment ceases and the soloist is accompanied by the continuo. This is because, when the A section is repeated, the soloist may take more time to improvise a cadenza at this point. The B section presents a marked contrast, with a change of key to C minor (the relative minor) and a continuous dotted rhythm. This ends in bar 66, leaving a dramatic silence and the soloist unaccompanied. The B section ends more like a recitative, with the unaccompanied vocal line followed by a perfect cadence in G minor. The B section also makes use of a circle of 5ths in bars 55–59.
Bass: 'The Trumpet Shall Sound'	This is also a da capo aria, but the music is repeated from the sign (bar 29), without the opening orchestral ritornello. As suggested by the words, the aria features obbligato trumpet. Handel wrote obbligato parts very differently from Bach; in Bach's works they are continuous, whereas Handel leaves space for the singer to be heard. The bass emulates the trumpet, outlining a tonic chord in the first phrase. Other points to note are the long melisma on 'change' (bars 60–66), hemiolas, continuo-only accompaniment in bars 139–140, and the contrasts in the B section.

Scores vary in their numbering of individual movements, so for clarity the first line of the movement being discussed is given.

Passions

Music of Holy Week

A passion tells of the crucifixion of Jesus, with words from one of the Gospels. Passions were written in Lutheran areas and are a distinct feature of the Protestant music movement. They were performed in Holy Week (the week before Easter).

The earliest passion settings used plainsong for the narration; as time went on these became recitatives with some choral writing, including polyphony, and non-biblical text was also used. Baroque Passions are like a special kind of oratorio.

Schütz

Heinrich Schütz (1585–1672) was one of the most important German composers before J. S. Bach, writing a significant amount of sacred music.

After a childhood as a choirboy, he spent time studying in Venice with Giovanni Gabrieli and Monteverdi, bringing back Venetian ideas to use in his music. As time went on, Schütz moved from being one of the most radical composers, using new ideas, towards a simpler style. His music uses the modal system, but at cadences elements of the tonal system can be heard.

Schütz: *Matthäus-Passion (St Matthew Passion)* SWV 479

- Composed 1666, first performed 1st April 1666 in Dresden (the Sunday before Easter)
- For SSATTTBB soloists and SATB choir (two choruses are for ATTB)
- Approximate performing time: 60 minutes.

Context

Matthäus-Passion was composed for the chapel of the Elector's court, for services during Holy Week. It is in German, using Luther's translation of the Bible. It is unaccompanied, as was traditional in Dresden (no instruments were used during Holy Week).

Schütz: *Matthäus-Passion*

Harmony

This early-Baroque Passion combines traditional and new elements. Passions traditionally used the Lydian mode on F, but here Schütz uses the **Dorian mode** transposed to G. Within a movement there are 'cadences' in several keys areas, e.g. the second chorus 'Ja nicht' has cadences on B♭, C, D, B♭ and G. Within the choruses the music is clearly melodically conceived, resulting in some powerful dissonances, e.g. in bar 16 of the Introitus (the opening chorus) the tenors have E♭ a semitone above the altos' D.

Text

With the exception of the choruses at the beginning and end, Schütz uses only words from the Bible; some of his contemporaries inserted non-biblical texts into their works. However, Schütz does occasionally include a newer idea of repeating words at times of tension, e.g. Jesus and the Evangelist both repeat 'Eli'/'Mein Gott' three times when Jesus is on the cross.

Solo narrative

The solo narrative and speaking parts are set to a kind of plainchant recitation – Schütz provides the pitch, but the performers choose the tempo and rhythm, as in plainchant. However, Schütz conveys the emotion and meaning of the words through the use of modes and the shape of the melodic line:

- Jesus, sung by a bass as was traditional, has melodic lines often in the shape of an arch, to give an impression of tranquillity, together with short melismas. For example, 'Nehmet, esset, das ist mein Leib' (Take eat, this is my body) begins with an ascending pattern, then descends, with two notes on most syllables.
- When the Evangelist sings about Peter's denial of Jesus, the music has a wide range (from F to D a 10th lower) and falls in paired notes for a description of Peter weeping.
- The two tenors in the role of the false witnesses ('Er hat gesaget') sing in canon a major 2nd apart, reflecting the untruthfulness of their statements. The first tenor also begins a tone higher than the 2nd tenor, but in the middle changes to sing a tone lower – the two characters really cannot get their stories straight!

Chorus

The chorus take several roles in the work; they are the disciples and later a Jewish crowd. The choruses are generally quite short, sometimes only three bars, but the music describes the action. When the chorus are disciples ('Die Jünger Jesu') their music is controlled and the points of imitation occur regularly. In contrast, when they are an angry crowd (e.g. in the chorus 'Barrabam') their imitation overlaps, sometimes occurring at the same time.

The flowing melodic lines of the final chorus sometimes create significant dissonances, such as in bar 4, with the A♭ in the bass and G in the alto.

J. S. Bach: *Matthäus-Passion (St Matthew Passion)* BWV 244

- Composed 1727, first performed Good Friday 1727 in Leipzig
- For double SATB choir, two groups of soloists and two orchestras
- Approximate performing time: 3 hours.

Context

J. S. Bach wrote several Passion settings, but only two (St Matthew and St John) survive complete today. The *St Matthew Passion* was performed during a service, with Part I before the sermon and Part II afterwards. Bach revised the work twice and it is the latest version which is performed now.

Bach sets words from the Gospel of St Matthew (chapters 26 and 27), interspersed with texts by the librettist Christian Picander used in recitatives, arias and the large-scale choral movements. As in his cantatas, Bach used chorale melodies familiar to the congregation, most often in four-part harmonisations, but also as the basis for other movements as a cantus firmus.

Performers

The work calls for singers and instrumentalists who were probably stationed in the two organ lofts in St Thomas Church in Leipzig, so their numbers would not have been particularly huge. The two groups are roughly equal, each having SATB choir, SATB soloists and orchestra, though the two most important soloists (the tenor Evangelist who narrates the work and Jesus, sung by a bass) are in Choir I.

Instruments include recorders, flutes and three types of oboe: two standard oboes, two oboes d'amore and two **oboes da caccia**. The string section includes a viola da gamba, (a bass viol).

The two choirs sometimes perform together (as in the chorales, when the instruments also play the vocal lines), sometimes separately, when a smaller group of people is represented (e.g. the disciples are played by Choir II), and sometimes in alternation, creating an antiphonal effect.

J. S. Bach: *Matthäus-Passion*

Overview	The Passion includes all the expected movements: secco and accompagnato recitatives, arias and choruses. The work opens with a chorale fantasia, with the existing chorale melody in the soprano in the ripieno part.
Jesus' recitatives	Jesus' recitatives are usually accompanied by strings, while the recitatives of the Evangelist and other characters are usually accompanied only by continuo. An example of this is in No. 15, where the Evangelist begins by singing 'he said' with continuo accompaniment, but when Jesus begins speaking the strings enter. This gives the words of Jesus a special atmosphere, which some have likened to a halo. The only time Jesus has a recitative with just continuo accompaniment is when he speaks his final words (No. 71).
Solo arias	Solo arias are usually preceded by a recitative by the same soloist. The work includes obbligato arias, e.g. No. 47 'Erbarme dich', with an obbligato violin part. In this sorrowful aria Peter (sung by an alto rather than bass) is regretting denying Jesus and is 'weeping bitterly' in a minor key with descending vocal lines. At the end of the aria the orchestra repeats the opening ritornello. Da capo arias are also used, such as in No. 75, 'Mache dich'.
Word painting	Bach often uses the music to heighten specific words or emotions in the text, particularly in the recitatives. When Jesus sings the word 'crucified' ('gekreuziget') in No. 2, it is over a diminished 7th chord with a chromatic melisma. The word 'Kreuzigen' ('crucify') is chromatic in the chorus No. 54. Thunder and lightning are portrayed in the chorus part of No. 33 ('Sind Blitze, sind Donner') by the descending arpeggio melody lines and rumbling instrumental bass line.
Chorales	Bach includes chorales in his Passions, which appear at significant points in the narrative: 'O Haupt voll Blut und Wunden' appears five times, in a different key each time and in four different harmonisations, the last of which is the most chromatic.

Two numbering systems are found for this work. Here the older BWV numbering system is used, in which there are 78 movements.

AoS4 Answers can be found on pages 358-361

AS Level (2017)

Exercise 1

Without referring to your notes, complete the table below, listing the significant features of each movement of Bach's Cantata No. 140 *Wachet auf, ruft uns die Stimme.*

	1. *Wachet auf, ruft uns die Stimme*	**2.** *Er kommt, der Bräut'-gam kommt!*	**3.** *Wann kommst du, mein Heil?*
Type of movement	Chorale fantasia		
Vocal forces		Tenor solo	
Instrumental forces			Violino piccolo, continuo
Key			
Time signature			
Melodic features (including word setting)			
Texture			
Harmony			
Other significant features (this may include structure)			

AS Level (2017)

Exercise 2

How does Bach use pre-existing music in his Cantata No. 140, *Wachet auf?*

AS Level (2018)

Exercise 3

Describe the timbres and textures used in Purcell's anthem *My Heart Is Inditing.*

(A Level students may like to compile a similar table for a different work).

4. *Zion hört die Wächter singen*	**5.** *So geh herein zu mir*	**6.** *Mein Freund ist mein!*	**7.** *Gloria sei dir gesungen*
$E\flat$ major			
	C		
		Lots of paired quavers, some melismas	
			Homophonic

A Level

Exercise 4

What is the difference between aria and recitative? Illustrate your answer with reference to at least two works of your choice.

Exercise 5

Compare two choruses from works you have studied.

Exercise 6

Compare one work from the early Baroque period with one from the later Baroque. What are the similarities and differences?

Exercise 7

Describe the ways in which a composer could create variety in a multi-movement work. Refer to any work(s) of your choice.

Exercise 8

Describe how Baroque composers conveyed the meaning of the text in their sacred works. Refer to at least two works in your answer.

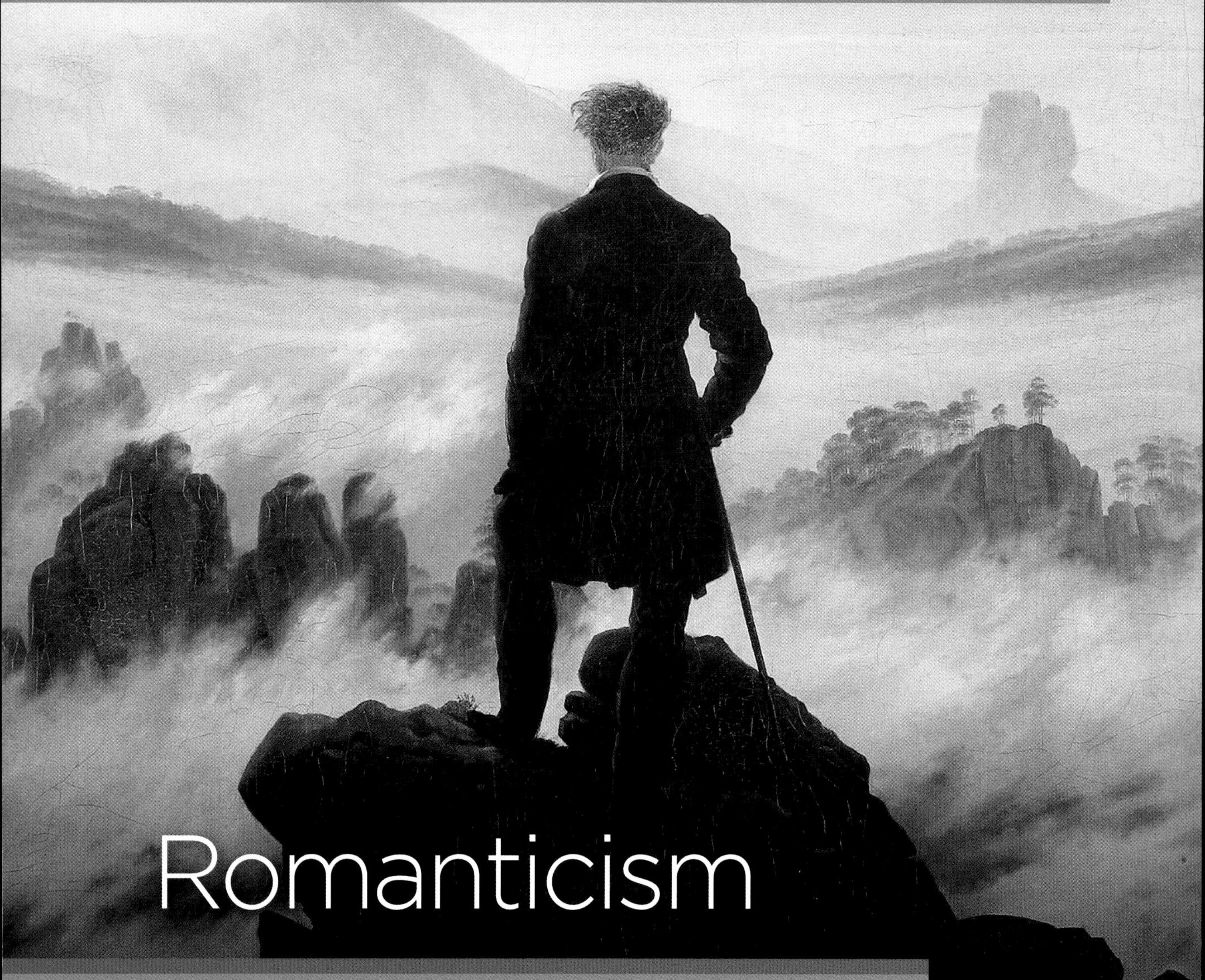

Romanticism

OVERVIEW

The years 1820–1910 are referred to in music as the Romantic period. Following the Classical period, composers wanted to break free from tightly controlled structures and to write music expressing moods and emotions.

Romantic composers sometimes saw themselves as heroes, creating original masterpieces for posterity, rather than as servants – as Haydn was – creating music for aristocratic employers. In the Romantic period audiences for concerts grew in size and performances became less intimate. Romantic composers increased the range of pitch, dynamics, instruments and harmonies.

Social changes

The French Revolution at the end of the 18th century changed society in Europe and beyond. With the decline of the aristocracy, composers were likely to be self-employed, receiving money for writing and publishing commissioned works.

The Industrial Revolution created a wealthy middle class, who wanted to see spectacular musical performances, by a soloist such as Liszt (a virtuoso pianist) or large orchestra. Concert halls were built in Europe and the United States. Bristol's Colston Hall was built in 1867 and Birmingham's Town Hall in 1834. Possibly the most famous concert hall in the UK, the Royal Albert Hall was built in 1871. The middle classes also wanted to perform music at home, particularly on the piano, creating demand for instruments and simple repertoire. There were advances in piano technology in the 19th century and pianos were produced in large quantities.

The Romantic orchestra

In the Romantic period the size of the orchestra increased significantly.

To the two horns and trumpets of the Classical brass section were added two more horns, trombones (taken from the opera orchestra) and later a tuba. The invention of the valve system (c. 1815) allowed horns, trumpets and the tuba to play a full range of notes.

The double woodwind section of the mature Classical period was improved by the invention of the key mechanism in the 1830s, initially for the flute, then later for other wind instruments, helping to increase the volume and improve the tone. The percussion section sometimes just consisted of timpani, as in the Classical period, but Romantic composers could include a range of other instruments. The larger brass and woodwind sections were balanced by an increase in the number of string players, resulting in orchestras numbering around 90 players.

Programme music

In the 19th century there were strong links between music and other art forms, such as literature and painting. Romantic composers often composed 'programme music'.

This is music which describes something or tells a story, with the subject being known as the 'programme'. Although descriptive music had been written earlier (e.g. Vivaldi's *Four Seasons* described poems in music) the term 'programme music' usually refers to descriptive music of the 19th century. Programme music itself does not use any words or lyrics – all description must be contained within the music.

Writers have long debated the extent to which it is possible to represent extramusical ideas in music. Romantic composers clearly thought that it was, though they varied in the extent to which they published the programmatic backgrounds to their music.

For programme music, composers took inspiration from the past, legends and fairy tales, nature and love. They explored these most often in pieces for orchestra or solo piano. Some composers, however, did not want their music to have any outside associations and composed absolute or **abstract** music.

What you should know

The OCR specification has the requirements for this Area of Study, together with suggested listening (two possible lists).

However, you and your teachers can choose music to listen to: from the specification, this study guide, or your own choice. Listening to as many examples of Romantic programme music as you can will be beneficial and, if possible, try to attend at least one live performance. Even better, try playing some of the music yourself.

You should cover the following:

- The concert overture
- The symphonic poem
- The programme symphony
- Solo works
- Works communicating an awareness of national identity.

For A Level you will need to know about all the above genres, be able to discuss aspects of the music (drawing on the music you have listened to), and also show an awareness of the background in which the music was created.

For AS Level in 2017 you will need to know about concert overtures and be able to discuss the music and explain the background using examples from Mendelssohn's *Hebrides Overture.*

For AS Level in 2018 you will need to know about concert overtures and be able to discuss the music and explain the background using examples from Tchaikovksy's *Romeo and Juliet.*

The concert overture

The concert overture grew from overtures to operas being performed on their own at concerts. It was therefore not a huge step for Romantic composers to write independent pieces of music, known as concert overtures.

Many Romantic composers adopted this idea, with Mendelssohn hailed as the most notable early composer. Typical Romantic concert overtures had a recognisable (though possibly modified) sonata form structure and pictorial or nationalist elements.

Felix Mendelssohn

'Fingal's Cave'

Mendelssohn (1809–1847) was a German composer from a wealthy background, benefiting from a good musical and general education from tutors at home.

AS PRESCRIBED WORK 2017

The Hebrides Overture, 'Fingal's Cave', Op. 26

- Final version completed June 1832
- Score published (with two other overtures) in 1835
- Dedicated to King Frederick William IV of Prussia (then Crown Prince of Prussia
- Allegro moderato (sonata form)
- Orchestration: two each of flutes, oboes, clarinets in A, bassoons, horns in D, trumpets in D, timpani (B and F♯), strings
- Approximate performing time: 10 minutes.

Context

As part of his education Mendelssohn undertook tours abroad and in 1829 visited the UK. After performing in London, Mendelssohn travelled to Scotland, spending the night of August 7, 1829 on the island of Tobermory. He wrote to his sister, saying how 'extraordinarily' the Hebrides islands had affected him, and included 20 bars of music he had been inspired to write. The following day he visited the uninhabited island of Staffa, and saw the famous Fingal's Cave. The cave, one of the natural wonders of Scotland, was named after Fingal, a Celtic hero invented by the 18th-century Scottish writer James Macpherson.

Following years of revisions, the bars of music Mendelssohn sent to his sister eventually became an overture. During the revisions the overture was given several names, including 'The Lonely Island'.

Instruments

Mendelssohn uses an orchestra similar to Beethoven's, with double woodwind, two trumpets and two horns.

The clarinets are in A (sounding a minor 3rd lower than written) and the trumpets and horns are both in D, but the trumpets sound a major 2nd higher than written while the horns sound a minor 7th lower. The strings are in five parts, with the cellos and basses having different music throughout. The scoring shows that Mendelssohn was relatively conservative in his instrumentation.

The programme

Other than the title(s), there is no programme. The music represents a journey at sea, the islands and caves visited, and the Scottish landscape.

Mostly the sea is calm, but there are stormy moments, suggested by ***ff*** passages with tutti scoring, dissonant chords and rapid modulations through distant keys (e.g. bar 169 onwards). Continuous semiquavers contribute to the feeling of the movement of the water (e.g. violas and cellos from bar 9). This is also reinforced by never having a break between sections; the transition leads straight into the second subject, which leads straight into the development, and so on. The rise and fall of the melodic lines, together with the use of crescendo and diminuendo, also add to the picture of the sea rising and falling.

Structure

The overture is in sonata form:

	Bars	Keys
Exposition	**1–95**	
First subject	**1–32**	B minor
Transition	**33–46**	B minor–D major
Second subject	**47–76**	D major
Codetta	**77–95**	D major
Development	**96–179**	B minor, G minor, D major, G major, F minor, B♭ minor, D minor, V7 in B minor
Recapitulation	**180–216**	
First subject	**180–201**	B minor
Second subject	**202–216**	B major
Coda	**217–268**	E minor, B minor, D major, C major, B minor

Much of the movement is built from the motif in bar 1 on the 1st bassoon, violas and cellos, representing the swell of the sea. The **first subject** consists of repetitions of this motif, twice at each pitch on the tonic, mediant and dominant, moving up a 3rd each time (bars 1 to 6). This progression contains hardly concealed parallel 5ths, which could be a reference to traditional Scottish music. In bars 7 to 8 the motif is stretched. Bars 9 to 16 are a repeat of bars 1 to 8, but with the melody played by 1st violins. The end of the first subject uses the opening motif with a new woodwind melody derived from the motif.

The transition takes the end of the woodwind accompanying theme (bar 29 in the 1st flute, 1st oboe and 1st bassoon) and passes it between different instruments. For most of the transition the music heads towards the key of F♯. Only in the final two bars (bars 45 to 46) is there a change of direction to V7 in D major, partly obscured by a diminuendo.

The **second subject** melody, played initially by bassoons and cellos with help from clarinets, is derived from the cello accompaniment figure in bar 3, based on a D major chord (the relative major). As before, this melody is repeated by the 1st violins, followed by more use of the opening motif.

The codetta uses the opening motif but very differently: the dynamic is now ***ff***, the rhythm is stronger and there are brass fanfares, using a simplified version of the rhythm.

The development begins in the tonic with the opening motif in the violas, sounding almost like a false recapitulation. However, from bar 112 the woodwind and brass present a dotted rhythm figure, related to the opening motif. The second subject melody is used from bar 123 and the motif from bar 29 appears from bar 135. The opening motif is used in another transformation from bar 149, now staccato, with imitation between wind and strings.

The recapitulation is significantly shorter than the exposition; the first and second subjects are not repeated and the transition is not really present (since the music has the same tonic note it is not required). The first subject, although having the same orchestration as the opening (melody in violas and cellos) has two extra bars between each statement (bars 182 to 183 and 186 to 187) and the motif is extended in bars 188 and 189 and played by the 1st violins, just as in bars 13 and 14. The two statements of the exposition are therefore combined into one in the recapitulation. The second subject is now played by clarinets and is in the tonic major, mirroring the major mode in the exposition.

The coda presents a new motif, heard in imitation between the 1st oboe, violas and violins, leading to another presentation of the opening theme from bar 226. However, it now descends by 3rds (B minor, G major, E minor), unlike the ascending opening. The opening motif reappears right at the end of the movement, played by the 1st clarinet from bar 264. In bar 266 the second subject is heard in the 1st flute at the same time, finally in the tonic minor.

Tonality and harmony

Although Mendelssohn follows the expected outline in terms of keys (first subject B minor, second subject relative major, recapitulation in B minor/major), he often moves to unexpected chords or keys.

As the opening presentation of the melody in B minor, D major and F♯ minor suggests, Mendelssohn uses mediant relationships (keys a 3rd apart) and the development centres around these keys. The development also explores the keys of G minor and G major, and a move to F minor followed by B♭ minor requires a new key signature (bar 138). There is also much use of major and minor keys with the same key note; B major in addition to B minor, D major and minor and G major and minor.

Mendelssohn uses diminished 7th chords to create tension and excitement and to help with modulations. There are examples of diminished 7th chords in the development in bar 35 (E, G, B♭ and D♭ as a **dominant minor 9th chord** in F without the root) and bar 144 (A, C, E♭ and G♭ as a dominant minor 9th chord in B♭ without the root).

The coda uses the key of B minor (the flattened 2nd of C major) from bar 249 to postpone the final appearance of the tonic key.

Orchestral textures

Mendelssohn's orchestration creates a variety of colours. The opening gradually adds wind instruments to subtly change the sound, with clarinets in bar 3, and oboes in bar 5. Similarly, when the melody is repeated by the 1st violins from bar 9, trumpets are added in bar 11 and bassoons in bar 13.

Full orchestral tutti textures are used in two ways. The first occurs from bar 15 and, with the increase in dynamic to ***f***, represents a swelling of the waves, but not yet a storm. The next tutti in the exposition occurs from bar 77 with the start of the codetta, together with an ***ff*** dynamic. Here the sea is clearly much stronger. Unison string writing from bar 85 and accents from bar 80 make this the climax of the exposition. Similarly, the climaxes of both the development and the recapitulation occur towards the end of each section (around bars 169 and 255) and both have unison strings.

The double basses are independent from the start, where they carry the bass line alone. They are also important at the start of the development, where the opening motif is introduced by the violas and passed to the cellos and basses. For much of the time the strings, particularly the violins, play continuous semiquavers, creating a shimmering effect, particularly when they play tremolo alternating between two notes (e.g. bar 37).

Mendelssohn wrote for natural horns and trumpets, capable of playing only a limited number of notes in the key of D major. This can be seen from the small number of pitches they play. However, the brass still has an important task to perform. The horns and trumpets introduce fanfares from bar 77, used by other instruments later in the work (e.g. woodwind bar 99). At the end of the exposition the brass plays D and F♯ alone – this can be interpreted either as the tonic and mediant in D major or the mediant and dominant in B minor. This chord forms a link between the two sections.

Mendelssohn uses the woodwind independently from the strings. When motifs are passed around the orchestra it is often between strings and woodwind (bar 33 onwards). When the strings are playing shimmering semiquavers or held notes the woodwind have the melodic interest (bar 70 onwards), and the woodwind is sometimes responsible for introducing a new melodic idea (bar 112 onwards). In the recapitulation the second subject, originally played by the bassoons and cellos with help from the clarinets, is entrusted to the 1st clarinet alone.

The end of the overture is rather surprising. After the ***ff*** in bar 265, there is an unexpected diminuendo with ***p*** and ***pp*** statements of the first and second subject motifs, and the movement ends on three unison tonic pitches, played by the timpani and pizzicato strings, under a flute held note.

FURTHER LISTENING

- **Mendelssohn wrote two programmatic overtures before *The Hebrides Overture*:**
- ***A Midsummer Night's Dream* (1826), together with incidental music, to be performed with a staging of the play; *Calm Sea And Prosperous Voyage* (1828) based on two poems by the German writer Goethe.**
- **Dvořák's *Carnival* Op. 92 is part of a group of three orchestral overtures.**

Pyotr Ilyich Tchaikovsky

Romeo And Juliet

Tchaikovsky (1840–1893) was a Russian composer, with some French ancestors. He was employed as a clerk at the Ministry of Justice and studied music in his spare time. In 1863 he began studying at the St Petersburg Conservatory and then moved to Moscow to teach.

In 1867 Tchaikovsky met Mily Balakirev, the informal leader of a group of Russian nationalist composers known as 'The Five' or 'The Mighty Handful'. For some years Tchaikovsky accepted Balakirev as his mentor, though his more Western musical training at the Conservatory resulted in music less nationalistic in flavour than that of 'The Five'.

AS PRESCRIBED WORK 2018

Romeo and Juliet (fantasy-overture)

- **Final version completed 1880, dedicated to Balakirev**
- **First performance (of third and final version) May 1886 in Tbilisi (now the capital of Georgia, but then part of Russia)**
- **Orchestration: Piccolo, two flutes, two oboes, cor anglais, two clarinets in A, two bassoons, four horns in F, two trumpets in E, two tenor trombones, bass trombone, tuba, timpani (E, B and F♯), cymbals, bass drum, harp, strings**
- **Approximate performing time: 20 minutes.**

Context

In 1869 Balakirev proposed that Tchaikovsky should write a piece based on Shakespeare's *Romeo And Juliet* and even devised a plan for it, including the main keys. Tchaikovsky's first version was premièred in March 1870. However, Tchaikovsky immediately made some changes and a second version was published in 1871. Much later, Tchaikovsky returned to *Romeo And Juliet,* producing a third (and final) version, published in 1881.

Although most writers refer to the work as a symphonic poem, Tchaikovsky described the work as an 'fantasy-overture'. The designation 'fantasy' in music had long implied a free structure, where the composer was free to follow his or her ideas. However, *Romeo And Juliet* is in sonata form, with a slow introduction.

Instruments

Tchaikovsky uses a relatively large orchestra.

To the double woodwind he adds a piccolo (sounding an octave higher than written) and a cor anglais (sounding a 5th lower). There are four horns in F (sounding a 5th lower), two trumpets in E (sounding a major 3rd higher), two tenor trombones (written in the tenor clef), a bass trombone and a tuba. The percussion section consists of three timpani, cymbals (possibly 'piatti' on your score) and bass drum (*gran cassa*). Above the strings on the score you will see two staves for the harp, and at the bottom the double basses have their own stave as their music is significantly different from the cellos. Some of the cello music may be written in the treble clef, an old-fashioned way of writing a high cello part, sounding an octave lower than written.

Structure

To standard sonata form Tchaikovsky adds Romantic harmonic twists and much development, both within and outside the Development section.

	Bars	Main Keys
Slow introduction	**1–111**	F♯ minor (modal), F minor, E minor, A minor, dominant of B minor
Exposition		
First subject	**112–160**	B minor, D minor, G minor, B minor
Transition	**161–184**	B minor, dominant of D major
Second subject	**184–243**	D♭ major
Codetta	**243–272**	D♭ major
Development	**273–352**	B minor, modulating, B minor, dominant of B minor
Recapitulation		
First subject	**353–366**	B minor
Second subject	**367–440**	D major
First subject and slow introduction themes	**441–484**	B minor, C minor, dominant of B
Coda	**485–522**	B major

The programme and themes

Tchaikovsky's music features three elements of Shakespeare's play:

- Friar Lawrence is represented by the music heard in bars 1–11. The clarinet and bassoon four-part harmony in F♯ minor with modal colouring sounds like a hymn (as befits a monk). The low register and dark colour of the clarinets suggest a tragic end.

- The feud between the Montagues and Capulets is the first subject theme, initially in B minor, with some immediate development of the theme in the exposition. This theme is loud and syncopated, and is scored for most of the orchestra.
- The second subject, first heard at bar 184 played by cor anglais and muted violas, signifies the love of Romeo and Juliet. It continues from bar 193 with the second subject second theme.

All the themes are heard a number of times during the work, sometimes alone and sometimes simultaneously. The use of the Friar Lawrence theme in the development, with and between fragments of the first subject, may represent the Friar trying to stop the fighting.

Tonality and harmony

Tchaikovsky explores some distant keys, often using an enharmonic change or moving a semitone. The first enharmonic change takes place in bars 20–21.

The C♯ in the bass (in D major) simply becomes a D♭ with the change of key signature. By the bass line moving from a pedal D♭–C (bar 36), the music moves towards F minor. Similarly, by the pedal C (bars 61–65) falling a semitone to B (bar 66) the music moves towards E minor.

A more complicated **enharmonic change** is used for the modulation at the end of the transition. As expected, the transition heads for the dominant of D major. However, the second subject is actually in D♭ major, a semitone lower than expected. The dominant 7th chord in D major (A, E, C♯ and G) is reinterpreted when the bass moves down to A♭ (A♭, F, C♯), leading to D♭ major.

Augmented 6th chords are used at the end of the codetta in bars 253 and 257 (B𝄫, D♭, E, G), and there is a similar enharmonic change to bars 20 and 21, but here in reverse (the D♭ in the bass then becomes a C♯).

Tchaikovsky's interest in keys moving by semitones is demonstrated in the development section, where the Friar Lawrence theme is heard several times. At bar 280 the theme begins on a concert A in the horns; in bar 302 the same passage is heard a semitone higher. Another example is found in bar 454, where the music from bar 446, originally in B minor, is repeated a semitone higher in C minor. Similarly, in the introduction the music from bars 1–38 is repeated from bar 41 a semitone lower (F minor instead of F♯ minor), together with fuller orchestration.

Tchaikovsky had been educated in Western harmony, but the modal opening and the alternating chords of B and G major in the Coda (bars 499–500) show a Russian influence.

Harmony point ↳ GOOD try to use

Orchestral textures

Tchaikovsky selects his orchestral colours carefully.

Imitation is used a number of times: in bars 90–96 the horns imitate the woodwind; in bars 115–117 the violas and cellos imitate the rising scales of the 1st violins in inversion. The imitation in the first subject continues with woodwind imitating the string syncopation from bar 122 and the variant of the first subject theme in the cellos and basses from bar 126.

The 1st inversion B minor chord played alternately by woodwind and strings at the end of the slow introduction, together with a crescendo and **stringendo**, is a striking moment.

The full tutti is saved for the really important climaxes: bars 151 and 353 (tutti statements of the first subject), where the cymbal crash on the third beat of the bar emphasises the syncopation in the rest of the orchestra, and bar 335, the climax of the development. The second subject is played by tutti from bar 411, where the melody in the piccolo, clarinets, bassoons and strings appears with a horn countermelody (played by all four horns), throbbing triplets and brass chords.

The tragic ending is clear in bar 462, where the Friar is unable to stop the fighting and the orchestra develops the first subject (even though this is the recapitulation). It is compounded by the only ***fff*** marking in the work, in bar 473. The music does then quieten down, but it is jolted with a sudden drum roll in bars 483–484, followed by the only silence in the work.

With nine bars of drum roll and fragments of the love theme, the coda sounds like a funeral march, followed by a chorale-like section from bar 495, based on the second theme of the second subject, played by woodwind and horns.

FURTHER LISTENING

Tchaikovsky wrote another 'fantasy-overture' based on a Shakespeare play: *Hamlet*. His *1812* overture – written in 1882 to commemorate Napoleon's retreat from Moscow – is very famous, due to its use of cannons, bells and the French and Russian national anthems.

SYMPHONIC POEM

By the 1840s, the composer Franz Liszt had ascribed the term 'symphonic poem' to a piece of music for orchestra in one movement. The music followed the events of the programme closely, rather than being constrained by sonata form. Many composers enthusiastically adopted the idea, with the more conservative staying with the concert overture. 'Tondichtung' in German and 'tone poem' in English were alternatives, if a composer wanted to avoid any symphonic implication.

The symphonic poem was very popular during the later 19th century but by about 1920 it had died out as composers moved towards more abstract ideas. Symphonic poems were written in Russia, France, Germany and other countries and typical themes included legends, historical events, poems by Goethe and Hugo and Shakespeare's plays.

Franz Liszt

Orpheus

The concept of 'thematic transformation' was exploited to the full in Liszt's works.

Liszt (1811–1886) – a Hungarian composer, pianist and teacher – spent much of his life in Germany and France. From 1848 he conducted the court orchestra in the German city of Weimar and had his orchestral compositions performed. Initially he employed copyists who helped him to orchestrate his works, but from 1854 he was confident enough to write alone.

Orpheus

- **Composed 1853–1854, first performed in Weimar in 1854, conducted by Liszt**
- **First published in 1856, dedicated to Princess Sayn-Wittgenstein**
- **Orchestration: Piccolo, two flutes, two oboes, cor anglais, two clarinets in A, two bassoons, four horns (in F and C, changing to E), two trumpets in C, two tenor trombones, bass trombone, tuba, timpani (C and G), two harps and strings**
- **Approximate performing time: 10 minutes.**

Context and programme

Although this is the fourth of Liszt's series of 12 symphonic poems, it was originally written as the overture to a Weimar performance of Gluck's 1762 opera *Orfeo ed Euridice,* as Liszt did not like the existing overture.

Liszt wrote a long introduction to the work, explaining that he had seen an Etruscan vase in the Louvre showing Orpheus taming wild beasts with his music. The symphonic poem does not tell the story of Orpheus and Euridice but portrays the idea of the Arts taming man's brutal instincts. This was typical of Liszt's approach to programme music; he wanted to convey general ideas rather than a narrative.

Structure

Though Liszt had invented the term symphonic poem for works that did not strictly follow Classical structures, this work is in abridged or modified sonata form, as found in some Classical second movements.

Though there appear to be several themes, Liszt used **thematic transformation**, where one theme is changed over the course of several presentations.

Liszt uses two main key areas, which help to define the sections. The music begins with 14 bars of introduction. Octave Gs are played three times by the horns, followed by an E♭ major chord, then an A7 chord. These first two key areas are a tritone apart, and their significance only becomes clear once the exposition begins: they are a minor 3rd above and below the main key of C major. This is the first of several mediant relationships.

The exposition begins in bar 15 with the final horn Gs in C major and a 1st horn and cello theme from bar 16.

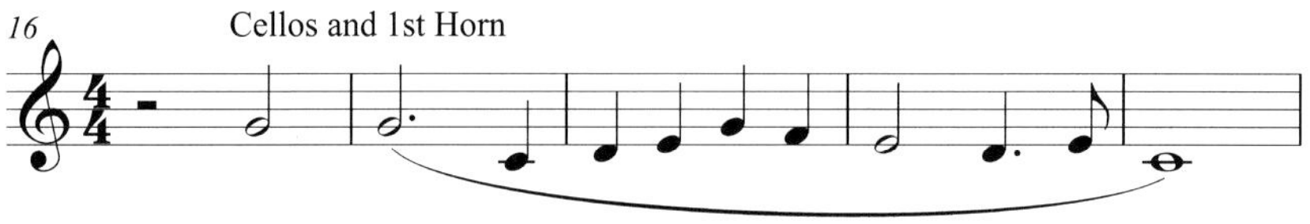

This opening melody is transformed from bar 38, played by the 1st violins.

Another example of a mediant relationship is heard here: once the melody has been heard twice (bars 38–43) it is repeated a minor 3rd higher (bars 44–50). The music from bar 55 is a repeat of the music from bar 38.

E major is the secondary key of the work - not the dominant, but the mediant major. Some writers suggest that the cor anglais melody from bars 72–75 is yet another transformation of the opening melody.

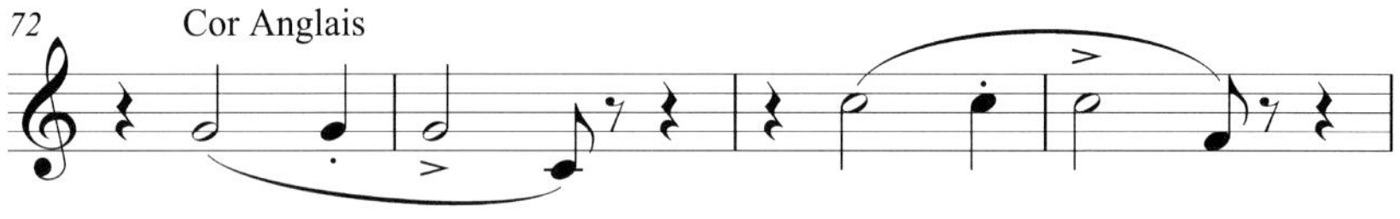

Bar 84 is the codetta, alternating chords of C♯ minor and major. Bar 102 restates music from bar 72, again in E major, with small changes in orchestration.

At bar 128 the key returns to C major, and bar 130 restates music from bar 38, with a clarinet countermelody. There is a powerful return of the main theme from bar 144, played by the whole orchestra, and bar 180 sees an unexpected return of the music from bar 72, now in B major. The main theme is restated from bar 195 and then, after a fast diminuendo, the music from the codetta at bar 84 returns from bar 206, this time with the alternating chords of C major and C minor. Bar 210 is a repeat from bar 206 in **augmentation**.

The work ends with a chord progression, beginning (in bar 214) with a C major chord and ending with a held C major chord. The chords used in-between are very chromatic, with the violins and violas ascending and the bass descending. The wind, playing only for the second half of each bar, adds a distinctive colour to the sound.

Orchestration

Though Liszt was initially unsure of his orchestrating abilities, the instrumental sounds have been carefully chosen. The prominence of the harp in the introduction refers to Orpheus's lyre, pictured on the vase in Liszt's preface. Solo players from each of the string instrument groups are heard, leading to a chamber music feel in places such as bar 122 (two flutes, two clarinets, two harps and solo violin).

FURTHER LISTENING

Three of Liszt's other symphonic poems concern significant men: *Tasso* (after the 16th-century Italian poet), *Prometheus* (from Greek mythology) and *Mazeppa* (after a real-life 'hero' from a poem by Victor Hugo).

Liszt also wrote programmatic solo piano music, for concert performance. *Au bord d'une source (Beside a spring)* is from the first suite of *Années de pèlerinage (Years of Pilgrimage)*. His set of 19 Hungarian Rhapsodies is based on Hungarian folk themes.

Richard Strauss

Don Quixote

Complex polyphonic writing and edgy chromatic writing marked Richard Strauss out as a leader in establishing a diverse harmonic palette for the 19th century.

Richard Strauss (1864-1949) - always referred to with his first name included to avoid confusion with Johann Strauss I and II - was regarded as the most important German composer of his day, although his use of chromatic harmony was not without controversy. He wrote a number of tone poems (Strauss' term for a 'symphonic poem'), which were some of his most successful works.

Don Quixote

- Composed 1897, first performed in Cologne in 1898
- Orchestration: Piccolo, two flutes, two oboes, cor anglais, two clarinets in B♭, bass clarinet, three bassoons, contrabassoon, six horns in F, three trumpets in D and F, three trombones, tenor tuba in B♭, tuba, timpani (D and A), bass drum, snare drum, cymbals, triangle, tambourine, wind machine, harp and strings (including significant parts for solo viola and solo cello)
- Approximate performing time: 40 minutes.

Don Quixote portrays episodes from the Spanish novel of the same name by Cervantes, published in two volumes in 1605 and 1615. It tells the story of a Spanish nobleman who, having read about knightly deeds, comes to believe that he is a knight and sets out on a series of adventures. He persuades a local farmer, Sancho Panza, to accompany him as his squire.

SCORES

The Dover score does not have bar numbers and the Eulenburg edition EE3504 begins numbering right at the beginning of the work, despite the fact that this is not a full bar. Eulenburg bar numbers are used here. German markings in the score are plentiful and there are many transposing instruments and clefs to negotiate.

Structure, programme and themes

***Don Quixote* is long and requires a large orchestra. It has an introduction, theme, 10 variations and a finale, with elements of a concerto, as there are prominent and virtuosic parts for solo cello and viola.**

These are not variations in the Classical sense, as they are different lengths (e.g. Variation 7 is just 11 bars, while Variation 3 is 135 bars) and do not share similarities in phrase structure. However, there are common themes which are heard in various keys and transformation throughout the work, a technique used by many other composers, including Liszt and Wagner.

The tables below will help you to locate significant features.

Introduction: (1–122) Don Quixote is at home reading about knights and becomes lost in fantasy.	
1–4	Quixote's first theme is heard in the flutes and oboes in D major.
5–13	Quixote's second theme is played by the 2nd violins, moving quickly from D major–A♭ major, a tritone from the opening key.
14–17	Two cadential progressions are heard, but they do not follow traditional rules of harmony and voice leading, although they finish on the tonic of D major.
19 onwards	Quixote's first theme is begun by the violas, but then loses its way, as Quixote's mind wanders further from reality.
24–33	A new theme is introduced: Quixote dreams of a lady (Dulcinea). This melody begins in G, but finishes in F♯ minor.

33–38	Muted brass and strings play a fanfare as Quixote imagines protecting the lady.
39–45	Quixote's and Dulcinea's themes are heard together and Quixote serenades her.
58 onwards	Three earlier themes - all connected with Quixote - are heard together, including his main theme in the violins and his fanfare theme in 3rd trombone. These begin in F major and lead into a section of complicated polyphony, which would have been new to late-19th century audiences.
83–85	After reappearances of Quixote's main theme and Dulcinea's theme in various keys, Quixote's theme is heard in augmentation in the brass in D minor.
113 onwards	After a build up in the texture, the ***fff*** dynamic and discords mark where Quixote descends into madness. Bar 113 has the notes E, G♯, B♭, D and F, which can be seen as B♭7 and an incomplete E7 chord together, or a German augmented 6th chord with the added root. From bar 117 the repeated note A is heard against a discord (E♭7) until finally in bar 122 it is heard alone.
Themes: (123–161) Don Quixote, the knight of sorrowful countenance and Sancho Panza.	
123–139	The solo cello is heard for the first time, representing Don Quixote, whose theme has been adapted to begin in D minor.
140–161	Sancho Panza is represented by solo viola and occasionally tenor tuba and bass clarinet. His first theme, played by bass clarinet and tenor tuba portrays the rustic side of his character (bars 140–142) while his second theme (bars 143–146) shows that he is very talkative.
Variation 1: (161–213) The adventures of the windmills.	
161–169	Quixote and Sancho set out.
169–178	Dulcinea's theme, guiding them on their way.
186–193	Flutter-tonguing in the piccolo and flutes represents the windmills turning in the breeze. Quixote attacks them, thinking they are giants. He falls from his horse.
194 onwards	After prayers and help from Sancho, Quixote can continue.

Variation 2: (214–248) The battle with the sheep.	
214–221	Quixote, played by three cellos, is determined to conquer the approaching armies (really a flock of sheep).
222 onwards	The sheep are bleating (minor 2nds and flutter-tonguing in the brass and clarinets) over tremolo violas, who represent the dust cloud created by the sheep.
227–232	The shepherds are piping (flute, cor anglais, bass clarinet and bassoon).
233–248	Quixote charges and, in Strauss's version, is victorious (not the case in the novel).

Variation 3: (249–383) Dialogue between knight and servant.	
249–319	Quixote talks with Sancho but becomes increasingly irritated by his questions and falls silent, letting Sancho prattle on.
320–331	Quixote breaks in, cross with Sancho.
332 onwards	Quixote is speaking of the wonderful deeds he will accomplish as a knight. The music is richly orchestrated in F♯ major and features the Dulcinea theme from bar 349, with some of the most romantic music of the whole work.
381–383	Sancho (bass clarinet) makes a cheeky query and Quixote turns on him furiously.

Variation 4: (384–431) Unfortunate adventure with a procession of penitents.	
384–397	Quixote is still angry with Sancho – Sancho's theme is not heard.
398	A procession singing a religious chant and carrying an image of Mary comes towards them. The semiquaver motifs sound a bit like the word 'Ave' being sung.
414	Quixote attacks the group as he thinks the picture of the Virgin Mary is an abducted maiden. He is knocked to the ground, unconscious.
423	Sancho mourns as he thinks Quixote is dead, but his mourning rouses Quixote.
426–431	Sancho shouts with delight and falls asleep with a snore (tuba and contrabassoon).

Variation 5: (432–471) Don Quixote's vigil.	
432	Quixote keeps vigil over his armour and thinks about his beautiful lady (the Dulcinea theme is heard in the horn and later in the solo cello).
452	The sound of the wind.
Variation 6: (472–514) Dulcinea's enchantment.	
472–475	The two men are looking for Dulcinea and come across three peasant girls on donkeys. Sancho tells Quixote that one of them is Dulcinea under a spell. The peasants' theme is played by the two oboes in 3rds in alternating time signatures.
476–487	Quixote makes himself known to the lady.
488–500	The peasant girls quickly hurry off.
501–514	Quixote is left confused.
Variation 7: (515–525) Ride through the air.	
515 onwards	Quixote sits blindfolded on a toy horse thinking he is riding a flying horse to rescue a lady. The sensation of flying is created by a wind machine, harp glissandi and orchestral arpeggios and runs, but the pedal D indicates that he is really on the ground.
Variation 8: (526–590) Voyage on the enchanted boat (barcarolle).	
526–551	Quixote and Sancho find a boat and set out in it.
552–557	They head towards a weir and catastrophe.
558–567	They are saved by the boat overturning.
567–581	They clamber out of the river and water drips off them (string pizzicato).
582–590	Sancho prays.

Variation 9: (591-616) Battle against the supposed enchanters.	
591-598	Quixote sees two monks on mules but thinks they are enchanters.
599-612	The monks talk to each other (bassoon duet).
611-612	Quixote creeps towards the monks - the start of his theme is played pizzicato in the lower strings.
612-616	The music from the start of the variation; the monks have hurried away.

Variation 10: (617-690) Duel with the knight of the shining moon.	
617-639	A duel is arranged with a neighbour of Quixote's, to bring him to his senses.
640	Following defeat, Quixote makes his journey home, the sound of his footsteps is the pedal on the timpani, below Quixote's and occasionally Sancho's themes.
649-657	Dissonance, as in the introduction, but resolved as Quixote's sense returns.
657-669	Quixote imagines being a shepherd and the piping music from Variation 3 returns.
670-675	Quixote's delusion and the dissonance return briefly.
676-690	Quixote's mind and the harmonies begin to clear.

Finale: (691-752) The death of Don Quixote.	
691-711	A gentle version of Quixote's theme as he takes to his bed for the last time.
712-714	Don Quixote is trembling.
741-742	The cadential progression from the introduction (bars 14-17) is now a clear, straightforward cadence.
743-747	A final phrase for the solo cello, then Don Quixote dies.
748-752	A quiet cadence, using Quixote's third theme.

Strauss makes full use of a range of orchestral timbres, including tuba and contrabassoon

Harmony

There is much chromatic harmony in this work, though it is still tonal. It opens in D major, the key of the whole work, with a perfect cadence in D in bars 4–5. However, the music then moves to A♭, a tritone away, as far as it is possible to be. This use of keys may emphasise the fact that Quixote is losing touch with reality. The tonic reappears with a perfect cadence in bars 12–13, followed by two cadential progressions in bars 14–17, which, although they end with a perfect cadence in D, do not follow standard progressions and voice leading.

The harmonic progressions follow the same pattern for the rest of the work: relatively rapid modulation through a wide variety of keys, with perfect cadences briefly establishing each new key. The dominant is not used as a contrasting key area, but A♭ (as seen in the Introduction) or the mediant of F♯ (used from bar 332, where Strauss is at his most romantic) could be seen in this role. The key of A♭ is also used in Variation 9, which begins in D minor, but uses A♭ major for the dialogue between the two monks from bar 599, reached via an interrupted cadence to the flattened VI in C major.

Discords (such as those from bar 113) are used at moments of tension or for programmatic effects (e.g. the minor 2nds from bar 227, representing the sheep). The use of chromatic harmony in the work emphasises Quixote's fragile mental state.

FURTHER LISTENING

This tone poem was the third written from 1894–1898. Strauss saw the fourth, *Ein Heldenleben*, as a companion to *Don Quixote*, portraying a different kind of hero.

Paul Dukas

The Sorcerer's Apprentice

***The Sorcerer's Apprentice* was one of the few works that escaped its creator's harsh judgement.**

The French composer Dukas (1865–1935) was very self-critical and left few works, having either destroyed or left incomplete those he didn't think good enough. Today, perhaps with the help of Walt Disney's famous *Fantasia* series of animations, Dukas is famous for just one piece of music, *The Sorcerer's Apprentice,* despite having written a symphony, ballet and opera, among other works. Dukas was particularly admired for his orchestration and his careful use of instrumental sounds is evident in this work.

The Sorcerer's Apprentice (a symphonic scherzo after a ballad by Goethe)

- **Composed 1897, first performed in May 1897**
- **Orchestration: Piccolo, two flutes, two oboes, two clarinets in B♭, bass clarinet, three bassoons, contrabassoon, four horns in F, two trumpets in C, two cornets in B♭, three trombones, timpani (F, C and F), glockenspiel, bass drum, cymbals, triangle, harp and strings**
- **Approximate performing time: 11 minutes.**

Context

Dukas closely based this symphonic poem on Goethe's 1797 poem *Der Zauberlehrling*. The score, when published, was accompanied by a French translation of the ballad.

It tells of a sorcerer's apprentice who is left to clean up. When he tires of working, he puts a spell on a broom to do the work for him. Unfortunately, there is soon far too much water and the apprentice cannot stop the broom. He chops it in half, but this only creates two brooms. Fortunately, the sorcerer returns and sorts out the mess. Though this work is subtitled a scherzo it is only a scherzo in style (lively triple time), not in structure.

Themes

The opening sounds very mysterious, reflecting the sorcerer. This is created by the use of artificial harmonics in the violas and cellos, and the 1st violins outlining a diminished 7th chord (C♭, A♭, F, D), not suggesting any particular key. Only once we hear the main motif played by the 1st clarinet in bar 3 does the tonality of F minor emerge. The motif of the busy apprentice is heard three bars before fig. 2, where the indication is 'vif' (lively).

A further important motif is played by the 1st and 2nd horns and trumpets from the fifth bar of fig. 3. This fanfare represents the casting of a spell, bringing the broom to life. The motif begins with an augmented triad (F, A, C♯/D♭), using notes from a whole-tone scale (F, G, A, B, C♯), moving to another whole-tone formation (E, G♯, A♯/B♭). The broom comes to life with the C7 chord four bars after fig. 5.

There is use of silence, with the broom beginning to stir, until it launches its own theme in the bassoons from fig. 7. Once the theme begins, the broom's movement continues to increase, growing from one note per bar to two and finally three.

For many bars the music moves constantly, with the broom's theme passed around the orchestra as it goes about its work. By fig. 38 the apprentice is aware that things have gone drastically wrong, and the fanfare theme returns shortly after this. The motif is repeated three times, rising in pitch, reflecting the apprentice's increasing panic.

Two loud chords in bars 10 and 13 of fig. 41 represent the apprentice chopping the broom, but the parallel 10ths of the bass clarinet and contrabassoon from 10 bars before fig. 43 portray the two brooms. The instruments play in different keys, the clarinet in D♭ major (A♭, B♭, C, D♭) and the contrabassoon in B♭ minor (F, G, A, B♭), adding to the sinister feeling.

The return of the fanfare theme just after fig. 49 could be the desperate apprentice calling to his master. A few bars later (the *a tempo* before fig. 50) we hear just how out of control things have become. The broom theme is heard clearly as it is played by many instruments, while the apprentice theme appears in cornets and 1st violins. At fig. 50 the broom theme moves to the trumpets and 1st violins, defeating the apprentice.

Fortunately, in the coda (*assez lent* after fig. 55) the sorcerer returns and the fanfare theme is in the full brass section as he commands the brooms to stop, with the two chords two bars before fig. 56 being the point where they become still. The viola solo after fig. 56 could represent the apprentice's apology.

FURTHER LISTENING

Dukas's French contemporary, Debussy, wrote the famous symphonic poem *Prélude à L'Après-midi d'un faune* in 1894. This sets scenes from a poem by Mallarmé, in which a sleeping faun dreams of nymphs.

***Danse Macabre* by Saint-Saëns (another French composer) is a symphonic poem for solo violin and orchestra, describing a churchyard on Hallowe'en.**

Bedřich Smetana

Vltava

During the second half of the 19th century, some composers felt there was excessive German influence on music and sought to do something different.

They created national styles, reflecting their own countries in a variety of ways, including folk music influences (scales and rhythms) or episodes from a country's history or legends.

Nationalist composers found many outlets for their style, including operas and symphonic poems. Nationalist composers include:

- Smetana and Dvořák in Bohemia
- Sibelius in Finland
- Grieg in Norway
- The 'Mighty Handful' in Russia

Smetana (1824–1884) was born in Bohemia, today the Czech Republic. Despite the fact that he was German-speaking, not learning Czech until he was nearly 40 and spending several years in Sweden, he became the first major Bohemian nationalist composer. His musical style reflected nationalist feelings in Bohemia at the time, with a revolution in Prague in 1848 and Czechs being allowed to give performances in the Czech language. Smetana composed nationalist operas and symphonic poems, though none of these use folk music.

Vltava from *Má Vlast (My Fatherland)*

- Composed 1874, first performed in April 1875
- Orchestration: Piccolo, two flutes, two oboes, two clarinets in C, B♭ and A, two bassoons, four horns in C, E♭, E and F, two trumpets in C, E, A and B, three trombones, tuba, timpani (E and B, C and G and D and A), triangle, bass drum, cymbals, harp and strings (including **divisi** cellos)
- Approximate performing time: 13 minutes.

Context

***Vltava* is the second symphonic poem in a series of six written between 1874 and 1879.**

Smetana had already written symphonic poems, influenced by Liszt, but with this set he chose to display important historical events, legends and scenes from Bohemia. He originally wrote a set of four, extending it to six later.

The programme

Smetana wrote programme notes for each of the symphonic poems in a letter in 1879, and added notes when the music was published in 1880. Vltava (also known as the Moldau) is the river that runs through Prague.

The symphonic poem follows the course of the river, from its beginning as two springs, past forests, a hunt, a wedding party, water sprites and a castle, through rapids and into a broad river through Prague, disappearing into the distance.

Structure

The music divides into eight sections, three of which use a 'river' theme, leading some to suggest that the structure of the music is a kind of free rondo form.

The Two Sources of Vltava	1–79	
Alternating flutes playing scalic passages, emphasising the tonic and dominant, introduce the first source and the sound of flowing water.	**1–15**	E minor
Clarinets represent the second source, playing the flute idea in inversion, and the two sources intertwine.	**16–35**	
Semiquavers transfer to the strings, with 2nd violins and violas and the two cello parts alternating.	**36–79**	
The main river theme for the first time, in 1st oboe and 1st violins; eight bars of melody are repeated.	**40–55**	
The river theme continues at a louder dynamic and with more instruments; the first phrase is repeated in sequence.	**56–63**	G major, E minor
Return of main river theme, but starting in the tonic major and reverting to the minor after two bars.	**73–79**	E major, E minor

The Forest and Hunting	80–117	
Hunting calls and fanfares in the horns and trumpets while strings continue the river semiquavers, now louder.	**80–117**	C major
Tutti ***ff*** and ***sf/rfz***.	**93**	F major
A tonic pedal, instruments gradually stop playing, and a *diminuendo*.	**102–117**	E major
Instruments change from compound time to simple time, beginning with cellos, then violas and 2nd violins, and then 1st violins.	**112–117**	
Rustic Village Wedding	**118–176**	
Only the note E is left from the previous E major chord (becoming the 5th of chord II in the new key).	**118–121**	
A woodwind and string melody in parallel 3rds, resembling a **polka** for the rustic wedding party.	**122–137**	G major
The celebrations become livelier as nearly the whole orchestra plays.	**137–153**	
Flutes, oboes and timpani play a dominant pedal, with accented syncopation in the flutes.	**153–169**	
Horns, cellos and basses play a tonic pedal; with the dominant pedal this gives a pastoral drone, after which the tonic pedal finishes the section.	**161–179**	
Moonlight and Dance of the Water Sprites	**177–238**	
Above the G tonic pedal of the previous section the woodwind adds a diminished triad, one note a time (G, B♭, D♭).	**177–184**	
Several ideas, with contrasting rhythms: 1. Flutes continue the gurgling of the streams in semiquavers. 2. Clarinets have rocking triplet quavers, outlining a broken chord.	**185–200**	A♭ major

3. 1st violins have a high theme in long note values. **4.** A dominant 7th chord in A♭ major (resolving in bar 187), with occasional harp arpeggios. The harmonic rhythm is very slow here.		
The ideas continue, but the key has changed and half of the cellos join the 1st violins, playing the slow melody two octaves lower.	**201–210**	C minor
The key returns to A♭ major and the brass add dotted rhythms.	**211–226**	A♭ major
Clarinets forsake their triplets to join the flutes in semiquavers.	**227–228**	E♭ minor
There is an enharmonic shift from E♭ minor to the dominant of E minor (B major). Although this new chord sounds very far away, the two chords have two notes in common (E♭=D♯ and G♭=F♯) so no preparation is needed. Smetana moves from E♭ minor straight to B major, with a pedal in the bass. The orchestration is gradually reduced, until only the flute and clarinet semiquavers are left over the dominant pedal.	**229–238**	Dominant preparation for E minor
Vltava	**239–270**	E minor
The music from bars 40–79 returns (without the repeat)		
St John's Rapids	**271–332**	
The loud dynamic and use of brass and percussion suggests faster-moving water. Strings have the semiquaver figure, ***ff*** and accented, and 1st violins have even faster triplet semiquavers. Two-bar sections of the Vltava theme are heard. There is much dissonance, with the A♯ in the bass forming a false relation with the A♮ in the other string parts.	**271–286**	
The very high piccolo over the full orchestra adds to the tension.	**287–295**	
The climax at ***fff*** dissipates with descending scales and a diminuendo.	**321–330**	Dominant preparation for E

The Broad River	333–358	
The main theme in the tonic major, played by the full orchestra.	**333–358**	E major

Coda	359–427	
The river flows past Prague Castle and a motif from the first symphonic poem (about the castle) is heard in the flute, bassoons and trombones, with the movement of the water still in the strings.	**359–373**	E major
A prolonged cadence moves to a tonic pedal and the river heads into the distance.	**374–425**	E major

Extended listening

- Rimsky-Korsakov, a Russian composer and member of 'The Five', wrote a five-movement suite of pieces for orchestra called *Capriccio Espagnol,* based on tunes and rhythms from Spanish folk music. It is not a 'nationalistic' piece, but has an exotic flavour and is famous for its brilliant orchestration.
- Sibelius wrote four symphonic poems called *Four Legends* or *The Lemminkäinen Suite,* based on the Finnish hero Lemminkäinen. The subject matter and themes were originally intended to be the basis for an opera.
- French composer Hector Berlioz's *Symphonie Fantastique* is a programme symphony – a symphony with a programme used in all the movements. Berlioz was inspired by Beethoven's 'Pastoral' symphony to write a programme symphony in five movements. It is thought to be an autobiographical account of Berlioz's unrequited love for the actress Harriet Smithson. To give the symphony unity Berlioz used *idée fixe,* where the same motif is used in a different form in each movement. This is another example of thematic transformation, and in this case the shape of the theme is dictated by the programme.

Music for piano

Grieg's *Lyric Pieces* and Schumann's *Kinderszenen*

In the Romantic period the piano was important, both in the concert hall and in homes. Piano manufacturing was a major industry, with pianos being produced in London, Vienna and Paris. Improvements to the mechanisms and structure meant that by the 1860s pianos were similar to modern ones.

Different manufacturers produced their own particular types of pianos, but universal changes included thicker strings, supported by an iron frame. Due to the piano's popularity much music was produced, particularly for people to play at home, including short pieces, transcriptions of orchestral music, and large-scale, flashy pieces for performance in the concert hall.

Many Romantic composers were virtuoso pianists (Liszt, Smetana, Schumann), but also wrote music suitable for those of a lower standard. Collections of short piano pieces were very popular: either character pieces expressing a single mood, or programmatic pieces with a descriptive title. These can almost be said to have been 'invented' by Schumann, with many other composers then also taking up the idea.

Edvard Grieg

Grieg (1843–1907) was a Norwegian composer who studied at the Leipzig conservatory in Germany.

Like Smetana, he was not initially a nationalist composer, but after meeting two important Norwegian musicians (the violinist Ole Bull and the composer Rikard Nordraak), Grieg decided that nationalism would be his way forward.

Grieg studied Norwegian folk music, producing many piano arrangements and using harmonic and melodic features of folk music in his compositions. He enjoyed creating musical pictures of the landscapes of Norway.
Grieg combined nationalism with other features of Romanticism, due to his training in Leipzig and his travels throughout Europe.

Lyric Pieces, Book 5, Op. 54

- Composed 1889–1891, published in Leipzig in 1891
- Six short pieces for piano.

Context

Grieg wrote 10 books of *Lyric Pieces* for piano, between 1867 and 1901. From the first book (Op. 12), there are signs of nationalism.

The series was very popular with pianists at home and made Grieg famous. The American conductor, Anton Seidl, made orchestral arrangements of four of the pieces under the title *Norwegian Suite*. After Seidl's death Grieg obtained the score, reorchestrated three of the works, removed 'Klokkeklang', and made an arrangement of 'Shepherd Boy' for strings, republishing the pieces under the title *Lyric Suite*.

Features

Op. 54 contains some of Grieg's most popular music. All the pieces make a feature of perfect 5ths, giving an immediate 'folk' feel. There is also use of pedal points, abrupt key changes and chromaticism. Grieg uses a wide range, including crossing of hands, and there are *una corda* and sustain pedal markings.

1. 'Gjetergutt' ('Shepherd Boy')

Features of this piece include:

- The falling leading-note in the opening, which is from Norwegian folk music
- Chromatic harmony from bar 17
- Bass in descending parallel 5ths from bar 30
- The coda (bar 46) features perfect 5ths piled up in the left hand.

2. 'Gangar'

This is a traditional Norwegian folk dance for couples, usually in duple time and sometimes performed at wedding ceremonies. It includes:

- Pedal notes, heard from the start, emulating the Norwegian Hardanger fiddle, which has sympathetic strings
- Parallel perfect 5ths which appear in bar 16 and are very prominent in the bass from bar 25
- A **circle of 5ths** from bars 25–40
- Offbeat accents, which appear throughout the piece and are first heard in bar 3
- A distinctive dotted crotchet beat, either as dotted crotchets or crotchets followed by a quaver rest.

5. 'Scherzo'

This piece is notable for:

- A perfect 5th, decorated in the left hand from bar 46
- The characteristic falling leading-note, heard from bar 198
- Its contrasting trio, from bars 71–134, with a change in tempo and texture. However, the melody in the right hand is an augmented version of the left-hand melody from bar 1. Grieg writes out the repeat of the scherzo, rather than just writing 'D.C.', even though the music is identical.

6. 'Klokkeklang' ('Bellringing')

The title is realised by:

- Bell-like parallel 5ths, which are a folk influence
- A programmatic reference to the sound of bells.

The lack of functional diatonic harmony in this piece led some to suggest that it looked forward to impressionism. Only in the coda (from bar 77) are 'proper' chords heard.

Robert Schumann

As a German composer, Schumann (1810–1856) was not a nationalist, though he wrote a great deal of programme music.

He had intended to become a virtuoso pianist, but an injury prevented this. He is more famous for his numerous collections of short pieces for piano than for larger works such as sonatas. Many of his pieces have descriptive titles, often added later. In many ways Schumann was the archetypal Romantic composer – a tortured soul who tried to commit suicide and was eventually confined to an asylum.

Kinderszenen, Op. 15

- **Composed 1838, published in Leipzig in 1839**
- **13 short piano pieces with descriptive titles (added after Schumann had composed them).**

Context

These pieces were written before Schumann had children of his own, so are reminiscences of his childhood. They are not intended for children to play, as some are rather difficult.

In print, the pieces were one of Schumann's first successes. They were written at the time when he was hoping to marry Clara Wieck, the daughter of his teacher, and are thought to have been inspired by her.

7. 'Träumerei' ('Dreaming')

This central piece is the most famous of the collection and was one of the most popular short piano pieces by any composer in the 19th century, being produced in many different editions.

Some 19th-century pianists liked to think they could hear Schumann's love for Clara (who eventually married Schumann) in the music. Though it has four-bar phrases throughout, it manages to not sound 'four-square' by using several modulations, syncopation and a polyphonic texture, with as many as seven simultaneous notes.

A	**1–4**	F major	The main musical ideas, ending with an imperfect cadence.
	5–8	F major–C major (dominant) via D minor (relative minor)	Begins as the first phrase, but modulates, ending with a perfect cadence in C major. Secondary dominant in bar 6, diminished 7th at the end of bar 7.
(Section A is repeated)			
B	**9–12**	F major–G minor	Continues with the same melodic ideas.
	13–16	B♭ major–D minor	
A¹	**17–20**	F major	Exact repeat of bars 1–4.
	21–24	F major	Changed from bars 5–8 to remain in the tonic key.

12. 'Kind im Einschlummern' ('Child Falling Asleep')

This is in E minor, with a middle section in E major and then a repetition of the E minor section. The $\frac{2}{4}$ time signature and repetition suggest the peaceful breathing of the child. The end of this piece features a circle of 5ths, but is left unresolved on the subdominant (A minor) until the first chord of the following piece 'Der Dichter spricht' (The Poet Speaks).

FURTHER LISTENING

Mussorgsky's *Pictures at an Exhibition* for piano is a set of 10 pieces describing a picture from an exhibition of the work of the Russian artist Viktor Hartmann.

Liszt's *Transcendental Étude* No. 4 in D minor, 'Mazeppa', is a very difficult piano piece based on a poem by Victor Hugo in which the hero Mazeppa is tied to a galloping horse. This leaves the horse and Mazeppa in a poor condition, but Mazeppa is eventually crowned king.

AS Level (2018)

Exercise 1

Complete the table below showing where Tchaikovsky uses each of the main themes in *Romeo and Juliet* and how the keys and orchestration are changed.

Friar Lawrence theme/slow introduction theme

Bar numbers	Orchestration	Key	Other features
1–11	Clarinets and bassoons	F♯ minor/ modal	Chorale, four-part harmony
41–51			
86–96			
280–284	Two horns		
293–297	Three horns		
302–307	Two horns		Semitone higher than bar 280
315–320	Three horns		
335–342	Two trumpets		Heard over rest of the orchestra because they are playing high notes
450–453	All brass and some woodwind		
458–461			

cybalyn

Montagues and Capulets theme/first subject

Bar numbers	Orchestration	Key	Other features
112–122			
126–130	Cellos/basses in imitation with woodwind	D minor	First subject with new rhythm
130–134			
151–161			
273–279			
302–305	2nd violins		Development of theme
321–342	Tutti		Fragments of theme developed
353–365			
441–445			With fragments of love theme inserted
446–449			
454–457		C minor	

Love theme/second subject first theme

Bar numbers	Orchestration	Key	Other features
184–192	Cor anglais and muted violas with horn, bassoon, cello and bass accompaniment	D♭ major	
213–243	Flutes and oboes with horn countermelody and woodwind and string accompaniment	D♭ major	Extended theme and added appoggiatura at the start
389–419	Piccolo and strings, horn countermelody now played by two horns to balance fuller melody, woodwind triplet accompaniment		With appoggiatura and extension of theme

419–435			Contrapuntal treatment of theme
436–438			Theme cut short
475–476	Violins and violas		In diminution
479–481	Cellos and basses		In diminution
486–492			Fragments of theme
510–518	Strings and bassoon		

AS Level (2017)

Exercise 2

Describe how Mendelssohn uses different timbres and orchestral textures in *The Hebrides Overture* ('Fingal's Cave').

A Level

Exercise 3

To what extent are Tchaikovsky's *Romeo and Juliet* and Liszt's *Orpheus* really symphonic poems?

Exercise 4

Which features of Strauss's symphonic poem *Don Quixote* demonstrate that it is from the end of the 19th century? Compare it with any other works of your choice.

Exercise 5

Compare Dukas's narrative approach to the composition of programme music in *The Sorcerer's Apprentice* with a piece of your choice that takes a different approach.

Exercise 6

Compare how at least two composers have depicted water in their programmatic compositions.

Exercise 7

How did composers display nationalism in their music? Refer to the work of at least two composers in your answer.

Exercise 8

Document the rise of short pieces of music for piano during the 19th century, referring to at least two different works.

Fragmentation of styles

OVERVIEW

The 20th century was a politically turbulent time. World wars and revolution changed Europe. Technology took the European tradition all over the world and brought in new influences. The sense of a world in chaos and the concept of freedom of choice led to new innovations and a fragmentation of styles.

A performance of Stravinsky's ballet, *Petrushka* (1912)

When Arnold Schoenberg submitted his composition *Verklärte Nacht* (*Transfigured Night*) for string sextet to the Vienna Music Society, it was rejected. One chord, it was said, did not exist. Innovation is an inevitable part of the creative process.

Young composers begin by learning the accepted musical styles of their time, but in time they develop their own voice. Audiences may take some time to accept new styles or techniques. Within a few years Schoenberg was writing compositions in which tonality had been abandoned.

In 1913 a Viennese audience rioted at a concert of music by Schoenberg and his pupils Berg and Webern. Again in 1913 another riot took place in Paris at the first performance of Stravinsky's *The Rite Of Spring*, which challenged conventional notions of rhythm and metre.

Composers were breaking away from accepted forms of music, finding new inspirations and developing new styles. Some of these styles were shared by like-minded composers and given general names that sum up their characteristics: **serialism**, **neoclassicism**, **avant-garde music**, **minimalism** and others. Some composers created unique, personal styles which cannot be easily categorised, such as Olivier Messiaen or John Cage. The fragmentation of musical styles since 1900 has contributed to the diversity found in music today.

What you should know

There is a summary of the requirements for this Area of Study in the OCR specification. There are also two lists of suggested listening, but you and your teachers are free to choose your own programme of listening to suit the requirements. You can use the suggested pieces in the specification or in this study guide.

You must find examples to cover the following:

- Styles of music since 1900
- Musical elements
- Conditions and context.

For A Level you need to know about all the styles listed, explain the music (using examples from your chosen listening) and be able to discuss the background from 1900 to the present day.

For AS Level in 2017 you need to know about the late Romantic style in music since 1900, explain the music (using examples from Part 1 of *The Rite Of Spring* by Stravinsky) and be able to discuss the background to the music.

For AS Level in 2018 you need to know about national styles (e.g. music based on folk traditions), explain the music (using examples from the first two movements of *Sinfonia Antartica* by Vaughan Williams) and be able to discuss the background to the music.

Listening to music is vital. The examples in this book are a starting point. If you can, find and explore other music. Listen to recordings, and locate scores to help you. If possible, go to live performances of music, including new music by composers working today. Better still, develop your own skills in performing music written since 1900 and use ideas from contemporary composers in your own compositions.

Keep a notebook or folder with details of your listening. For the essay question in the examination you will need to show that:

- You are **familiar with the music**. Aim to learn the music well enough to be able to discuss it confidently.
- You have **listened carefully** and **analysed** the music. This means being able to explain overall features and discuss details of the music and the performances.
- You know the **technical language** to discuss the music convincingly.
- You know the **background** to the music and its composers. Some of the information is given in this study guide. Find out more about these topics. Conduct your own research.
- You are able to make **critical judgements**. Use your knowledge of the music and the background to express an opinion. This includes being able to discuss change over time, strengths and weaknesses, and successes and failures. You have to support your opinions with reason and evidence.

Igor Stravinsky (1882-1971)

Late Romantic style

Mahler and Elgar

Intense musical expression was the focus of the late Romantic style.

The music of Richard Wagner (1813–1883) was a dominating influence on composers at the end of the 19th century and at the beginning of the new century. His music dramas (as he called his operas), particularly *Tristan und Isolde* and *Der Ring des Nibelungen*, set the pattern for much of the musical thinking of composers from all over Europe. The harmony and tonality of *Tristan* was far ahead of its time, but by 1900, constantly shifting keys and chromatic chords were largely accepted by audiences.

The characteristics of the late Romantic style are:

- Chromatic harmony. Chromatic appoggiaturas and passing notes are used much more freely to achieve intense expressive feeling. There is still plenty of diatonic music, but chromatic passages can be used for contrast.
- Increased use of modulation or passing modulations, weakening the sense of key.
- Less use of periodic phrasing or clear cadences, making the music continue for longer periods without coming to a rest.
- Wider melodic intervals, e.g. falling 6ths or rising 7ths.
- Sophisticated techniques of orchestration, with much attention to instrumental colours and richness of texture. Composers experimented with texture, sometimes creating chamber-like textures within an orchestral piece, or writing rich, complex textures for smaller chamber ensembles.
- Piano music becomes much more elaborate in texture, covering the full range of the instrument and including complex inner parts, sometimes requiring notation on three staves.
- Large symphonic structures, calculated to achieve an overwhelming build-up effect on the audience.
- A chorus could be used in addition to the orchestra to add colour or volume.

Mahler: Symphony No. 6

The Symphony No. 6 in A minor (1905) by Gustav Mahler (1860–1911) shows many of these characteristics in practice.

Like almost all of Mahler's nine symphonies it uses a large orchestra and lasts well over an hour in performance. Unlike some of the others there are no solo voices and no chorus: it is purely instrumental.

The first movement is in sonata form, complete with an exposition repeat. The march rhythm at the beginning is typical of much of the work. The melodic writing uses compound intervals (intervals larger than an octave), characteristic of the emotionally charged expression of the late Romantic style.

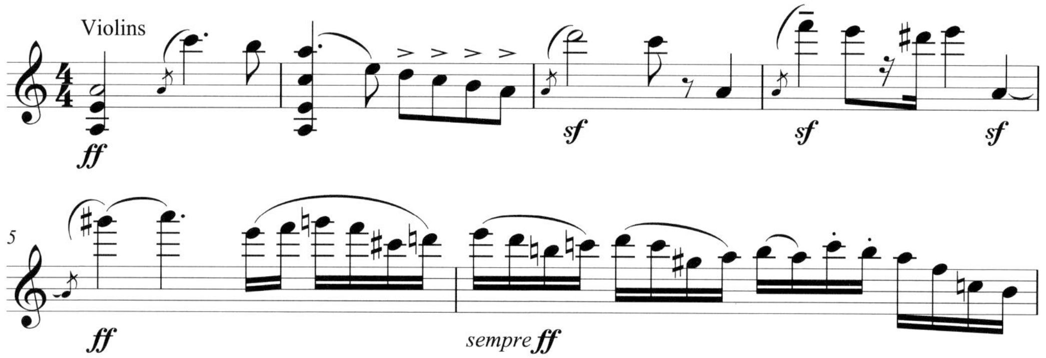

Mahler's music is often regarded as very personal, even autobiographical. This work is sometimes known as the 'Tragic' symphony. Although this label was not Mahler's, he uses the full orchestra to achieve a powerful musical impact, which is serious and driven. Contrasting with the exposition's 'march of fate' mood is the atmospheric passage in the development, suggesting a distant alpine scene. He uses the instruments with sensitivity and delicacy, including the use of cowbells, celesta and harp to provide the mountain atmosphere.

For much of the 20th century Mahler's lengthy symphonies were regarded as gigantic oddities, but now they are standard repertoire for modern orchestras.

FURTHER LISTENING

Richard Strauss (1864–1949) and Giacomo Puccini (1858–1924) were respectively the leading composers of German and Italian opera in the late Romantic style.

Strauss's *Salome* (1905) created a sensation for its treatment of the Biblical story and its dissonant musical style. A good introduction to the work is the orchestral 'Dance Of The Seven Veils', which appears near the climax of the opera. Puccini's *Turandot* was his last opera, unfinished at his death but first performed in 1926. The music is bold and colourful, exploiting the pentatonic scale to suggest the Chinese setting of the story. It is best known for the tenor aria 'Nessun dorma'.

Elgar's Cello Concerto

The Cello Concerto in E minor, Op. 85 (1919) by Edward Elgar (1857–1934) shows some of the characteristics of the late Romantic style.

The concerto is more compact than his two symphonies and violin concerto as the first three movements are short. Only the fourth movement has a large-scale design.

Elgar is careful to allow the sound of the cello to be heard clearly over the orchestra. There are only a few orchestral tuttis, and they only occur when the cello is not playing. At the end of the finale the fast, rondo-like music gives way to a slow passage of intense expression.

Jacqueline du Pré, a celebrated performer of Elgar's Cello Concerto

Schoenberg: Chamber Symphony No. 1

Elgar's writing is effective and technically accomplished, using a heavily Romantic harmonic style. By comparison, Schoenberg's Chamber Symphony No. 1 in E, Op. 9, composed over a decade earlier in 1906, departs from the Romantic style.

Within the work, the four movements of a typical symphony have been compressed into one, lasting just over 20 minutes. The large symphony orchestra is replaced by a smaller group: flute, oboe, cor anglais, three clarinets (D, A/B♭ and bass clarinet), bassoon, contrabassoon, two horns, two violins, viola, cello and double bass (contrabass).

The more adventurous harmonic style is clear from the opening:

Theme 1

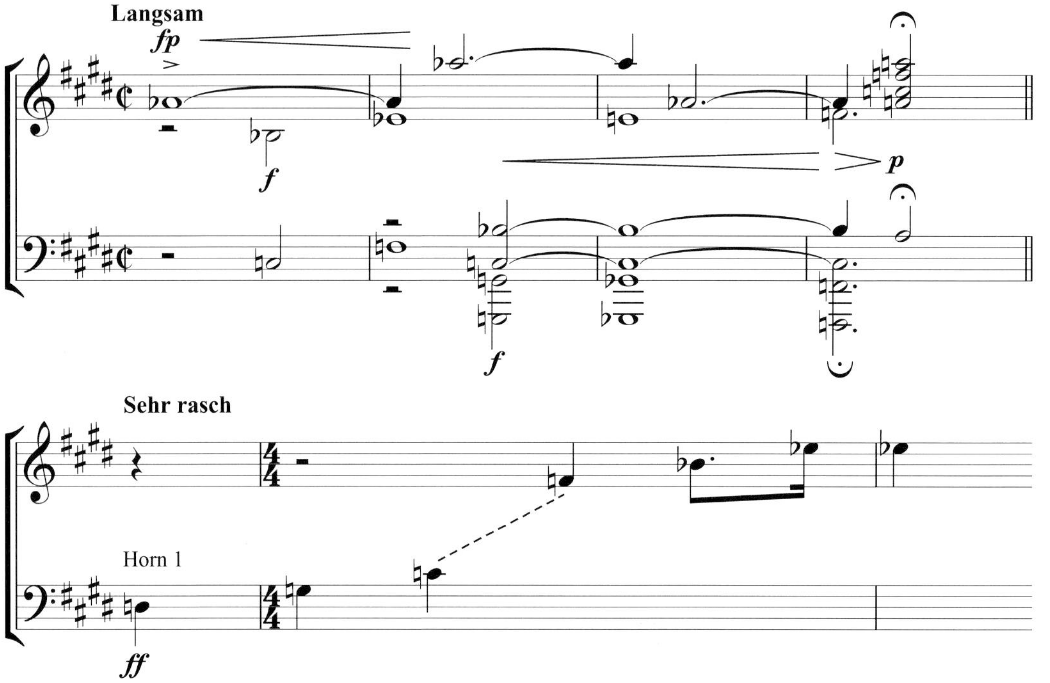

Although the key signature is E major, the opening harmonies are very remote from this. Notice how the opening chord is built up from dissonant notes, with intervals of a 7th between the notes of the opening chord, and intervals of a 4th (known as quartal harmony) in the second bar, resolving to a pure F major chord. The 4ths then become the defining feature of the main theme, first heard in the solo horn.

Theme 2

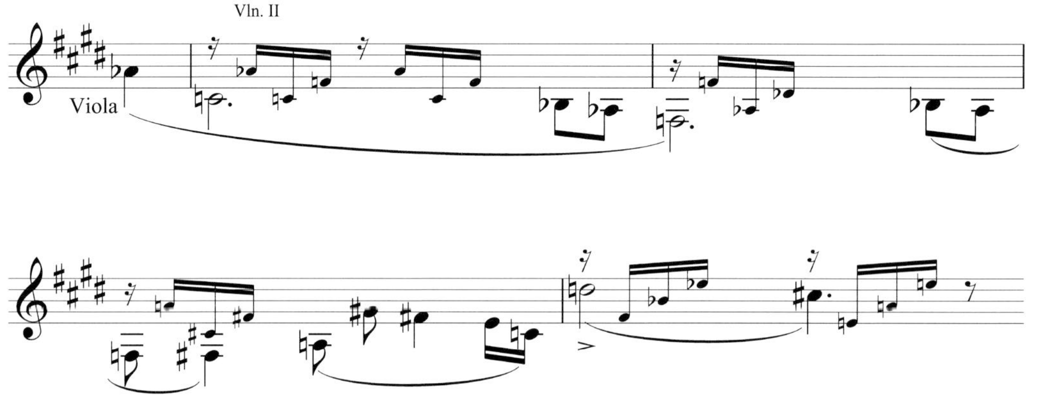

The second subject is a more lyrical melody, with the same wide intervals characteristic of late Romantic melody (which we noticed in the music of Mahler and Elgar). It begins in the remote key of F minor but the tonality changes quickly.

Impressionism

Debussy's *La Mer*

Claude Debussy (1862–1918) gave many of his works illustrative titles. His work is often compared with that of the French impressionist painters, such as Monet and Renoir.

Obvious links between Debussy's compositional style and the impressionist art movement are:

- Debussy's pictorialism (creating images through music)
- The way he uses colourful harmonies and textures in music
- The fact that he was French.

As with all labels, sometimes describing his music as impressionistic is not particularly helpful or revealing.

Debussy made a number of important contributions to the development of post-Romantic music:

- Moving away from the intense, late Romantic influence of Wagner
- Allowing music to be introspective, exploring new sounds and ideas, but also able to explore moods, thoughts and feelings in the way that dreams move from one idea to the next
- Turning away from large structures and working through themes by repetition and development. Allowing music to unfold and refresh itself by adding new ideas
- Using extended chords (7ths, 9ths, 11ths, etc.) for their sound alone, moving away from traditional functional harmony (where chords have implications of movement to and from tonal centres)
- Freedom to be influenced by new sounds, (e.g. from Spain or the gamelan music of Bali), and the exploration of new scales (e.g. whole-tone, modal influences).

'Jeux de vagues'

The second movement of *La Mer* (1905) is titled 'Jeux de vagues' ('Play of the waves').

Note how Debussy introduces a succession of ideas and motifs, shifting quickly between distantly related keys and chords:

- Beginning, F♯m9
- Bar 9, fig. 16, Cmaj7, with the sharpened 4th (F♯) in the cor anglais melody
- Bar 18, fig. 17, F♯maj7 over a G♯ pedal, the melody in the oboe
- Bar 28, fig. 18, B♭9
- Bar 36, fig. 19, Emaj7, alternating between C♮ and B.

At the end of the movement Debussy builds up to a powerful climax, combining melodic motifs in a rich orchestral texture. He uses a pedal G♯, lasting 44 bars. This changes to B♭ at the decisive moment in the music.

Modernism

Stravinsky's *The Rite Of Spring*

AS PRESCRIBED WORK 2017

The Rite Of Spring (1913) is the third of the ballet scores that Igor Stravinsky (1882–1971) wrote for Sergei Diaghilev's Ballets Russes.

Stravinsky was brought up in St Petersburg, where his father was an opera singer at the Mariinsky Theatre. Stravinsky half-heartedly embarked on a law degree while taking music lessons from the composer Rimsky-Korsakov. After attending a performance of *Fireworks*, the impresario Sergei Diaghilev asked Stravinsky to do some orchestrations for him. In Paris, Diaghilev had exhibited Russian art and arranged concerts of Russian music. There was a vogue for Russian culture. Now he planned to bring Russian ballet to Paris.

Set up in 1909, the Ballets Russes created a sensation for the quality of its dancing. It never performed in its native Russia, but its Russian-trained dancers set new standards for ballet in western Europe. Its famous male dancers included Vaslav Nijinsky, who choreographed *The Rite Of Spring*. Diaghilev commissioned works from leading composers, including Debussy and Ravel. From Stravinsky, three ballet scores were to

launch his career as a composer: *The Firebird* (1910), *Petrushka* (1912) and *The Rite Of Spring*, often referred to by its French title, *Le sacre du printemps*.

The scenario for *The Rite Of Spring* was developed by Stravinsky and the painter and anthropologist Nicholas Roerich (who designed the costumes). The setting is prehistoric times. Pagan tribes celebrate the Spring. Part II is centred on 'the chosen one,' who dances herself to death in a wild sacrificial ritual.

DISNEY

An abridged version of the music was used for the Disney animated movie *Fantasia* (1940). The scenario was changed to cover the creation of the Earth, the evolution of life and dinosaurs.

The Rite Of Spring score

The orchestral score is not easy to follow. There are many instrumental parts, often divided or combined into complex textures.

If you are listening to the music, the melody can be hard to locate in the score. The complex rhythms and the irregular bar lengths are an extra challenge.

You will find something new every time you look at the score:

- The layout of the score is the same as in Haydn, Mozart and Beethoven. Woodwind are at the top, then brass and percussion, with strings at the bottom.
- Try following individual instruments. The 1st violin can often be heard clearly and the bright tone of trumpets and flutes tend to stand out. In some passages cellos and basses are easy to follow.
- Try counting the beats in each bar, using the top number in the time signatures as a guide.

The orchestra

The orchestra is very large:

- Extra woodwind includes two piccolos, alto flute, two cor anglais, two bass clarinets, clarinets in D and E♭ (labelled in the score as piccolo clarinet) and two contrabassoons.
- There are eight horns (two horn players doubling tenor tubas). The trumpets include a high trumpet in D and a bass trumpet. There are two bass tubas.
- The percussion requires two timpani players. Look at 'Ritual Of The Rival Tribes' (fig. 57–60) to see how they divide between high and low pitches.
- Other percussion is limited: bass drum, guiro, tam-tam (gong), triangle and antique cymbals (pitched to A♭ and B♭). Cymbals and side drum are not used.

Transposing instruments

The added woodwind and brass parts have their own transpositions. The score lists the instruments in Italian, with their transposition in French.

In score	English	Sounding
Cl. in La	Clarinet in A	Minor 3rd lower than written
Cl. in Sib	Clarinet in B♭	Major 2nd lower than written
Cl. bas in Sib	Bass clarinet in B♭	Major 9th lower than written
Cl. picc. in Re	Clarinet in D	Major 2nd higher than written
Cl. picc. in Mib	Clarinet in E♭	Minor 3rd higher than written
C. ing.	Cor anglais	Perfect 5th lower than written
Fl. alto	Alto flute	Perfect 4th lower than written
Cor. in F	Horn in F	Perfect 5th lower than written
C. Fag.	Contrabassoon	Octave lower than written
Cb.	Double bass	Octave lower than written
Tr. picc. in Re	Trumpet in D	Major 2nd higher than written
Tr. in Do	Trumpet in C	At pitch
Tbe./tbe. bas	Bass tuba	At pitch
Tbe. ten. in Sib	Tenor tuba in B♭	Major 9th lower than written

Structure

The Rite Of Spring is made up of separate dance sections, played without a break.

There is an overall accelerando shape in both Part I and Part II, beginning with a slow introduction, with more movement as the action is developed, and ending with a fast, wildly energetic final dance.

Part One: 'Adoration Of The Earth' ('L'adoration de la terre')

	Score ref.	Tempo indication	
Introduction		Lento Più mosso Tempo I	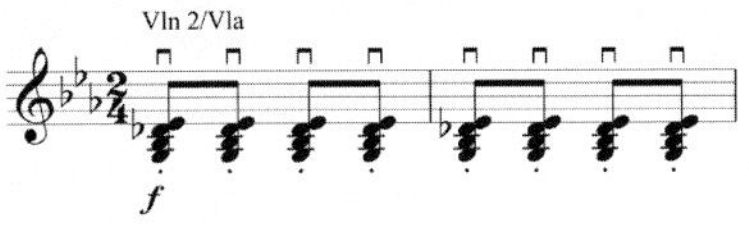
'The Augurs Of Spring: Dances Of The Young Girls'	Fig. 13	Tempo giusto	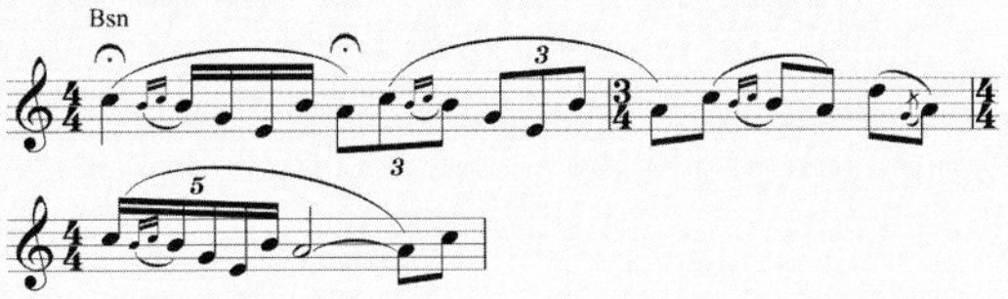
'Ritual Of Abduction'	Fig. 37	Presto	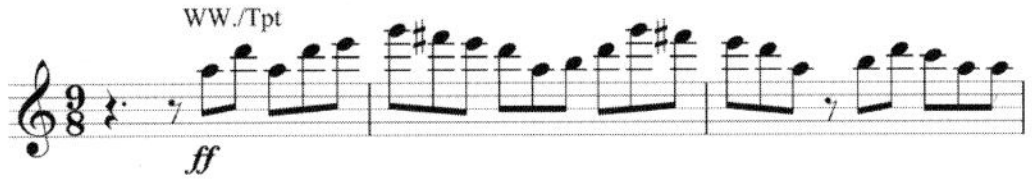
'Spring Rounds'	Fig. 48	Tranquillo Sostenuto e pesante Vivo Tranquillo	
'Ritual Of The Rival Tribes'	Fig. 57	Molto allegro	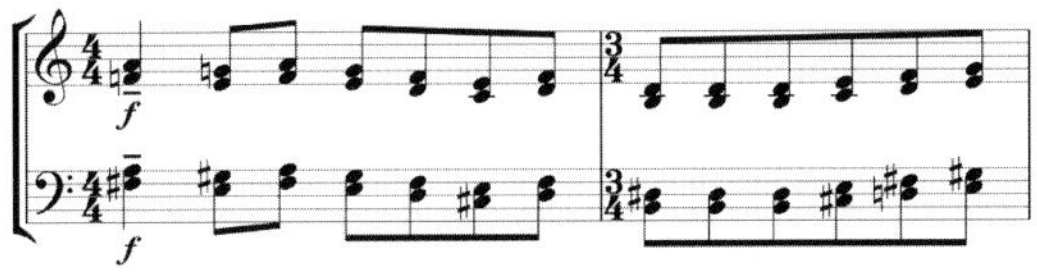
'Procession Of The Sage'	Fig. 67		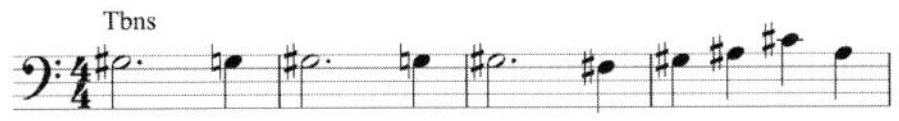
'The Sage'	Fig. 71	Lento	
'Dance Of The Earth'	Fig. 72	Prestissimo	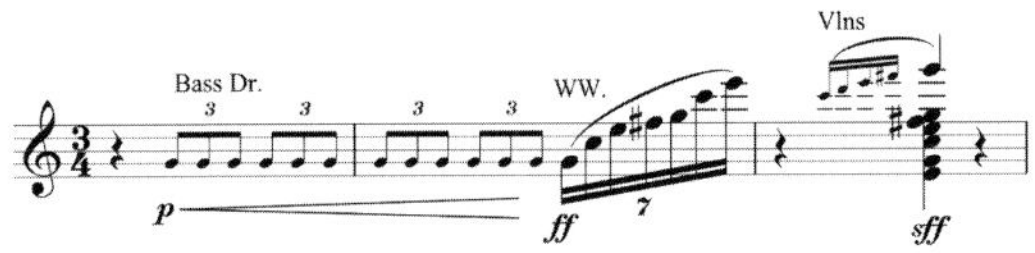

Introduction

The opening solo is very high in the bassoon's range. The melody is adapted from a folk melody – it is ornamented, and its pulse is disguised by pauses and varied subdivision of the beat into triplets, semiquavers or quintuplets. Solo woodwind sounds dominate this section, suggesting the sounds of nature and of early humans. The strings are used very sparingly, for example a trill in the violins (fig. 6) or the delicate use of six solo double basses at fig. 10, playing a muted (*con sordino*) chord of harmonics over a pizzicato syncopated triplet B.

The melodic material is introduced in stages:

- Fig. 2, a pentatonic melody in the cor anglais
- Fig. 4, an expressive descending chromatic motif in the D clarinet
- Fig. 5, a motif on the notes of a C♯ minor triad in the oboe
- Fig. 9, an elaborated calling melody in the oboe, beginning with the descending 4th, answered two bars later by an inverted version in the clarinet in D.

The use of ornaments and rapid decoration is typical of the melody lines in this section. The music builds up to a complicated texture at fig. 11 before stopping abruptly for the return of the opening melody. A new four-note motif (in pizzicato violins) provides the ostinato figure for the next section.

'The Augurs Of Spring: Dances Of The Young Girls'

The 'Augurs' chord

The harmony for this section is based on two superimposed chords: E♭7 and F♭. The strings repeat the chord in quavers, each one played with a down bow, **non divisi** (which means playing both notes at once). The sforzandi in the eight horns (bass clef horns sound a perfect 4th higher than written) reinforce the syncopated accents in the strings. The first three sforzandi are on offbeats, the next two on the beat and then a final offbeat again. The combination is unpredictable.

The four-note ostinato motif (with notes from the E♭7 chord) is taken up by the cor anglais at fig. 14, where it remains for most of the section. The harmony includes a C major broken chord here and in the new viola motif at fig. 16. Rimsky-Korsakov and other Russian composers were interested in using new scales at this time. These included eight-note scales (sometimes known as **octatonic** scales), which can be heard in the harmony here. New varieties of scales provided interesting possibilities for composers.

The scale here is made up of the notes of two diminished 7th chords. One tetrachord (a four-note segment of a scale) begins on B♭, the other on E (an augmented 4th higher). The diminished chords and the tritone make it more unstable harmonically compared to major and minor scales.

Tetrachords

Scale

Ostinato

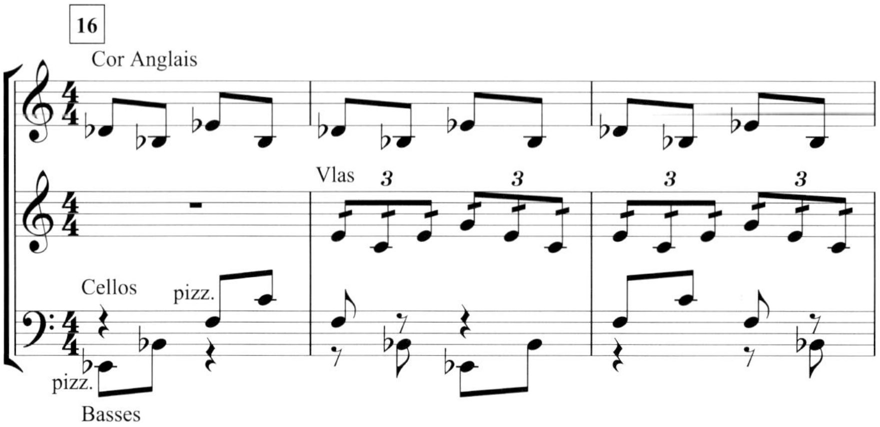

The opening string chords return at fig. 18 for a longer, more settled passage of 35 bars. A simple folk-like melody is added in bassoon and double bassoon. The four-note motif returns in cor anglais. At fig. 25 a new melody strikes up in the horn, made up of two four-bar phrases.

The melody becomes one of the strands in the passage at fig. 28:

- Melody in the flutes and alto flute
- Constantly moving semiquavers and trills in the clarinets
- The four-note ostinato in trombone and timpani
- Sustained chords in low woodwind.
- Quaver movement in the strings: 2nd violins *col legno* (hitting the strings with the wood of the bow), pizzicato 5ths in basses and cellos, creating a cross-rhythm of three crotchet beats against the $\frac{2}{4}$ time signature.

Having set up this rich accompanying texture, the four trumpets (with three solo cellos doubling the melody) introduce a new procession-like melody in close harmony:

This four-bar melody is repeated in shorter versions, with unpredictable phrase lengths: four bars (quoted above) + two bars + three bars + three bars + two bars.

The harmony is unchanged for long periods. It is based on a scale of E♭ minor, with a flattened 7th (D♭), giving it a modal feel (**Dorian mode**).

'The Ritual Of Abduction'

'The Ritual Of Abduction' is the first fast section of the work. Note the dissonance at fig. 37 with the clash between E♭7 in the trumpets and C major in the horns.

TEMPO

Listen to the fast speed Stravinsky takes for this passage in his recording of *The Rite Of Spring* with the Columbia Symphony Orchestra. Also note the swift, unsentimental phrasing of the 'Tranquillo' section at fig. 48.

The $\frac{9}{8}$ time signature is not always clear. It is disrupted at the beginning by the timpani in $\frac{3}{4}$, which has its F♯s syncopated (on the second and sixth quavers). Cellos and basses double the timpani tuplet at fig. 38. At fig. 43 the folk-style melody is played by the full orchestra in a homophonic texture. The changing time signatures are violent and disruptive: (in quavers per bar) 6+6+7+3+6+4+6+6.

At fig. 46 the fanfare melody from the beginning of this section is given similar treatment:

- The melody is arranged in irregular patterns. At first 5+5, then 4+5+6+5.
- The melody is punctuated by ***sff*** bass drum and cellos/basses, notated as a single $\frac{3}{8}$ bar.
- The punctuation transfers to full orchestra, now as $\frac{2}{8}$ bars interrupting the $\frac{6}{8}$ in the strings.

'Spring Rounds'

The procession melody from fig. 28 of 'The Augurs Of Spring' returns. Note Stravinsky's use of the orchestra's resources for colour and contrast:

- The melody at fig. 50 is scored for a delicate combination of four flutes and four solo violas.
- The tutti version at fig. 53 is reinforced by timpani, bass drum and tam-tam on the first beat of the bar.
- The trumpets and trombones are held back until the ***sff*** quavers at the end of the $\frac{5}{4}$ bar. The trombones slide (glissando) between the chords.

'Ritual Of The Rival Tribes'

The melody in trombones from fig. 64 is another example of the octatonic-type scale. Here it sounds as if it is in a different key from the strings: a C scale with a flattened 7th (B♭). The trombone ostinato continues without a break into the next section, 'Procession Of The Sage'.

Dance Of The Earth

The final section is the fastest of Part I. The three-beat pulse is set up in the ascending ostinato figure in the bassoon, violas and basses. Against this, strings, woodwind and horns have fast arpeggios or glissandi rushing up to single chords or triplet rhythms. The music alternates unpredictably between glissandi and chords or repeated triplets.

At fig. 75 the music goes suddenly quiet. The build to the end features a constant movement of semiquavers and triplets, at first in the lower strings and two horns. The crotchet pulse is in bass clarinets, repeating the first three notes of a major scale before extending to a whole-tone scale (A♭ – B♭ – C – D – E – F♯). Extra layers are added to the texture. For example, the bursts of repeated trumpet semiquavers are built step by step: firstly F in trumpet 4, then C is added in trumpet 3, then a higher F in trumpet 2.

The whole-tone ostinato repeats to the end. Finally, in bass clarinet, four bassoons, tuba and tenor tuba, it extends to two octaves for an abrupt finish on the last beat of the bar.

Stravinsky is commonly regarded as one of the most influential composers of the 20th century. His three early ballet scores for Diaghilev made him famous.

Continuous exploration

The Russian revolution prevented Stravinsky from living in Russia again. In the 1920s he pioneered the neoclassical style of music.

Pieces from this later period include the Octet for woodwind and the *Symphony Of Psalms*. By the 1950s he had become interested in serial methods and experimented with atonality.

Neoclassical styles

Tonality

For many composers, abandoning tonality was unthinkable. After the First World War there was a reaction against large-scale works and the excessively Romantic thinking of the pre-war era.

In France the later works of Debussy and Ravel provided the lead, using smaller forms, borrowing ideas from earlier eras and reinterpreting them in a 20th-century style.

Features of the new style were:

- A return to Baroque and Classical ideas of style and structure - shorter, easier to follow
- Clear textures, often writing for small groups of instruments (such as chamber music), highlighting solo sounds, especially woodwind
- An 'objective' style, emphasising craftsmanship and order
- Simpler, repetitive rhythmic patterns, returning to earlier composers such as J. S. Bach and F. Couperin for their dance rhythms
- The use of titles from older forms of music: sonata, suite, partita, concertino
- Exploration of tonality and harmony, use of dissonance, **bitonality**
- Restrained expression, grace, wit, humour, but also seriousness and emotion when required.

Germaine Tailleferre

Germaine Tailleferre (1892–1983) was the only woman of 'Les Six', the group of Paris-based composers identified in 1920 by the critic Henri Collet as representing a new movement in French music. Of the group, the most well-known are Francis Poulenc, Darius Milhaud and Arthur Honegger.

Tailleferre had studied at the Paris Conservatory, despite the opposition of her father, gaining several prizes and became part of the circle of young composers associated with Eric Satie.

Concertino For Harp And Orchestra

Tailleferre wrote a number of pieces for harp. Her *Concertino For Harp And Orchestra* dates from 1927. The work is laid out like a Classical concerto in three movements. The harp part is busy and inventive, supported by a light orchestral texture that allows it to be heard. The solo part is mostly an equal partner with the accompaniment, with little virtuosic writing, although the first movement has an elaborate, fully written cadenza.

The third movement is a short, lively rondo, structured **ABACABA**. The harp melody is clearly set out in regular phrases. The ascending glissando which opens the movement becomes a recurring feature of the work, returning, for example, at the end of **A**^{1} just before the fugal **C** episode. The movement ends with a solo march rhythm for the side drum before a short tutti final chord.

She worked on commissions for most of her life, including writing for film and television. Struggling to bring up her daughter and to make a living during the the Second World War, she managed to get to Portugal and then to the United States. She returned to Paris after the war. Much of her work is unpublished.

William Walton

As a young man William Walton (1902–1983) had early success with *Façade* (1923), a chamber piece for reciter and six instruments.

Described as an 'entertainment', it set poems by Dame Edith Sitwell, who gave the first performance reciting through a megaphone from behind a screen. Walton drew on a variety of styles, including popular music and quotation from other composers. In wit and lightness of style, *Façade* has much in common with the work of Satie and Les Six.

Belshazzar's Feast

By contrast Walton's oratorio *Belshazzar's Feast* (1931) is a large-scale work, first performed at the Leeds Festival. Despite the difficulties of the choral writing, the work was a great success. Its main features include:

- Dramatic and expressive writing for chorus, sometimes divided into two choruses
- A large orchestra, including two brass bands placed **antiphonally** left and right
- A baritone soloist, singing with the chorus and orchestra but also with extended unaccompanied recitative
- The overall key structure moves from D minor at the beginning for the captivity of the Israelites, to D major in praise of the Babylonian king, and finally to F major for his downfall. Dissonance is used for dramatic effect, such as in the opening chorus for divided tenors and basses, 'Thus Spake Isaiah'.
- Walton refers to other styles of music, for example the jazz-inspired rhythms at 'Praise Ye The God Of Iron' and the British Empire style march (similar to his later coronation marches) at the beginning and end of the 'Praise Ye' section.

FURTHER LISTENING

The 'neoclassical' label soon outgrew its associations with early classical composers. It can be loosely used to describe any 20th-century style that is essentially tonal, and was the dominant form for European and American composers in the first half of the 20th century. There are plenty of examples to listen to:

- **Hindemith: Concert Music For Strings And Brass, Op. 50**
- **Copland: *Appalachian Spring*, ballet suite**
- **Prokofiev: *Romeo And Juliet*, ballet**
- **Shostakovich: Symphony No. 5 in D minor**
- **Martinů: *Memorial To Lidice***
- **Poulenc: Organ Concerto**
- **Britten: *War Requiem***

Serialism and the Second Viennese School

Schoenberg, Berg and Webern

The Vienna of the early 1900s was a melting pot of intellectual and cultural activity. The 'expressionist' style in the arts explored intense emotional and psychological states, interested in dreams and the subconscious rather than everyday life. For Schoenberg the expressionist style led inevitably to atonality.

Schoenberg grew dissatisfied with his method of composition. His pieces were getting shorter. Without tonality it was getting difficult to write longer works. Even successful full-length atonal works, such as *Pierrot Lunaire* (considered one of his most original works), were made up of shorter sections. His pupils Alban Berg and Anton Webern faced the same challenge.

The name 'Second Viennese School' is a deliberate reference to Vienna's 'First School' of Haydn, Mozart and Beethoven. Schoenberg regarded his music as continuing their tradition.

Berg: *Wozzeck*

Berg's opera *Wozzeck* (1922) uses a number of methods to organise the music:

- Leitmotif - musical ideas associated with a character or idea
- The use of Classical structures to shape the music. Act 2 is a symphony in five movements; Act 3 is made up of six inventions
- The communication of text and story through spoken passages and **Sprechgesang** (a vocal technique between singing and speaking, used by Schoenberg in *Pierrot Lunaire*).

Wozzeck:
Act 3, Scene 4
pp
3
A - ber der Mond___ ver - rät mich,
Der Mond ist blu - tig.

Translation: But the moon betrays me, the moon is bloody.

Wozzeck is a soldier. He is exploited by everyone around him but he is too inarticulate and poor to control his own destiny. At the end of the opera he murders his wife and drowns himself. The orchestral interlude - an invention on a key (D minor) - is a powerful and expressive climax to the work. The final scene cuts to Wozzeck's child, told by the other children that his mother is dead. He carries on playing.

The opera was very successful and Berg was able to live off the royalties. Following its first performance in 1925 it was performed in many opera houses in Germany (before it was banned by the Nazis) and in Austria, Philadelphia, Leningrad and Prague. The BBC broadcast extracts from a London concert performance in 1932.

Serialism

Schoenberg's solution was to develop a new method of composition, known as serial or 12-tone technique. He aimed to be able to write longer works.

The main features of serialism were:

- A row of 12 pitches is constructed, using each note of the chromatic scale
- The order of pitches stays the same, giving a melodic identity to the music
- Pitches can also be combined vertically into chords, providing a harmonic identity to the music
- 48 versions of the row (sometimes called a set or series) are available. The row can be played:
  - in **retrograde** (in reverse order from the last note to the first)
  - in **inversion** (ascending intervals become descending intervals, e.g. ascending minor 3rd C–E♭ becomes descending minor 3rd C–A)
  - in **retrograde inversion**
  - each form can be **transposed** to begin on any of the 12 notes of the octave.

Berg vs. Webern

Two contrasting approaches to serialism can be found in Alban Berg's Violin Concerto (1935) and Anton Webern's String Quartet Op. 28 (1938). Both composers design a row that will help them to create a particular sound world.

Berg's Violin Concerto

Berg uses a succession of 3rds, ending with notes rising in steps of a whole tone scale.

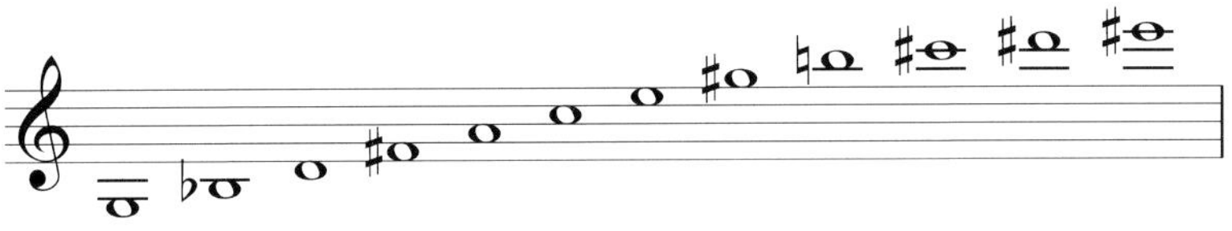

The 3rds are used to create tonal-sounding chords. The row also provides the open string 5ths that the violin plays at the beginning. As in Schoenberg's Chamber Symphony, Berg is able to contrast a powerful use of dissonance with highly expressive use of chords built from 3rds. The whole tones at the end of the row develop in the second movement into Bach's chorale melody, 'Es ist genug!' ('It is enough). Berg interprets the serial rules freely and allows himself to quote Bach's rather chromatic harmony (played *pianissimo* by a quartet of clarinets).

The concerto is dedicated 'To the memory of an Angel', a reference to Manon Gropius, the 19-year-old daughter of Alma Mahler, who died in 1935. Although the work was a commission for the violinist Louis Krasner, the highly expressive music is a response to her tragic death. Berg himself died before the end of the year.

Despite incorporating serialism, Berg's Violin Concerto is highly expressive and melodic, showing a strong Romantic influence.

Webern's String Quartet Op. 28

Webern's approach is strikingly different. Like Berg, his row is carefully organised: a four-note motif of pairs of semitones, inverted, then transposed. The intervals are limited to only 3rds and minor 2nds.

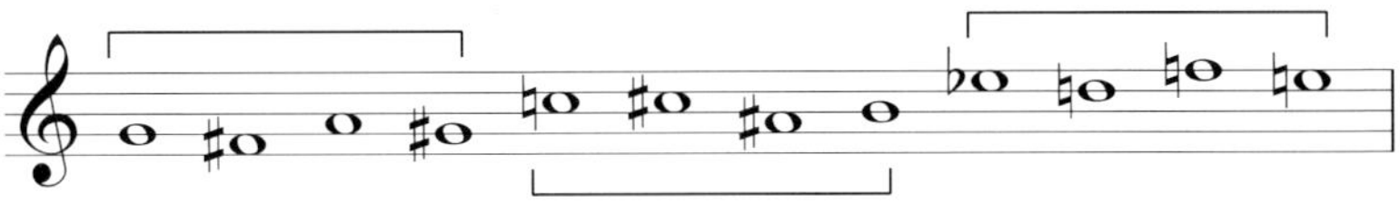

The notes of the original row can be traced at the opening of the quartet, up to the E in the viola (numbered 1-12 in the example). The pizzicato G♯ in the 1st violin is the first note of an inverted version of the row.

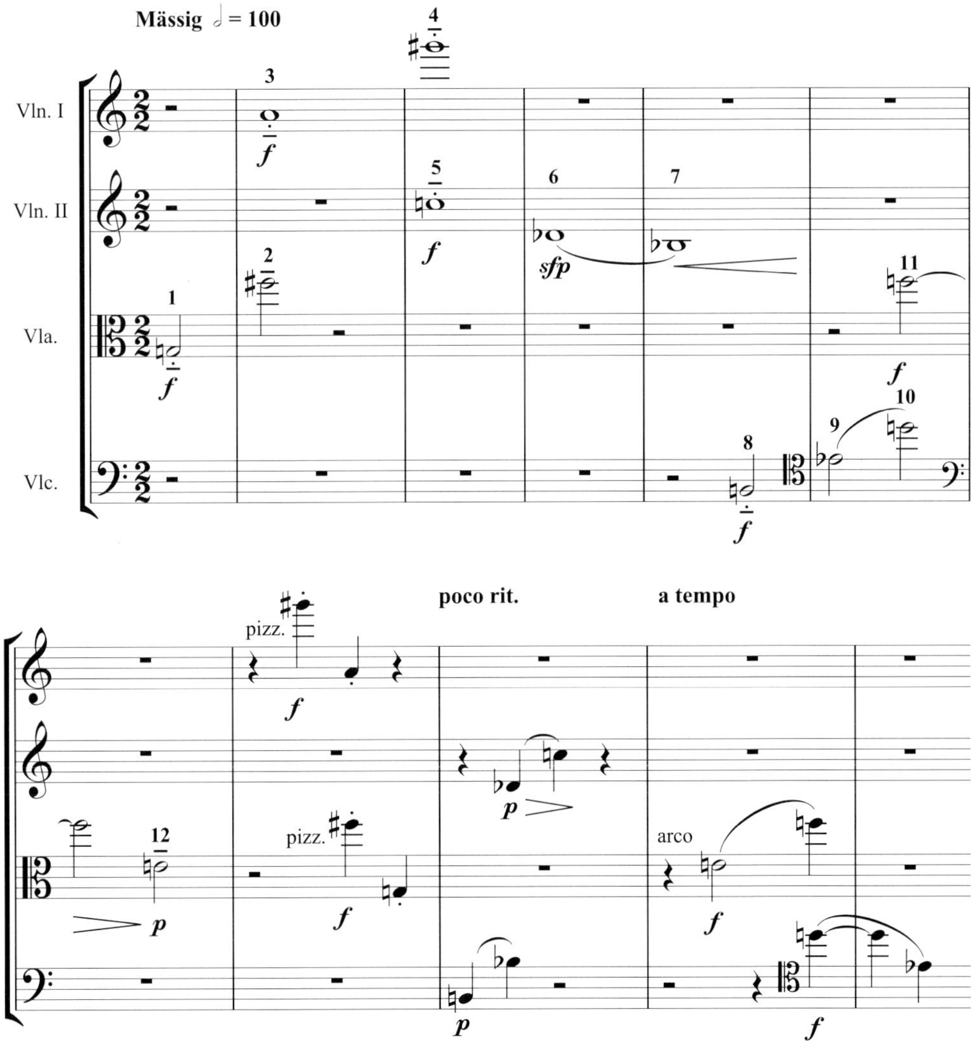

Webern deliberately avoids any suggestion of melody or any phrasing that would suggest Romantic forms of expression. The opening is built of exchanges of pairs of notes. Webern sets up canonic patterns, later in the movement made up of six-note phrases.

As in Mahler, wide intervals are intensely expressive: the opening semitones are stretched to two octaves. Each pair is treated with its own dynamics, articulation and string technique. Every note counts. The String Quartet is one of Webern's major works. Even so, it lasts for barely 10 minutes.

Webern was accidentally shot in 1945 by an American soldier. When musical life began to return to normal after the war, younger composers regarded Webern as an inspiration for a new style of music to replace the traditional thinking of pre-war composers.

National styles

Bartók and Vaughan Williams

Béla Bartók, composer and folk song collector

In the early 1900s the study of traditional music was just beginning in Europe. In *The Rite Of Spring*, Stravinsky used rhythms and melodies rooted in the traditional music of Russia.

For composers looking to move away from the musical style of Germany and Austria, the folk music of people in rural areas - away from the educated and refined tastes of the towns and cities - offered what they regarded as an authentic taste of their own national identity.

Composers such as Béla Bartók in Hungary and Jean Sibelius in Finland came to be associated with expressions of national identity at a time when both countries were parts of larger empires.

While Sibelius looked to the Finnish national epic the *Kalevala* for his inspiration, his style remained mostly unaffected by the traditional music of Finland. A tone poem such as his *Tapiola* is an atmospheric evocation of the forests and lakes of Finland, but Sibelius does not use folk melodies as sources for his scales and rhythms.

Bartók: String Quartet No. 5

The music of Bartók (1882–1945), however, shows the clear influence of folksong from his native Hungary and further afield (for example Bulgaria, Turkey and North Africa).

His String Quartet No. 5 (1934) shows how his music uses features of traditional music in a highly personal style.

The work is in five movements, symmetrically arranged. The first and last movements are fast, and there are two slow movements either side of a central Scherzo:

- Allegro
- Adagio molto
- Scherzo - Alla bulgarese
- Andante
- Finale - Allegro vivace.

The first movement begins with fast, aggressively syncopated, repeated B♭s, establishing the tonal centre of the work. The music is driven forward by complex cross-rhythms and intricate polyphonic writing.

The repeated quavers return (but never exactly the same) at important points in the structure:

- Just before the second subject (as a repeated double-stopped semitone, D and C♯), and after it (on C)
- At the beginning of the development (on E), before the music becomes even faster
- In clashing semitones (F and E) for the climax at the end of the development
- At the end of the movement, back to the home key of B♭.

The first movement has a similar structure to sonata form, but the recapitulation repeats material in reverse order. The distinctive repeated B♭s of the opening material return at the end of the movement (from bar 159) and in the coda. This creates an overall arch structure, sometimes called 'bow' (or in German 'Bogen') form.

The second and fourth movements are examples of Bartók's fondness for 'night music': slow moving, whispering sustained chords or tremolos, fragments of melody, trills suggesting night-time sounds. He exploits the textures and techniques of the strings fully. The *tranquillo* section that concludes the fourth movement uses a duet between a muted viola and the cello, under sustained chords in the violins. The repeated demisemiquavers slow to staccato sextuplets and reduce from ***mf*** to ***p*** to ***pp***, the last played col legno (with the wood of the bow). The movement ends with pairs of pizzicato chords, with glissandi between each pair of chords.

The faster third and fifth movements employ the dance rhythms characteristic of traditional folk music. The Bulgarian rhythm in the third movement involves a time signature of 4+2+3 quavers, changing in the trio to 3+2+2+3. The fast and exciting finale builds up to a climax (from bar 673) based on repetitions of a dissonant chord combining F♯ major and F♯ minor. The music then breaks off into a startling tune in A major over a drone (imitating the sound of a traditional instrument such as the hurdy-gurdy). The first violin repeats the tune in B♭ major (while the A major chord continues) to create a polytonal effect.

AS PRESCRIBED WORK 2018

Vaughan Williams: *Sinfonia Antartica*

Ralph Vaughan Williams (1872–1958) wrote the *Sinfonia Antartica* in 1949–1952. It was based on his music for the Ealing Studios film *Scott Of The Antarctic* (1948), which tells the story of Captain Robert Scott, the first British explorer to reach the South Pole.

Scott had narrowly failed to beat a rival Norwegian expedition to be first to the Pole. Exhausted and out of supplies, Scott and his men died on the return journey.

By 1948 Vaughan Williams was regarded as the leading English composer of his day. Like Bartók, he had begun composing in the German tradition but developed a personal style based partly on the folk traditions of his own country. As a young man, Vaughan Williams followed the example of English folk song collectors such as Lucy Broadwood and Cecil Sharp in collecting, arranging and publishing traditional melodies. The modal nature of many of the melodies influenced Vaughan Williams' own style.

Vaughan Williams believed that composers had a duty to be useful and contribute music that served the wider community. He edited the *English Hymnal*, writing new melodies himself and adapting folk melodies as hymn settings. He wrote choral and instrumental music for both professional and amateur musicians.

He had written the music for a number of films. In this case he did not see the film of *Scott Of The Antarctic* while writing the music. He was shown some still photographs and he composed several short sections. The music was then recorded, with Ernest Irving conducting, and edited to suit the scenes in the story. This suited the composer, who preferred in his film music to 'ignore the details and to intensify the spirit of the whole situation by a continuous stream of music'.

Vaughan Williams was much taken by the story of Scott, a popular heroic figure. He also responded to the opportunity to create original atmospheric and powerful music to convey the heroism of the film's subject and the power and danger of the Antarctic landscape. He seems all along to have intended to make a symphony out of the film music.

WORKING TITLE

Sinfonia Antartica **is the seventh of Vaughan Williams' nine symphonies. It is usually known by this title, not 'Symphony No. 7'.**

Movements

There are five movements, loosely following the story:

- Prelude*
- Scherzo*
- Landscape
- Intermezzo
- Epilogue

Movements with * are the prescribed movements for AS Level in 2018.

For each movement Vaughan Williams chose an epigraph (a quotation that goes at the beginning of a section), which is printed in the score. These are sometimes spoken in recordings of the work.

The opening theme of the symphony returns in the Epilogue (a title which Vaughan Williams used for the finale of other works). The opening is heroic and defiant, but the movement ends with the wordless chorus and the rise and fall of the wind machine. The direction is '*niente*' – fading away to nothing.

Orchestration

The orchestral scoring provides much of the colour and atmosphere of the music and is an essential feature of the symphony:

- The wind machine is a cylinder of wooden slats. It is covered in canvas and rotated with a handle to make the sound of the wind.
- The chorus of women's voices and the solo soprano, singing only 'ah', are used in the first and last movements. Voices are also used in the film score, but the wind machine is not.
- The percussion section includes glockenspiel, xylophone and vibraphone. A celesta, harp, piano and (in the third movement) organ are also included. This selection gives the composer a range of pitched timbres that he can add, for example to suggest the glitter and danger of ice and snow.
- Tuba and double bassoon play for much of the time, adding depth to the bass. Look at the second theme at bar 59^3, which is played in octaves: the tuba and double bassoon double the melody four octaves below the 1st violins.

Vaughan Williams was well into his seventies when he wrote the music. Critics recognised the vigour and inventiveness of the music, but there were suggestions that the orchestration was the work of Roy Douglas, who assisted the composer from 1947 to his death. Vaughan Williams was proud of his orchestration and he was irritated at the idea that he did not do it himself. Douglas wrote out the fair copy of the score that was used for the first performance, deciphering the composer's untidy original manuscript. In the process he made many minor corrections. It was typical of Vaughan Williams to discuss his work and listen to suggestions from others, but the final work was his own.

I. Prelude – outline

	Score ref.	Tempo indication	
Main theme	bar 1	Andante maestoso	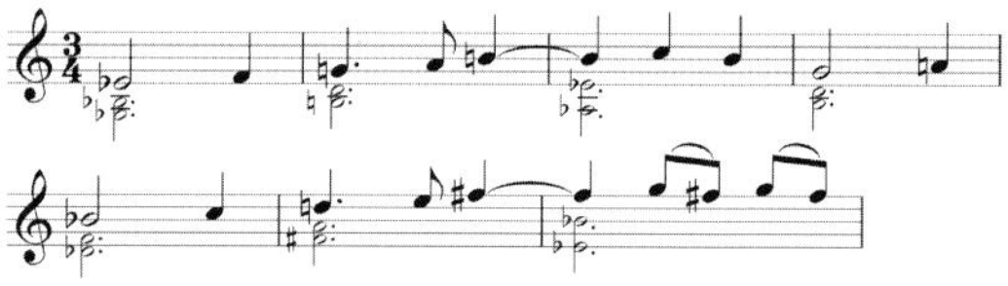
4/4	bar 57	Lento	
	bar 68 (fig. 7)	Poco più mosso	
	bar 86	Tempo primo	
	bar 94	Poco animato	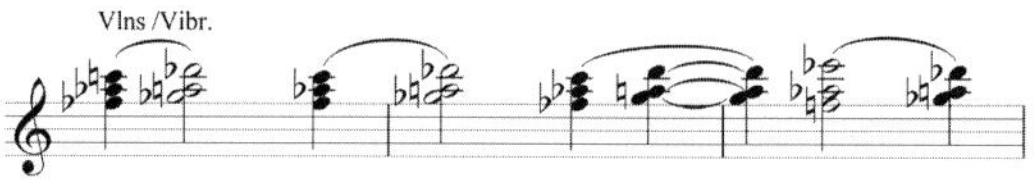
	bar 102	Più mosso	
Fanfare theme	bar 116	Meno mosso	
Flutes/ clarinets in 4ths	bar 126	Tranquillo	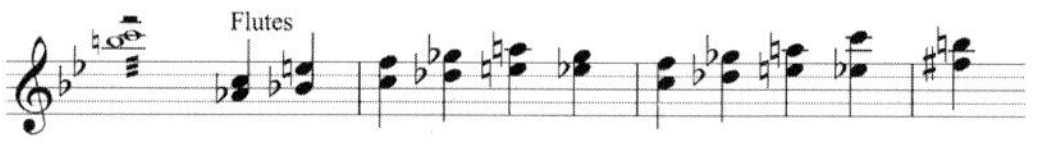
'Death' motif	bar 133		
Voices/wind machine	bar 141		
Coda: New fanfare E major, then G major	bar 158	Andante moderato con moto	

Structure

The Prelude begins with music from the opening titles of the film. There are some similarities with first movement sonata form. Bars 1–56 can be regarded as a first subject, with the second subject at bar 57 (leading into the passage with the voices). The return of the opening theme (in the bass at bar 86) suggests the beginnings of a development. However, what follows (bar 86–end) is mostly made up of sections of largely new material. There is little sense of a Classical development that works through themes introduced in the exposition. There is no obvious recapitulation. When the opening theme returns (at bar 163) it is very different. It is introduced with a more optimistic fanfare and moves quickly to a bright, full orchestra conclusion in G major.

The structure of the first movement is clearly different to the sonata form in the works of Haydn, Mozart and Beethoven or later works such as Mahler's Sixth Symphony. Composers in the 20th century moved towards freer interpretations of symphonic form. The origin of the symphony in film music may account for its episodic form. It is possible to debate if *Sinfonia Antartica* is really a symphony or a five-movement symphonic poem.

REANALYSIS

An alternative is to consider the structure of the Prelude as a type of arch ('Bogen') shape. Compare the movement to the Bartók quartet or to other symphonic examples, such as the concise first movement of Sibelius' Symphony No. 4 in A minor.

Harmony and tonality

The 'Main titles' theme at the beginning uses juxtaposed combinations of unrelated triads: E♭ minor, G major, A♭ minor, G major, B♭ minor, D major, E♭ minor. The use of parallel triads (ignoring any rules about parallel 5ths and octaves) is common in his music. Notice how the bass follows the shape of the melody in parallel octaves, rather than behaving as a functional bass with a shape and direction of its own.

The opposition between keys of E♭ minor and G major in the opening bars is a feature of the work as a whole:

- Flat keys are associated with the nature of the Antarctic itself. They feature **octatonic** scale patterns (similar to those in Stravinsky's *The Rite Of Spring* - see page 302), chromatically shifting, with many intervals of a semitone.
- More diatonic music is in major keys. This is the music of human endeavour and is heroic and striving.

Chords often shift by a semitone, the 3rd of the major chord becoming the 3rd of the minor chord. For example, in bars 2–3 the B is common to both G major and A♭ minor. Similarly, in bars 21–22 the C♯ is the 3rd of both A major and B♭ minor. Such 'enharmonic' harmonies (changing between different spellings of a note) are common in this music.

The 'triad + semitone' shape derives from the octatonic scales. Motifs made up of 3rds and an added semitone link together much of the melodic and harmonic material. For example:

- The accompaniment chords at the second subject (bar 57) are triads of C major and F♯ major, each with an added semitone.

Ralph Vaughan Williams
(1872–1958)

- The F♯ major + D is used again in the *sul ponticello* (playing on the bridge) tremolos when the voices enter (from fig. 7).
- At the *poco animato* (bar 94), where the glockenspiel and vibraphone are first used, there are dissonant chords built up of 3rds, with the melody moving in semitones.
- The horn fanfare at the mid-point climax in bar 116 (later used for the scherzo theme) is built on a C major triad, with an A♭ added at bar 117^2.

The last movement of the symphony ends with an E♭ in the voices left unresolved over a tonic G pedal.

The integration of musical material and the large-scale planning of harmony and tonality is evidence of 'symphonic' thinking.

II. Scherzo

The second movement is more pictorial, using the sections of the film score that depicted the sea, whales and penguins. Compare the music in the film (from about 26:42 in the Optimum Classic/StudioCanal DVD), which begins from the clarinet solo at bars 38–41 in the Scherzo.

It continues into an extended version of the passage at bars 42–56, as Scott's ship is off the coast of Antarctica and has to break through the ice (the flute/piccolo demisemiquaver figures at bar 53 in the symphony). The horn motif from the end of the Scherzo appears at 30:46 in the film, scored for muted trumpets. The penguins provide a brief moment of light relief, but their music is repeated and reordered compared to the symphonic version.

SOUNDTRACK

The recorded soundtrack is also available on Classic Film Scores. The sound quality is better than on the film release. There is more music than is used on the film. The cheerful 'Pony March' features in the film but is not included in the symphony.

The Scherzo's three-part structure is similar to that of a classical scherzo. The penguin music provides a contrasting trio section, followed by only a shortened return to the opening material, with the themes in reverse order.

	Score ref.	Tempo indication	
A Main theme	bar 1	Moderato	
	bar 19[2]	Poco animando	
	bar 42	Moderato	
	bar 59	Poco animato	
B Penguins	bar 66	Moderato scherzando	
A[1]	bar 123	Meno mosso	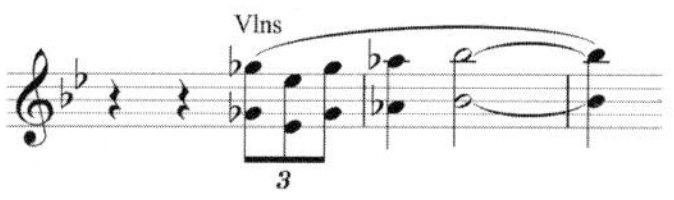

The horn fanfare at the beginning is based on an augmented chord: B♭, D, F♯. The atmosphere of the sea is made up of tremolo strings, harp glissandi and whole-tone scales in the clarinets and bassoons. The unstable tonality contrasts with the firm D major key (the close harmony chord is a D major triad with C♯ added in the bass) for the forte fanfare in full orchestra at bar 9. The movement of the waves is suggested by the brief use of duplets against the $\frac{6}{8}$ time signature.

From bar 42 there is a return to the ascending semitone motif used in the first movement from bar 94. A texture of scales and arpeggios is set up in the large tuned percussion group. The melody (octaves in low woodwind, tuba and cellos) emphasise tritone intervals (B/F and E/B♭).

The melody for the penguin music (from bar 66) is also based on an augmented chord (all in major 3rds), giving an oddly amusing feel to the music. The melody in solo trumpet and trombone is accompanied by triplet repeated chords (B♭ - D - E - F♯). At bar 84 the accompaniment chords are extended to make a middle section, leading to the return of the penguin tune in the full orchestra at bar 95. The slower section at the end, now piano in violins and solo clarinet only, makes the original scherzo music seem far away. The final chord (D - G♭ - B♭) is unsettled, fading away to nothing.

Experimental approaches after 1945

Avant-garde

By the end of the Second World War in 1945, much of Europe had been destroyed, atom bombs had been dropped on Hiroshima and Nagasaki in Japan and the truth of the Nazi Holocaust had emerged in full as the death camps were liberated. Western European composers began to work freely again, but in a world that had been radically transformed.

In eastern Europe the Soviet Union ensured that composers provided music that met the requirements of the Communist Party. In Russia the leading composers, such as Dmitri Shostakovich and Sergei Prokofiev, were expected to provide scores for propaganda purposes, even after the war was over.

A performance of Stockhausen's *Stimmung*

Extended listening

Shostakovich's later music was barely accepted by the Communist Party. Even outwardly propagandist works such as his Symphony No. 11 (subtitled *The Year 1905*) seem ambiguous in their presentation of history. Symphony No. 13 (subtitled *Babi Yar*) gives a nod to a setting of poems, written the previous year in 1961 by the banned Russian poet Yevgeny Yevtushenko, whose work was a protest to the Soviet Union's refusal to recognise Babi Yar as a Holocaust site. Symphony No. 14 for soprano, bass, strings and percussion is a sequence of poems on the theme of death.

In western Europe, young composers such as Pierre Boulez and Karlheinz Stockhausen met regularly in Darmstadt, Germany. They aimed to rebuild modern music for the post-war world. They rejected the conventions of pre-war music. Much of their work was challenging to audiences, but the composers regarded their work as difficult and necessary. The movement became known as the 'avant-garde'.

Pierre Boulez

Pierre Boulez's *Le marteau sans maître* (*The Hammer Without A Master*) is a chamber work, setting surrealist poems by René Char for voice and five instruments.

Boulez extends the use of a series to cover note values and dynamics. The instrumentation – **xylorimba**, vibraphone, guitar, alto flute, viola – is unusual, lacking a proper bass and showing an openness to the music of Asia.

Karlheinz Stockhausen

Karlheinz Stockhausen's *Stimmung* (1968) is for six solo voices amplified by microphones. It is based on a single chord, focusing on vocal timbres.

It uses chance procedures, so that some events in each performance take place in a different, random order.

György Ligeti

György Ligeti escaped from Hungary in 1956, following the Russian repression of the Hungarian uprising.

Under Communist rule composers had to follow strict guidelines for composition in order to be paid and have their work performed. Ligeti composed more experimental works in secret. Once he was in the West, he was free to immerse himself in the new music associated with Boulez, Stockhausen and the 'Darmstadt School'.

Ligeti's *Études*, Book 1

Ligeti's *Études* (1985) follow in the tradition of technical studies for solo piano by Chopin and a series of Préludes (with programmatic titles) by Debussy. There are six pieces in the first book:

I. 'Désordre' (Disorder)

II. 'Cordes à vide' (Open strings)

III. 'Touches bloquées' (Blocked keys)

IV. 'Fanfares'

V. 'Arc-en-ciel' (Rainbow)

VI. 'Automne à Varsovie' (Autumn in Warsaw)

I. 'Désordre'

The first piece, 'Désordre', shows Ligeti's interest in generating musical material from the principles of fractal mathematics and chaos theory. He read Benoît Mandelbrot's book on fractals in 1985 and worked closely with mathematicians to explore its potential for musical composition.

The melody in octaves in the right hand is repeated 14 times, rising a step higher each time. Only the white notes of the piano are used, so there is a modal effect.

The rhythm changes on each playing, with a scalic *moto perpetuo* of ascending quavers, played ***p***, filling in the length of each melody note. To begin with, each bar adds up to eight quavers, made up of unpredictable groupings of three and five quavers (3+5, 3+5, 5+3), similar to the rhythmic groupings in Bartók's Fifth Quartet (which Ligeti knew well – he wrote the analytical preface to the published score).

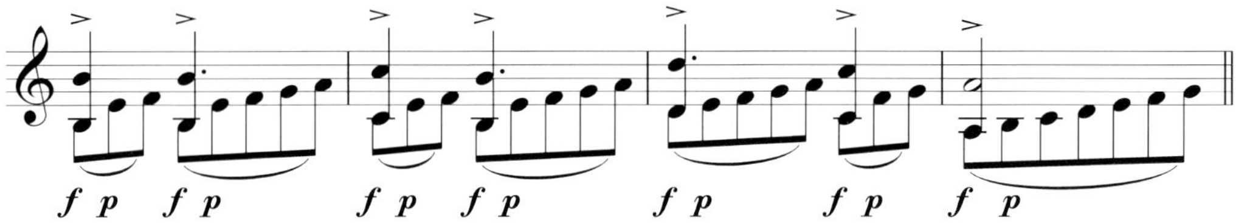

A longer phrase is played by the left hand, using only the black notes.

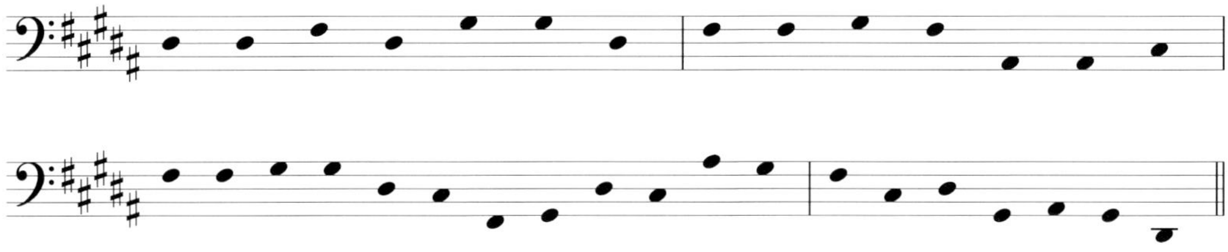

The left-hand melody descends in step each time, so the two hands are pushed further apart as the piece progresses. Ascending pentatonic scales fill in the quavers between the notes of the left-hand melody. Between both hands all 12 notes of the octave are covered.

Each repetition has different groupings of quavers. As groupings of two and four quavers are introduced, the melody becomes faster. The repetition of the phrases in different rhythms creates a constantly changing, chaotic pattern. It should be noted that Ligeti makes changes to his own rules at times, for example to make sure that he has 3rds, 6ths and tritones as harmony notes. At the climax of the piece, when the hands are furthest apart and the music is at its loudest, the dynamics suddenly drop and both hands move to the treble clef, reverting to the slower rhythmic patterns of the opening.

FURTHER STUDY

- ***György Ligeti: Music of the Imagination*** **by Richard Steinitz. Faber, 2003. Includes a detailed discussion of the Études.**
- **Tōru Takemitsu: *A Flock Descends Into The Pentagonal Garden* (1987).**

Witold Lutosławski

Lutosławski (1913–1994) graduated from the Warsaw Conservatory in piano and composition. When the Nazis invaded Poland in 1939 he was in the army as a radio operator. He was captured but managed to escape and walk 250 miles back to Warsaw. He managed to scratch a living as a café musician, performing his own arrangements. After the Second World War, Poland was controlled by a Communist government under the direction of the Soviet Union. Lutosławski won prizes for his music for children, but his Symphony No. 1 was banned as 'formalist', the term used to describe music classified as elitist and not accessible to ordinary people. After the death of Stalin the musical climate in Poland thawed and became more open to contemporary music.

Piano Concerto

Lutosławski's Piano Concerto (1987) begins with an example of the composer's aleatoric writing. The fast overlapping lines in the woodwind are each marked 'ad lib', so the player is free to play the notes at will.

The conductor signals the beginning and end of sections. However, the Piano Concerto uses less of this technique than Lutosławski's other works. The work was written for the Polish pianist Krystian Zimerman, a leading interpreter of Chopin. Some passages in the piano solo part use textures that are characteristic of Romantic piano music, e.g. fig. 20 where, over a sustained 11th chord (F – C – G – B♭) in the strings, the piano right hand is in octaves and the left hand alternates between an octave bass and chords in the middle of the texture. The first movement ends with dramatic, dissonant fanfares in the full orchestra, as if the Romantic piano style were being rejected. A short, fast-moving scherzo follows, then a slow movement.

The fourth movement has some of the characteristics of a chaconne, a Baroque dance form in triple time over a ground bass. The bass is played 17 times, each time scored differently. The first statement in the doubles basses begins on C:

After that the next statement begins on F, then on B♭, working through a pattern of descending 5ths (with a few detours before the pattern is restored) to cover all 12 notes of the octave (similar to the 'circle of 5ths'). The instrumentation works through lower-sounding instruments at first. Listen for the sixth statement in the horns, widening the original semitones of the statement to 4ths. The violin statement that follows uses glissandi between the semitones. The tenth statement is for percussion only.

The piano provides an example of a 'chain' structure, a feature of much of Lutosławski's music at this time. In a conventional variation design (e.g. Rachmaninov's *Rhapsody On A Theme Of Paganini* or Lutosławski's early *Variations* on the same theme), the piano and the accompaniment change to a new mood, style of figuration, key, or similar, for each variation. In this movement the piano begins new material at a midpoint in the orchestra statement. The orchestra and piano material overlap, making up the links in a chain:

	Fig. 83	**Fig. 85**	**Fig. 87**	**Fig. 89**
Orchestra:	Statement two: Cellos and basses	Statement three: Add bassoon and double bassoon	Statement four: Trumpets, then flutes	Statement five: Add trombone and oboe

	Fig. 84	**Fig. 86**	**Fig. 88**	**Fig. 90**
Piano:	Chromatic demisemi-quavers and detached chords	Semiquavers and sustained chords	Chords in quavers	Arpeggio figuration in rapid sextuplets

Minimalism

Steve Reich's *Different Trains*

Minimalism originated in the United States in the 1960s and has become a widely recognised style of composition. Minimalist composers often work within the framework of tonality, using consonant harmony, unlike their serialist counterparts.

Steve Reich's *Different Trains* (1988) is written for string quartet and pre-recorded performance tape. As a boy Reich travelled frequently by train between Los Angeles and New York, where his separated parents lived. The title of the work comes from the idea that had he been in Europe, as a Jewish child, he might have been on a train taking him to a concentration camp and death.

Reich recorded the reminiscences of his governess and a retired train porter who worked in New York at the time. He also recorded the memories of survivors of the Holocaust. From the recorded speech he selected short rhythmic phrases that generated the melodic material for the work. The intonation of the spoken voice provides the melodic shape:

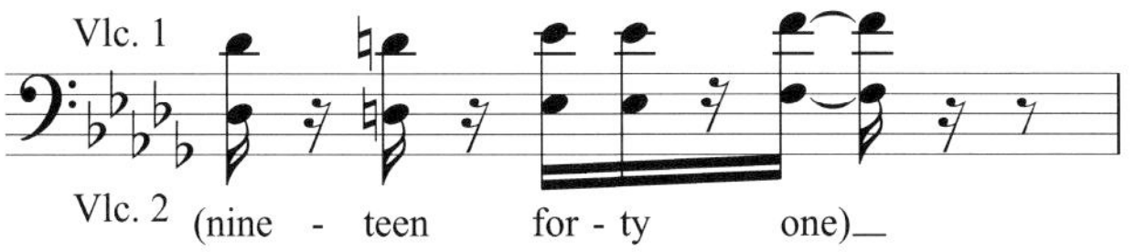

The pre-recorded tape comprises:

- The speech samples, transferred using a sampling keyboard and a computer
- Train sounds from the period, for example bells and whistles
- Three separate string quartets.

The live performance consists of an amplified live string quartet and the pre-recorded material. There are detailed instructions for a sound engineer to control the sound during the performance, for example to ensure that the live quartet is louder than the recorded quartets.

The first movement, 'America – Before The War', uses only 11 samples of speech, not enough for a continuous story. The melody is introduced in viola or cello before being heard spoken. The second movement, 'Europe – During The War', has a darker tone, with longer fragments of speech and a clearer narrative emerging. The final movement is titled 'After The War'.

FURTHER LISTENING

Compare Steve Reich's approach to other examples of works which respond to war and violent persecution. Schoenberg's *A Survivor From Warsaw* uses a spoken narration in English and ends with a setting of a Jewish prayer for male chorus. Contrast Schoenberg's intensely powerful, emotional writing with Reich's cooler, more objective style.

A string quartet

Contemporary music

Judith Weir and Thomas Adès

Judith Weir's *The Consolations Of Scholarship* (1985) is a short music-drama for mezzo-soprano and a chamber ensemble of nine players.

The story is adapted from 14th-century Chinese plays. It tells the story of General K'an and the virtuous civil servant Chao Tun. K'an plots the downfall and death of his rival. Chao Tun's orphaned son is brought up to value peace and scholarship. He gets the opportunity for revenge when visiting the library in the capital, 20 years later. The illiterate General gets a message from the Gods, which he cannot read. The boy's deliberate mistranslation ensures the defeat and death of K'an.

The singer sings all the parts. There are no sets or costumes. The singer is placed among the instrumental players so that they too are characters in the drama. In 'Last Moves' the pianist is instructed to play detached chords 'as if they were chess moves', carefully studied before the next chord is played.

The mezzo-soprano adopts a variety of vocal styles to suit the various characters:

- Rhythmic speech for narration, dramatic effect ('Revenge!') and the writing of a letter
- Abrupt repeated notes in a low register for the gruff General, more lyrical as he dreams of power
- Elaborate and grand for the 'Shining Immortal' from heaven, in a more human middle register when in disguise, and disappearing back to heaven with a 'Whoosh!' (marked 'either exaggeratedly animated or restrained and slightly unconvinced').

In the opening section, 'A Traveller In The Desert', the accompaniment shadows the rhythm of the recited text of the voice exactly. The voice and woodwind begin and end phrases together, with silences rather than linking instrumental passages between phrases. The music picks up pace as the General is introduced over a pedal G in octaves in the piano. In 'The General's Aria' the close relationship between voice and instruments is continued. The General begins fiercely on repeated Ds, followed by silence. As he gets into the story of his plots against Chao Tun, there are more extended passages. His music begins to expand up a whole-tone scale, before returning to the D.

FURTHER LISTENING

- The piece manages to engage with the characters and tell a good story while maintaining a satirical and ironic tone. Judith Weir uses a similar approach in *King Harald's Saga* (1979), 'a grand opera in three acts' for unaccompanied solo soprano.
- James Macmillan: *The Confession Of Isobel Gowdie* (1990).

Thomas Adès: *Asyla*

Thomas Adès' *Asyla* (1997) was commissioned by the John Feeney Charitable Trust for the City of Birmingham Symphony Orchestra and its conductor Sir Simon Rattle. It was his largest orchestral work up to that time.

Look at **www.thomasades.com** for details of Thomas Adès' working life. Investigate the role of commissions from all over the world, the work of his publishers, his period as 'Composer in Residence' with the Hallé Orchestra in Manchester, and his roles as a conductor (not only of his own music) and with the Aldeburgh Festival.

Adès expands the orchestra by adding instruments and techniques to the standard symphony orchestra of the early 20th century:

- Six percussionists are required. The instruments include a large selection of drums and cymbals, tuned rototoms, large tins (paint tins are suggested), tuned cowbells and gongs (including a water gong, which can be lowered into water to reduce its pitch by a semitone).
- Two piano players, covering grand piano, two upright pianos with practice pedals (one tuned a quarter-tone flat) and celesta.

Asyla has four movements, similar to a symphony. The second movement is slow. The third movement is a modern dance equivalent of a minuet, taking influences from 1990s dance music. The overall approach might be termed 'postmodern'.

Asyla incorporates influences from 1990s dance music

The second movement begins with the delicate sounds of two upright pianos played with the practice pedal, celesta, harp and tuned cowbells. As in Mahler's Sixth Symphony the cowbells represent another, distant place. The expressive bass oboe melody consists of a descending sequence:

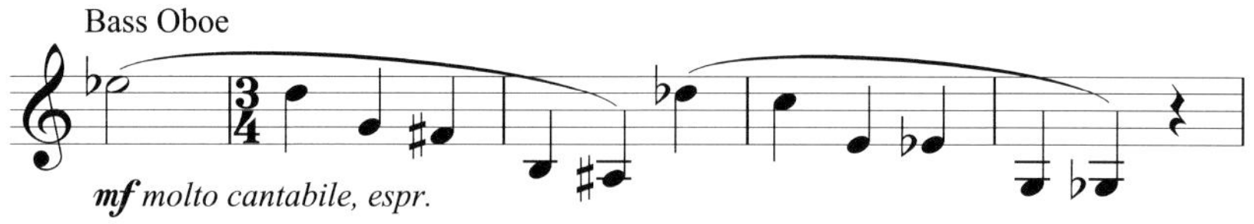

(The time signature in bar 1 is $\frac{2}{6}$ - there is a triplet bracket under the E♭ minim.)

Harmony and texture

The harmony is tonal. The strings explore a range of timbres, so that the use of a full tone stands out when it occurs. At the beginning of the third movement, for example, the violins play harmonics very quietly, often split into desks.

A crescendo is created by adding solo players to a note. The tremolo in the cellos at fig. D moves rapidly from *sul ponticello* (on the bridge) to ordinary tone, with a diminuendo to *sul tasto* (played over the fingerboard). After the detailed pianissimo textures, the traditional sound of orchestral strings playing in octaves at fig. H is a striking contrast.

The third movement is titled 'Ecstasio', referring to the music and atmosphere of London clubs in the 1990s.

Section C

Essays

AS Level (2017)

The Rite Of Spring and the late Romantic style.

1. What does Stravinsky's music for *The Rite Of Spring* have in common with late Romantic orchestral works?
2. Explain how revolutionary Stravinsky's music was in 1913.
3. Describe the factors which influenced the creation of *The Rite Of Spring*.
4. Assess the importance of *The Rite Of Spring* in the development of music since 1913.

AS Level (2018)

Sinfonia Antartica and national styles.

5. What are the distinctive features of the musical style of Vaughan Williams?
6. How successful is *Sinfonia Antartica* as a symphony? Is it more successful as film music?
7. Describe the use of harmony and tonality in *Sinfonia Antartica*.
8. Evaluate the contribution of Vaughan Williams to the development of English music in the 20th century.

A Level

9. Describe some of the factors that led to the emergence of serialism.
10. Write about one composer who made a decisive contribution to music since 1900. Refer to examples from at least one work by this composer.
11. Explain the impact of politics or persecution on the music of one composer of this period.
12. To what extent is the Second World War (1939–1945) a significant dividing line in the history and development of music?
13. Outline the main features of minimalism, referring to at least one work that is in your view a successful example of the style.
14. Describe the opportunities and challenges for composers working today.

Writing about music

Introduction

People often talk about the 'language' of music. What they often mean is that music can exist independently of language. Before Haydn visited England for the first time, his friend Mozart asked how he would manage without languages. Haydn replied that he had the language of music.

A common language is needed for discussion. For Haydn and Mozart, Italian was the most commonly understood language for musicians, even though they were German speakers. Today Italian terms for expression, dynamics and tempo are standard for musicians all over the Western world.

Being able to talk about music is a natural part of making music, including:

- Learning how to sing and play, and discussing technique and repertoire with a teacher.
- Rehearsing with other musicians in a group or ensemble, and being able to give an opinion about how to improve a performance.
- Collaborating with other musicians to create new music, and explaining our intentions as a composer.
- Communicating our opinions and understanding about music, and sharing views and knowledge as listeners.

Writing in the examination

Section A

Short answers, e.g. from one word answers (1 mark) to longer answers requiring a few lines (3, 4, 5 marks or more).

Section B

Four medium length answers of a few paragraphs each, for 10 marks each; there will be roughly a page of lines for each answer, but this is only a guide. A shorter answer is perfectly acceptable if you have covered all you want to say. If you need more space, use the extra lines at the back of the question/answer paper. Ask for extra paper if this is not enough.

Section C

This is the essay section. At AS Level there will be one essay to complete for 20 marks. At A Level you have to write two essays for 25 marks each.

Section A

Two extracts or pieces of unfamiliar music

The extracts will be divided as follows:

- **One from Area of Study 1: Instrumental music of Haydn, Mozart and Beethoven.**
- **One from Area of Study 2: Popular vocal music – blues, jazz, swing, big band.**

Questions will require short answers, ranging from one word to a few sentences or a paragraph. There may be a list of words from which you choose the correct answer.

Some questions may ask you to notate your answer. For example, you may be asked to listen to a section of the music and notate the melody, bass or rhythm. A few bars of the score will be printed in the question paper for you to write in a melody, bass or rhythm. You may be asked to write in other details, e.g. dynamics, articulation, chord symbols and so on.

READ THE QUESTIONS CAREFULLY

Make sure that you understand what the question is asking for. Usually questions will have 'command' words at the beginning, e.g. 'Identify', 'Describe', 'Explain', 'Evaluate', 'Compare'.

Follow instructions about how many answers are required.

Example: Identify two instruments in the introduction. (2 marks)

Correct answer: trumpet and trombone.

- Brass. (0 marks)
- Horn and trombone. (1 mark)
- Trombone, horn, bassoon. (0 marks)
- Horn, tuba, trumpet, trombone. (0 marks)

Check how many marks are awarded for the question. If there are two marks to be gained then at least two pieces of information are needed in your answer.

In longer answers use bar numbers to identify exact places in the music. This will show that you are listening carefully to the music.

UNDERSTANDING SUPERSCRIPT

Superscript numbers refer to beat numbers, e.g. bar 24^3 is the third beat of bar 24.

Tone

Use straightforward language to express your knowledge and ideas. You should use the style of language expected from a student at A Level. It will be formal and educated, but you don't need to be too academic in tone.

You have a limited amount of time in the exam. Use your time to write what you know and to give your opinions. There is no need to spend time thinking up complicated sentences or using unnecessarily long words. Be clear and direct.

Avoid the temptation to chat to examiners, especially about irrelevant issues. They will only be interested in your answer to the question.

Be confident about your opinion. Avoid adding 'I think...' or 'In my view...' or 'I feel...'. These make you sound unsure of your ability. Any statement you make will be taken as your judgement.

Refer to composers and performers by surname (or first and last names) - Beethoven or Ludwig van Beethoven, not Ludwig!

Technical language

At AS and A Level you are expected to understand and use the technical language and terminology of music.

Some of these may be Italian words (or French or German) - pizzicato, crescendo, leitmotif, etc. Others may be English words which have a specific meaning when applied to music - sequence, dominant, modulation. If you can't remember the exact term, you may get some credit for describing it.

Expressive language: music as sensations, emotions and imagery

It is an old idea that music can express ideas and emotions in a way that words cannot.

If we are in the right frame of mind, a piece of music or a song can speak to us personally. It can set up a train of thought or feeling in us.

At times a composer may invite us to respond in a way that matches his or her intention. For example:

- In AoS5, Berlioz writes a detailed description of the story of his *Symphonie fantastique* so that the audience follows what he means to express.
- In AoS4 the religious meaning is provided by a text or a common form of worship which the congregation understands.

In writing about music, using imagery is a way of expressing our knowledge and understanding of the music. This could be a picture or an event. It communicates easily with the reader in language that can be understood.

As an example we could describe the transition from the Scherzo to the Finale in Beethoven's Symphony No. 5 like this:

> The Scherzo is linked by an extended transition, moving from darkness into light. The dynamics are piano. The timpani repeats the rhythm of the theme from the first movement. There is a long build up over a dominant pedal, with a crescendo in the last few bars into the last movement. The full orchestra chord of C major, with the theme outlining the notes of a C major triad, is a moment of blazing triumph after the dark C minor of the Scherzo.

Note the use of metaphorical language:

- 'Moving from darkness into light'.
- 'A moment of blazing triumph after the dark'.

The use of metaphor in describing the passage is helpful:

- It persuades the reader that you have listened to the music.
- It shows your insight into the expressive qualities of the music.
- It invites the reader to share your enthusiasm and provides a moment of relief from technical analysis.

You may think the metaphor in the example is overdone. After the 'darkness into light' in the first sentence, 'blazing triumph' in the final sentence is not adding anything new.

In using expressive images:

- Avoid over-extending your ideas.
- Simple metaphors work best.
- Make sure that most of your writing shows technical knowledge, analysis of the music and relevant social and historical context.

Referring to example A and motif X

Labelling a musical idea – a melodic or rhythmic motif – as 'X' or 'A' can be a useful shorthand. It is easier than describing it in full every time.

Take care to let the examiner know what your label means (e.g. with a full description or a brief musical example), then you are free to use it, knowing that you will be understood.

For example, you might be discussing the first four notes of Beethoven's 5th Symphony by writing out those notes and describing them as 'the rhythm of the theme from the first movement'. You would label your musical example as 'Motif X'. After that, when you write 'the timpani repeats Motif X', the examiner will understand.

Writing about harmony and tonality

Try to be specific about keys and chords. When writing about tonality, single capital letters mean major keys, unless the word 'minor' follows.

Chords can be written in Roman numerals or in chord symbols:

- Roman numerals: chords are identified according to their relationship to the key of the music. Capital letters for major, lower case for minor, but not all writers are consistent about this. For example: in C major, I = chord of C major, ii = D minor, iii = E minor, IV = F, V = G, vi = A minor.
- Chord symbols: capital letters are used for major and minor, with 'm' added to indicate minor. Example: A = A major, Am = A minor, A/C♯ is A major with C♯ in the bass.
- Chord inversions: in Roman numerals, use 'b' for first inversion, 'c' for second inversion, 'd' for third inversion. In the key of C major, the chord of G major with B in the bass is Vb. In guitar chords this is G/B. You can also use figured bass, in which $^{6}_{3}$ indicates the inversion.

Locate examples accurately

Use the bar numbers on the score to give the location of specific examples in the music.

Section B

10 mark questions

In this section of the examination paper you will have four questions to answer. These will be about the prescribed work you have been set (Haydn, Mozart and Beethoven, and Popular Vocal Music), and the background to it, including related listening to the Areas of Study.

Examples of the type of questions include:

A. Style and techniques of composition

Examples:

- Discuss the use of harmony and tonality in this extract.
- Identify features of this extract that are typical of sonata form.
- Describe the use of instruments in the accompaniment to this song.

B. Comparison of performances or arrangements

Examples:

- Compare the two different performances of the extract.
- Compare the prescribed performance of this song with a version of your choice by another singer.
- How effective is the recorded performance of this song?

C. Historical or social context

Examples might be:

- Explain the reaction of audience and critics to the music of the composer.
- How do period instruments differ from modern instruments?
- Discuss the role of the record company in producing the album from which this song is taken.

USE OF TIME

Work out how much time to spend on the whole of Section B. As a guide, divide this into four equal lengths of time. Some questions may take longer to answer, for example if you have to listen to two different performances. You may be able to make up the time on other questions, e.g. on historical or social context. Try to stick to your schedule. Answer all the questions in this section.

Here is guide to allocating your time in the examination. Allow enough time to complete the essays, especially at A Level.

AS Level - 2 hours		
Section A	40 marks	50 minutes
Section B	40 marks	40 minutes
Section C	20 marks	30 minutes

A Level - 2½ hours		
Section A	30 marks	40 minutes
Section B	40 marks	40 minutes
Section C	50 marks	70 minutes

Section C
Essay questions

Essay responses require a number of writing skills which are easy to acquire if you follow the guidelines below.

Extended writing

You may be required to do some or all of these in extended writing questions:

- Recall the facts. Give information about the background of the music you have studied.
- Show that you are familiar with the music. Discuss it in detail.
- Link up ideas. Show that you can compare different music and styles. Show that you can connect ideas about the background, e.g. what was happening at different times or in different countries, or how a musical style develops.
- Put forward opinions and make judgements of your own. Back up your ideas with evidence from the music you have listened to and the background information you have studied.

Read the questions carefully. Do this a few times until you are sure you understand what you have to do:

- The first word of the question is often a command word. Examples: **Identify, Describe, Explain, Evaluate, Compare.**
- Command words can appear twice in a question, telling you there are two tasks. Example: **Describe** the features of a religious cantata of the Baroque period. **Illustrate** your answer with examples from the work of at least one composer.
- Sometimes the first sentence gives you background information. The command word then comes at the beginning of a later sentence. For example:

> Billy Strayhorn's phrase 'the Ellington effect' is often used in connection with Duke Ellington and his band. **Explain** to what extent Ellington's methods were unique and personal to him.

What examiners are looking for:

- Knowledge and understanding of the background.
- Familiarity with the music, including relevant examples.
- Ability to make evaluative and critical judgements.
- An understanding of context.
- Careful analysis and appraisal in relation to the question.
- Development of and ability to sustain a line of reasoning.
- Relevant and substantiated responses.

An example question from A Level AoS6

Explain the challenges for composers from 1900 to the present day in writing music for dramatic performance on stage or in film. Refer in detail to the music of at least one work for the stage (opera, musical or ballet) or one film score.

Do I choose this question?

Checklist:

- What background information do I know?
- Do I know one work well enough to go into detail about the music? Can I refer to other works? Can I discuss examples?
- What are the issues? Are there chances for me to give opinions? Is there an argument to be made?

Example answer

I chose this question because I know West Side Story really well. I want to discuss how innovative it is compared to other musicals.

Example plan. My ideas are:

- Intro – West Side Story, how it is innovative (summary), consider use of different musical styles.
- Para 1 – background, New York-set version of Shakespeare R&J.
- Para 2 – link to previous musicals, Rodgers and Hammerstein Oklahoma! Frontier setting, dramatic storyline, colourful choruses. Escapism for Broadway audience.
- Para 3 – Prologue of WSS sets mood. Dance elements rivalry of gangs.
- Para 4 – musical details, dissonant chords (semitones), tritones in melody, jazz/bebop style melodies, dance rhythms.
- Para 5 – mixture of styles in WSS. Latin-Cuban dance patterns, comedy vaudeville (Sgt Krupke), jazz/blues dance ('Dance At The Gym').
- Para 6 – romantic style solo songs and duets ('One Hand, One Heart'), discuss contrast of style—does it work?
- Para 7 – Influence? Strengths and weaknesses?
- Conclusion—WSS attempts to be relevant, social issues, but still escapist, romantic melodies. Innovative use of jazz/Latin music in a musical.

Reduce the plan to a simple outline to write on the exam paper. This will help you to keep on track as you write.

- Intro – Innovative
- WSS background
- Oklahoma
- Prologue
- Music – dissonance, tritone, jazz
- Mix of styles
- Romantic features
- Strengths and weaknesses
- Old and new – strong jazz/Latin styles.

Plan

Make a note of the points you want to cover in your chosen essay.

Single word prompts will be fine. Get the order of your points sorted out: try to make a good first impression and leave a strong point to the end. Think about how much evidence you have for each point, e.g. where you can show your knowledge of the music with specific detail.

Some essay questions may ask you to give an opinion or make a judgement. You have to write persuasively and use evidence. Write a short plan. Decide how you are going to approach the argument. Examples:

- Present your opinion in the opening paragraph; then paragraphs of evidence in favour; deal with arguments against, either in each paragraph or at the end; conclusion repeating your opinion.
- Outline the issues in the opening paragraph; either paragraphs in favour followed by paragraphs against, or each paragraph has evidence for and against; longer conclusion (possibly more than one paragraph) giving your final opinion and the reasons why.

You should practise writing essays of this sort during your course. Develop your own style of persuasive writing.

Keep introductions short, the bare outlines only. At A Level you may need to identify the music, composer or style which you have chosen for your answer.

Similarly a conclusion should be a short summary. It should add something new, if you can.

Quotations

Musical quotations are allowed. Use musical quotations if they really help your argument or illustrate a point. Don't just write out all the themes in a movement because you happen to know them. Make it relevant.

You do not have to use quotations. You will not lose marks by not doing so. However, a quotation from a historical source can be useful. For example:

(AoS3) 'Some jazz musicians from the previous generations found it difficult to accept bebop, feeling that it was "like playing Scrabble with all the vowels missing" (Duke Ellington).'

(AoS4) 'The choruses in *Messiah* show Handel's ability in Beethoven's description to "create vast effects from simple means".'

(AoS5) 'Berlioz's situation is summed up in David Cairns' neat phrase: "Journalism pays on the spot, composition is an investment".'

(AoS6) 'Stravinsky told Robert Craft that Britten's *War Requiem* featured "patterns rather than inventions... an absence of true counterpoint".'

Bebop players Tommy Potter, Charlie Parker, Miles Davis and Duke Jordan

Use quotes for the following if possible:

- In the introduction, as an interesting starting point, to show that you have read about this topic.
- In support of one of your ideas, especially if it is unusual or controversial.
- To present an idea that you disagree with.

EXACT QUOTES AND REFERENCES

Use quotation marks (“ ”) if you remember the exact words. Alternatively, summarise in your own words (without quotation marks) and refer to the author or source by name.

Paragraphs

Break your writing up by dividing it into paragraphs. Make sure each paragraph is clearly set out. A new line is a good way of highlighting that you have a new idea.

PEEL METHOD

One way of organising your ideas is to use the **PEEL** method.
Each paragraph is built up in this way:

P - Point

E - Evidence (or Example)

E - Explanation

L - Link

Example:

P - Although we think of Beethoven as a composer of abstract music, some of his music makes use of pictorial or dramatic effects.

E - An example is the ‘Pastoral’ symphony.

E - Each movement has a subtitle to indicate the story of the symphony. The last three movements begin with a peasant dance, which is interrupted by a storm before the happy conclusion in the finale.

L - Scenes in the country are a common theme in Romantic music. Examples include Rossini’s ‘William Tell’ overture (which also has a storm section) or the ‘Scène aux Champs’ in Berlioz’s *Symphonie fantastique*.

Answers

Area of Study 1

Exercise 1

1. Strings
2. G major
3. Broken chord
4. 
5. Each small note takes half the value of the following note, so the rhythm is heard as two quavers followed by a crotchet each time (though interpretations of this may vary between recordings).
6. Perfect
7. Bar 22
8. D major
9. Dominant

Exercise 2

Section/ theme	Bar numbers	Key(s)
Exposition	1 to 40	D major and A major
1st subject	1 to 8	D major
Transition	9 to 16	D major
2nd subject	17 to 35	A major, A minor
Codetta	35 to 40	A major
Development	41 to 61	A major and B minor
Recapitulation	61 to 103	D major
1st subject	61 to 73	D major
Transition	74 to 79	D major
2nd subject	79 to 98	D major, D minor
Coda	98 to 103	D major

Exercise 3

1. a. Acciaccatura, e.g. bar 1 (1st note in the right hand) – sometimes called a 'crushed note', this note is to be played very quickly before the larger note
   b. Mordent, e.g. bar 1^3 – play the note above, the main note, the note above and then the main note again
   c. Trill, e.g. bar 34 – rapid alternation of the written note with the note above
2. a. Staccato, e.g bar 1 (2nd, 3rd and 4th notes in the right hand) – the note is to be played very short and detached
   b. Slur, e.g. bar 1 (5th and 6th notes in the right hand) – on the piano the first note is to be joined to the second note (played legato), but the second note is lifted off
   c. Staccatissimo, e.g. bar 1 (1st note in the right hand) – the note is to be played as short as possible
   d. Accent, e.g. bar 10 (1st note in the left hand) – attack the note with emphasis
3. a. Appoggiatura – the small note 'steals' half the value of the large note
   b. Turn – the note above, the main note, the note below and the main note again
   c. Inverted/lower mordent – the main note, the note below and the main note again.

Exercise 4

Section	Bar numbers	Total number of bars	Key(s)
A (rondo theme)	1 to 20	20	D major – A major – D major
B (Episode 1)	21 to 40	20	D minor – F major – G minor – D minor
A	41 to 60	20	D major – A major – D major
C (Episode 2)	61 to 80	20	G major
Link	81 to 93	13	E minor – D major – A major
A	94 to 134	21	D major – A major – D major

Exercise 5

1.

2. Alberti bass
3. Ascending and descending scales in a descending sequence
4. Dominant
5. Transition.

Exercise 6

1. Dominant minor
2. It is in the subdominant key, rather than the expected tonic key
3. a. e.g. bars 18-21
   b. e.g. bars 26 to 27
   c. e.g. bars 27 to 28 (in G major).

Exercise 7

A Scherzo		B Trio		Coda	
a	1 to 16	c	65 to 72	Coda	106 to 128
b	16 to 39	d	72 to 80		
a	39 to 55	c	81 to 88		
Codetta	55 to 64				

2. The trio begins in the relative minor of A minor. Unlike the scherzo, which begins with thematic material presented in imitation, the trio is built on triplet quaver broken chords and arpeggios with no distinct thematic material.

   The scherzo has a variety of textures, from monophonic to polyphonic and then homophonic with some very dense chords. The texture of the trio is the same throughout, with the triplets in the right hand and octaves in the left hand.

   In the trio Beethoven makes changes when material recurs - e.g. section **c** when it reappears at bar 81 is an octave higher than in bar 65, and the repeat of sections **d** and **c** is written out so that Beethoven can make further changes.

   Finally, the scherzo begins on an upbeat whereas the trio begins on the downbeat.

Exercise 8

Answers to exercise 8 will depend on the music being studied.

Exercise 9

Variation 1 - This is for piano alone. The melody has been decorated and is presented as continuous semiquavers. The harmonic structure is the same, but the accompaniment pattern has been changed and is sometimes an octave lower than in the theme.

Variation 2 - To begin this variation the piano has the original violin melody, with an accompaniment very similar to the theme, while the violin plays decorative triplet semiquavers above, making the variation sound faster, even though the pulse is the same. After the double bar in the middle, the piano and violin begin to pass the triplet semiquavers between them and there are some changes to the harmony: the second section begins in D minor instead of the original D major. However, by the end of this variation the original harmonic pattern has returned.

Variation 3 - The piano now has continuous demisemiquaver movement, for the first half following the harmony of the theme. Over the top the violin plays a decorated and higher version of the original melody. Again, after the double bar there are further changes as the piano has loud demisemiquavers in octaves and the music begins in D minor rather than the original D major.

Variation 4 - This variation is in the tonic minor (G minor) which leads to other harmonic changes. Many of the rhythms of the theme are now dotted and are accompanied by triplet semiquavers in the left hand of the piano.

Variation 5 - There is a change in tempo to adagio, and the violin now plays pizzicato, very much in an accompanying role. The highly decorative piano melody shadows the original melody, adding long scalic flourishes. The original chord scheme is mostly present, with the exception of the first and third bars after the double bar, which have minor rather than the original major chords.

Exercise 10

1. Your examples may vary, but could include:
   - Bars 1 to 6 - the cello opens the sonata alone, with the main melodic material.
   - In bar 17 the piano and cello are equal, playing the melody in unison, but then the cello continues with the melody while the piano plays the accompaniment.
   - In bar 24 the cello has a virtuosic flourish, while the piano is silent (this also happens at the corresponding point in the recapitulation).
   - In bars 55 to 57 and 71 to 78 the piano has a repeated accompaniment pattern (scales follow, then an Alberti bass figure), while the cello has the melody.
   - In bars 58 to 65 the piano right hand and cello play a melody and countermelody, which then becomes a conversation in which the melody is passed between them (bars 61 to 62).
2. In the Mozart sonata there are many occasions on which the violinist could remain silent and not play the printed notes, and it would not make a huge difference to the music. Indeed, in variation 1 in the final movement the violinist does not play at all anyway.

   In the first movement both the 1st and 2nd themes are presented first by the piano and in the 2nd theme the violinist joins only for the final three bars.

   In the Beethoven the piano and cello play nearly continually, with just a few bars rest occasionally, whereas in the Mozart the violin has many bars of rest while the piano plays a solo.

Exercise 11

1. Four movements: **I** Sonata form, **II** Scherzo and trio, **III** Slow movement, **IV** Rondo
2. E♭ major
3. **I** Tonic, **II** Tonic, **III** B♭ major (dominant), **IV** Tonic
4. **I** Sonata form

   II Scherzo and trio - overall ternary form **ABA** with **aba** scherzo and **cdc** trio

   III No clear form - repeated melody with contrasting episodes and melody repeated with decoration

   IV Rondo
5. **I** E♭ major to B♭ major, A♭ major, F minor, C minor (false recapitulation), E♭ major

   II Scherzo: E♭ major to B♭ major (with dominant minor 9th, C♭, in bars 5, 23 and 29), E♭ major
   Trio: E♭ major to C minor, E♭ major

   III B♭ major to G minor, F major, B♭ major

   IV E♭ major to B♭major, A♭ major, F minor, E♭ major
6. **I** The 1st violin has most of the melodic material, with very occasional contributions from the other three parts.

   II Again, it is mostly a 1st violin melody, with occasional fragments of melody in the other parts.

   III The melody is first presented by the viola, which again has the melody from bar 32. For the rest of the movement the melodic interest is mainly in the 1st violin.

   IV This movement is completely dominated by the 1st violin.
7. The most common texture is that of melody (usually in the 1st violin) with accompaniment by the other three instruments, e.g. **I** bars 1 to 4. However, there are also examples of monophony, with just one instrument, e.g. **I** bar 25. Haydn sometimes writes music in which the melody is doubled in 3rds and 6ths (e.g. **I** bars 79-80) and in 10ths (e.g. **II** bars 16 to 18). There are also examples of music where the melody is passed between different instruments, often in imitation (e.g. **I** bars 76 to 77, **II** bars 10 to 14). There are also examples of 2-part writing (e.g. **III** bars 1 to 10) and 3-part writing, (e.g. **III** bars 32 to 35).
8. Comparison with earlier Haydn quartets:
   - Although the 1st violin is still the most important part in the music, it does not dominate completely, unlike in Haydn's earlier quartets.
   - Most of the time the music is in four clearly separate parts; in his earliest quartets Haydn often wrote music that was in just two really distinct parts.
   - Haydn has perfected the conversational style of quartet writing by the time of writing these quartets, with all players taking an active part in the discourse.
   - This quartet includes a scherzo and trio; Haydn's earlier quartets had a minuet and trio instead.
   - Some of Haydn's earlier quartets, such as some of those of Op. 20, included fugal movements. While there is some imitative writing in this quartet, there is not a fugue.

Exercise 12

1. 

2. 

3. Imperfect and perfect
4. An antecedent and consequent phrase, each of four bars
5. Transition
6. Dominant/F major
7. Trill
8. At the start of the extract the 1st violin has the melody with the other instruments accompanying, playing mostly the same rhythm as the melody, and the 2nd violin playing in 3rds with the 1st violin some of the time. In bars 9 to 10 and 13 to 14 the texture is reduced to three parts. In bars 20 to 21 the two outer parts (1st violin and cello) have held notes while the two inner parts (2nd violin and viola) have the melodic interest in 3rds. At the end of the extract, from bar 26, while the 1st violin plays a long trill the 2nd violin and viola play the opening melodic idea in 3rds, with the cello joining for the cadences.
9. This quartet is similar to Haydn's Op. 33 No. 2 quartet ('The Joke'), which might be expected, as Mozart wrote this quartet after getting to know Haydn's Op. 33 quartets. In both quartets the 1st violin has the dominant share of the melody and there are times where the 2nd violin plays the melody in 3rds with the 1st violin. In both quartets most of the time there is a four-part texture, but occasionally this is reduced to a three- or even two-part texture. Mozart's quartet has a stronger feel of an idea being passed around the whole ensemble, with instruments other than the 1st violin getting to have more of the melodic interest than in Haydn's quartet.

Exercise 13

1. The music in bar 1 of the minuet is heard in inversion in bars 1 to 2 of the finale.
2. The motif is heard a huge number of times in the finale:
   - It is used to build the subject for the fugato (the start of a fugue) which opens the movement.
   - It is heard in bars 1-2, bars 2-3 a tone lower and bars 3-4 at the original pitch within the subject presented initially by the viola.
   - The motif is then heard in the same way in the entry from the 2nd violin, cello and finally the 1st violin.
   - From bar 100 the motif is heard in the 1st violin initially in F minor and at the same time in inversion in the cello.
   - From bar 108 the motif is heard in 3rds in the 1st and 2nd violins in D♭ major, imitated in 3rds one beat later by the viola and cello.

- From bar 176 the motif is passed down the quartet, from the 1st violin to the 2nd violin and then the viola.
- The fugue returns in bar 210 and the motif is used in the subject and presented by the instruments in the same order as before.
- From bar 305 the motif is heard first in the 2nd violin with the viola playing it in inversion, and then in the 2nd violin and viola (which is actually higher than the 2nd violin at this point) and in inversion in the cello.
- The 1st violin picks up the motif at the end of bar 309, passing it then to the viola and finally the 2nd violin.

Exercise 14

Jansons	Hogwood
Large orchestra with modern instruments.	Period instruments, a smaller orchestra and at a lower pitch.
Large string section making a full, rich sound, using vibrato.	Quieter, with fewer string players and sounds more tentative. Makes more of the staccato, detaching the notes more.
A large crescendo in bar 8 and accents on the upbeat G natural and G sharp at the end of bar 10 and the middle of bar 11.	A diminuendo in bar 8.
In the tutti in bar 14 the wind and brass do not enter particularly quietly and following a large crescendo are extremely loud by bar 16.	The wind and brass enter more quietly and there is a large crescendo, but they do not reach the volume of the Jansons recording.
In the tutti at the end of the slow introduction the flutes are very audible.	Like the other recording, the flutes are audible, but it is also possible to hear the oboes.
The tempo of the Allegro section is faster.	The tempo of the Allegro section is slower.
The string entry in bar 32 is not really the marked ***p***.	The ***sf*** markings from bar 52 are heard, but then there is an added diminuendo from bars 53 to 55.

Exercise 15

Monothematicism:

- Literally means 'one theme'.
- Refers to use of one theme for both 1st and 2nd subjects (though other themes may also be present).
- The 1st movement of the 'Military' symphony is monothematic, in that the opening of the slow introduction is the same melodic shape as the start of the 1st subject in the exposition.
- When the music reaches the 2nd subject at bar 75, in the key of the dominant, the 1st subject theme is heard again. However, there is a new 2nd subject theme heard slightly later.
- Haydn's trumpet concerto is also monothematic in the sense that the 1st subject (in both the orchestral and solo expositions) and the 2nd subject in the solo exposition start in the same way.
- Mozart's String Quintet K. 593 is monothematic as the 1st and 2nd subject in the exposition of the first movement use the same melody in different keys.

Exercise 16

- 1st subject is first heard played by the cellos from bar 3, after two loud tonic chords played by the full orchestra.
- Cellos play the first part of the melody and it is continued by the 1st violins from bar 9.
- The theme is then extended by sequence.
- The start of the theme is then heard tutti and ***ff***, firmly establishing the tonic key.
- Just before the end of the exposition the theme returns in the dominant.
- In the development the theme is used in the minor (C minor and C sharp minor) over tremolo strings and is heard with a transition theme as a countermelody, modulating frequently.
- There is also use of the theme in C major, C minor and E♭ major in the development, making it sound like the end of the development section, but Beethoven then moves swiftly to a statement in E♭ minor (the tonic minor).
- At the very end of the development the theme is heard played by the 2nd horn, as though they have started the recapitulation four bars too early.
- In the recapitulation the theme returns initially as in the exposition, but only for six bars. After the cellos have played their dissonant C sharp, it is resolved differently. In the exposition they moved up from the C sharp to a D, but in the recapitulation they move down to C.
- The theme is then extended by sequence as before and presented tutti.
- In the Coda the theme is heard with a new 1st violin countermelody.
- There is a presentation of the theme with a large *crescendo,* created not just by the orchestra increasing in volume but also by the gradual addition of instruments to the texture.
- In the final statement of the theme played by the brass, the trumpets do not play the top note at the end, playing down the octave instead. It could be that Beethoven is suggesting that the hero of the title still has some work to do.

Exercise 17

- Although both Mozart and Haydn used chromatic chords in their music, Beethoven increased their use considerably.
- Mozart and Haydn used chromatic chords sometimes, often to achieve a modulation.
- In the first movement of his 'Military' symphony Haydn uses a diminished chord and also a German 6th chord.
- In the first movement of Mozart's clarinet concerto there is also a German 6th chord and a Neapolitan 6th chord.
- Beethoven uses chromatic harmonies much more frequently.
- As early as bar 7 in the first movement of the 'Eroica' symphony there is a chromatic C sharp in the melody line, harmonised with just the note G above, creating a dissonant tritone.
- There are occasions where Beethoven increases the already strong dissonance of the diminished 7th chord by presenting it over a pedal note in the bass.
- Sometimes Beethoven highlights dissonant chords by giving the two notes a semitone apart to the two flutes, so that they can be heard very clearly.
- Beethoven often repeats very dissonant chords, sometimes with accompanying rhythmic instability, creating a feeling of great tension and drama.

Exercise 18

Tadeusz	Karajan
Fortepiano with a small period instrument orchestra	Grand piano with a large orchestra
A slightly lower pitch	A slightly faster tempo
Piano acciaccatura in bar 6	No piano acciaccatura in bar 6
The first tutti in bar 9 is loud	The first tutti in bar 9 is very loud
The bassoons are heard very clearly in bars 29 to 31 and 47 to 49	The sound quality is slightly muffled, suggesting an older recording (it actually dates from 1951)
The quavers in the piano part in bars 74 to 76 in the right hand are much clearer, partly due to the use of the fortepiano and the more modern recording	The dynamic contrasts are greater
There is a small crescendo in bars 70 to 73 in the wind	
Both observe the reduction in dynamic to ***p*** in bar 16	

Exercise 19

- The form of this movement is sonata-rondo, so features of both sonata form and rondo form are present.

Features that correspond to sonata form:

- 1st subject themes presented in the tonic
- Modulation to the dominant
- 2nd subject themes in the dominant (though initially the dominant minor)
- Middle section which corresponds to a development, though there is no actual development as Mozart introduces new themes instead, in the related keys of F sharp minor (relative minor) and D major (subdominant)
- Recapitulation of themes in the tonic, but not in the order in which they appeared in the exposition
- 2nd subject themes all appear in the recapitulation in the tonic or tonic minor

Features that correspond to rondo form:

- Alternating new themes with themes which recur
- The first theme from the 1st subject is heard again at the end of the exposition

Exercise 20

Hogwood	Davis
Lower pitch	Slightly faster
	The clarinet has a more mellow and slightly more muffled tone
The soloist is playing a basset clarinet and is playing the full range of notes	The soloist is playing a standard clarinet as the lower notes in bars 134 to 137 are not heard and bars 145 to 147 are transposed up an octave
Notes are staccato as marked, such as the third and fourth notes in bar 130	More of the soloist's notes are slurred together
The virtuosic Alberti bass pattern in bars 134 to 137 is played detached	The virtuosic Alberti bass pattern in bars 134 to 137 is played slurred
Both soloists add slurs in bar 142	
The orchestra is smaller	The orchestra uses more vibrato
The orchestra add a small crescendo in bars 147 and 147 but then a diminuendo into bar 148	

Exercise 21

Comparison of Mozart's Clarinet Concerto and Haydn's Trumpet Concerto.

- Both written for friends of the composers, who were virtuoso performers on their instruments.
- Both written for new versions of an older instruments: a basset clarinet (which could play lower notes that a standard clarinet) and a keyed trumpet (which could play more notes than a standard natural trumpet).
- Both the invented instruments became obsolete.
- Both concertos are in three movements.
- Mozart's concerto was written in 1791, Haydn's in 1796.
- Both concertos have three movements with a ritornello/sonata-form 1st movement, ternary form 2nd movement and sonata-rondo 3rd movement.
- Both 1st movements reduced the number of different themes presented, but in different ways. In Mozart's concerto there is no orchestral 2nd subject; instead the 1st subject is repeated in imitation. In Haydn's concerto the 2nd subject in the solo exposition begins in exactly the same way as the 1st subject (which is the same in both the solo and orchestral expositions).
- Both composers wrote music to display the full capabilities of the new instruments. Mozart wrote passages covering a very wide range of notes in a short space of time, including the extra lower notes; and Haydn took full advantage of the chromatic notes the keyed trumpet could play.
- Haydn's orchestra is slightly larger than the one used by Mozart as in addition to the 2 flutes, 2 bassoons and 2 horns used by Mozart, Haydn also has 2 oboes, 2 trumpets and timpani.

Area of Study 2

Popular song: blues, jazz, swing and big band

Section A: Unfamiliar music

Frank Sinatra: 'Love Walked In'

a. Pizzicato

b. Walking

c. Bar 1: unaccompanied/monophonic. Shortened to minim/crotchet, detached/staccato. Harp chord on 3rd beat. No clear indication of tempo.

Bar 5: syncopated/sung on 2nd beat/(crotchet) rest on 1st beat. Sustained/legato. Accompanied. Tempo/pulse now established.

d. Bar 3: 'drove' made longer, e.g. dotted crotchet with 'the' as a quaver. Bar 3 'shadows a-' even rhythm/triplet. Bar 6: anticipates/pushes the rhythm for 'walked right in'. Bar 7: delays/holds back 'and brought'. Bar 7: faster movement on 'sunniest'. Anticipates bar 8 'day'. Approximately notated:

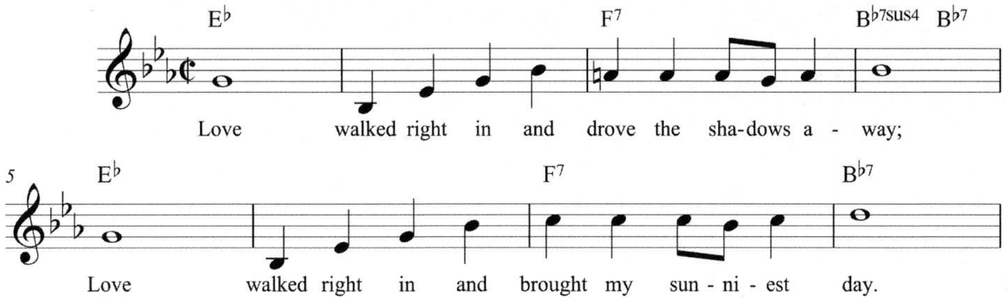

e. Trombones

f. 1st time bars are cut/repeat of melody in the band begins on the singer's final note. 2nd time bars are extended/a coda (outro) is added.

g.

h. Vibraphone

T-Bone Walker: 'Call It Stormy Monday'

a. Verse 1, even tone, mid-range, sung clearly and simply. Verse 2 begins on a high G, wider range to the melody, more relaxed and carefree; dynamic and melodic contrast for 'Sunday', sung gently. Verse 3, high register, falling phrases, downhearted and repentant.

b. Choose one blues singer for comparison. Refer to a blues recording you have heard – title, name of singer, technical or expressive detail to compare with Walker. May include: rougher tone of earlier blues, projected vaudeville style of Twenties blues queens, sophisticated vocal delivery of jazz singers who sang blues.

c. Beginning of electric guitar/amplification, example of developments in Memphis blues style. T-Bone Walker was one of its first exponents (influence on B. B. King). Use of a band (e.g. reference to Chicago blues style), similar to a jazz band (saxes, trumpets), playing riff during guitar solo. Light bass and drums, more amplification later. Light, elaborately decorated piano background, improvised figurations, tremolo. Muted trumpet in Verse 2, jazz influence/crossover with blues.

Section B

Ella Fitzgerald: *The Cole Porter Songbook*

1. Fitzgerald's success as a recording artist; Norman Granz, setting up Verve Records, taking over as her manager; development of LP album format, longer collections of music; themed/concept album, e.g. songs of Cole Porter; Buddy Bregman arrangements.
2. Background in musical theatre from Twenties; educated, wealthy background; wrote his own lyrics, witty, clever, ironic, references to contemporary events; use of rhyme, internal rhyme; melodic structure, harmony.
3. Fitzgerald steady tempo, clear diction, expressive, well-shaped and projected, light swinging feel, humour. Choose one other version to compare (e.g. Sinatra, Paige). Comment on the key features. Compare the two, e.g. faster, slower, vocal qualities, expression of the lyrics. Not too much on accompaniment: the question asks about 'Ella Fitzgerald's performance' and 'any other artist'.
4. Comment on two songs: (i) 'Anything Goes': minor key introduction, change to major for 'today'; major key, tonic chord with I–V bass, main focus on melody and humour of lyrics; bridge in submediant major; (ii) 'Too Darn Hot': minor key, fast tempo, slow harmonic movement, allows focus on words/humour; repetition of minor 'Too darn hot', contrasts with faster lines in major key; bridge in tonic major; (iii) 'Let's Do It': major key; ambiguous first chord – minor or 6th chord, melody then descends chromatically to harmony note, teasing humour; sequence in bridge section; (iv) 'Ev'ry Time We Say Goodbye': major key, reflective mood of loss in minor chords, e.g. 'I wonder why a little', changes mood to major for 'begin to sing about it'; 'change from major to minor' in lyrics and harmony.
5. Fitzgerald: controlled, natural communication, able to sustain phrases and keep the listener's interest. Unexaggerated, sensitive treatment of the music, keeps the music flowing at a steady speed. One other song (e.g. Washington, Bentyne). Comment on their qualities in this song: timbre of voice, phrasing, concentration, ability to connect with the audience, effect of a slower speed.
6. Development of LP, longer recording lengths leading to album format, collections of random songs; Norman Granz, founding of Verve Records, first of a series of Songbooks; successful commercially and artistically, e.g. themed composer albums by other artists.

Frank Sinatra: *Classic Sinatra 1953-1960*

1. Riddle worked with Sinatra from 1953, 'I've Got The World On A String'; new style compared to earlier string-based arrangements; technique (e.g. allowing voice to be heard, using fills, concern for structure/pacing of the music); worked on a series of Sinatra albums for Capitol.
2. Choose one song for discussion of vocal technique: phrasing, legato style, natural even tone throughout range, rich baritone timbre and projection (e.g. compare to thinner sound of 1920s/1930s), expressive, clear diction.

3. Rich harmony, e.g. added 6th, chromatic chords, chord extensions (7ths, 9ths, 11ths, 13ths); clear strong bass (e.g. strong feeling for tonic and dominant, clear modulations, use of secondary dominants). Varied treatment of harmony and tonality in B/bridge sections, e.g. change of key to B minor from tonic D of 'I've Got The World On A String'; faster or slower harmonic movement. Use of static pedal in 'I've Got You Under My Skin' (modelled on Ravel's Boléro).
4. Long career, beginning with Dorsey band, 1940s Sinatra craze, diversifies into acting, dip in singing career but recovers with Capitol albums. Early success builds on achievements of Bing Crosby; conversational, direct style, intimate and expressive; explores musical theatre song repertoire, encourages arrangers to develop new versions of old sets, set example of achievement for other male singers.
5. Sinatra: treatment of the introduction, confident and direct, colouring of vocal tone and rhythmic freedom/rubato in responding to lyrics. Choose one other version to compare (e.g. Billie Holiday, Steve Tyrell). Describe briefly and comment on features that communicate with the audience.
6. LP album format developed, allowed collections of songs, expansion of recorded material needed for an album, exploration of standards from 1930s/1940s, with new arrangements; Capitol/Sinatra developed themed albums (concept album, e.g. *Songs for Swingin' Lovers*). Singles, radio/jukebox hit songs, popular songs, competition with mass market of young people (e.g. rock 'n' roll).

Sammy Davis Jr.: *Greatest Hits Live*

1. Warmth of tone, rhythmic, phrasing, able to time anticipation or delay; range, able to shape a song, build to a climax; ability as an actor, dancer, comedian; able to communicate successfully with audience, storytelling, treatment of lyrics; use example from one or more songs.
2. Piano accompaniment in introduction, cabaret-style voice/piano, decorated chords, keeps movement of music during a long, slow passage; able to respond to changes by the singer; full band, strong backing for powerful singing; reharmonisation, strong harmonies, use of chromatic chords over tonic pedal; saxophone countermelodies, brass/drums/cymbals provide rhythmic backing, working to a big finish; faster-moving fanfares in final tag.
3. Davis version: shorter, fewer verses, chorus sung once only; whistled intro and outro; expression, personal way with the story, characterisation (e.g. hoarse voice of Bojangles); vocal skills, range of tone, dynamics; accompaniment. Compare with one other version (e.g. Walker, Diamond). Comment on more verses at a faster tempo, delivery of story, vocal performance, country style, guitar accompaniment.
4. Segregated nature of music business as radio began; 'race records' for black audience; business largely in the hands of white management, possibilities of exploitation; Davis as an example, breaking down barriers by talent as a singer, entertainer; friendship and support of Sinatra; guest television appearances, unusual for black performers to have their own show (Nat King Cole, NBC 1954); later has his own show (1966, NBC).

Nina Simone: *I Put A Spell On You*

1. Details of Simone's version, e.g. expressive, vocal qualities, feeling of swing, shaping of phrases; treatment of chorus, expressive qualities of low register, ability to communicate meaning of lyrics, individual timbre; arrangement, jazz style. Compare with another version (e.g. Aznavour, Giddens) – slower, waltz treatment, expressive differences, etc.
2. Simone's success built on recording contracts; release of singles and albums; first major success with 'I Loves You Porgy', single from first album. Link between recordings and radio air-time; publicity, increased concert audiences. Album *I Put A Spell On You* recorded for Philips; more pop material; promotion of image, e.g. 1967 album *High Priestess Of Soul.*
3. Arrangement by Hal Mooney; large orchestra available. Strings used in introduction, melody in violins; later sustained string chords; crescendo to support build-up to climax. Rhythm section; swing rhythm on cymbal, rim on snare drum. Piano countermelody, Simone credited as pianist; elaborate blues-style, tremolo. Tenor sax solo in Verse 2; player not identified on record sleeve (Jerome Richardson or King Curtis); use of double-tongued repeated notes.
4. Refer to qualities of singing: vocal timbre, expression, influences of jazz, soul, etc. Jazz repertoire, also embraces pop, folk. Specific detail on songs; ability to put her own stamp on a song (e.g. 'I Put A Spell On You', compared to Hawkins version); influence on later performers of these songs.

Area of Study 3

Duke Ellington, early jazz and swing

1. **You should mention:**
   - Big band (15 players), using sections of reeds, trumpets and trombones (e.g. chordal, riffs, antiphonal writing).
   - Pre-written sections; 'Ellington effect', using characteristics of players, solo improvisation, muted sounds, vocal effects.
   - Short three-minute recordings, attempted longer pieces.
   - Dance numbers, ballads, mood or character pieces.
   - Jungle style, Cotton Club origins.
2. **You should mention:**
   - Some of the key players in the Ellington band, e.g. Ben Webster, Cootie Williams, Jimmy Blanton, Johnny Hodges.
   - Reputation as noted soloists in their own right, recordings, European tours.
   - Ellington's skills in exploiting their musical personality.
   - Cootie Williams' solo in 'Concerto For Cootie'.
   - Development of signature techniques, e.g. Joe Nanton's 'ya-ya' sound in 'Ko-Ko'.
   - 'Ellington effect', flexible rehearsal methods, including melodic ideas from bandmates.

3. **You should mention:**
   - Musical skills as pianist, composer, arranger.
   - Opportunity of contract at Cotton Club, including regular radio spot (usually for white bands only).
   - Management role of Irving Mills, e.g. publicity emphasising artistic qualities as a composer.
   - Skill in managing personnel in the band.
   - Ability to attract the leading players and to retain them, sometimes for many years.
   - Commitment to life of touring, e.g. by train all over the United States, concert tours to Europe.
4. **You should mention:**
   - Early rhythm section (before Ellington), piano, banjo or guitar, tuba (e.g. for a stronger bass on recordings) or plucked double bass.
   - March rhythm, tonic-dominant bass, piano/banjo fills in chords (comping).
   - Refer to other rhythm sections, e.g. Count Basie.
   - Ellington rhythm section: bass and guitar provides forward momentum and swing; Jimmy Blanton on bass; firm, projected tone, able to take solos; walking bass; Ellington's piano, sparse, occasional chords, some solos.

Miles Davis, cool jazz and bepop

1. **You should mention:**
   - Davis's move away from bebop towards cool jazz.
   - Trumpet style (e.g. *Porgy And Bess* or other albums with Gil Evans, *Birth Of The Cool*).
   - Individual tone, softer, Harmon mute.
   - Approach to melody, phrasing, use of silence.
   - 'So What': reduces chords to very simple pattern, allows time for melodies to be developed.
   - Modal scale for melody.
   - Detail on his solo.
   - Collaboration with important soloists, e.g. John Coltrane, Bill Evans.
   - Commercial success, contract with Columbia, television appearance, high profile.
   - Artistic integrity, role model for black musicians.
2. **You should mention:**
   - Slower tempo compared to bebop.
   - Slow introduction, influence of impressionist/modern composers.
   - Simplicity of material, bass melody, with 'So What' chords, only two chords over **AABA** structure.
   - Davis's solo, pure in tone, thoughtful, expressive, build-up of phrasing, effective use of swing, carefully paced and structured.
   - Contrast to Coltrane and Adderley, more bebop style; discuss if the contrast in style is effective.

3. **Choose two soloists to compare:**
   - Davis, modal, typical of cool jazz, relaxed, begins with simple phrases separated by silences.
   - Coltrane, use of arpeggio-based figures ascending and descending, begins simply, develops into more double time than Davis.
   - Adderley, more bebop influenced, continuous semiquavers, also slower melodic motifs (e.g. repeated crotchets).
   - Evans, shorter solo, one solo chorus but also playing in rhythm section. Style of introduction, parallel chords in 'impressionist' style.
   - Add specific detail on solos; also background information, e.g. links to other work by these artists (Davis's *Porgy And Bess*, later fusion works; Coltrane's later saxophone influence; Bill Evans' later albums, piano trio).
4. **You should mention:**
   - Davis's leading position as a recording artist, contracts with Columbia, publicity about his music and life, coverage in magazines and TV documentary.
   - Previous albums in the 1950s, collaboration with Gil Evans.
   - Small groups, working with the best sidemen; background to recording, 30th Street Studio in New York, individual microphones.
   - LPs, stereo recording.
   - Background to cool jazz, discussion of jazz theory, artistic and social context.

Jazz history

1. **This question is not about the origins of jazz. There were many important and influential New Orleans musicians, such as Jelly Roll Morton, Louis Armstrong, Sidney Bechet, etc.**

   New Orleans spread its influence through bands such as Fate Marable's steamboat band, which trained many musicians; movement of musicians to Chicago and New York. You should discuss the music of at least one in some detail:
   - Morton: recordings are carefully rehearsed, preferred working with New Orleans Creole musicians; feeling of swing, intended for dance.
   - Armstrong: strong tone, range up to high notes, fluent and exciting improvisations, much-imitated solo style.
2. **You should mention:**
   - War-time loss of players to armed forces, strike in radio/recording, companies aiming for more popular vocal market, post-war decline of big bands, rise of small groups for bebop.
   - Growth of new popular styles to replace jazz (rock 'n' roll, R&B).
   - As economy recovers, a youth/teenage market grows, but jazz is not the automatic first choice.
   - Jazz bands survive (Ellington and Basie the longest), but competition is fierce.
3. **Choose one musician only.**

   British can include Ted Heath, Ivy Benson, Johnny Dankworth, John McLaughlin, Keith Tippett, Evan Parker, Deirdre Cartwright, Courtney Pine.

European includes Django Reinhardt, Misha Mengelberg, Barbara Dennerlein, Jan Garbarek.

You should know at least one example of music to discuss in detail. You are expected to make a case for your chosen musician to be widely known. Explain the qualities of their work, why they are important, and write about their reputation and influence. Include weaknesses to make a balanced discussion, but mostly explain their strengths.

4. **Note the date: the first half of the 20th century is before 1950. You should mention:**
    - Musical challenges, i.e. technique, improvisation, learning the changes for standards, their transpositions, adapting to the demands of playing in a band.
    - Responding to demands of fashion (e.g. rise of the big band means less work for small groups).
    - Keeping up with technical advances (e.g. imitating solo styles of Louis Armstrong, Charlie Parker).
    - Highly competitive scene in Chicago and New York.
    - Contracts for engagements, recordings.
    - Dealing with publishers, managers, recording companies.
    - Economic challenges such as 1930s Great Depression and fewer recordings during the war.
5. **Choice of works including:**
    - Latin Jazz music by Mario Bauzá and Tito Puente, including salsa, mambo pieces with jazz solos.
    - 'Caravan' by Juan Tizol and Duke Ellington.
    - 'Manteca' by Dizzy Gillespie.
    - 'Song For My Father' by Horace Silver.
    - Describe the music in detail.
    - How often are Latin features found in music by this composer?
    - Background information on rhythms, clavé patterns, song forms, use of percussion (timbales, conga, etc.).
    - Cultural background, Latin influence on southern states of USA, immigration.
6. **Any choice of free jazz. 'Evaluate' means you are asked to comment on the quality of the piece.**

    Issues include: what is meant by free jazz, the interpretation that is applied to your chosen work, limitation of what is meant by free. e.g. Ornette Coleman, swing rhythm, walking bass, pre-notation of solos. Success of his ensemble in creating convincing jazz. Or 'Weather Report', free jazz without solos and a focus on timbre and texture.

    To what extent is this jazz? Response of audience, critics, other musicians; commercial viability of experimental styles.

Area of Study 4

Exercise 1

See the table below.

	1. *Wachet auf, ruft uns die Stimme*	**2.** *Er kommt, der Bräut'gam kommt!*	**3.** *Wann kommst du, mein Heil?*
Type of movement	Chorale fantasia	Secco recitative	Obbligato aria
Vocal forces	SATB choir	Tenor solo	Solo soprano and bass
Instrumental forces	Two oboes, taille, strings, continuo	Continuo	Obbligato violino piccolo, continuo
Key	E♭ major	C minor	C minor
Time signature	3/4	C	6/8
Melodic features (including word setting)	Most vocal phrases ascend, reflecting the 'waking up'. Syllabic until alleluias, which are melismatic, then back to syllabic	Disjunct melody, syllabic, follows spoken rhythm of words	Flowing violin melody, syllabic vocal lines
Texture	ATB in imitation, instrumental accompaniment using two motifs	Melody and accompaniment	Obbligato and sung melody with accompaniment Voices rarely sing together
Harmony	Oboe suspensions; modulates to dominant, relative minor, subdominant	Dissonant chords over opening tonic pedal; perfect cadences in various keys	
Other significant features (this may include structure)	Sopranos sing cantus firmus; Verse 1 of chorale melody in longer note values; Da capo of opening ritornello		

4. *Zion hört die Wächter singen*	**5.** *So geh herein zu mir*	**6.** *Mein Freund ist mein!*	**7.** *Gloria sei dir gesungen*
Chorale	Accompanied recitative	Obbligato aria	Chorale
Tenors	Solo bass (the voice of God)	Solo soprano and bass	SATB choir
Strings and continuo	Strings and continuo	Solo oboe and continuo	Instruments play 'colla parte'
E♭ major	E♭ major to B♭ major	B♭ major	E♭major
C	C	C	C
Tenors sing 2nd verse of chorale; upper strings play obbligato countermelody in unison, using several motives in varying orders	Syllabic, some unexpected notes representing tribulations	Lots of paired quavers, some melismas, flowing oboe melody	The chorale has very irregular phrase lengths
Melodies with continuo accompaniment	Melody and accompaniment	Two melodies with continuo accompaniment	Homophonic
Cadences in tonic, dominant, G minor	Diminished 7th chords; cadences in various related keys		Bach's harmonisation of the melody
Was later used for a piece of organ music		Traditional da capo structure	The final verse of the chorale melody

Exercise 2

Points could include:

- *Wachet auf* is a chorale cantata, meaning that it takes the music of an existing chorale and uses it as the basis for some of the movements.
- The chorale is *Wachet auf* by Nicolai, written in 1599.
- The chorale melody and words are used in the 1st, 4th and 7th movements, while the other movements set words by an unknown poet.
- The 1st movement is a chorale fantasia - an extended movement is built around the chorale melody
- In the 1st movement the sopranos sing the chorale melody line by line in long note values; this is known as a cantus firmus ('fixed song')
- The alto, tenor and bass sing imitative lines, initially entering after the cantus firmus, then at the same time, and finally before the cantus firmus.
- The lower vocal parts use the words sung by the sopranos, but repeat them many times.
- The orchestra has its own melodic material, used in ritornellos and as accompaniment.
- In the 4th movement the tenors sing the chorale melody (Verse 2) while the violins and violas play a unison obbligato melody and the continuo accompanies.
- In this movement the vocal and instrumental phrases do not begin and end together.
- The obbligato melody is made up of several short motives, which are repeated in different orders.
- In the 7th (and final) movement Bach harmonises the chorale melody in four parts, which the choir sings accompanied by the instruments playing the vocal parts.

Exercise 3

Points could include:

- This was a coronation anthem, so Purcell had large and capable instrumental and vocal forces at his disposal: eight soloists, eight-part choir and instruments including a brand new organ!
- The verse anthem structure immediately gives variety of timbres and textures: sections for soloists only are contrasted with sections for full choir.
- The work opens with a 'symphony', a movement for instruments (strings and continuo) only. The first half of this is homophonic, and at the change of metre the texture changes to polyphonic, with imitative entries (1st violin, followed by 2nd violin, viola and then cello).
- The first two choruses continue with a polyphonic texture and the number of parts singing at any one time varies from one (at the start of each of the choruses) to the full eight parts, accompanied by the strings playing both with the vocal lines and extra melodic lines too.
- In the first verse section, as well as reducing the number of singers, the texture changes to homophonic and three higher parts are answered by three lower parts, before they sing together. Only seven different voice parts are used in this movement and it moves into an imitative polyphonic texture.
- The chorus 'Praise The Lord, O Jerusalem' has a homophonic opening, again moving to imitative polyphony.
- The final chorus contrasts two different melodic ideas in different voices at the same time: faster-moving alleluias in 3rds and 6ths and a slower-moving 'amen'.

Throughout the movement the texture gradually builds, with more voices singing simultaneously and the accompaniment increasing from just continuo at the start of the movement to all the strings.

Exercise 4

Points could include:

- Recitative is used to move the action forward and to describe what is happening while arias are often more reflective and convey the emotions or the 'effect'.
- Recitative has much more text, which is set to reflect the rhythms of speech. In arias the text is shorter overall, but words and lines are often repeated.
- In recitative the word setting is syllabic; in arias it can be syllabic and melismatic.
- *Secco* recitative is accompanied by the continuo only. *Accompagnato* recitative is accompanied by strings and continuo. Arias often have fuller accompaniment and sometimes an obbligato instrument playing a flowing countermelody.
- The fact that arias were reflective meant that a da capo form was sometimes used, in which the first section was repeated again at the end (giving an overall ternary form).
- Recitatives are through-composed and often modulate quickly through a range of keys. Arias do modulate, but not usually so quickly.
- Both can include examples of word painting, using harmony, melody and rhythm to convey the meaning of the words.
- Refer to any examples of your choice.

Exercise 5

This question could be answered by comparing any two choruses, but would be easier if two very contrasted choruses were selected, such as one by Schütz with no accompaniment and one by a later composer with fuller accompaniment and in a different number of parts. Answers should cover a range of features including word setting, texture, accompaniment, harmony and word painting.

Exercise 6

Works such as Schütz's and Bach's St Matthew Passions would work well here, as they have clear similarities and differences. Another alternative would be to compare a Purcell anthem with a Handel anthem.

Exercise 7

This would be best answered by limiting the references to different works and to giving detail about the individual movements. Works using a range of soloists and instruments would be best, such as Bach's *St Matthew Passion*, with a range of forces.

Exercise 8

Later Baroque composers used word painting more than early Baroque composers, so would be a better choice for answering this question.

Area of Study 5

Exercise 1

Friar Lawrence theme/slow introduction theme

Bar numbers	Orchestration	Key	Other features
1–11	Clarinets and bassoons	F♯ minor/ modal	Chorale, four-part harmony
41–51	Woodwind	F minor	Repetition of bars 1–38 more fully scored and a tone lower
86–96	Woodwind	A minor	Increasing tempo
280–284	Two horns	B minor/ F♯ minor	
293–297	Three horns	Modulating	Echoed by flutes and clarinets
302–307	Two horns	G minor	Semitone higher than bar 280
315–320	Three horns	Modulating	Echoed by flutes and clarinets
335–342	Two trumpets	B minor	Heard over rest of the orchestra because they are playing high notes
450–453	All brass and some woodwind	C minor	Accompanied by runs in strings and woodwind
458–461	All brass and some woodwind	C♯ minor	Semitone higher than 450

Montagues and Capulets theme/first subject

Bar numbers	Orchestration	Key	Other features
112–122	Full orchestra	B minor	Presentation of first subject
126–130	Cellos/basses in imitation with woodwind	D minor	First subject with new rhythm
130–134	Cellos/basses with woodwind imitating	G minor	New rhythm
151–161	Full orchestra	B minor	Climax

273–279	Strings	B minor	Rapid crescendo
302–305	Second violins	G minor	Development of theme
321–342	Tutti	B minor	Fragments of theme developed antiphonally
353–365	Tutti	B minor	Recapitulation, shorter than in exposition
441–445	Tutti	B minor	With fragments of love theme inserted
446–449	Tutti	B minor	Theme in full
454–457	Tutti	C minor	

Love theme/second subject first theme

Bar numbers	Orchestration	Key	Other features
184–192	Cor anglais and muted violas with horn, bassoon, cello and bass accompaniment	D♭ major	Second subject
213–243	Flutes and oboes with horn countermelody and woodwind and string accompaniment	D♭ major	Extended theme and added appoggiatura at the start
389–419	Piccolo and strings, horn countermelody now played by two horns to balance fuller melody, woodwind triplet accompaniment	D minor	With appoggiatura and extension of theme
419–435	Cello and bassoon imitated by flute and oboe	Modulating	Contrapuntal treatment of theme
436–438	Tutti	E major	Theme cut short
475– 476	Violins and violas	B minor	In diminution
479–481	Cellos and basses	Dominant of B	In diminution
486–492	1st bassoon, 1st violins and cellos	B major	Fragments of theme
510–518	Strings and bassoon	B major	

Exercise 2

Points could include:

- Mendelssohn was not using a large orchestra – it was the same size as that used by Beethoven.
- The double basses are independent from the cellos, often playing the bass while the cellos have a melodic role.
- The work begins with a gradual increase in the number of instruments playing: clarinets join in bar 3, oboes in bar 5.
- Tutti textures are used to represent when the sea is stronger.
- The tutti texture at the end of the exposition is the climax of the section, with unison string semiquavers.
- There are similar textures at the climaxes in the development and recapitulation.
- The brass can play only limited notes but are used in loud tutti passages.
- The woodwind are independent from the strings, sometimes having the melodic interest while the strings play the accompaniment.

Exercise 3

Points could include:

- Though writers describe *Romeo And Juliet* as a symphonic poem, Tchaikovsky described it as a fantasy-overture.
- *Romeo And Juliet* uses sonata form, rather than a structure following a narrative.
- Tchaikovsky takes elements of the play to use in a sonata form structure.
- Liszt invented the term symphonic poem and used it to describe *Orpheus.*
- The work was written to serve as an overture to a performance of an opera, as Liszt didn't like the existing overture.
- *Orpheus* is in abridged sonata form.
- *Orpheus* does not follow a narrative, but aims to give an overall impression of music taming man's brutal instincts.

Exercise 4

What features of Strauss's symphonic poem *Don Quixote* demonstrate that it is from the end of the 19th century? Compare it with any other works of your choice.

Points could include:

- There is use of a very large orchestra.
- The work is long.
- Strauss takes the Romantic idea of transforming themes to use in different circumstances, as invented and used by Liszt and others.
- Though structured in the form of introduction, theme and variations, they are not variations in the Classical sense as the music does not follow the same phrase or harmonic structure.
- The music serves to follow the narrative and to portray Quixote's adventures.
- Strauss uses wide-ranging harmony: the music passes quickly through a huge number of keys, briefly stabilised with perfect cadences before moving on.
- Cadential progressions are often unusual, with distant chords and unexpected voice-leading.
- Distant keys are used; the opening features keys a tritone apart.
- The dominant of the main key of D major does not really feature in the work, though to a certain extent the mediant of F♯ fulfils this role.

Exercise 5

Points could include:

- Taking a narrative approach means portraying the events of the programme in order in the music.
- Though Dukas described the work as a scherzo, it does not have the structure of a scherzo: the structure is created by the events in the programme.
- Dukas first sets the scene with a mysterious opening, reflecting the sorcerer.
- The apprentice also has a theme, which is faster.
- A fanfare-style theme is used to signal the casting of spells.
- The broom is heard coming to life with its theme gradually taking shape.
- The apprentice chopping the broom is depicted by two loud chords and then the broom theme played in 10ths, representing the two brooms.
- Dukas can hint at unspoken parts of the programme in his music. The work ends with four notes from the broom theme – does this imply that the broom has been stilled only temporarily?
- Mendelssohn does not take a narrative approach in his overture *The Hebrides.*
- There is not a programme with a list of events for this work, only the title.
- It is an evocation of a journey at sea and the islands and caves visited.
- The lack of a narrative means that the music can conform to sonata form.

Exercise 6

Suggested comparison: Mendelssohn's *The Hebrides* (portraying the sea) and Smetana's *Vltava* (following the course of a river).

Exercise 7

Suggested works: *Vltava* by Smetana and *Lyric Pieces* Op. 54 by Grieg.

Exercise 8

Points could include:

- The piano was a popular instrument, both for people to listen to in concerts and for people to play at home.
- The piano had been developed since the Classical period.
- Wealthy people in the newly created middle class could afford to have a piano at home and wanted music to play on it.
- In addition to transcriptions of orchestral works, composers wrote short pieces of piano music for performers of varying standards.
- Short character pieces often had descriptive titles, though these were sometimes added after the works had been composed.
- Schumann's *Kinderszenen* is a set of 13 short pieces for piano, which is an evocation of childhood for adults to play.
- The pieces have descriptive titles such as 'Child Falling Asleep' and 'By the Fireside'.
- Grieg wrote 10 books of *Lyric Pieces* for piano, each a contained set of short pieces of music.
- Grieg's music includes nationalist elements, such as references to traditional dances and use of melodic and harmonic ideas from Norwegian folk music.
- Grieg also took ideas from the scenery and folk tales of his country.
- Grieg's *Lyric Pieces* helped him to become famous and are still popular today.

Area of Study 6

1. You should mention: size of orchestra, elaborate and colourful orchestration; Russian music, e.g. Rimsky-Korsakov (Stravinsky's teacher), influence of distinctive Russian approach, (e.g. including folk melodies or melodies in a primitive style, scene-setting rather than symphonic); pushing boundaries of harmony and tonality. Possibly include Debussy. Include specific detail from *The Rite Of Spring*. Refer to other late-Romantic works if you can.
2. You should mention: rhythm and metre, cross-rhythms, examples of changing time signatures, challenging for dancers; use of traditional melody, with expressive use of ornaments; polytonal and octatonic harmony/melody, (e.g. Augurs chord); role of woodwind, complex textures, alto flute solo; expanded use of percussion; string writing, (e.g. divisi harmonics, repeated down-bows).
3. You should mention: background to Diaghilev and Ballets Russes; impact of dancers (Massine, Nijinsky) on western European ballet; cultural life of Paris, fashion for Russian art, music; Stravinsky's earlier ballets, *Firebird* and *Petrushka*; influence of Russian school of composers, such as Rimsky-Korsakov, (e.g. exotic and elaborate orchestration), choice of subject material; collaboration with Roerich; circumstances of choreography, rehearsals and first performance. Refer to specific detail from the music.
4. You should mention: impact of Stravinsky's use of rhythm and metre; size and power of orchestra, use of colour and instrumental effects; use of folk melody and primitive elements; repetition of rhythmic figures, use of ostinato, e.g. for industrial, machine-like effects; dissonance, polytonal writing. Include specific detail from *The Rite Of Spring*. Refer to other related works if you can, e.g. large orchestra in Holst's *Planets* (use of $\frac{5}{4}$ ostinato in 'Mars'), aggressive elements in Bartók (e.g. Allegro barbaro).
5. You should mention: melodies from English folksong, modal/pentatonic character (flattened 7ths); triadic/diatonic harmony, parallel 5ths/octaves, e.g. between bass and melody; unexpected sequences of unrelated chords; large orchestra, adding tuned percussion in later scores; music for a practical purpose, e.g. film music. Refer to specific detail from *Sinfonia Antartica* and if you can another work by Vaughan Williams.
6. You should mention: background on the film music origins of the symphony; pictorial elements in music, (e.g. Antarctic, ice, penguins); overall structure of symphony (e.g. related to usual format); compare Prelude and Scherzo with a first movement/Scherzo of another symphony (e.g. Mahler, or Beethoven from Area of Study 1). The question asks for your opinion: back up your judgements with detailed evidence from the music. Be positive and appreciative if you can. If you are negative about both the symphony and the film music, don't just criticise: compare with an example that you do value (e.g. (i) Vaughan Williams' Symphony No. 4 is a better symphony because..., or (ii) Korngold's score for *The Adventures Of Robin Hood* is better than the music for *Scott of the Antarctic* because...).
7. You should mention: unrelated triads from G major and E♭ minor in opening theme; parallel movement of bass and harmony; dissonant chord formations, (e.g. major chord + semitone, similarity to octatonic patterns); chords for the penguin music; contrast with diatonic heroic figures (e.g. fanfare); overall key structure, changes of key, ending in G major.

8. You should mention: background to Vaughan Williams, lack of tradition of English composers, education in German tradition of teachers (Parry, Stanford); study with Ravel; Vaughan Williams establishes distinctive English voice, based on folk song, 16th/17th-century English composers (e.g. Thomas Tallis); philosophy of role of composer within society, music for amateur performers or social use (e.g. *English Hymnal*), film music, including as part of the war effort; successful career as a serious composer sets an example for younger British composers (e.g. Britten). Refer to specific detail from the music.
9. You should mention: gradual breakdown of tonality under pressure from increasing modulation and chromaticism; atonal music before serialism, trend to extreme brevity, (e.g. Schoenberg, Webern); musical solutions or text-based pieces, (e.g. *Pierrot Lunaire, Wozzeck*); 12-note series to guarantee consistent atonality, create melodic unity with order of intervals. Refer to specific detail from at least one work.
10. You may choose any composer but you should give reasons for their 'decisive contribution', such as an example of their influence (examples include Stravinsky on rhythm, Schoenberg on pitch, Richard Rodgers on the development of the American musical, Steve Reich on minimalism). Discuss detail from at least one work, explaining typical features of the composer's style.
11. You may choose any composer affected by 'politics or persecution'. Many European composers fled to America (Schoenberg, Bartók, Martinů, Tailleferre, Hindemith, Korngold) before and during Second World War. Other examples are composers whose work was written under threat. Messiaen wrote *Quartet For The End of Time* as a prisoner of war. Shostakovich's Fifth Symphony was written in response to criticism by Stalin, at a time of terror in Soviet Russia. Include specific information on the music.
12. You should look at the development of music before the war and after it. Using the evidence, you need to judge what changed after the war or as a result of it. You might include: the development of the European avant-garde, composers meeting at Darmstadt (e.g. Boulez, Stockhausen), rejection of pre-war culture and values; rebuilding of Britain and the end of Empire; musical response to war, the Holocaust and the dropping of the first atomic bomb. Include specific detail on the music.
13. ou should mention: explanation of 'minimalism'; origins in the United States (La Monte Young, Terry Riley, Steve Reich, Philip Glass), later practitioners (John Adams, Michael Nyman); techniques such as phasing, layering, addition or subtraction of notes, ostinato loops, metamorphosis. Include detail from at least one work you know well.
14. You should mention: how composers work today, commissions, sponsorship; challenge of appealing to audiences, music for film or television, crossover styles; possibilities of new styles, computers, electronic, sampling; commercial challenges, recordings, live performances. If you can, refer in detail to the working life of one living composer.

Glossary

Abstract music. Music that is not obviously 'about' anything, effectively the opposite of programme music. Also known as 'absolute' music.

Aeolian mode. A scale that is reproduced by playing the white notes from A to the A an octave above. It has a minor key sound, but does not function like a normal minor scale.

Alberti bass. A type of broken-chord accompaniment used extensively in the Classical period.

Antecedent-consequent. Two linked phrases in a question-and-answer style, where the first ends in a weak cadence (e.g. I–V) and the second ends in a strong cadence (e.g. V–I).

Anacrusis. If a phrase begins before the first downbeat of a bar, the notes or notes preceding the downbeat are known as an anacrusis.

Antiphony. A method of performance in which two or more groups of singers/ instrumentalists are heard alternately.

Aria. An extended vocal solo in an opera, **oratorio** or **cantata**.

Asyla. As well being the title of Thomas Adès' orchestral piece, 'asyla' is the plural of 'asylum', with the double meaning of 'place of refuge' and 'madhouse'.

Augmentation. Lengthening the time values of a musical theme (often by doubling the length).

Aural familiarity. A term used by examiners to refer to evidence in your work that you are listening perceptively and becoming familiar with the music of others

Avant-garde. (Jazz) This term is often used to describe the experimental jazz styles of the 1960s and 1970s. Literally French for 'advance guard', it is used for cultural styles that push the boundaries. Musicians associated with this style include Cecil Taylor, Charles Mingus, Sun Ra, and The Art Ensemble of Chicago.

Avant-garde. (Classical music) The term 'avant-garde' is used to describe the modernist composers of the 1950s and 1960s, including Boulez and Stockhausen.

Baryton. A bowed stringed instrument, similar to a bass viol.

Basso continuo. A bass part (with accompanying chord indications) found in almost all Baroque ensemble music. The term can refer to the bass part or to the ensemble itself (usually a cello with an accompanying harmony instrument, such as a harpsichord or a lute).

Bitonality. The simultaneous use of two different tonalities.

Black Bottom. A popular dance from the 1920s.

Bombs. Accented hits on the snare or bass drum.

Bossa nova. A Brazilian style, which fuses samba and jazz music and which was popularised in the 1950s and 1960s. Bossa nova tends to be played 'straight' rather than 'swung'.

Cadenza. A passage of music (usually in a concerto) for the soloist alone in which they could display their technical brilliance.

Cantata. The word cantata literally means 'to be sung'. In the Baroque period it referred to a piece of sacred or secular music in several movements involving soloists, a choir and an orchestra. Although music was not used in services during Lent and Advent, Bach would have performed about 60 cantatas per year. Bach wrote many sacred cantatas; some have been lost, but over 200 have survived.

Cantus firmus. A pre-existing melody used as the basis for otherwise freely composed polyphonic music.

Chalumeau register. The lowest pitch register of the clarinet.

Charleston. A popular dance from the 1920s, which uses the rhythm

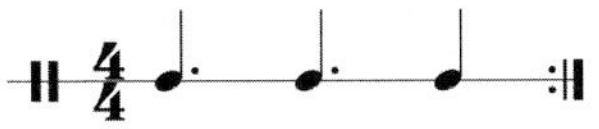

Chorale. A Baroque secular or sacred composition in several sections or movements.

Circle of 5ths. A series of notes or chords that are all a (perfect) 5th apart.

Clavichord. A soft-toned keyboard instrument, used from the Medieval era until the Classical period.

Collect. A short prayer used in Christian churches.

Commission. A formal request for a specific piece of work.

Contralto. The lowest female voice range.

Cup. (Brass) A common form of mute for brass instruments.

Diminished 7th. A four-note chord made up of a diminished triad plus a diminished 7th above the root.

Dissonance/dissonant. Notes that 'clash'. The opposite of **consonance**.

Dominant minor 9th chord. A dominant 7th chord, plus the note a minor 9th above the root. On C, this would be: C E G B♭ D♭.

Divisi. A string section which is divided into two or more separate groups.

Doit. (Jazz) A note sliding upward indefinitely.

Dorian mode. A scale that can be reproduced by playing the white notes from D to the D an octave above. It has a minor key sound, but does not function like a normal minor scale. It is heard on a lot of folk music, especially from the British Isles. The mode can centre on any note, so on G it would include G, A, B♭, C, D, E, F and G.

Doxology. The doxology is the form of words often used at the end of psalms: *Glory be to the Father,* etc.

Enharmonic change. Changing the name of a note without changing the sound (e.g. C♯ and D♭ are actually the same pitch).

Fall-offs. A long glissando down, played on a brass instrument. A good example of this is the final chord of *The Pink Panther* theme.

Falsetto. This involves the singing of notes above the normal range of the human voice, normally by male singers.

Flageolet. The term to describe **falsetto**, when used by female singers.

Found sound. A 'non-musical' sound, often used in electronic composition. This can come from a variety of sources: it might be a recording of a natural environment or an object that is struck to create a percussive sound.

French augmented 6th. A type of augmented chord, containing the root, major 3rd, 4th and augmented 6th.

Fugal. Containing some of the characteristics of a **fugue**.

Fugue. A sophisticated form of composition which explores the potential of a theme (called the 'subject') in a variety of imitative, contrapuntal textures.

Fugato. A fugal passage within a larger structure.

German 6th. A type of augmented chord, containing the root and notes of a major 3rd, perfect 5th and augmented 6th.

Goethe. A German writer (1749–1832), best known for his plays (including *Faust*) and poetry.

Harmon mute. (Brass) Generally refers to a 'wah-wah' sounding mute.

Harpsichord. A keyboard instrument of the 15th to 18th centuries, which was superseded by the piano.

Hauptstimme. The principal vocal or instrumental part.

Head. The main melody or theme in a piece of jazz music.

Horn. In jazz and pop music, the term 'horn' is loosely used to mean any blown instrument.

Idiomatic. Well-suited to the expressive and technical capabilities of the instrument or voice.

Jazz-rock fusion. A genre of music, most popular in the late 1960s and 1970s, which combines elements of jazz and rock music, often with an emphasis on improvisation and unusual timbres and instrumentation.

Jukebox. A music-playing device, found in bars and diners throughout the 1950s and 1960s. They are commonly associated with rock 'n' roll music.

Klangfarbenmelodie. 'Tone-colour melody' – a melody consisting of a succession of changing instrumental timbres.

Mediant. The third degree of a major scale (e.g. the note B, in G major).

Minimalism. A form of music that was developed in the late 20th-century. It uses minimal music material, often employing unusual textures, harmony that is rooted in tonality or modality, and a heavy use of repetition.

Mixolydian. A scale that can be reproduced by playing the white notes from G to the G an octave above. It has a major key sound, but does not function like a normal major scale.

Monody. A single melodic line with accompaniment

Motet. A sacred choral composition with a text chosen by the composer. Words were usually in Latin, though Bach wrote motets in German and English motets were known as anthems.

Musical elements. These are explained fully in the specification. They include concepts of pitch, tonality, rhythm, structure, sonority, texture, tempo, and dynamics.

Neapolitan 6th. A major chord on the flat 2nd degree of a diatonic scale (usually a minor scale) in first inversion. For example, in D minor, this would be an E♭/G. The chord usually resolves to the dominant.

Nebenstimme. In a complex, atonal piece, the term that describes the second most important instrument/vocal part (after the **Hauptstimme**).

Neoclassicism/neoclassical. A 20th century style and 'movement' that sought to reinstate a tonal language deriving from pre-Romantic (often Baroque) music.

Non divisi. On an orchestral score, a request for each player (in a particular section) to play all the printed notes of the chord.

Obbligato. An obbligato part is 'obligatory' – an instrumental part which is essential in creating the particular effect or mood of the music.

Oboes da caccia. An oboe da caccia is a tenor oboe, rather like today's cor anglais.

Oboes d'amore. An oboe d'amore sounds a minor third lower than a normal oboe and has a pear-shaped bell like a cor anglais.

Octatonic scale. An eight-note scale. The term often refers to a particular eight-note scale, where the intervals ascend in alternating intervals of a semitone and a tone.

Oratorio. A sacred text set to music and intended for concert (rather than theatrical) performance.

Passaggio. Italian for 'passageway'. It describes the feeling of a moving from one register to another. Often, for less experienced singers, this can feel like a 'tightening' in the voice.

Pastiche. In music, a type of composing that seeks to fully imitate the language and technical characteristics of a genre, style, tradition, or of a specific composer's work.

Phrygian cadence. An imperfect cadence in a minor key, where the dominant chord is preceded by the subdominant in 1st inversion, so the bass line moves down a step to the dominant.

Plainsong. An unaccompanied single melody, to which the Latin text of a Roman Catholic church service was first sung in the Medieval period.

Plunger. (Brass) Similar to a cup mute, and capable of creating voice-like sounds.

Polka. A fast duple-time dance, which originated in Bohemia in the early 19th century.

Pointillism. A texture made up of individual 'points' of sounds and melodic fragments.

Recitative. A type of vocal music in which the text is the most important element. The singer declaims the words, using natural speech-rhythms.

Restoration. the period of history after the English Civil War in which the Stuart monarchy was restored with the enthronement of Charles II.

Scoop. (Jazz) Sliding up ('scooping') to a note from a lower pitch.

Scotch snap. A two-note dotted rhythm which has the shorter note on the beat. Usually an on-beat semiquaver followed by an off-beat dotted quaver. Also known as lombardic rhythm.

Sequence. The immediate repetition of a motif or phrase of a melody in the same part but at a different pitch.

Serialism. Music based on a predetermined succession of musical elements such as durations and dynamics, and most commonly, pitches of notes.

Sforzando. A strong accent, marked ***sf*** or ***sfz***.

Shakes. A trill, played on a brass instrument, usually with a harsh, brash tone and imprecise intonation.

Smear. A glissando (up or down) played on a brass instrument, usually with a harsh, brash tone.

Sprechgesang. A type of vocal performance halfway between speech and singing.

Stride. A style of piano playing, similar to ragtime, involving wide left-hand leaps between the bass notes and the corresponding chords.

Stringendo. 'Hurrying', i.e. getting .

Sul G. For string players, this marking stipulates that they should play on the G string. On the violin this is the lowest, warmest-sounding string.

Stop-time. A rhythm pattern where the accompaniment stops on the first beat of the bar, allowing the focus to shift to the soloist/vocalist. Used frequently in jazz and blues music.

Style galant. This refers to the style of early Classical music, which was a reaction to the complicated polyphonic textures of the later Baroque period. Music in the galant style is light and elegant, homophonic and ornamented.

Swing. A performance style whereby the first quaver in a pair is lengthened, and the second quaver is shortened. Very common in jazz and blues music.

Tailgate. (Jazz) A trombone glissando.

Thematic transformation. A compositional technique in which the pitches of a theme heard earlier in a work are retained, but other musical parameters (such as rhythm, tempo, key, instrumentation, etc.) are changed.

Tremolo. Playing fast, repeated notes. Often used on string instruments as a device for creating tension.

Tritone. An interval that is equivalent to three tones (an augmented 4th or a diminished 5th).

Vaudeville. A type of popular entertainment combining comedy, song and dance. Vaudeville was popular in the USA in the early 20th century.

Visitation. The Visitation (from the Gospel of Luke) celebrates Mary, who is pregnant with Jesus, visiting her cousin Elizabeth, who is pregnant with John the Baptist. The words of the Magnificat are Mary's song in praise of God, beginning 'My soul doth magnify the Lord and my spirit doth rejoice in God, my Saviour'.

Xylorimba. A xylophone with an extended (lower) pitch range.

Acknowledgements

Rhinegold Education is grateful to the following publishers for permission to use printed excerpts in their publications:

Anything Goes, words & music by Cole Porter
© Copyright 1934 Harms Incorporated, USA
Warner/Chappell North America Limited.
All Rights Reserved. International Copyright Secured.

Asyla, music by Thomas Ades
© Copyright 1997 Faber Music Limited.
All Rights Reserved. International Copyright Secured.

The Birth Of The Blues, music by Ray Henderson, words by Lew Brown & Buddy DeSylva
© Copyright 1926 T B Harms Company all rights assigned to Warner Chappell Music Inc.
Redwood Music Limited for the Commonwealth of Nations, Germany, Austria, Switzerland, South Africa and Spain. All Rights Reserved. International Copyright Secured.

Ca, C'est L'amour, words & music by Cole Porter
© Copyright 1957 Chappell & Co., Inc.
Warner/Chappell North America Limited.
All Rights Reserved. International Copyright Secured.

Call It Stormy Monday (But Tuesday Is Just As Bad), words & music by T-Bone Walker
© Copyright 1963 Gregmark Music Incorporated/ Lord And Walker Publishing.
Burlington Music Company Limited/Wixen Music UK Ltd.
All Rights Reserved. International Copyright Secured.

Come Fly With Me, music by Jimmy Van Heusen, words by Sammy Cahn
© Copyright 1958 Maraville Music Corporation, USA/ Cahn Music Company, USA.
Chelsea Music Publishing Company Limited/ Imagem Music. All Rights Reserved. International Copyright Secured.

Désordre (From '18 Preludes'), music by György Ligeti
© Copyright 1985 Schott Musik International GMBH Co KG. Schott Music Limited. All Rights Reserved.
International Copyright Secured.

Different Trains, music by Steve Reich
© Copyright 1988 Hendon Music Limited.
All Rights Reserved. International Copyright Secured.

Ev'ry Time We Say Goodbye, words & music by Cole Porter
© Copyright 1946 Chappell & Company Incorporated, USA. Warner/Chappell North America Limited.
All Rights Reserved. International Copyright Secured.

Feeling Good, words & music by Leslie Bricusse & Anthony Newley
© Copyright 1964 Musical Comedy Productions Inc.
Concord Music Limited. All Rights Reserved.
International Copyright Secured.

Chamber Symphony No. 1, music by Arnold Schoenberg
© Copyright Universal Edition AG (Wien)
Universal Edition (London) Ltd. All Rights Reserved.
International Copyright Secured.

I Put A Spell On You, words & music by Screamin' Jay Hawkins
© Copyright 1956 EMI Unart Catalog Inc.
EMI United Partnership Limited. All Rights Reserved.
International Copyright Secured.

I've Got The World On A String, music by Harold Arlen, words by Ted Koehler
© Copyright 1931 (Renewed) EMI Mills Music Inc./ S.A Music, Co/Koehler Music Inc.
EMI Music Publishing Ltd/Redwood Music Limited for the Commonwealth of Nations, Germany, Austria, Switzerland, South Africa and Spain. All Rights Reserved.
International Copyright Secured.

I've Got You Under My Skin, words & music by Cole Porter
© Copyright 1936 Chappell & Company Incorporated, USA. Warner/Chappell North America Limited.
All Rights Reserved. International Copyright Secured.

Let's Do It (Let's Fall In Love), words & music by Cole Porter
© Copyright 1928 Harms Incorporated.
Chappell Music Limited. All Rights Reserved.
International Copyright Secured.

Love Walked In, words & music by George Gershwin & Ira Gershwin
© Copyright 1938 Chappell & Company Incorporated, USA. Warner/Chappell North America Limited.
All Rights Reserved. International Copyright Secured.

Mr Bojangles, words & music by Jerry Jeff Walker
© Copyright 1968 Mijac Music/Cotillion Music Incorporated. Sony/ATV Music Publishing/Warner/ Chappell North America Limited. All Rights Reserved.
International Copyright Secured.

One Word, music by John McLaughlin
© Copyright 1973 Chinmoy Music Incorporated, USA/ Warner-Tamerlane Publishing Co. Warner/Chappell North America Limited. All Rights Reserved.
International Copyright Secured.

Picture credits:
Adobe Stock: 27, 32, 43, 323, 332; Alamy: 35, 121, 283 (AF archive), 66 (INTERFOTO), 73 (Adrian Sherratt), 110, 117, 118, 119, 143, 151, 166, 183, 187, 207, 213, 316 (Pictorial Press Ltd), 111 (Glasshouse Images), 122 (AFT History), 124 (Granamour Weems Collection), 182, 195, 295 (Everett Collection Historical), 188 (Photo Researchers, Inc), 210 (MARKA), 219 (Adam Rowley), 223 (Terese Loeb Kreuzer), 230 (© chrisstockphotography), 247 (Gavin Rodgers), 265 (Photos 12), 275 (Harold Smith), 276 (United Archives GmbH), 290 (ITAR-TASS Photo Agency), 292 (Archive Pics), 291, 298 (SPUTNIK), 338 (PF-(bygone1)); Getty Images: 39 (Robbie Jack / Corbis), 310 (DEA/A.DAGLI ORTI), 318 (Hulton Archive); iStock: 20, 240, 259, 270, 278, 333; Rex Features: 137 (Warner Bros/Shutterstock), 154 (ITV/Shutterstock); 234 Creative Commons: © Jebulon ('Baroque Organ' entry on Wikipedia)